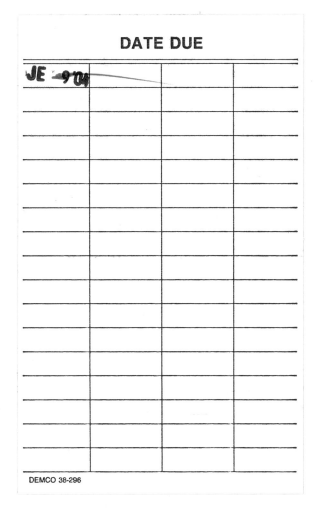

DATE DUE

JE -9'04			

DEMCO 38-296

MADE BY HONG KONG

THE MADE BY HONG KONG RESEARCH TEAM

Senior Researchers

Alice H. Amsden
Suzanne Berger
Andrew B. Bernard
Richard K. Lester
James C. Leung
Helen Meng
Rafael Reif
Charles G. Sodini
David L. Tennenhouse
Daniel I. C. Wang
I-Ching Wu
Victor W. Zue

Student Researchers

Joseph Bambenek
Kheng Leong Cheah
Nicholas Gao
David Gartner
Mary Hallward-Driemeier
Kevin Karty
Jake Seid
Hemant Tejani
Trudy Wilcox
Kathy Yuan

Hong Kong Executive Director

Monique Viengkhou

MADE BY HONG KONG

Edited by
Suzanne Berger and Richard K. Lester

Made By Hong Kong Study Leaders

Alice H. Amsden
Suzanne Berger
Andrew B. Bernard
Richard K. Lester
Rafael Reif
Charles G. Sodini
Daniel I. C. Wang
Victor W. Zue

HONG KONG
OXFORD UNIVERSITY PRESS
OXFORD   NEW YORK

:sity Press
w York
:ok Bogota Bombay
)e Town Dar es Salaam
ng Istanbul Karachi
Madrid Melbourne
Mexico City Nairobi Paris Singapore
Taipei Tokyo Toronto
and associated companies in
Berlin Ibadan

Oxford is a trade mark of Oxford University Press

First published 1997
This impression (lowest digit)
3 5 7 9 10 8 6 4 2

Published in the United States
by Oxford University Press, New York

© Oxford University Press 1997

British Library Cataloguing in Publication Data
available

Library of Congress Cataloging-in-Publication Data
available

ISBN 0-19-590358-7

Printed in Hong Kong
Published by Oxford University Press (China) Ltd
18/F Warwick House, Taikoo Place, 979 King's Road,
Quarry Bay, Hong Kong

Contents

Tables, Figures, and Appendices

Figures

Appendices

Preface

The *Made by Hong Kong* report grows out of a unique collaboration between public and private leaders of the Hong Kong community and researchers at the Massachusetts Institute of Technology. The MIT group are faculty, research staff, and students from across the departments and laboratories of the Institute who have in common an interest in comparative industrial performance. We share the belief that working at the frontiers of knowledge in science, social science, and technology today requires us to become deeply involved with societies other than our own. To do well ourselves in a global economy, we realize there is much to learn from how others respond to the challenges of using new technologies both to gain competitive advantage and to provide good and equitable opportunities for all in society.

On the Hong Kong side, our interlocutors come from both government and the private sector. Many people—including three MIT alumni: David S. Y. Wong, Chairman, Dah Sing Financial Holdings Limited; Kenneth Fang, Chairman, Hong Kong Productivity Council; and Victor Fung, Chairman, Hong Kong Trade Development Council, as well as Raymond Ch'ien, Chairman, Industry and Technology Development Council; Lily Chiang, Executive Director, Chen Hsong Group; Andrew Leung, Deputy Chairman, Federation of Hong Kong Industries, and Herbert Liang, Chairman, Chinese Manufacturers Association of Hong Kong—took the initiative in introducing us to their friends and colleagues in industry and public life. We are especially grateful to them for their trust in us and for their encouragement to let our conclusions and recommendations fall as they would—no matter how politically awkward they might be, no matter that they themselves might not agree with us. This encouragement to speak our minds was one we received throughout the study from many different people: from Henry Tang, the Chairman of the Federation of Hong Kong Industries (who at the outset exhorted us: 'Just tell us what your conclusions are! We can always agree or not. But be honest with us!') to those in the government who supported our project—Donald Tsang, Financial Secretary; Denise Yue, Secretary for Trade and Industry; Regina Ip, then Director-General of Industry, now Director of Immigration; and Francis Ho, current Director-

General of Industry, all of whom urged only that we support our positions with the most solid evidence available. We also were encouraged in meeting Chan Yuen Han, leader in the Democratic Alliance for the Betterment of Hong Kong and the Hong Kong Federation of Trade Unions; and Martin Lee, leader of the Democratic Party, who in listening to an early account of our efforts, approved our 'hopeless objectivity.' To all of the sponsors and to the many others who encouraged us to believe that the honest effort of outsiders could contribute to Hong Kong at this critical moment, we owe a special debt, for we realize that the faith they expressed in us inevitably carried its own risks.

The Hong Kong funding for the project was about evenly divided between public and private sources. On the public side, we received a grant from the Hong Kong Productivity Council, drawing on funds received from the Industry and Technology Development Council. On the private side, the Hong Kong Trade Development Council, the Chiang Industrial Charity Foundation Company Limited, the Better Hong Kong Foundation, the Hong Kong Industrial Technology Centre Corporation, the Chinese Manufacturers Association of Hong Kong, and the Federation of Hong Kong Industries supported the project. A steering committee of sponsors, chaired first by Regina Ip, then by Francis Ho, provided valuable counsel to the researchers throughout. At MIT, the project was located at the Industrial Performance Center (IPC), the director of which is Richard Lester. The IPC is supported by a grant from the Alfred P. Sloan Foundation. The Freeman Foundation, through a grant to the MIT International Science and Technology Initiative/China Program (MISTI/China), contributed the funds that allowed eight MIT students to carry out research in Hong Kong as part of the project.

Our Hong Kong sponsors asked us to focus on the future of industry. At the outset we made three decisions: to carry out research from the firm level up, and, as in the research a number of us had previously carried out for the study *Made in America: Regaining the Productive Edge* (MIT Press, 1989), to attempt to understand the range of possibilities for transforming the productive system by identifying the best practices of good companies as well as targeting the strengths and weaknesses of the system as a whole. Secondly, we decided to look not only at those industries that are commonly seen as high-technology candidates—biotechnology, information technology, electronics—but also at the core industries of Hong Kong's past industrial success, including textiles and clothing, and plastics. We were doubtful that the core industries were inevitably doomed, since we found them still strong in other advanced societies. So we wanted to understand how new products embodying unprecedented combinations of manufacturing skills and services might transform these old industries as well as create new ones. Finally, we rapidly became convinced that the line between industry and services obscured precisely that change in manufacturing that was most important: the emergence of new generations of products that tightly link services and manufactured goods. It became clear that including information technology within our study was vital.

This book presents our findings and recommendations in two parts. Part One, 'Hong Kong Industry and Its Future,' draws together the common themes that cut across the sector studies and outlines the general recommendations. This part has been written by the two editors, but it draws heavily on the discussions that the entire group of researchers held weekly over the period of the study. Part Two contains the special studies which provide the basis for the report: sector studies of the textiles and clothing, electronics, information technology, and biotechnology industries, and cross-cutting studies of Hong Kong capital markets and of Hong Kong manufacturing capabilities. Each of these chapters appear under the names of its principal authors, who alone bear responsibility for it. As the reader will observe, our researchers saw Hong Kong through quite different lenses, and we hope that the diversity in their perspectives—as well as their special professional expertise—may prove interesting and useful. We have attempted to develop a consensus on certain central issues; we have not erased the differences in emphasis and interpretation that characterize the views of our team members.

We wish to acknowledge the special contributions of a few among the very many who have helped us along the way: V.C. Davies, Director-General, Hong Kong Federation of Industries; Francis T. M. Lau, Executive Secretary, Chinese Manufacturers Association; Annie Choi, Assistant Director, Hong Kong Government Industry Department; S. K. Chan and James Fok at the Hong Kong Productivity Council; Ruth Schindler, and the group of energetic Hong Kong students who volunteered their efforts, Anna Chan Kar-on, Helen Li, and Clarence Leung. At MIT, we are indebted to Betty Bolivar, Dori Digenti, Anita Kafka, Kate Noonan, and Deborah Ullrich for their heroic contributions as members of the team. Their energy and commitment were invaluable to the entire enterprise. We gratefully acknowledge the help of Mary Child and Joan McCandlish in bringing the book to publication.

A New Direction for Hong Kong Industry

An Executive Summary

Hong Kong stands at a time of unique challenge and transition. On July 1, 1997, the People's Republic of China resumes its sovereignty over a territory that is one of the wealthiest and freest economies on the globe. Under the eyes of all the world, Hong Kong will be trying to preserve its way of life and expand its economic power as one of two systems that will live together within one country. The world's attention is riveted on the political stakes of this historic moment: Can Hong Kong remain a free and open society? In Hong Kong, we have learned, many are also asking about their economic future: Can the Hong Kong system operate as it has over the past 40 years to build growth and affluence? Will the engines of development that worked so well in the past continue to generate prosperity? These are the questions that are addressed in this study by a team of researchers from the Massachusetts Institute of Technology.

The wealth of Hong Kong stands on a foundation built by industry and trade. But today, Hong Kong statistics report that industry contributes only 9.3 percent of the gross domestic product, compared with 23 percent just 13 years ago. Over this period, much of Hong Kong's manufacturing has shifted out of Hong Kong proper in search of lower-cost land and labor. Hong Kong enterprises now own and manage a far-reaching network of activities in the Pearl River Delta, further inland in China, and beyond. This transformation has been enormously profitable for many. The scale of Hong Kong's manufacturing activities has greatly expanded, even as production within Hong Kong itself has shrunk. 'Made *by* Hong Kong' has grown, even as 'Made *in* Hong Kong' has declined.

In this study, we use the term 'Made By Hong Kong' to refer to the products manufactured by Hong Kong-owned and/or managed enterprises wherever they are located. Hong Kong firms make goods through long production chains that may start in Hong Kong but use manufacturing sites in the Pearl River Delta, further inland in China, and beyond: in Indonesia, the Philippines, Burma (Myanmar), Malaysia, Mauritius, Africa, and more recently even in Latin America. 'Made By

Hong Kong' designates in a phrase the international chains of networked production that link Hong Kong-owned and managed companies, inside and outside of Hong Kong proper. In terms of gross output and employment, 'Made By Hong Kong' manufacturing now far exceeds the product of the manufacturing sector within Hong Kong itself. But products 'Made By Hong Kong' depend, as we shall show, on inputs that are 'Made *in* Hong Kong.'

'Made in Hong Kong' refers to goods and services that are produced within the territory of Hong Kong proper. Many of these goods and services serve as inputs into the production networks of 'Made By Hong Kong.' These inputs include management, design, product development, marketing, logistics, telecommunications, quality control, testing and certification, financial services, and a wide array of component parts—from software to buttons—that are 'Made in Hong Kong.'

Even as traditional manufacturing in Hong Kong has shrunk, financial, trade, transportation, and other services have flourished. Hong Kong's leap into the future of information technology-driven connectivity and organization ranks it among world pioneers in creative uses of the new technologies. The question is whether industry still has a future in this dynamic, prosperous society and whether industrial activities can generate a high standard of living for Hong Kong people: this was the charge to the MIT research team. This book presents our findings, conclusions, and recommendations at the end of a year's explorations and 516 visits to 350 Hong Kong companies and organizations.

Our central conclusion can be simply stated: We see a future for Hong Kong as a world-class industrial power. To realize such an ambition, Hong Kong needs to strike out in a new direction, as a leader in the production of new generations of products. The high-value-added goods of the twenty-first century will be *service-enhanced* products. Such products bring together manufacturing and services in ways that defy our conventional statistical categories. They bundle together in desirable combination the capabilities of advanced manufacturing systems and new possibilities in design, customization, rapid delivery, quality, and product novelty and uniqueness—all enabled by information technologies. The services that make these new generations of products possible depend heavily on information and its rapid diffusion. Hong Kong's outstanding telecommunications infrastructure, its creative software designers, its pioneering on-line services, and Hong Kong people's enthusiastic interest in acquiring novel products and services all create a fertile terrain for experimentation with these new products.

The services which create the high value added in the new generations of manufactured goods are not only the result of technological advance; they are also the product of societal capabilities. Consumers in both the advanced rich countries of the West and the new consumers of China and other emerging economies seek assurances of quality, purity, reliability, and brand reputation—and each of these depends not only on the activities of private firms but also on the capacity of public institutions to set and enforce standards, to repress intellectual property and brand-name violations, and to provide a 'safe harbor ' which attracts innovators and investors. Hong Kong's public institutions today provide solid foundations for creating such protection, but need strengthening in certain areas.

Hong Kong's great opportunity lies in its manufacturing capabilities, a burgeoning information technology sector, and liberal and respected public institutions. The challenge is to strengthen each of these components and to bring them together to create new generations of products. Will such an evolution take place spontaneously? Perhaps for a small number of leading firms. But not on a scale that would galvanize Hong Kong industry and make it a world leader in the new century, as it has been a leader among emerging Asian societies in the second half of the twentieth century. What would this take? We believe that industry, government, and the educational community in Hong Kong must now dedicate themselves to the development of six vitally important and interrelated capabilities.

First, the capacity to create new products and processes in Hong Kong must be strengthened. More of Hong Kong's firms should follow the example set by a few leaders and devote new efforts to building independent capabilities for product and technology innovation. More of them need to build brand identity for their products. Industry must also work more closely with Hong Kong's universities on industrially relevant research and development. The overall level of private and public investment in research and development should be substantially increased. A larger fraction of university research funds should be allocated to applied research and development, and there should be greater reliance on competitive mechanisms in allocating these funds.

Second, the capabilities of Hong Kong's industrial workforce must be upgraded. This means overcoming the widespread lack of commitment to the development of human resources at all levels of Hong Kong industry. It means reversing the decline of English language competence among primary and secondary school children. It also means developing new capabilities for product and process innovation and design among Hong Kong's university student population. Industry and the universities should work together to create a new cadre of university students and faculty in engineering and management with the ability to work as members of teams creating and designing new products, processes, and systems. They should be able to operate effectively beyond a single discipline and to combine deep knowledge of scientific and engineering fundamentals with practical, real-world knowledge and hands-on experience.

Third, Hong Kong must strengthen the public institutions of 'safe harbor'. If investors and innovators are to develop new product concepts in Hong Kong itself and if they are to bring ideas from elsewhere for trial and adaptation in Hong Kong's bracing commercial environment, they must be assured that intellectual property rights will be fully respected and enforced. Hong Kong must continue to cultivate and safeguard one of its most valuable assets—the worldwide reputation of Hong Kong-created products for meeting standards of quality and integrity. The agencies that enforce intellectual property rights need vigorous strengthening. For this they require new public outreach programs like those of the Independent Commission against Corruption (ICAC) in order to change public attitudes about the value of intellectual property.

Fourth, Hong Kong must increase the rate of formation of new technology-based enterprises. There is a critical need for more true venture investing activity, that is, equity investment in new enterprises that have yet to sell their first product. Broadening the range of exit options for venture investors is an important step toward promoting such investment. The current proposal to set up a NASDAQ-type second stock exchange for technology companies should be pursued. Because this may face practical obstacles in the near term, leaders of industry, government, and finance should explore the creation of a new class of 'T shares' in such companies that would be tradable on the Hong Kong stock exchange as an intermediate step toward the formation of a second exchange. In addition, the government's proposed Science Park initiative should be accelerated by creating a decentralized, 'virtual' science park for start-up, early-stage, and small technology-based enterprises.

Fifth, more technological competence must be brought into government. The increasingly technological nature of society and the economy demands a high level of technical expertise within the public administration. The Hong Kong Government should introduce a rotation mechanism allowing specialists from industry and academia to serve in full-time administrative positions on temporary assignment.

Sixth, the ability to bring technological expertise to Hong Kong from the West and from the People's Republic of China must be strengthened. This means solving the problem of affordable housing for such personnel. It will also require a review of immigration policies concerning highly skilled people from the PRC.

These recommendations and the many others advanced in the body of this book share the characteristic that implementation will require actions by both private and public institutions. More important than any single proposal is the need for concerted action on multiple fronts. We believe that Hong Kong industry has arrived at a critical fork in the road. Which route it will take depends on many separate choices by different organizations and individuals.

As researchers, we hope to show where the obstacles lie in the existing system, and what the map of policy options might be. As individuals who have tried to contribute to change in the American economy and society, we recognize that the contribution of researchers is ultimately a limited one, and that the real choices must be seized by the participants themselves. We see the vital role that Hong Kong's new leaders will have to play in such a development; most important of all, they will have to engage the energies and commitment of broad sectors of the community. To such an endeavor, we offer an analysis that builds on our observations of Hong Kong industry and our efforts to understand it in the light of emerging best practice in other advanced industrial societies around the world.

Part One
Hong Kong Industry and its Future

1   Why Study Hong Kong Industry?

In 1996, a group of researchers from the Massachusetts Institute of Technology set out on a study of Hong Kong industry that would bring them into hundreds of factories, laboratories, and headquarters in Hong Kong and China. MIT professors in electrical engineering and computer science, economics, urban studies, chemical engineering, political science, and nuclear engineering went with senior research colleagues and graduate students into Hong Kong companies and their China-based plants to try to discern the future of industry in East Asia from a firm-level-up perspective. Many have asked us why senior faculty and researchers from an institution known for its contributions to education and research in technology and science would devote so much effort to analyzing activities in China and Hong Kong. At a time when the American economy is booming and when the US lead across a broad spectrum of high-technology industries is greater than at any point since the 1960s, why focus on China, except as a market for US exports?[1] Within China, why study Hong Kong?

Those of us who have chosen to work on the *Made By Hong Kong* project believe that to remain a world leader in advancing science and technology for the common good, MIT needs to work on the frontiers of knowledge creation and application, wherever they are. After World War II, the US economy and market, as well as its research enterprises, dominated the world, and there seemed to be little need to look abroad for innovation and opportunity. Over the half century since the end of the war, other nations have emerged alongside the United States as strong independent centers of science, technology, and industry. Americans can no longer afford—if ever they could—to remain focused exclusively on the domestic market or on domestic sources of new ideas and processes. Rather, to derive the fullest range of benefits from our engagement in the global economy and in the worldwide knowledge creation, we need to be able to learn in diverse national settings, to work in centers of innovation outside our own society, and to problem-solve beyond our own borders. These imperatives first became clear to American society in the

1980s, as we saw Japanese industry and technology pose major competitive challenges to the best US companies. The MIT Commission on Industrial Productivity, authors of *Made in America: Regaining the Productive Edge* (MIT Press, 1989)—a study in which a number of us on the Hong Kong team participated—emphasized the importance of moving beyond parochialism to understand industry and technology abroad.

Today the emergent frontier in industry and technology is East Asia.[2] Its extraordinary growth rates and large market constitute a major draw for American and multinational industry. Between 1974 and 1993, the annual average rate of GDP growth in East Asia was 7.5 percent per year, in contrast to only 2.9 percent in the advanced industrial world.[3] Today Asia accounts for close to a third of world trade, and between 1993 and 2000, the World Bank has estimated, Asia will account for half the growth in world trade. Asians will comprise 3.5 billion of the world's estimated 6.2 billion people by the year 2000.[4] There will be about a billion middle-class consumers in Asia by 2000.[5] But beyond the potential of this vast emerging consumer base, we see an enormous potential for scientific, technological, and industrial achievements that we need to understand in the making. The rapid advances of Korea, Taiwan, and Singapore in the electronics field show the potential of this region to equal the industrial prowess of the West. The ambitious research agendas of the laboratories of leading Chinese institutions of science and technology, the strength and depth of their reservoir of scientific personnel, the new and growing ability to attract back home students who have been trained in the best Western universities, and the concentrated effort on pulling advanced technology from multinational companies—all these factors are working to build technological capabilities that will be formidable in the future, however uneven they are today. For all these reasons, anyone with an interest in the forces that will drive the global economy of the twenty-first century needs to focus on Asia.

If Asia, why Hong Kong? Three broad sets of considerations drew us to conclude—and we believe should convince others—that Hong Kong is a privileged site for observing the emergence of Asia as a major player in the global economy. First, Hong Kong provides a unique window onto China. No society in the world has more experience investing and producing in China. Hong Kong has been the largest source of foreign direct investment in China since the mid-1980s. Although the exact figure is impossible to determine, various statistical sources estimate Hong Kong's contribution to realized foreign investment in China by 1994 to comprise about two thirds of the total. By comparison, the Japanese share was about 13 percent. In Guangdong Province the dominance of Hong Kong capital was greatest, with about 90 percent of all foreign-invested companies.[6] About 35 percent of China's international trade (43 percent of exports and 25 percent of imports) is handled by Hong Kong.[7] Overseas Chinese investors—often Hong Kong companies, or investors operating out of Hong Kong—employ some 14–15 million people in China.[8]

As we observed on our visits to the Hong Kong-owned and managed plants in the Pearl River Delta and elsewhere in China, Hong Kong managers have an unparalleled fund of knowledge about what it takes to operate production systems distributed across long distances and to turn out high-quality goods in a wide range of industries in 'greenfield' sites in China. Some have argued that Hong Kong entrepreneurs are uniquely qualified to operate in China—because of linguistic, cultural, and family ties—and that others are likely to fail where Hong Kong managers succeed. The more recent successes of some of the Taiwanese, Korean, Japanese, and American joint ventures who are now operating on the same terrain suggest to us that such a claim is exaggerated.[9] But Hong Kong's experience still stands as a benchmark for working in China and thus provides an extraordinary chance to learn what the potential opportunities and pitfalls may be of shifting some part of the activities of advanced industrial societies into China.

The second factor that drew us to this study of Hong Kong industry was the importance to the United States of Hong Kong as an economy and society. On the barren rocks of a small trading port and fishing village with about half a million people at the end of World War II, Hong Kong has built a first-rate world manufacturing power. The dynamism, growth rate, and world reach of this economy is today vitally connected with American interests. Depending on the source, Hong Kong ranks either as the world's third most competitive economy (in the Institute for Management Development's 1996 *World Competitiveness Yearbook*) or as the second most competitive (by the World Economic Forum's reckoning).[10] Over the 15-year interval 1980–95, Hong Kong's annual average rate of growth of GDP was 6 percent; and by 1994 its GDP per person (calculated in purchasing power parity) was US$23,080, topping Singapore ($21,430), South Korea ($10,549), and Taiwan ($13,022).[11] Moreover, unlike the other 'little dragons,' Hong Kong's growth pattern was one in which government eschewed any direct role in promoting industry. This fact was reflected in Hong Kong's heading a list of countries ranked by their economic freedom.[12]

As Hong Kong became a powerful and rich economy, it became increasingly more important to the United States: today it is its 13th largest trading partner and the 11th biggest market for US exports.[13] The US Commerce Department estimates that direct US investment in Hong Kong is US$13.8 billion. As the *United States–Hong Kong Policy Act Report* of March 31, 1996 described, US stakes in Hong Kong are multiple and significant: 'Last year's exports to Hong Kong, many of which are re-exported to China, total over US$14 billion. We have US$12 billion investment in Hong Kong. Some 1,000 resident US firms employ 250,000 Hong Kong workers (10 percent of the workforce), and Hong Kong's open society and attractive living environment are home to over 36,000 American citizens.'[14] There are 198 regional headquarters and 228 regional offices of US companies in Hong Kong, and the American Chamber of Commerce in Hong Kong is the largest one outside the United States, with over 1,200 members. In last year's debates over renewing China's most-favored-nation status in the US Congress, one source calculated that the exports to Hong Kong of 15 key US states total US$8.3 billion alone and that, together with the US$7.9 billion exports of these states to China, they create over 800,000 jobs in the United States.[15] For Hong Kong, only China is a bigger partner than the United States.

At this point, given the massive Hong Kong investment in productive facilities in China and the major role that Hong Kong plays in re-exporting goods made in China to the outside world and re-exporting the world's goods into China, it is extremely difficult to disentangle US interests in Hong Kong from those in China. As Barry Naughton, an expert on US–China relations, has explained, conventional trade accounting overstates China's exports and understates Hong

Kong (and Taiwan)'s contributions to the US trade deficit with China.[16] Foreign-invested firms generate a large share (41 percent) of China's total exports. Hong Kong is the major foreign investor in China, hence is directly responsible for a large component of those Chinese exports. Naughton traces the continuity between today's US trade deficit with China and earlier trade deficits between the United States and Hong Kong and Taiwan. 'For a whole series of commodities such as footwear, toys, and bicycles, declining US market share for Taiwan or Hong Kong has been matched by increasing market share for the PRC. Thus underlying the dramatic growth in US–PRC trade is the substantial continuing role of Hong Kong and Taiwan businesses as intermediaries in this trade.'[17]

Naughton examines further the 'value-added chain' of production which brings inputs (fabric, electronic devices, materials, and so forth) from Hong Kong into China; assembles products in China; then returns the products to Hong Kong for packaging, marketing, and shipping. He estimates that of imports arriving at the port in Long Beach California, value added in China may be 20 to 25 cents or less per dollar of c.i.f. [cost, insurance, and freight, or cost in full] imports.[18] Thus much of the large US deficit in trade with China should be attributed to Hong Kong (and Taiwan).[19] In sum, Hong Kong's economic importance to the United States is greater than the trade or investment figures that relate directly to Hong Kong-based activities reflect, for Hong Kong inputs create a large part of the economic flows within the US–China economic relationship.

A third—and for us compelling—reason to focus on Hong Kong's experience is that it may help us address one of the most important questions confronting American society: What is the impact of globalization on the productive and innovative capabilities of firms which shift some part of their activities across national borders into low-cost labor markets and retain others in domestic markets in close proximity to skilled personnel and centers of research and development? Is it possible to break up production systems geographically and to separate physically the functions of research, product conception and design, development, production, and commercialization without losing efficiency and the ability to design products that can be manufactured well? What are the effects of globalization of production on employment in home territory? Can production be located very far from ultimate end users without losing a vital feedback possibility that drives improvement and new products?

These questions first entered debates over industrial performance in the 1980s, when the issue was to explain the significance of differences between the American and Japanese systems of production. At that time, much of the Japanese industrial superiority—in developing and bringing to market new generations of products rapidly and in continuously improving the processes of production—seemed to derive from the closeness of R&D, product development, and production. It also derived from the intense interactions and frequent rotations of personnel among these activities. In the United States, by contrast, many of the weaknesses of our industrial system seemed to derive from its compartmentalization and from the fact that ideas conceived in R&D labs were 'tossed over the transom' to manufacturing with little regard for how they could be produced or modified.[20]

Today, Japanese, Americans, and Europeans alike are moving parts of their productive activities out of their own societies into Asia, East Europe, and Latin America, driven by a search for lower costs, or to gain market access, or to stay close to vital customers. Globalization seems to be fragmenting production systems everywhere. But which activities are shifted and separated and which are retained in close proximity in order to sustain the capacity for future innovation and growth—these decisions are made differently in various companies and in various countries. Their consequences may shape critical differences in capabilities, hence determine the performance of firms in the future. They may also matter for the quality and number of jobs that remain in the home country.

We believe that a firm's ability to perform well and to continue to turn out a solid stream of innovations will, increasingly, depend on the decisions it makes on the location of design, research, product development, and manufacturing. But we still know little about the consequences of these patterns of outsourcing. The early findings of a University of California/San Diego research team on US, Japanese, and Asian firms in the hard disk drive industry suggest very great variations in the decisions firms from different countries make about the location of production and employment.

These differences raise major questions about the proximity of manufacturing and product development and its implications for locating R&D abroad.[21] The San Diego team argues that manufacturing tolerances may be growing tighter with technological advances in hard disk drive production, so co-locating design and manufacturing—instead of distributing them at geographically distant sites—may become increasingly important. If this were true in other high-tech sectors as well, then maintaining real manufacturing capabilities in close proximity to design and R&D may be a source of competitive advantage.

There are real trade-offs between the advantages to be gained from lean production and the cost savings to be gained from distributed network production systems, as geographic distances and delays between units associated in the production of goods greatly reduce the possibility of very low inventories, of seamless collaboration with suppliers and customers, and of monitoring in ways that rapidly halt defects. As David L. Levy reports in a recent analysis, these two strategies cannot be completely married, and hard choices need to be made among them.[22] Hong Kong's rich experience in this domain has great interest for many who are beginning to discover the difficulties of interacting with vital parts of their production network which are not within close geographic reach.

For those seeking to learn the lessons of early globalizers who organized their production in networks extending in distributed chains out from headquarters in high-wage societies into low-cost labor manufacturing sites in emerging countries, Hong Kong, in fact, represents a kind of critical case.[23] Since China's opening and the economic reforms of the late 1970s, Hong Kong manufacturing industry has been transferring activities to China on a massive scale. At its peak in 1984, Hong Kong had a manufacturing workforce of 905,000 (41.7 percent of the active labor force); by 1995 those employed in industry had shrunk to 386,000 (15.3 percent of the Hong Kong workforce). There were 48,992 manufacturing establishments in Hong Kong in 1984 and only 31,114 by 1995. Manufacturing, which had been the largest component of GDP in the 1970s and 1980s—about 23 percent of GDP—now represents only 9.2 percent.[24] But while 'Made in Hong Kong' manufacturing declined, 'Made By Hong Kong' manufacturing—that is, manufacturing in Hong Kong-owned and managed plants operating outside Hong Kong proper but using significant Hong Kong inputs—flourished. By shifting parts of their operations to China, Hong Kong industrialists vastly increased the scope of their enterprises. By 1997, Hong Kong manufacturing companies were estimated to employ some 5 million in their plants in Hong Kong and China—over five times the workforce they had employed in Hong Kong at the peak of manufacturing in the territory in 1984. Manufacturing productivity in Hong Kong itself had risen from US$25,501 (gross output per employee) in 1984 to $87,789 in 1994.[25]

We can observe, in effect, a roughly decade-long natural experiment with distributing the activities of a production system between Hong Kong, a high-wage society with a per capita GDP in 1993 of US$18,530 and China, a poor country, whose most prosperous province, Guangdong had a per capita GDP in that same year of US$826.[26] What have been the effects on the profitability of Hong Kong companies? On the levels and kinds of employment opportunities in Hong Kong? On Hong Kong's societal well-being? On Hong Kong's innovative and managerial capabilities? On Hong Kong's chances of developing new higher-value-added industries in high-technology areas? On Hong Kong's ability to sustain a high-growth trajectory over time? What would be the consequences if all manufacturing activities shifted out of Hong Kong across the border and only services remained in Hong Kong? It was this last issue above all that troubled the Hong Kong groups that offered to support our research, for they worried about the sustainability of Hong Kong's prosperity and autonomy if all their industry should move out. These worries are hardly Hong Kong's alone, but are voiced with greater and greater insistence everywhere in the developed world. These are the questions we hoped to answer by examining in the microcosm of Hong Kong a set of relationships that all of the advanced societies are entering into with the emerging economies.

Finally, why study Hong Kong industry, others asked us—and we wondered ourselves—on the eve of Hong Kong's return to Chinese sovereignty? On July 1, 1997 Hong Kong will become a Special Administrative Region (SAR) within China, after 154 years as a British crown colony. What reason is there to believe that the fundamental conditions that supported the extraordinary societal and economic flourishing of the past will persist? These societal foundations are the rule of law, limited government, honesty and transparency in administration, private enterprise, public commitments to relatively high levels of social goods and equity, and protection of individual freedoms of expression, association, and belief. In the words of newly chosen Chief Executive for the Hong Kong SAR, Tung Chee-hwa, 'The success of Hong Kong is the freedoms we enjoy. Freedom of every nature—freedom of thought, freedom of movement, freedom of the press, freedom of information, freedom to be creative.'[27] But if these freedoms were to be significantly eroded, what basis would we have for laying out scenarios for possible new directions in the Hong Kong economy?

In the course of our research in Hong Kong and China, we heard a range of very different views about Hong Kong's political future. Many in Hong Kong repeated to us the commitments that China's highest leaders have expressed over the years to the framework of 'one country, two systems.' They also emphasized China's enormous material stakes in Hong Kong's prosperity and explained that these interests make it likely that the foundational conditions of a prosperous and innovative economy and social stability will be preserved. Equally sanguine, some argue that the transition has really already taken place gradually during the 13 years since the British and Chinese signed the Joint Declaration, as Hong Kong people have taken the eventual change in sovereignty into account. On this reading, 1997 has only a symbolic value. Others, more pessimistically, doubt that China truly understands the links between these political and societal foundations and the vital motors of the Hong Kong economy—that even if China wants to keep alive the goose that lays the golden eggs, it doesn't understand what kind of food· the goose eats, in Thomas Friedman's pithy expression.[28] Still others see a dark future, because they believe that China's fears about political and social unrest in Hong Kong spilling into the mainland are so great that the leadership's priority for political survival will overwhelm the concerns for preserving the economic *status quo*.

As outsiders and as researchers, we did not attempt to reach consensus on these issues. Since the best informed of those we were privileged to meet during our research did not agree among themselves, we do not believe that we can do so. The

absence of an analysis of Hong Kong's prospects as a free society in this report does not mean that we care less about this
matter than about others which receive extended discussion
here. Nor do we think Hong Kong's economic prosperity
could continue, let alone be enhanced, if its historic freedoms
were to be abridged. Whatever claims may be made about the
compatibility of authoritarian rule and economic growth in
other societies, this is not Hong Kong's legacy and we cannot
conceive it as a plausible future scenario. On the contrary: our
analysis, prognosis, and recommendations for Hong Kong
depend on two basic assumptions—without any certainty
that they will prove warranted. We assume that within the
framework of 'one country, two systems,' Hong Kong can
maintain the *status quo* of its commitments to high levels of
societal well-being and equity, to individual freedoms, to a
market-driven economy, to limited government, to the transparency and integrity of the civil service, and to the rule of
law. Secondly, we assume, as the condition of the rest, that
there exists a real will on the part of both the Hong Kong people and the Chinese to find ways of working together that
provide mutual benefit.

Notes

1   In contrast to the situation a decade ago, the 1995 report of crit-
    ical technologies compiled by the White House Office of Science
    and Technology Policy lists no area in which the United States
    lags behind any other country. (Office of Science and
    Technology Policy, *National Critical Technologies Report,*
    Washington, DC: US Government Printing Office, 1995.)
2   See, for example, the M. Porter and W. R. Timken presentations
    to the Council on Competitiveness describing these emerging
    economies as the real challenge for the United States. Reported
    in *The Daily Yomiuri,* October 24, 1996, p. 15.
3   *The Economist,* 'War of the Worlds,' A Survey of the Global
    Economy (October 1, 1994): 3. See World Bank, *The East Asian
    Miracle,* New York: Oxford University Press, 1993.
4   *The Economist,* 'A Billion Consumers,' A Survey of Asia (October
    30, 1993): 3.
5   *The Economist,* 'The Search for the Asian Manager,' A Survey of
    Business in Asia (March 9, 1996): 23.
6   Enbao Wang, *Hong Kong, 1997: The Politics of Transition,* Boulder,
    Colo.: Lynne Rienner, 1995, pp. 146–7.

7   East Asia Analytical Unit, Department of Foreign Affairs and Trade, Australia, *Overseas Chinese Business Networks in Asia*, Canberra: AGPS Press, 1995, p. 205.

8   Ibid., p. 217. This source also cites an estimate of 15 million in early 1994 from C. Zhang, 'A Memorandum on the Workers' Situation in Foreign Capital Enterprises,' *Chinese Industrial and Commercial News* (June 24, 1994): 6.

9   On the experience of these companies, see the very interesting survey carried out under the auspices of the Academy of Social Sciences, Asia Pacific Research Center, *Survey of Hong Kong, Macau, and Taiwan Investment in the PRC* [Gang tai ao zai zhong guo da lu tou zi qing kuang wen juan diao cha fen xi bao gao] (Beijing, August 1995). We are grateful to Professor Zhang Yunling for sharing the results of this study.

10 IMD International, *The World Competitiveness Yearbook 1996*, Lausanne, 1996; *The Economist* (June 1, 1996): 76.

11 *The Economist*, 'Survey, Business in Asia' (March 9, 1996): 4.

12 K. R. Holmes; B. T. Johnson; and M. Kirkpatrick (eds.), *1997 Index of Economic Freedom*, Washington, DC: Heritage Foundation and *Wall Street Journal*, 1997, p. 222.

13 K. B. Richburg, 'Hong Kong is America's Business,' *Washington Post*, February 3, 1997, pp. A1, A13.

14 *United States–Hong Kong Policy Act Report*, as of March 31, 1996, as required by Section 301 of the United States–Hong Kong Policy Act of 1992, 22 U.S. C. 5731, as amended, p. 8.

15 P. Cheng, 'Don't Forget MFN,' *South China Morning Post*, March 15, 1996, p. 25. The trade figures are attributed to the Hong Kong Government Trade Department and the employment figures to the US Department of Commerce.

16 B. Naughton, 'The United States and China: Management of Economic Conflict,' unpublished paper, 1996, pp. 8, 6, 16. See also F. Lemoine; A. de Saint Vaulry; and M. Dramé, 'Hong Kong–Chine: un dragon à deux têtes,' *Economie Internationale*, 57 (1er trimestre, 1994).

17 Ibid., p. 6.

18 Ibid., p. 16.

19 Because Taiwan has no direct diplomatic or trade relations with the People's Republic of China, much of its investment in and trade with China moves through Hong Kong and cannot be readily separated from Hong Kong-generated components.

20 See M. Dertouzos; R. K. Lester; and R. M. Solow (eds.), *Made in America: Regaining the Productive Edge*, Cambridge, Mass.: MIT Press, 1989; and J. P. Womack; and D. T. Jones; and D. Roos, *The Machine that Changed the World*, New York: Rawson Associates, 1990.

21 P. Gourevitch; R. E. Bohn; and D. McKendrick, 'Who Is Us? The Nationality Problem in Globalization of Production,' The Data Storage Industry Globalization Project, Report 96-01, December 1996. Important work is being carried out on this subject at the Berkeley Roundtable on the International Economy: see M. Borrus, 'Left for Dead: Asian Production Networks and the Revival of U.S. Electronics,' in E. M. Doherty (ed.), *Japanese Investment in Asia: International Production Strategies in a Rapidly Changing World*, San Francisco: BRIE, 1994; J. Zysman; E. M. Doherty; A. Schwartz, 'Tales from the 'Global' Economy: Cross-National Production Networks and the Re-Organization of the European Economy,' San Francisco: BRIE, 1996.

22 D. L. Levy, 'Lean Production in an International Supply Chain,' *Sloan Management Review* (Winter 1997).

23 On production networks, see G. Gereffi and D. L. Wyman (eds.), *Manufacturing Miracles: Paths of Industrialization in Latin America and East Asia*, Princeton, NJ: Princeton University Press, 1990; and G. Gereffi, 'Commodity Chains and Regional Divisions of Labor in East Asia,' February 1996 (forthcoming in *Journal of Asian Business*).

24 Statistics for the 1980s and 1996 are from Hong Kong Government Industry Department, *1995 Hong Kong's Manufacturing Industries*, 1995, pp. 8, 9, 22, 23; and from Hong Kong Government Industry Department, *1996 Hong Kong's Manufacturing Industries*, 1996, pp. 23–4.

25 These estimations of the combined workforces of Hong Kong and Hong Kong-managed China plants come from *Far Eastern Economic Review* (January 9, 1997): 5, which cites as its sources Vision 2047 Foundation, Hong Kong Government Information Services, and M. Enright; E. Scott; and D. Dodwell, *The Hong Kong Advantage*, Hong Kong: Oxford University Press, 1997.

26 Sung Yun-Wing; Liu Pak-Wai; R. Wong Yue-Chim; and Lau Pui-King, *The Fifth Dragon: The Emergence of the Pearl River Delta*, Singapore: Addison Wesley, 1995, p. 227.

27 Interview in *Business Week* (December 23, 1996): 54.

28 T. Friedman, 'What the Goose Eats,' *New York Times*, December 15, 1996, p. 13.

Industry in Hong Kong: A Short History

To build scenarios for Hong Kong's future as an industrial economy requires understanding its industrial past.[1] The history of Hong Kong as a manufacturing power dates to the postwar years, when a massive inflow of immigrants and capital catalyzed a process of rapid economic growth. The entrepôt economy of the century between British acquisition of the territory and the outbreak of World War II had been dominated by the banking and trading interests of the 'hongs,' most notable among them Jardine Matheson and Swire, by the rising importance of a class of Chinese traders, the 'compradors,' who emerged out of the world of European trading houses, and by the vitality of a set of activities associated with a deep-water port commerce: shipping, boat-building, cargo services, and insurance. The war and the occupation inflicted heavy damage on these industries, and Hong Kong's population declined, as people retreated into unoccupied zones of China to escape life under the Japanese.

The return of those who had fled Hong Kong during the war was followed by a wave of refugees in flight from the civil war on the Chinese Mainland, then by another wave of immigrants after the Communist victory in 1949, then by still other flows in the 1960s and 1970s. Between September 1945 and December 1949, about 1,285,000 refugees poured into a territory whose prewar population (March 1941) had been only 1,640,000. The strain on Hong Kong's basic infrastructure, housing stock, social services, and labor market was enormous. Despite the colonial administration's resistance to social provision, the hazards to public health and safety of sprawling refugee shanty dwellings would eventually lead the government to a large-scale program of public housing. This would mark a major break with the *laissez-faire* past. But in the first years after the war, the government tried to find ways to make the newcomers capable of generating their own jobs and sustenance. In this way the crisis created by the massive influx of migrants proved a catalyst for a rapid process of industrialization.

First, the British colonial administration, anxious to avoid unemployment and social unrest and unable to draw significant new resources from London to cope with the situation, began to lay out policies more favorable to industry than in the past in order to make the colony self-sufficient. Leases on land for industrial uses were set below market rates. This shift in colonial land policy would gradually evolve into a more active use of public control over land to encourage industry, which led to the creation in the mid-1970s of industrial estates at Tai Po and Yuen Long. There was a (modest) expansion of the government services that dealt with industry, with the creation in 1949 of the Department of Commerce and Industry and an Assistant Director to encourage and advise industrial expansion.[2] The new industries that emerged were predominately cotton spinning and weaving firms. Inevitably in the 1950s and 1960s, these commercial interests came into conflict with those of the British textile industry. In a departure from old practices, the British government allowed the Hong Kong government to negotiate internationally as a separate voice in defense of its industries, and this development would lead to a *de facto* autonomy for Hong Kong as a separate customs territory in bilateral and multilateral commercial negotiations. Thus out of a crisis which threatened to swamp Hong Kong's basic societal infrastructure grew a set of public policies that provided a more favorable climate for industry than the old colonial framework.

The second major spur to industry that dates to the postwar crisis was the influx of capital along with the immigrants from China. As the situation of private capital in China fell apart, there was massive capital flight to Hong Kong. Wong Siu-lun, in *Emigrant Entrepreneurs* cites estimates of a flow of capital that financed approximately two thirds of the initial expenditures of Hong Kong industrialization.[3] A sizeable amount of the capital arrived in the form of new machinery for spinning mills, which the Shanghai industrialists had ordered at the end of the war, but which had not yet been delivered. As the Communists moved into Shanghai, many of the Shanghai textile entrepreneurs decided to leave China for Hong Kong, and they diverted the machinery—still en route from England and the United States—to the new destination. The result, as Wong describes, was to create 'some of the most modern spinning factories that Hong Kong, or even the whole of Asia, had ever seen.' To the assets of modern equipment, the Shanghai textile industrialists added a capability for raising the bank finance needed to provide working capital for the companies.

The Shanghai industrialists who played so prominent a role in the process of rapid industrialization brought with them not only modern machinery and advanced technology, but a sense of industrial vocation and commitment that has been remarkably analyzed in Wong's *Emigrant Entrepreneurs*.[4] Many of the enduring traits—and characteristic strengths and weaknesses of the Hong Kong industrial class—can be located in the values of these immigrants. The spirit of entrepreneurship of these industrial pioneers continues to be a strong feature of Hong Kong capitalism and it fosters an environment that is extremely favorable to new enterprise formation. The passion for autonomy and disinclination to bureaucratic organization continues to favor organizational systems that are strong at the top and weak in middle levels of management—indeed, these values make it difficult to develop strong management systems.[5]

Finally, and perhaps most important, these immigrants brought with them a distinctive determination to build businesses as family enterprises. This characteristic is common not only to the Shanghai business elite, but to overseas Chinese entrepreneurs as a group. [6] Conceiving the firm as a family affair has produced tremendous strength and resilience in the Chinese business enterprise, first of all, because of the long time horizons a multi-generational perspective induces. A high proportion of profits tend to be reinvested in the business. Family connections extend across national frontiers, and as businesses organize network production and locate their assets in geographically separated locations, the ties of trust and kinship substitute for the formal institutions and infrastructure that are often lacking in less developed markets. As an Australian analysis of the overseas Chinese economic success explained:

> Ethnic Chinese entrepreneurs could be characterised as fillers of economic potholes on the road to development. Developing markets are imperfect and incomplete, giving rise to market niches and opportunities to make higher than normal profits. The ethnic Chinese specialise in markets where competition is not atomistic, and where their products benefit from a degree of market power (such as traded manufactures.) This allows them to accrue oligopolistic rents, i.e., higher than normal profits. . . . Market nich-

es arise not only in embryonic markets, but in markets constrained by external factors . . . [an] example is the Sino-
Thai Bangkok Bank, which in the 1960s and 1970s lent to
ethnic Chinese businesses, filling a niche across South-East
Asia left by Western banks who would not lend to many
ethnic Chinese entrepreneurs, citing as the reason their
often unsatisfactory book-keeping practices.[7]

Wong, reviewing the literature on family-controlled businesses, points out that their performance and expansion can rival
that of other business forms. But from the early days of Hong
Kong industrialization, certain weaknesses of these family
enterprises were apparent. First, in Wong's words, this is a pattern that 'is strong in entrepreneurship but weak in management. The supply of entrepreneurs outstrips the supply of
managers and executives. The Chinese who enter into industrial competition, as exemplified by the Shanghai spinners,
take pride in proprietorship but disdain salaried employment.
They pursue technical expertise, but not managerial profes-
sionalism.'[8] Next, issues about family control, particularly at
the time of succession are extremely difficult to resolve.
Finally, across a whole range of business functions, the family ownership pattern promotes a particular set of solutions
which, depending on circumstance and context, may or may
not be appropriate. It favors:

> highly centralised decision-making, low-margin, and high
> volume as a means of penetrating markets; rigorous control
> of inventory to achieve low capital investment and high
> rates of stock turnover; reduction of 'transaction costs'(i.e.,
> the costs of doing business) through a preference for doing
> business within ethnic Chinese networks: preference for
> internal financing; tendency to undervalue services and
> other intangibles, such as legal and other advice and R&D
> (and a preference to internalize these costs where possible.)[9]

That the patterns of entrepreneurial familism of Hong
Kong's first wave of industrialization have survived largely
intact is reflected today in the domination of family control
even in companies listed on the Hong Kong stock exchange.
In 1988, ten family groups controlled 54 percent of Hong
Kong's stock market capitalization; of them, seven were ethnic
Chinese, three, British.[10] The Hong Kong Society of
Accountants recently reported on changes in the family dom-
inance of boards of listed companies: only 9 percent now
have a majority of directors that are members of families with

major shareholdings. But most listed companies still have a single individual or a family holding most of the issued shares.[11]

Out of the turmoil and crisis of the momentous changes in China flowed the human and capital inputs that fueled the first wave of Hong Kong industrialization. It was a second crisis—a disastrous collapse of entrepôt trade triggered by the Korean War and the United Nations embargo on trade with China in June 1951—that led to reorganization of the colony's economy as a manufacturing economy. From 1950 to 1960, the number of manufacturing establishments grew from 1,478 to 5,346; the numbers employed in them, from 81,718 to 218,405. In 1961 manufacturing employed 40 percent of the Hong Kong workforce and accounted for about one-fourth of GDP. [12]

The distinctive characteristics of this industrialization experience diverged sharply not only from the patterns of the West and Japan, but even from those of Hong Kong's neighbors in the region, as Chiu, Ho, and Lui have analyzed in their notable comparison of Hong Kong and Singaporean growth.[13] First of all, Hong Kong's industrialization has been propelled by small and medium-sized companies. The average number employed in these firms declined even as their numbers climbed and industrial growth accelerated, thus demonstrating a very great ease of new enterprise formation. In 1994, 95.6 percent of Hong Kong's 34,068 manufacturing establishments employed fewer than 50 employees.

Second, these firms have been heavily concentrated in labor-intensive, light consumer industries: textiles and clothing, electronics, watches and clocks, printing, metal products, plastics, and food have been the major sectors (see Table 2.1). Over time, these enterprises demonstrated a phenomenal ability to identify new markets and to upgrade their products. Starting from plastic flowers, wigs, cheap garments sold in low-end discounters, and wind-up toys, the Hong Kong companies shifted their products and improved their quality, partly under the tutelage of the buyers, and partly in response to the imposition of trade quotas by the West. By the end of the 1970s, Hong Kong garments were heading for the better department stores in the United States and Europe and the toys had become TV and hand-held electronic games. The electronics industry which had barely existed in 1960 (183 workers) was booming by 1980 (93,005 workers; almost one-fifth of Hong Kong's industrial output).[14]

Table 2.1
Gross Output of Hong Kong's Leading Manufacturing Industries, 1984 and 1994

Industry	1984	1994
	(Value in HK$ Millions) (%)	
Clothing	49,453 (26.1)	70,386 (23.8)
Electronics	36,776 (19.4)	56,218 (19.0)
Printing	6,786 (3.6)	24,431 (8.2)
Textiles	19,235 (10.1)	23,495 (7.9)
Watches and Clocks	11,726 (6.2)	17,864 (6.0)
Food and Beverages	6,767 (3.6)	16,328 (5.5)
Metal Products	8,106 (4.3)	12,912 (4.4)
Industrial Machinery	2,464 (1.3)	9,607 (3.2)
Plastics	16,864 (8.9)	8,460 (2.9)
Chemicals	2,886 (1.5)	8,396 (2.8)
Jewellery	3,513 (1.9)	8,261 (2.8)
Packaging Products	1,546 (0.8)	6,425 (2.2)
Toys	10,988 (5.8)	3,271 (1.1)

Source: Hong Kong Government Industry Department, *1996 Hong Kong's Manufacturing Industries*, p. 46.

Finally Hong Kong industrialization was unique among postwar East Asian growth 'miracles' because the state played so limited a role. The Hong Kong government was not exactly the hands-off state of *laissez-faire* dreams. Its ownership of all land in Hong Kong and use of land sales to finance much of governmental expenditure; its role in the provision of physical and social infrastructure; its concession of monopoly rights in telecommunications and public utilities, and much else made the state a major presence in the economy. But in comparison with other governments in the region, Hong Kong's interfered minimally: tax rates were low; there was virtually no 'industrial policy' in any form, nor any subsidies for new industries or for bailing out old ones; and no incentives to foreign companies to locate in the territory. Even public support for research and development, a virtually universal policy in modern societies, was absent in Hong Kong.[15]

Three decades after the war, Hong Kong's economy was racing ahead at an annual average growth rate of over 10 percent. It had become the leading exporter of manufactured goods in the developing world, and in per capita exports far outstripped the United States and Japan. [16] But already there were concerns about the future of this pattern of industrial development. In October 1977 the Hong Kong government charged a high-level commission of civil servants and private individuals with a study of how to maintain the growth rate of the economy. The Committee on Diversification was to consider factors that could attract new activities and the role of policies that might encourage industrial diversification. In particular, it was to recommend 'whether existing Government policies could be either modified or replaced to facilitate and stimulate this process.'[17] Looking back on this effort nearly 20 years later, we find it striking that many of the issues the Committee on Diversification signaled at that time remain unresolved today, and that many of their recommendations anticipate the recommendations that will be advanced in our own report.

The 1979 recommendations range from: proposals to facilitate cooperation and links with China—which the committee members saw as opening to the outside; suggestions to increase the supply of industrial land and to improve infrastructure on this land, making it more attractive to new industries; recommendations on education and training, above all, providing better information on links of education to work; links with industrialists and technical schools, and opportunities for combining work and tertiary education. The committee urged raising the level of inputs into industrially oriented research; making stronger efforts to promote foreign industrial investment in Hong Kong; and bringing more technological competence into government. A number of the proposals were implemented: the recommendation to develop a Standards and Testing Centre led to the establishment of a primary standards laboratory and to a standards and calibration laboratory that supported the generalization of ISO 9000 qualification and the emergence of local certifiers. Many of the recommendations for an Industrial Development Board have been picked up by the Industry and Technology Development Council. But in the main, the road map laid out for reorienting and upgrading Hong Kong's industry lay unused.

The reason was that from the late 1970s on, Hong Kong industrialists found a vast arena in which to deploy the assets and skills they had developed in low-cost, low-end manufacturing.[18] With the opening of China to foreign direct investment and the new market-oriented experiments in coastal regions and special economic zones from 1978 on, Hong Kong manufacturers found an enormous field for expanding their operations. In lieu of technological upgrading of companies, it became possible to increase profits by transferring and expanding production facilities into South China, thereby solving the problems of rising labor and land costs in Hong Kong.

At the time of the 1978 reforms, Guangdong was a poor and marginal province—its per capita GDP below the Chinese average; its population almost five times larger than that of Shanghai, but its GDP only 68 percent of Shanghai's.[19] Guangdong received special autonomy and reform status in 1979 and the authorization in 1980 to experiment with 'special export zones,' later to be renamed 'special economic zones' (SEZs). Three of these are located in Guangdong: Shenzhen, Zhuhai, and Shantou. The influx to Guangdong of Hong Kong capital jump-started a process of industrialization and growth that produced an average annual growth rate of 19 percent (nominal) from 1979 to 1991.[20] Guangdong was to play a vital role in the rapid growth of China in these opening years of reform. In foreign trade, Guangdong has accounted for over 40 percent of China's exports, with 70 percent of it from the Pearl River Delta.[21] Guangdong has attracted about one-third of all utilized foreign investment in China (20 percent of it in the Pearl River Delta). By far the largest share of this came from Hong Kong.[22] Eighty percent of Guangdong's exports were re-exported through Hong Kong.

On the Hong Kong side of the equation, Guangdong has been equally important. It was to be the principal terrain for Hong Kong's relocated production facilities. A survey carried out in 1994 by the Federation of Hong Kong Industries, *Investment in China*, found, for example, that of the 912 factories set up by the respondents outside Hong Kong, 86.4 percent were in Guangdong. Of those who had invested in China, very few (5 percent) had investment in other countries.[23] In the '1996 Survey on the Hong Kong Manufacturing Environment,' 26.8 percent of the respondents reported production facilities outside Hong Kong, of which 96 percent were in China, overwhelmingly concentrated in Guangdong. Of those firms planning to expand outside Hong Kong (11.5 percent of the respondents), the large majority were focusing on Guangdong.[24] Most of the firms (96.7 percent) still maintained some product manufacturing in Hong Kong as well.[25]

In Guangdong, Hong Kong industrialists found cheap labor and land. Wages (including basic wages, bonus, subsidies, and fringe benefits) to unskilled or semi-skilled workers in the four major cities of Guangdong in 1994 were RMB580–680; for skilled workers and technicians, RMB1,400–1,600. And when the Guangdong natives started to find opportunities for work outside the Hong Kong-owned and managed factories, workers from other parts of China were brought in to staff the positions. There are no accurate statistics on numbers of workers in Guangdong employed outside their home localities, but the Planning Commission of Guangdong estimates the total to be 5 to 6 million. Every year before the Chinese New Year, about 1.7 million workers leave Guangdong to return home to visit families, and return bringing others.[26]

The 'lock into labour-intensive manufacturing,' in Chiu, Ho, and Lui's terms, emerged not only in response to the vast opportunities that opened up in joint ventures and outward processing operations in China after the 1970s, but also because of a new wave of unskilled immigration—legal and illegal—into Hong Kong from the mid-1970s.[27] This, too, served to make it possible and profitable to continue on the same production trajectory, with only limited innovation in products and processes, by shifting most of manufacturing out of Hong Kong into the low-cost labor zones of China. Hong Kong industrialists' emphasis even today on labor costs as the major issue for decisions on locating new investments is clearly evident from a 1996 survey carried out by the Hong Kong Government Industry Department. The survey found that in ranking twelve factors affecting evaluations of investment climate, all industries except one ranked labor cost as the most important factor.[28]

The Hong Kong workforce employed in manufacturing fell from a peak of 46 percent in 1980 to 15.3 percent in 1995; the proportion of GDP generated in industry, from close to 24 percent in 1980 to 9.2 percent in 1996.[29] But though Hong Kong's real annual GDP growth rate in 1991–5 was 5.5 percent, the combined real growth rate of Hong Kong and Guangdong was 9.5 percent. Hong Kong employs eight times as many workers in Guangdong as in Hong Kong proper, and its investment in Guangdong is 22 percent as much as its domestic investment.[30] Profitability and high growth rates thus have been maintained without significant innovation. The opening of China and ensuing opportunities there for Hong Kong firms averted the pressure to move off the trajectory of labor-intensive, low-cost labor manufacturing and to find ways to upgrade and to develop higher-value-added manufacturing. Hong Kong industrialists' decisions can be understood as rational responses to market opportunities at that time; but the warnings for the future raised by the Committee on Diversification and the new directions it suggested were choices postponed and not avoided.

Today Hong Kong stands at a major fork in the road. It faces the challenges not only of an unprecedented political transition, but of choices that are critical to its future as a great industrial power. Twenty years after the Report of the Committee on Diversification, the context has been transformed by the rapid growth of China and the vast opportunities it offers. But many in Hong Kong are asking the same question that the Committee addressed: What kind of future is there for industry in Hong Kong?

Notes

1   On Hong Kong's industrial history see the following: S.W.K. Chiu; K.C. Ho; and T.L. Lui, *City-States in the Global Economy: Industrial Restructuring in Hong Kong and Singapore*, Transitions: Asia and Asian America, Boulder, Colo.: Westview Press, 1997; S.

Chiu, 'The Politics of Laissez-faire: Hong Kong's Strategy of Industrialization in Historical Perspective,' Hong Kong Institute of Asia–Pacific Studies, Chinese University of Hong Kong, 1994; Advisory Committee on Diversification, *Report of the Advisory Committee on Diversification 1979*, 1979; East Asia Analytical Unit, Department of Foreign Affairs and Trade, Australia, *Overseas Chinese Business Networks in Asia*, Canberra: AGPS Press, 1995; Lau Siu-kai, *Society and Politics in Hong Kong*, Hong Kong: The Chinese University Press, 1982; T.L. Lui and S. Chiu, 'A Tale of Two Industries: The Restructuring of Hong Kong's Garment-Making and Electronics Industries,' *Environment and Planning*, 26 (1994); Yin-Ping Ho and Tzong-Biau Lin, 'Structural Adjustment in a Free-Trade, Free Market Economy,' in H. Patrick, with L. Meissner (eds.), *Pacific Basin Industries in Distress*, New York: Columbia University Press, 1991; E.F. Vogel, *The Four Little Dragons: The Spread of Industrialization in East Asia*, Cambridge, Mass.: Harvard University Press, 1991; Wong Siu-Lun, *Emigrant Entrepreneurs: Shanghai Industrialists in Hong Kong*, Hong Kong: Oxford University Press, 1988.

2   See Wong, *Emigrant Entrepreneurs*, p. 25.

3   Wong, citing the calculations of E. Sczepanik *(Emigrant Entrepreneurs*, pp. 42–47).

4   The literature on the big leap forward of Hong Kong industrialization in the 1950s emphasizes the role of the Shanghai industrialists. Our own interviews of the past year have turned up far more cases of dynamic enterprises whose founders came from South China than we had been prepared to find. Among the best known are Li & Fung and Yangtzekiang, but there were many others as well.

5   T. C. Chu and T. MacMurray, 'The Road Ahead for Asia's Leading Conglomerates,' *The McKinsey Quarterly*, 3 (1993).

6   See on this point Wong, *Emigrant Entrepreneurs;* and East Asia Analytical Unit, Australia, *Overseas Chinese Business Networks in Asia*, pp. 126–137.

7   *Overseas Chinese Business Networks in Asia*, pp. 126–7.

8   Wong, *Emigrant Entrepreneurs*, p. 170.

9   *Overseas Chinese Business Networks in Asia*, p. 3.

10 Ibid., p. 93.

11 *South China Morning Post*, Weekly Edition, January 25, 1997, Business, p. 2.

12 See Hong Kong Government Industry Department, *1995 Hong Kong's Manufacturing Industries*, pp. 22–3; also, Chiu, Ho, and Lui, *City-States in the Global Economy*, pp. 30–77.

13 Chiu, Ho, and Lui, *City-States in the Global Economy*.

14 Hong Kong Government Industry Department, *1995 Hong Kong's Manufacturing Industries,* pp. 68, 70.

15 The best account of the differences is Chiu, Ho, and Lui, *City-States in the Global Economy.*

16 Annual average rate of growth of GDP at constant market prices, 1961–1987. Per capita GDP growth over the same period was close to 8 percent. (Ho and Lin, 'Structural Adjustment,' pp. 258–9.)

17 *Report of the Committee on Diversification,* p. 7.

18 A clear discussion of this period is to be found in Chiu, Ho, and Lui, *City-States in the Global Economy,* Chapter 3, 'Hong Kong: Locked into Labor-intensive Manufacturing,' pp. 51–77.

19 Sung Yun-wing; Liu Pak-wai; R. Wong Yue-chim; Lau Pui-king, *The Fifth Dragon: The Emergence of the Pearl River Delta,* Singapore: Addison Wesley, 1995, p. 15. See the pioneering study of Guangdong's growth by E.F. Vogel, *One Step Ahead in China: Guangdong under Reform,* Cambridge, Mass.: Harvard University Press, 1989.

20 Ibid., p. 30.

21 Ibid., p. 230.

22 Ibid., p. 211.

23 Federation of Hong Kong Industries, *Investment in China,* 1994, p. 9.

24 Hong Kong Government Industry Department, 1996 *Hong Kong's Manufacturing Industries,* pp. 280–1.

25 The numbers now operating only outside of Hong Kong may be larger than the replies indicate, since 569 of the 3,269 sampled establishment did not return questionnaires because they had been relocated or could not be traced. (Ibid., p. 273.)

26 Sung *et al.,* p. 118.

27 Chiu, Ho, and Lui, *City-States in the Global Economy,* pp. 54–6.

28 Hong Kong Government Industry Department, *1996 Hong Kong's Manufacturing Industries,* pp. 273–4. The one exception was photographic goods, a small industry employing 0.9 percent of the total manufacturing workforce. (Ibid., p. 251.)

29 Statistics for 1980, 1995, 1996 from Ibid., pp. 24, 23.

30 The estimations of Hong Kong plus Guangdong growth come from Merrill Lynch, 'Hong Kong Economic Focus, Comment,' *South China Morning Post,* October 28, 1996, Business, p. 8.

3 Manufacturing and Services in Hong Kong

Twenty years ago, it would have been rare indeed to find anyone who believed that industry in Hong Kong had no future at all. Today, however, such a view is common. In the course of our research we encountered a widespread belief—among government officials, in the universities, in the press, and even in industry itself—that high land and labor costs and the lack of technological investment are making industry in Hong terminally uncompetitive, that the territory's economic future rests entirely with services, and that Hong Kong is indeed already well on its way to becoming a 'post-industrial' society.

The rapid growth of services has reinforced this view. Growth has been particularly strong in the financial sector, and by almost any measure Hong Kong is now one of the world's leading financial centers. Other service industries have flourished too, and today services as a whole account for more than 80 percent of Hong Kong's GDP, compared with less than 10 percent for manufacturing.

But the statistical picture of industrial decline is misleading, not only because of the growth of 'Made By Hong Kong' outside the territory, but more importantly because it rests on a distinction between manufacturing and services that obscures the growing convergence between the two. On the input side, activities traditionally thought of as services are key inputs to manufacturing processes, while manufacturing industries are the source of many of the most important innovations in the production of services. The convergence is even more evident on the output side. On the one hand, for today's consumers the value of manufactured products increasingly hinges on intangible attributes—design, convenience, reliability, innovativeness, fashion, customization, timely delivery, and so on—that, were they not embodied in the product, would be classified as 'services.' On the other hand, the traditional characteristic of services—that they can neither be stored nor transported, and therefore must be produced where and when they are consumed—is also breaking down. Today many services can be stored electronically, transported over long distances using telecommunications technology, and delivered on demand, making them much more like manufactured products in many ways.

Information technology is playing a key role in promoting this convergence, and the information technology (IT) industry itself illustrates better than any other why the traditional distinction between manufacturing and services is less and less useful. The IT industry encompasses the manufacturing of equipment that enables information to be manipulated and accessed (such as computers and communication devices), the transportation of information (telecommunications network operations), and the information 'content' itself (newspapers, television programming).

As the boundary between manufacturing and services becomes increasingly blurred, preserving the statistical fiction of a sharp distinction between the two creates two kinds of confusion. First, it leads to what is almost certainly a significant undermeasurement of the real scale and scope of manufacturing industry in Hong Kong. Second, it obscures the special possibilities for growth that arise out of Hong Kong's distinctive capabilities and potential as an industrial power.

The measurement problem arises because large numbers of Hong Kong firms that are today classified as service businesses are in reality intimately connected to the manufacturing sector, provide vital inputs to it, and surely could not survive in its absence. Many actually were classified as manufacturing firms until recently. But according to statistical convention only those firms that operate manufacturing assembly or other processing facilities in Hong Kong itself are counted in the manufacturing sector. So when large numbers of Hong Kong manufacturers moved their factories across the border to China they were reclassified as services firms. Though most have retained functions such as design, engineering, marketing, sales, and production planning in Hong Kong, these now count as services. It is likely that many thousands of firms, and perhaps hundreds of thousands of employees, have been reclassified in this rather arbitrary way.[1]

In the rest of the service sector, too, many firms are deeply involved in manufacturing. Think of the thousands of Hong Kong trading companies that take orders for manufactured goods from buyers, locate and contract with suppliers in Hong Kong and elsewhere to produce the goods, and support the transactions with a variety of value-added services. Or

Figure 3.1
Manufacturing and Services

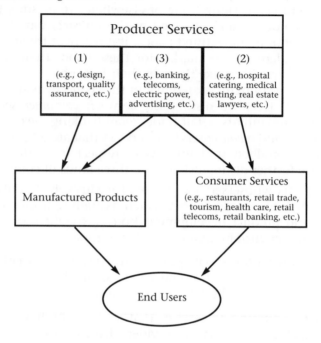

(1) Producer services for manufacturing exclusively
(2) Producer services for services exclusively
(3) Producer services for manufacturing and services

The importance of taking this broader view is all the greater in light of the global trend towards what we call here *service-enhanced manufacturing*—the growing significance of intangible product attributes in manufacturing competition. In a very wide range of markets, factors such as convenience of use, speedy delivery, brand identity, fashion, quality, reliability, and a variety of services designed to enhance the experience of buying and using the product are featuring more and more prominently. The key to success in manufacturing competition in the coming decades will be the ability to bundle together a tangible good with an array of intangible services to produce the most desirable product.

The trend towards service-enhanced products has roots in both the demand side and the supply side of manufacturing markets. Increasingly sophisticated and well-educated consumers in both the affluent and the emerging economies are demanding it, while the new technologies of customization and quick response are bringing these products within reach of vast numbers of consumers at reasonable cost. New technologies are forcing firms to pay ever-closer attention to the vagaries and unpredictable dynamics of customer demand, and to differentiate themselves and their products on the basis of intangible product attributes. These technologies include: point-of-sale information systems providing immediate information about changing consumer tastes; computerized inventory control systems facilitating just-in-time production strategies; rapid prototyping and simulation technologies that enable new, customized products to be brought to market much faster. Consider the following examples, each drawn from a different industry in which Hong Kong is involved:

- Manufacturers of denim jeans seeking high returns in high-wage societies need to deliver not just a carefully sewn pair of jeans in a sturdy denim at a reasonable price, but jeans that can be delivered rapidly to retailers who hold no inventory; jeans that can be restocked quickly to catch a fashion trend; jeans made for diverse new customers located with new electronic technologies; jeans made to fit the different body shapes of, say, Japanese and German women and men; jeans made with materials and accessories located with new electronic databases; jeans custom-cut to a consumer's individual measurements that are electronically transmitted to the sewing site (as Levi Strauss now does in the United States); jeans laundered with a fabric finish that requires laboratory monitoring; jeans with a label telling the consumer that her purchase expresses her social and environmental preferences as well as her fashion sense, and so on.

- Consider as a second example the emerging markets for Traditional Chinese Medicine products in the United States and Europe. Consumers in these countries want these medicines to be backed by meaningful guarantees of purity. They want to know that what they are buying is indeed what the label on the package says is inside. (In this case, of course, the embodied service—the guarantee of purity—can most likely only be provided by credible government regulatory inputs.)

- The concept of service-enhanced products also extends to the industrial goods sector. Manufacturers of industrial machinery today sell not just hardware but integrated systems, consisting of the equipment itself, electronic controls, information systems, software packages, reliability guarantees, and operating and maintenance support. (It is not unusual for them to second their employees to customers' factories for a year or more at a time to help operate and maintain their products.) Such firms see themselves as providing 'processes' and selling 'solutions,' rather than only selling hardware.

These examples are drawn from three industries in which Hong Kong is well represented. But it is important to recognize that the trend towards service-enhanced products can be observed across the entire spectrum of manufacturing industries, including many in which Hong Kong is only peripherally involved. To take just one example, consider the automobile industry, where the world's leading car manufacturers, traditionally preoccupied with issues of cost, quality, and reliability have recently also begun to focus on making the purchase of a new car a more efficient and satisfying experience for the customer. Thus, electronic communications systems linking dealers to assemblers and suppliers will in due course make it possible for customers to order cars with customized features and take delivery within a few days. In the view of one leading automobile executive, 'the great battleground between successful and unsuccessful manufacturers will be the process of selling, financing, maturing, servicing, warranting, and very importantly, disposing of a vehicle bought from a manufacturer.'[2]

To summarize: First, the view that manufacturing industry is a relatively minor and rapidly shrinking part of Hong Kong's economy is mistaken. Manufacturing plays an important role in the economy, and will likely continue to do so for the foreseeable future. The confusion about manufacturing's role stems partly from limitations in the economic statistics. There is an urgent need for a new system for collecting and classifying economic data that can better capture the changing realities of Hong Kong's industrial structure. Second, the key to success in world manufacturing competition in the coming decades will be the ability to bundle together tangible goods with intangible attributes to produce the most desirable products. Hong Kong's great potential as an industrial power lies in its capacity to serve simultaneously the well-to-do consumers of the West and the new consumers of the emerging economies, especially China, with service-enhanced products.

The rest of this book is devoted to an analysis of the strengths and weaknesses of Hong Kong industry today, and the steps that will need to be taken in order to realize its potential.

Notes

1   According to one source, more than 6,000 firms were reclassified from manufacturing to services in 1992 and 1993 alone because they closed their Hong Kong factories. These firms continued to employ nearly 50,000 people at their Hong Kong headquarters, and so all of these employees were reclassified as service workers, even though the nature of their activities had not changed in any fundamental respect. See M. Enright; E. Scott; and D. Dodwell, *The Hong Kong Advantage,* Hong Kong: Oxford University Press, 1997.

2   A. Trotman, CEO of Ford, cited in B. Sharfman, 'The Long View: Six top executives make some pretty surprising predictions about the state of the auto industry in ten years' time,' *Automobile,* 11, 1 (April 1996): 117.

4 The Strengths of Hong Kong Industry

What foundations are needed to build the new manufacturing economy of the future? What are the legacies of four decades of rapid economic growth and manufacturing prowess? In order to understand the strengths and weaknesses of Hong Kong industry today, the MIT research team started from detailed observations of companies in major sectors of Hong Kong manufacturing: electronics, pharmaceutical products, textiles and clothing, software and telecommunications, optical products, plastics and toys, industrial machinery, and food products. Together these sectors account for 63 percent of Hong Kong's manufacturing employment, 65 percent of gross manufacturing output, and 73 percent of manufacturing exports. We supplemented these industry studies with assessments of Hong Kong's industrial capabilities that cut across specific industries, including capital markets, the labor market, education and training, manufacturing capabilities, the research and development infrastructure, the services offered by government and industry associations, as well as investigations of the agencies dealing with trade, intellectual property, anti-corruption, and customs—all critical services for Hong Kong industry. In all, we visited more than 350 firms and other organizations mainly in Hong Kong and China (see Table 4.1) and spent nearly 700 person-days at work in Asia. Reports on the four industry sectors on which we concentrated our efforts—biotechnology, electronics, information technologies, and textiles and clothing—and on the two major cross-cutting studies—capital markets and manufacturing capabilities—constitute the second part of this book. They provide the basis for the findings, conclusions, and recommendations of Part One.

In the remainder of this section, the principal strengths of Hong Kong industry are summarized. In Chapter 5 we consider whether a continuation of Hong Kong's industrial development along the same path that it has followed over the past 15 years is sustainable. Our conclusion is that it is not, and that new challenges will need to be overcome in order to move the Hong Kong system towards the service-enhanced products of the twenty-first century. These challenges are discussed in Chapter 6, and the public and private strategies that we believe will be most effective in addressing them are presented in Chapter 7.

Table 4.1
Research Visits by the *Made By Hong Kong* Team

Sector	Total Number of Organizations Visited	Total Number of Research visits
Biotechnology	60	71
Electronics	36	66
Information Technologies	58	113
Textiles and Clothing	72	95
Other industries (Plastics and toys, optical products, food products, industrial machinery)	21	26
Capital Markets	47	53
Other Cross-Cutting	56	92
TOTAL	350	516

Flexibility in Production

Compared with excellent companies of similar size that we have studied in the United States and Europe, most of the Hong Kong businesses we visited display remarkable flexibility. There are multiple dimensions to flexibility in manufacturing: the ability to produce products for customers with very diverse needs; the ability rapidly to detect changes in trend and to respond to them with new products; the ability to get goods to customers quickly; the ability on the plant floor to work on many different products at the same time and to switch lines rapidly from one product to another. We discovered abundant evidence of all of these capabilities in the companies we visited.

The changes in customers and markets required major adjustments in these firms. Overall, in 1984, 45 percent of Hong Kong's domestic exports went to the United States; and less than 10 percent of domestic exports was destined for China. By 1994, the value of the domestic exports heading for the United States had fallen and that of the goods sold to China had risen; they were each about 28 percent of Hong Kong's domestic exports. (In other markets, there was reasonable stability over time, with a slight decline in exports to Germany and the UK, and a slight increase in goods going to Japan.)[1] Many of the firms in our sample reported working almost exclusively for the American market in the past. Over the past decade, with the opening of the China market, the best of these companies kept their Western customers and began to develop a new array of products for China. In one of the plastics firms, the founder and CEO told us that when his company first entered the China market, it experienced big problems, because the products were 'too Western.' So it designed 150 new items for the China market, targeted in terms of price and design for these new consumers, and the company manufactures these alongside the goods it continues to make for the United States. China at this point represents only 4 percent of its sales (the United States still 75 percent); still, the company has provided a specific array of products for its China customers.

The researchers studying the textiles and clothing industry visited a knitwear company working on 20 different styles at the same time. This firm was trying to expand its business in Japan, was engaged in a new joint venture with a Japanese trading company, and described the demanding nature of its new clients with respect to quality, delivery times, and requests for small orders. This firm can provide its Japanese customers orders as small as 150–350 garments. A denim manufacturer operating wholly within Hong Kong reported that his company had moved from making one to three items simultaneously a decade ago to 300 different items all within the same plant today.

Yet another dimension of flexibility is the ability to detect changes in customer needs and preferences and to develop new products. In the 16 Hong Kong software companies the MIT researchers visited, this emerged as a major characteristic. The degree of customization to meet specific requirements of particular customers was striking. Even those firms that started with the idea of making a standard packaged product, ended up customizing. On one hand this ability to meet the needs of sophisticated users creates a well-protected niche market where regional competitors are disadvantaged. For example, one five-year-old firm has specialized in software solutions that incorporate research and application of options, futures, warrants and other derivatives products and combines real time IT with an understanding of financial markets. The high technical barriers to entry in the financial engineering software area, plus this firm's customization skills, assure it a secure market. But on the other hand, the fragmentation of these niche markets makes it costly for firms to support the customized software they have developed for various customers and for different divisions within the client firms, rendering it even more difficult to sell in foreign markets.

The issue of location on the spectrum between customization and niche production on one end and the production of standard goods is a recurrent theme in Hong Kong manufacturers' decisionmaking. One very successful plastic machinery manufacturer contrasted the firm's strategy with that of European companies working in the same industry and attributed profitability to being able to turn out a more standardized, hence less expensive, product but one whose quality satisfied the most demanding customers. The company's slogan is 'Japanese Quality at PRC Cost.' In fact, in order to get machines of reliable quality to their most demanding customers, it is the machines made in the Hong Kong plant that are exported to the West. In order to get feedback on the strengths and weaknesses of new generations of machines, the newest models are placed with leading-edge users in Hong Kong.

The ability to detect the customer's emerging desires is hardly confined to the high(er)-tech segments of Hong Kong industry. For example, the senior executive of one very successful toy company explained to us how a company lives or dies on one season—Christmas—in their industry. The rapidity with which they pick up shifts in trends and desires makes a success or failure of the year. He commented: 'Having the most accurate market information, the most efficient production lines, and the best rapid development and design tools is all facilitated by information technology.' Some of the classic examples of the agility of Hong Kong manufacturers in developing new products in response to external stimuli involve changes in trade rules and quotas. Sweaters made with ramie—not pure cotton or linen—and jackets with zip-off sleeves are garments ingeniously designed to enter markets blocked by trade regulations. Some of the adaptive product responses we learned of involved significant technological advances, thus one of the large original equipment manufacture (OEM) electronics firms described how they had first learned to make circuit boards from a large Japanese games manufacturer, who had required the Hong Kong firm to work for it exclusively. When the Japanese customer went into crisis, the Hong Kong company rapidly found new customers to teach it how to make components for personal computers.

The speed with which Hong Kong companies get the goods to their customers is another striking mark of their flexibility. Hong Kong was ranked first in the world in 'time to market' by the IMD's 1996 *World Competitiveness Yearbook*.[2] There has been great pressure from American retailers to shorten delivery times in order to reduce inventories and to reduce risks by delaying orders into later in the year. Satisfying these demands is particularly important in the apparel business. With the development of low-cost labor manufacturing facilities in Mexico operating under free trade within the North American Free Trade Agreement (NAFTA) or in East Europe under the duty-free outward processing arrangements of the European Union, Hong Kong companies now have more to fear from competitors located closer to American and European customers. The distances (and the costs of air freight) make it unlikely that Hong Kong will be able to match the delivery times of these competitors. Still, virtually all the companies we visited have been able to compress their production cycles. A senior manager in a trading company noted that 'if production is coming out of non-Hong Kong-controlled plants—even if they are no further away than Hong Kong-controlled plants—it'll still take about 70 percent longer to get the goods.'[3]

The flexibility of Hong Kong industries, however, for the large majority of companies has involved making OEM products. Very few Hong Kong firms have tried to create or to acquire a brand name and to manage it over time—let alone attempted to sustain a balance between production under their own labels and OEM production. As the head of one firm that does produce both brand-name goods and OEM products for clients explained: 'With a label, you take on a series of challenges. It's a baby to continuously enhance. If you work only OEM, if you work only for others, you're taking commands from them. You're on the hand-me-down side. You're not in the decisionmaking seat.' Today some of the most successful Hong Kong companies are devoting large-scale resources to acquiring brands (for example Gold Peak's acquisition of Clipsal or Novel Industries' partnership with Tommy Hilfiger) or to developing their own labels. Goldlion, VTech, Jeanswest, and Episode are names that are coming to be well known in Western markets, while a new set of brand names is being developed for the China market, for example, by firms making plastic products. But these experiences with brand production are still limited to a few pioneers, even among the larger companies. It is only the rare Hong Kong firm—under 10 percent of the firms we interviewed—that enjoys both the protection of the barriers to entry that brands provide and their extra profitability, as well as the advantages of speed, diversity, and flexibility. A number of the OEM manufacturers we interviewed described their short cycle time and fast turnaround as substitutes for the barriers to entry of products with reputations consolidated by brand names.

Coordination

The globalization of production means that companies in all advanced industrial societies are learning to master the coordination of development, design, marketing, production, and distribution in sites that are widely separated in space. Hong Kong entrepreneurs have been doing this for longer than most and their experiences have made them superb coordinators of production, trade, and services. Victor Fung, chairman of the Hong Kong Trade Development Council, chairman of Li & Fung and of Prudential Asia, describes this as a 'middle man role,' which encompasses putting together buyers and sellers as well as production. 'In [the] competitive race,' he writes, 'there is a constant need for Hong Kong traders to find and manage new sources of supply. This means going further into undeveloped hinterlands. The gap between

production line and end-market is widening in all respects-
language, culture, technology. The middle ground is, therefore, opening up for Hong Kong traders. They provide the
essential human bridge, the interface between different parties who are worlds apart.' He imagines 'Hong Kong traders
dressed in safari jackets with pin-striped pants. In one hand
they each carry a machete, to hack their way through the
wilderness to new sources of supply. In the other, a laptop
through which to communicate with their customers in
North America and Europe via the Internet.' He explains that
this is far more than trade, for Hong Kong manages sourcing
and manufacturing all over Asia, locating various activities in
different sites to achieve low cost and efficiency. About one-
third of trade within the region, he notes, takes place within
companies, as they move materials and parts of products
between production sites in different countries.[4]

These coordination strengths can be described as the capability to use 'Made in Hong Kong' inputs to create and sustain
a geographically distributed 'Made By Hong Kong' system of
production. Consider, for example, the case of a Hong Kong
optical company we visited. It buys machinery components
in the United States; assembles the machinery in Hong Kong,
down to all the wiring and lighting and tracks that the equipment will move on; then ships the assembled production system to China where it is sold to a Chinese company. The
Hong Kong company supervises the factory in which the
machinery is installed for two years, providing on-site personnel for two months, then monthly and bimonthly visits
to insure quality control. They teach the buyer how to conduct random quality checks, how to package the goods, and
how to manage sales. The product being manufactured in this
complexly coordinated process is an integrated production
system that is an assemblage of machines and services; and its
value to the customer derives from the Hong Kong company's
ability to bring all of these elements together in a timely fashion. In the case of a large Hong Kong noodle maker, the coordination skills involve making different products in its plants
in the United States, Brazil, Singapore, and trading many of
the products between the production locales, since the product ranges do not entirely overlap.

Coordinating production among various sites may require
judgments about the technical capabilities of the workforce in

different locales. In dyeing and finishing plants, for example, the need for care and consistency at every step of the process means that the most complex jobs and those requiring the highest quality are likely to be carried out in Hong Kong. In garment making and sweaters, however, many of the companies reported that they can achieve equal quality in any of their plants after about a year, and so location decisions tend to be driven by labor costs. Some activities need to be carried out in particular places to establish their country of origin, and then are to be combined with the inputs of plants in other regions. The international trade regulations for textiles and clothing are thus major drivers of coordination chains.

Each shift in the arcane and complex set of foreign national rules governing quota and rules of origin—and there have been many changes over the years—determined shifts in the locational decisions of textile, apparel, and watch manufacturing and required exceptional organizational capabilities for coordinating fragmented activities. When, for example, in 1984 the United States changed the rules of origin to require knitted goods with Hong Kong origin to be knitted in Hong Kong, instead of simply assembled there, the Hong Kong manufacturers had to quickly build up their knitting capacities. Coordination also demands combining activities that might be carried out in any one of a number of different sites with those that cannot readily be moved to other locales. Foreign buyers want to remain in Hong Kong, for example, and are reluctant to operate in the PRC. Thus working with customers—for the approval of designs and prototypes—usually takes place in Hong Kong, and the rest of the production process has to be geared to that fact. The General Manager of a large finishing and dyeing company explained that his company needs to keep printing in Hong Kong because the buyers come in to monitor the final results before fabric enters into full production.

Managers

Of all the coordination problems that Hong Kong companies solve, the most demanding—and the one in which their level of achievement seems the most remarkable—is staffing plants outside Hong Kong with managers able to master the complex problems of production in territories with little industrial experience and big political machines. The abundance of Hong Kong managers is a product of the enormous expansion of manufacturing in Hong Kong from the 1960s through the 1980s. With the shift of manufacturing out of Hong Kong from the mid-1980s on, the managers who once worked in Hong Kong plants are available for such assignments. The multifaceted skills of these managers derive from: education in engineering and science in Hong Kong and abroad; years of work in Hong Kong in plants with skilled workforces; multiple close contacts with demanding and sophisticated buyers in Hong Kong and abroad; experience in international markets; and job rotation through a number of Hong Kong companies, across different parts of the industry.

These managers now face the challenge of replicating the performance of Hong Kong's best plants in settings that lack many of the basic ingredients of the Hong Kong environment. In Hong Kong, manufacturing expanded in a context with rule of law, a relatively unobtrusive and honest bureaucracy, an infrastructure of highways, telecommunications, water and electric power services that improved rapidly in pace with industrial expansion, and a low tax regime. From early days, the Hong Kong environment was a cosmopolitan one that regularly brought managers into contact with their foreign buyers. As in other small territories with large manufacturing sectors—like the 'third Italy' (the industrial districts of north central Italy), or the areas of medium-scale industries in Germany—there was a density of interactions among people in various sectors that fed diffusion of new ideas and mutual learning. As important as the context within which they developed was the *internal* environment of the Hong Kong plant, which produced a particular kind of manager. The Hong Kong labor force offered a range of different capabilities, from workers with low-skill levels seeking first jobs, workers with experience of various factories and positions, technicians and mechanics trained in technical institutes or vocational education programs, seasoned workers suitable for supervisory positions—in short, men and women able to fill in all the layers of responsibility of a comprehensive, mature factory.

Given the absence at the plant level of trade union representation or of collective bargaining, the authority of plant managers was certainly less challenged than in comparable settings in Europe and the United States. But still, the accounts we heard from managers about the early days of manufacturing in Hong Kong suggest that there was a real collaboration in production with workers who brought long experience and varied skills to a process of rapid learning—one which Hong Kong companies either mastered, or else, they failed. A significant segment of the workforce was stable. Managers and workers felt a certain sense of mutual responsibility.

On virtually every one of these key dimensions, the environment Hong Kong managers find in the Pearl River Delta is radically different and more difficult. There are many problems in operating in this environment: poor infrastructure, nonexistent banking services, changing and uncertain customs regulations governing the importation of machinery and supplies, the need to obtain licenses from government officials that too often are arbitrary or corrupt, and so forth. But of all the challenges in the Pearl River Delta that require high levels of managerial skills, the most difficult factor is the character of the workforce. The several million workers recruited for the Hong Kong-owned and managed plants in the Pearl River Delta are rarely natives of the region. Many come from China's inland provinces, hired by their provincial labor offices. Many are young women in their teens and twenties working at their first industrial job. The workers are housed eight to twelve to a room in dormitories the companies provide. They eat in company cafeterias. Most of these workers will stay in the plants no longer than a year or two. Their contacts with the local Guangdong community are nonexistent, or very limited, and the localities do not seek to integrate the newcomers. On the contrary: even in these economic reform zones which are the most liberalized in China, there are major restrictions on the possibilities for outsiders to acquire the residence status that would, for example, allow their children to attend local schools. The mindset of the workforce is one shaped by the temporary nature of the job and the objective of returning to the home locality with savings to finance some project back home, such as marriage, care for elderly relatives, or investment in a small business.

This situation produces extremely high rates of turnover in the Pearl River Delta plants. One Hong Kong-owned garment plant in the Pearl River Delta, 'Company Alpha,' which employs about 5,000 workers, tracked its worker and staff turnover on a monthly basis through the first eight months of 1996; it found worker turnover was about 80 percent and staff turnover, close to 30 percent. Some of the electronics companies report workers staying as long as five years. But figures like those of Company Alpha are not unusual, we learned in the other visits we made to plants in China. With such short stays in the factory, the level of training of the workforce is quite low, for few of the workers have been around long enough to acquire more than a few skills—or even the basic abilities to cooperate with others in a factory setting, to solve simple problems as they arise, or to repair simple machine breakdowns. The flow of new workers through these plants means a continuous process of providing the same basic skills and socialization for factory life to rapidly passing generations of workers. The possibilities of upgrading the skills of such workers—and the incentives to do so—are very low.

Under these difficult conditions, Hong Kong managers produce goods of a quality high enough to be acceptable to most buyers in all markets. This is true not only of designer sportswear like that which 'Company Alpha' produces for sale in top-of-the-line department stores and boutiques. It is also true of high-tech products like audio equipment, telephones, and circuit boards. For those of us on the *Made By Hong Kong* team who had observed workplaces in the United States, Japan, and West Europe, it was this finding which stood in greatest contradiction to the expectations with which we had started our research. Our previous studies had suggested that producing high-quality goods at reasonable costs requires a capacity at the level of the shop floor to solve such tasks as equipment breakdown, resetting machines, setting up the production line quickly to make another kind of product, and detecting errors rapidly to avoid repairs and rejects without having constantly to refer to the senior authority.[5] The levels of self-coordination and decentralized problem-solving that characterize the best plants in the West require skilled, experienced, and motivated workers; and the levels of training needed by such workers seem to be on the rise. We had thus anticipated finding that plants with low-skilled workers would at best only be capable of manufacturing rather simple products with rather low levels of quality. This anticipation was confounded by what we observed in the plants and learned from the comparisons managers drew between what they could produce in China and what they still could produce only in Hong Kong. While the large majority reported that the flexibility of the Hong Kong plants—the ability to produce a larger array of different products over a given period of time and to do so rapidly—was far greater than that of the China plants, the quality of any given product turned out in Hong Kong or in China, most managers told us, was quite similar.[6]

In analyzing the high performance standards of these plants, the single factor that seems most important are the managers who are burdened with the enormous responsibility of making the factories outside Hong Kong operate well. In the absence of a stable workforce with the natural habits of cooperation, group leaders, and professional standards that develop over years of working together, an unusually large managerial presence is needed to coordinate the plant, balance the line, and produce consistent results in quality and productivity. The process of institutional learning in such plants is severely constrained by the transient nature of the labor force, and for this reason as well, the managers shoulder a burden that is quite unlike that in the mature plants of Hong Kong or the developed world.

Our conclusions about the critical role of managerial inputs are supported by the observations others have made of successful operations in China. Ayala and Lai report in *The McKinsey Quarterly* that one of the key factors of success for the companies they studied was a heavy reliance upon expatriate managers.[7] They discuss the weaknesses of the local joint-venture partners (which lack product and market knowledge, distribution reach, and financial resources), the dearth of skilled local managers, and staff turnover rates of 30 percent per year. 'Don't be too quick to localize,' they conclude.[8] 'These companies recognize that expatriate managers provide the critical experience and leadership required to build well-functioning business processes and manage unruly distributors. Hence, they treat expatriate costs as essential investments, not as operating expenses.'

Public Institutions

The strengths derived from flexibility, coordination, and managing industry are assets that individual companies develop and enhance over time. It would be impossible to appreciate the legacies of the past and how they may serve as foundations for a new industrial system, however, without taking into account two societal strengths: Hong Kong's public institutions and Hong Kong's internationalism. The Hong Kong companies we studied benefit not only from the fruits of their own efforts, but from a political framework that is unique in the region. The rule of law, limited government, the protection of individual rights, and the exercise of such public freedoms as the freedom of information and association have created a public environment that supports economic growth and innovation and is open and secure for foreign investors. As Chiu, Ho, and Lui show, Hong Kong's government is distinctive in the region for its noninterventionism in the economy, but hardly *laissez-faire* in the classic sense.[9] It did provide a very low tax regime, but it also offered business a very good transportation and telecommunications infrastructure and, as they describe, education, cheap medical services, and a public housing program that supplied low-cost housing for much of the working class, effectively subsidizing the costs of industrialization.

Among Hong Kong's greatest assets as a society is its civil service, which has earned a high measure of public respect for integrity, efficiency, transparency, and authoritative decision-making. The territory's government institutions—and the traditions, values, and international reputation they embody—have evolved over time. Hong Kong's reputation as a society in which officials are honest, and entrepreneurs need not face the choice between engaging in corrupt practices or else meeting insuperable hurdles and delays in doing business, is a relatively recent creation. The Independent Commission Against Corruption (ICAC), established 20 years ago, tackled and reversed long-standing corrupt practices that reached deep into the public administration.[10] Today it stands as one of the outstanding examples of the regulatory and implementation capabilities of Hong Kong government. It recruits an independent staff with roles that include enforcement, advising other

government agencies on the design of regulations and procedures to pre-empt and prevent corruption, and public outreach. The public outreach activities employ a staff of 200 and
involve, in addition to programs in schools and in community organizations, producing ads and a very popular television
drama based on real ICAC cases ('ICAC Investigators,' which is
watched by an audience of almost two million).[11] The ICAC
has succeeded in reversing a legacy of public indifference and
resignation about corruption. One measure of public trust in
this institution is the number of persons who call to report
problems and are willing to identify themselves: some 65 percent today, compared with 33 percent in 1974.[12] While the
ICAC is in some respects an exceptional institution, some
important elements of its success recur across the public service: the developed sense of public mission that motivates
officials, tough enforcement, and an ability to project public
norms in a free-wheeling and open society.

As we shall suggest in the sections below, it is vital to build
on this public legacy in tackling the issue of intellectual property protection. This is a prerequisite for local and foreign
investment in innovation in the production of service-
enhanced goods. To signal issues that will be detailed in later
sections: if information technology is to achieve its potential
as an industry in Hong Kong, government will need to reinforce its capabilities to protect intellectual property; if a new
biotechnology industry is to emerge, regulatory agencies will
have to provide guarantees of purity and reliability for new
drugs; if Hong Kong is to maintain autonomous memberships
in international organizations, hence a differential access to
Western markets, its customs and trade agencies need to
maintain strength and credibility. These public institutions
are, in fact, a major provider of the services that will be incorporated into the new products of Hong Kong industry.

Internationalism

Finally, Hong Kong companies benefit from a set of intangible, but valuable collective norms that are usually called
'internationalism.' At the firm level, internationalism means
the ability to understand, interpret, and translate into specific

and diverse products the preferences of many different national societies. One measure of Hong Kong's capabilities in this respect is the range of different markets to which individual firms sell, and their ability over time to add new, emerging or opening markets (see Table 4.2). The key new markets for Hong Kong firms have been China, Japan, and Southeast Asia. The best Hong Kong companies have made striking advances in each of these areas, while still retaining their old customers in the West.

Table 4.2:
Hong Kong's Domestic Exports by Major Markets (and Value of Re-Exports)

Market	1985	1995
	(Value in HK$ Million)	
China	15,189 (11.7)	63,555 (27.4)
USA	57,687 (44.4)	61,250 (26.4)
Singapore	2,233 (1.7)	12,236 (5.3)
Germany	7,998 (6.2)	12,178 (5.3)
Japan	4,480 (3.4)	11,877 (5.1)
UK	8,546 (6.6)	10,941 (4.7)
Taiwan	1,252 (1.0)	7,971 (3.4)
Others	32,496 (25.0)	51,649 (22.3)
Total	129,882 (100.0)	231,657 (100.0)
Re-exports	105,270	1,112,470

Source: Hong Kong Government Industry Department, *1996 Hong Kong's Manufacturing Industries*, p. 37.

What are the sources of this internationalism? We believe that it derives in part from the cosmopolitanism of Hong Kong society: the presence in daily life of people from different ethnic and national groups and the capacities for social and business interaction that develop out of societal heterogeneity. There are many advanced countries with substantial foreign worker populations, where the migrants hold low-status jobs and thus rarely interact on terms of equality with citizens. This would be true of the 128,000 Filipino workers in

Hong Kong, most of whom are domestic workers. What is unusual in Hong Kong, however, is the presence of a large, foreign community from affluent countries. The nationals from these countries have educational attainments and incomes that locate them in middle ranges of Hong Kong society at a minimum. They have easy access to much of Hong Kong society, and a high density of social and business relationships. There were 438,200 foreign nationals in Hong Kong in December 1996, up from 370,000 in February 1996. The largest single group was the Filipinos, and the next two largest groups were 34,700 Americans and 30,600 Canadians, followed by substantial numbers from other developed countries, including 25,500 British, and 21,800 Japanese. [13] Hong Kong's internationalism builds on its openness to people from many different countries, who can easily enter the territory and freely exchange information, ideas, projects, and products.

Hong Kong has not only large communities of foreign nationals, but large numbers of foreign firms headquartered within the territory. Ten percent of the Hong Kong workforce is employed by 1,000 resident US firms.[14] There is a significant presence of European and Japanese regional headquarters and regional offices. (Hong Kong has 780 Japanese firms.) And there is a growing and very strong presence of PRC firms in Hong Kong. Mainland companies have invested US$25 billion in Hong Kong, making them the second largest foreign investor in the territory after Britain. There are at least 1,802 wholly owned Mainland-controlled enterprises in Hong Kong. The Bank of China Group's assets make it the second largest banking group after HSBC Holdings. The Bank of China's deposits represent nearly one quarter of total bank deposits in Hong Kong. Mainland traders account for 22 percent of Hong Kong's foreign trade volume. PRC companies listed on the Hong Kong stock exchange represent 8.2 percent of market capitalization; they account for 25 percent of cargo transportation and handling. With Citic Pacific's acquisition of a 20-percent stake in China Light & Power, they have a major role in Hong Kong utilities.[15]

Hong Kong's bilingualism is yet another support of internationalism. Our interviews revealed a substantial concern over a perceived decline of the English language skills of recent graduates. There is clearly a division within the community of teachers and educational administrators about the relative roles of English, Cantonese, and Mandarin in instruction.[16] Despite these controversies, the perception of the importance of English to future career chances is still great enough that in January 1996, 218 out of 394 (55 percent) of secondary schools chose English as the medium of instruction in contrast with Chinese, the choice of 72 schools (18 percent). The skewed result of these choices apparently reflects parental pressures. While there seems to be considerable doubt about the schools' capacity to implement this option, it is a measure of Hong Kong society's understanding of the importance of providing children with the resources to communicate with a dynamic and technologically advanced international community outside the Chinese-speaking world.

Notes

1   Hong Kong Government Industry Department, *1995 Hong Kong's Manufacturing Industries,* Chart 11, 'Relative Share of Hong Kong's Domestic Exports by Major Markets, 1984 and 1994,' p. xi.
2   IMD International, *1996 World Competitiveness Yearbook,* Lausanne: 1996, p. 511.
3   Company 15 in Textiles and Clothing Sector Study, Chapter 9.
4   V. Fung, 'Territory Standing at New Threshold of Opportunity,' *South China Morning Post,* Weekly Edition, February 1, 1997, Business, p. 8.
5   See M.L. Dertouzos; R.K. Lester; and R.M. Solow, *Made in America: Regaining the Productive Edge,* Cambridge, Mass.: MIT Press, 1989. See also, C. Ichniowski, T. Kochan; D. Levine; C. Olson; and G. Strauss, 'What Works at Work: Overview and Assessment,' *Industrial Relations,* 35 (1996): p. 299–333.
6   There are important exceptions to this generalization, particularly from companies in which quality in production requires a close attention to specifications across a lengthy production process—for example, dyeing and finishing plants and plastic injection machinery manufacturers. A few companies claimed they achieved higher quality in their China plants.
7   J. Ayala and R. Lai, 'China's Consumer Market: A Huge Opportunity to Fail?' *The McKinsey Quarterly,* 3 (1996).
8   Ibid., p. 68.
9   S.W.K. Chiu; K.C. Ho; and T.L. Lui, *City-States in the Global Economy: Industrial Restructuring in Hong Kong and Singapore,*

Transitions, Asia and Asian America, Boulder, Colo.: Westview Press, 1997, pp. 42.

10 See R. P. L. Lee (ed.), *Corruption and Its Control in Hong Kong,* Hong Kong: The Chinese University Press, 1981.

11 Interview with Mrs. Rosanna Ure, Assistant Director of Community Relations, Independent Commission Against Corruption, September 27, 1996.

12 Ibid.

13 *South China Morning Post,* Weekly Edition, February 9, 1997, 3.

14 See K. B. Richburg, 'Hong Kong is America's Business.' *Washington Post,* February 3, 1997, pp. A1, A13

15 Wang Xiangwei, 'Territory Turning a Deeper Shade of Red,' *South China Morning Post,* Weekly Edition, February 8, 1997, Business, p. 8.

16 On these issues and for a view critical of the schools' option for bilingualism, see G. C. L. Mak, 'Primary and Secondary Education,' in Nyaw Mee-kau and Li Si-ming (eds.), *The Other Hong Kong Report 1996,* Hong Kong: The Chinese University Press, 1996, especially, pp. 395–6. See also Cheng Kai-ming, 'Education: Crises amidst Challenges,' in S. Y. L. Cheung and S. M. H. Sze (eds.), *The Other Hong Kong Report 1995,* Hong Kong: The Chinese University Press, 1995, especially pp. 494–5.

5 How Sustainable is the Hong Kong Model?

Given the enormous achievements of Hong Kong society and economy and the great human and material resources that undergird its prosperity, many would argue that development along the same path will produce an equally bright future. This view has been clearly articulated by Enright, Scott, and Dodwell, in *The Hong Kong Advantage.*[1] Hong Kong's economic advantages—its continuing growth and low inflation, strengths in the China market, superior infrastructure, its entrepreneurship, and the industry strengths we have highlighted—all suggest that this view should not be dismissed lightly. But our analysis of firm-level performance in Hong Kong and in the China-based Hong Kong plants has led us to conclude that further economic success will require a major thrust forward of the technological and human capabilities of the 'Made By Hong Kong' system. We do not think that the present system can be sustained on its current trajectory. Why?

First, we doubt that the current strategy of achieving value in manufacturing by the continuous relocation of facilities to the lowest-cost labor markets can be indefinitely extended into the future. Hong Kong industrial and economic expansion over the past 15 years has above all involved expansion in the Pearl River Delta. As we discussed above, the overwhelming preponderance of manufacturing facilities owned and managed by Hong Kong companies outside of Hong Kong are in Guangdong.[2] It is true that Hong Kong companies have also moved into inland China and have production facilities elsewhere in Southeast Asia, and even in Africa and Latin America. Still, the success of Hong Kong businesses outside their home territory remains mainly a story of operating in Guangdong. And there are many reasons to doubt that expansion in the Pearl River Delta can continue at the same rate and in the same ways that it has over the past 16 years.

Labor and land costs are rising quite rapidly in the parts of Guangdong Province that are suitable for industrial development. As Sung Yun-wing *et al.* report, wages in Guangdong Province which at the beginning of the economic reform years were comparable to those in neighboring provinces, by 1992 were 45–76 percent higher.[3] The present average monthly wage for workers in the Pearl River Delta is between RMB300–500. In addition, foreign firms must pay into an insurance fund, provide dormitories and meals, and contribute to a wage fund.[4] Average monthly wages in Shenzhen rose rapidly over the past decade; the annual rate of increase ranged from 9 percent to 26 percent per year.[5] Wages would have grown even more rapidly, had it not been for an enormous influx of workers from outside the province, most of whom were working under one-year contracts.[6] The Labour Bureau of Dongguan, for example, estimates that the local labor force numbers 730,000 but workers from outside the Dongguan district number between 500,000 and 600,000. The migrant worker population in Guangdong Province (some 5–6 million) are part of an even larger transient population. This group, estimated in 1990 to be one-tenth the total population, has grown rapidly and today may be as large as one-fifth the total population of Guangdong. [7] Accounts vary on whether these workers are paid as much as the locals, but in any event, without the outsiders, either wages would rise even more rapidly, or industrial jobs would go unfilled. The presence of so large a number of migrants—mostly without families and without permanent ties to the local communities—has stirred up tremendous local tensions.

Not only labor costs but the costs of land, and conflicts over the appropriation of land are rising quickly. As Sung *et al.* report, 'Per capita income and savings in the Pearl River Delta have been increasing rapidly. There is a large demand for properties and a huge domestic market ready for development. The property market in Guangdong has boomed in recent years. Total transactions doubled annually in the Delta since 1990.'[8] Peter Cheung refers to a 'craze of real estate development in the Pearl River Delta [which] has sunk billions of dollars from the coffers of local governments which would otherwise be used for more productive purposes, such as education and infra-structural development.'[9] More generally, Cheung questions whether Guangdong can continue to grow unless it finds a more adequate political and administrative framework for resolving the complex social problems that have developed as a legacy of high growth. As other regions of China develop the ability to turn out the products that Guangdong makes today, can Guangdong upgrade its capabilities? Here, Sung *et al.* are rather pessimistic and point to Guangdong's limitations as a possible center for high-technology products. They draw a comparison between Hong Kong, which in 1971 had 282 tertiary graduates per 10,000 population and in 1991 had 891 tertiary graduates per 10,000, and Guangdong, which in 1991 had only 133 tertiary graduates per 10,000. They conclude that the endogenous prospects for high-technology development in Guangdong in the short and medium terms are limited for lack of appropriate human resources, and that other parts of China, like the Shanghai region, are far better endowed for such an evolution.[10] In short, for Hong Kong companies to continue to derive strong benefits from their implantation in the Pearl River Delta, operations they will need to shift from an emphasis on cheap labor and land (since these will be less and less cheap) to one based on other productive capabilities, even while continuing to be low-cost producers. To the extent that these new capabilities involve new products, processes, and technologies, many of the resources required for this shift to a different path of development will need to come from Hong Kong over the next decade, for local Guangdong capabilities will not suffice to build the new model.

If, on the other hand, Hong Kong companies wish to continue on the old industrial path, they will have to move deeper inland in order to find cheap labor and land. Yet to do so would require the same heavy managerial inputs as were required to make a success of the plants in the Pearl River Delta. As Hong Kong companies move further and further away from Hong Kong, it becomes more and more difficult to bring the Hong Kong managers along. Indeed, a number of the companies we studied reported greater difficulties in managing those of their plants that are located outside the Pearl River Delta region. The same staffing problems reported as acute for the multinational companies operating in other regions of China will become more challenging for Hong Kong firms as well. And, in fact, where will the new generations of Hong Kong managers come from? The current cohort are men and women who were trained by experience in Hong Kong-based plants and offices. But with the rapid wind-down of Hong Kong-based manufacturing, no successor generation is being groomed to take on assignments in the hinterlands of future industrialization. The extreme slowness of the promotion of PRC managers to top positions within the Pearl River Delta plants we have observed means it will be some time before they are ready to assume the reins of managerial power or to move out to play the roles in inland China that Hong Kong managers performed in the industrialization of Guangdong.

The second set of considerations that leads us to question whether Hong Kong industry can afford to continue on the same trajectory of development with low-cost labor mass manufacturing have to do with the growing prowess of Hong Kong's competitors. Hong Kong entrepreneurs, and the overseas Chinese ethnic business elite more generally, have benefited greatly from their linguistic and cultural closeness to the populations in South China, as well as from networks of family and old relationships that ease problems of trust and reliability. While these cultural affinities have been a major asset for Hong Kong, it would be a mistake to generalize from anecdotes about failures of entrepreneurs from other countries that companies from other nations cannot learn how to do business in this part of the world. The prevalent optimism we heard in Hong Kong about the unique capabilities of Hong Kong managers to perform well in China (and the rapid dismissal of Japanese, or Korean, or Singaporean, or American and European advances in this territory) reminded us of our own illusions in the 1960s and 1970s about the unique capabilities of Americans in mass manufacturing. This is worrisome, for the evidence is overwhelming that the competition is learning rapidly. Walter Hatch and Kozo Yamamura draw extremely negative comparisons between ethnic Chinese networks and Japanese production alliances. They see the overseas Chinese capitalists as pursuing a 'strategy of turning quick profits, rather than investing for the long run and thereby acquiring . . . dynamic technological efficiency. More often than not, they become embroiled in rent-seeking,' in contrast with the 'well-oiled *Japanese* production alliances.' They conclude that 'it is Japanese business, not ethnic Chinese business, that is embracing Asia, drawing together the different economies of the region.'[11]

One need not endorse Hatch and Yamamura's rather harsh conclusion to find quite impressive some of the evidence that they and others present for the rapid advance of non-Chinese groups along the learning curve of Asian production. Consider only the case of American and Japanese industrial-

ists—neither group of which is known for well-developed language skills or cultural sensitivities in China (the Japanese facing the additional challenge of a legacy of anger over their
country's wartime behavior in China). Recent research shows
the remarkable progress that firms from both these countries
have made in shifting production into East Asia and in using
both their own nationals and locals in managing these
plants.[12] Hatch and Yamamura present evidence that Japanese
manufacturers in Asia do even better than their affiliates in
Europe and the United States in procuring supplies locally,
even though they could conceivably bring in Japanese-made
components from Japan at lesser transportation cost than
from across the Pacific.[13]

Japanese firms in Asia are investing heavily in training programs, especially within the company, and they gradually
have been able to develop local managers. Japanese have been
slower than American or European firms to promote locals
into top management positions, but then Hong Kong companies, too, have been unable or reluctant to promote PRC
managers into top slots quickly.[14] Even in the most traditional of the industries in our study—textiles and clothing—
where there is a large reservoir of well-educated PRC professionals with experience in the industry and advanced degrees
from university programs in chemical engineering and textiles, we found few cases in which PRC managers had
assumed the top positions.

The case of one textile plant is quite typical: the plant was
set up in Guangdong in 1984 with 388 workers and today has
4,035. The general manager and three deputy general managers are from Hong Kong; one deputy general manager is a
local. Of the foremen, supervisors, and mid-level managers,
15 percent are from Hong Kong. Another company that
began China operations in 1978 now has 17 factories in
China, 15 of which are joint ventures. All the general managers come from Hong Kong. Among the 100 persons next to
the top in the organizational structure (assistant general managers, supervisors), 30 percent are from Hong Kong; of the
foremen, 100 percent are PRC Chinese. The figures seem quite
comparable to those Hatch and Yamamura report for Japanese
enterprises in Thailand and Malaysia.[15] From the above we
would conclude that Hong Kong companies' capabilities in
operating in China, enhanced by culture, language, and rela-

tionships in common, may only provide an initial advantage; but this edge will narrow as firms from other countries, under pressure to reduce their costs, throw massive resources into mastering network production in Asia. To maintain their competitive advantage, Hong Kong companies need to build on their initial positions of strength and to do so by adding higher-value-added products.

Finally, our doubts about a future for Hong Kong industry in which companies continue to move along the same trajectory of labor-intensive, low-technology mass manufacturing are compounded by a sense of opportunities foregone. Among the risks of clinging to the successful patterns of the past by trying to replicate them in ever more distant hinterlands, is the danger of missing out on a rich lode of opportunities that are present closer to home—in Hong Kong itself, and in the Hong Kong-owned and managed plants of the 'Made By Hong Kong' system. The best of the Hong Kong companies the MIT researchers visited—companies such as VTech, TAL Industries, Johnson Electric, Group Sense, and Chen Hsong—are producing new generations of manufactured goods in Hong Kong with attributes that make them especially valuable to customers and especially difficult for competitors to displace. These companies, and a few others like them are today producing the kinds of service-enhanced products that are likely soon to become the mainstay of global manufacturing markets. What challenges need to be overcome in order to move the Hong Kong system as a whole toward these products? And what public and private strategies would enable such an evolution? These are the questions that will be addressed in the next two chapters.

Notes

1   M. Enright; E. Scott; and D. Dodwell, *The Hong Kong Advantage,* Hong Kong: Oxford University Press, 1997.
2   Of the 27 percent with plants outside Hong Kong, 96 percent were in China, most in Guangdong. (Hong Kong Government Industry Department, *1996 Hong Kong's Manufacturing Industries, pp. 280–1.)*
3   This description of changes in Guangdong draws heavily on P.T.Y. Cheung, 'Prosperity and Politics: Guangdong,' presented at the 92nd American Political Science Association meeting,

August 29–September 1, 1996; Sung Yun-wing; Liu Pak-wai; R. Wong Yue-chim; and Lau Pui-kai, *The Fifth Dragon: The Emergence of the Pearl River Delta,* Chapter 6 'Labour Market,' Singapore: Addison Wesley, 1995, pp. 109–133, and Table 6.4, p. 116. See also C. Ikels, *The Return of the God of Wealth,* Stanford: Stanford University Press, 1996.

4   Ibid., p. 110.
5   Ibid., Table 6.2, p. 112.
6   Ibid., p. 117.
7   *Guangdong Gonganbao,* September 13, 1995, cited in P. Cheung, 'Prosperity and Politics: Guangdong,' paper presented at the 92nd American Political Science Association meeting, August 29–September 1, 1996, p. 9. See infra. for a discussion of the social tensions generated by this large 'floating' population, the hostility of the natives to these newcomers, and the difficulties anticipated if employment opportunities should close down for them.
8   Sung *et al.,* p. 163. See Chapter 8, 'Development of Property Markets,' pp. 163–184.
9   Cheung, 'Prosperity and Politics: Guangdong,' p. 36.
10   Sung *et al.,* p. 125.
11   W. Hatch and K. Yamamura, *Asia in Japan's Embrace,* Cambridge: Cambridge University Press, 1996, p. 96.
12   See earlier references to the San Diego study of US and Japanese experience in the globalization of hard disk drive production; on Japanese experience, see especially R. F. Doner, *Driving a Bargain: Automobile Industrialization and Japanese Firms in Southeast Asia,* Berkeley: University of California Press, 1991; and Hatch and Yamamura, *Asia in Japan's Embrace.*
13   Hatch and Yamamura, *Asia in Japan's Embrace,* pp. 158–9, especially Table 10.1.
14   Ibid., pp. 152–7.
15   Ibid., p. 156.

6   Challenges to Hong Kong Industry

In Chapter 4 we described the main competitive advantages of Hong Kong industry today. Any successful evolution of the 'Made By Hong Kong' system must build on these strengths. In the course of our research on Hong Kong's firms and industries, however, we also discovered recurring attitudes and practices that present significant obstacles to industrial upgrading. As we pieced together the evidence from our interviews and plant visits, six broad problem areas stood out:

- gaps in human resource development systems;

- low investment in new technology development;

- the limitations of family ownership of business enterprises;

- the low rate of formation of new technology-based enterprises;

- the scarcity of specialized technological knowledge in government;

- high labor and land costs.

Education, Training, and Human Resources

Education, training, and the continuous upgrading of worker skills are vital to the improvement of industrial productivity and performance. Public authorities, business enterprises, and private individuals share responsibilities for education and training and human resource development in combinations that vary considerably from one society to another. In Hong Kong both public and private initiatives over the past two decades have raised the average skill level of the industrial workforce. But our findings raise major questions about whether the new skills that Hong Kong industry will need to upgrade the global networks of 'Made By Hong Kong' production will be available.

During the last 20 years Hong Kong's educational system has been radically overhauled. Since 1978 all children stay in school for at least nine years, and today more than 90 percent stay for a further two. (By contrast, 46 percent of the population over the age of 25 has had no secondary schooling at all.) The tertiary education sector has also grown. In 1995 more than 18 percent of the relevant age group entered a first-degree course at one of Hong Kong's universities, up from 6 percent in the late 1980s, and just 2 percent in 1980. With an additional 7–8 percent enrolled in non-degree courses, and an estimated 3–5 percent studying abroad in tertiary institutions, roughly 30 percent of the relevant age cohort is now engaged in higher education of some kind.[1]

In industry educational qualifications have been rising too, though the explanation has much less to do with the education sector's growth than with the massive migration of low-skilled manufacturing operations to China. As already noted, the number of unskilled and semi-skilled positions in Hong Kong has been declining rapidly since the mid-1980s, but most manufacturing firms have maintained headquarters operations in Hong Kong, and the demand for managerial staff, engineers, technicians, and other skilled workers has continued to rise.[2] Industry's hiring profile in Hong Kong has therefore become sharply skewed towards more highly educated workers. According to a recent survey of its members by the Federation of Hong Kong Industries, two thirds of the new hires planned by these firms over the next three years will be for managerial, engineering, marketing, and R&D positions, with production engineers and technologists and R&D personnel topping the list.[3]

These trends notwithstanding, we have found three problems in Hong Kong's human resource development strategies and practices that put the goal of continued workforce upgrading at risk:

- the pervasive lack of commitment to the development of human resources at all levels in Hong Kong industry;

- frequently expressed perceptions of a decline in the quality of primary and secondary education;

- the weak links between Hong Kong's higher education institutions and industry.

None of these issues is wholly new, but as the demands on Hong Kong's human resource development system mount during the coming decade, the consequences of each are likely to become much more significant.

Human Resource Development in Hong Kong's Firms

Our research suggests that many Hong Kong manufacturing firms are today only weakly committed to the idea of investing in human resource development. Most Hong Kong firms have yet to make the kinds of investments in in-house and external education, training, and human resource development that characterize the world's leading manufacturing enterprises. Interviews carried out by the *Made By Hong Kong* team point to a widespread pattern of limited in-house training resources and scant attention to career development and planning. This pattern could be found at all levels, from production workers, to engineers, to managerial and other professional employees. In-house training often seemed to amount to little more than watching someone else perform a task, and employers typically provided few resources for employees to take classes outside the company. The results of the interviews were strikingly congruent on this point; similar findings were reported across the entire range of industries. The pattern was particularly pronounced in the textiles and clothing sectors, which out of all Hong Kong's manufacturing sectors are least likely to provide in-house training.[4] The human resource practices within these two industries contrast especially sharply with those of their counterparts in countries like the United States and Germany, which are devoting increasing resources to training managers and production workers. But even in new industries like software, our researchers reported a lack of attention to human resource development.

The general picture suggested by our research is confirmed by other data. A survey of manufacturing firms conducted recently by the Federation of Hong Kong Industries found that 60 percent of the responding firms provide no in-house training for their staff and workers.[5] According to the Institute for Management Development's 1996 *World Competitiveness Yearbook,* Hong Kong firms spend much less on training, on average, than do their counterparts in the other leading East Asian economies.[6] A recent survey of Hong Kong and Singaporean firms in the garment and electronics industries points to a similar pattern, with the Hong Kong firms significantly less likely to invest in training than their counterparts in Singapore (even after correcting for size differences between firms).[7] Judging by their recruitment policies, in fact, Hong Kong's manufacturing firms would appear to have a below-average commitment to education and training even by the modest standards of Hong Kong as a whole. Despite the trend toward hiring more highly educated workers in industry, local university graduates are still estimated to account for only 2.7 percent of total manufacturing employment in Hong Kong, compared with about 8 percent in the Hong Kong labor force as a whole.[8]

Explanations abound. The prevalence of small and medium-sized firms, the social acceptability of job-hopping in Hong Kong, and uncertainties over the 1997 transition have all contributed to a relatively high level of employee turnover, and to the tendency of employers and employees alike to take a short-term view of the employment relationship. Many Hong Kong firms remain under the direct control of their founders or the founders' families, and these companies typically pay less attention to developing the leadership capabilities of a cadre of mid- to senior-level management professionals than do other firms, for whom succession planning is a more deliberative exercise.

Another contributing factor is the pervasiveness of original equipment manufacture (OEM) strategies among Hong Kong's manufacturing firms. Operating with the narrow margins characteristic of OEM manufacturing, such firms have had fewer resources to allocate to the development of managerial and other workers. More importantly, most OEM manufacturers do not maintain in-house design and R&D functions, and they have been relatively slow to introduce new manufacturing technologies. They have therefore had little reason to invest in upgrading the technological skills of either workers or managers. They have been further deterred from such investments by their high rate of employee turnover, which, in turn, is at least partly attributable to the relatively unattractive, low-paying jobs typically associated with OEM production strategies.

From this perspective, then, the characteristic pattern of low human resource investment by OEM firms can be understood as a rational approach, a logically consistent element of a larger—and, until now, highly successful—business strategy. To be sure, if the huge new supply of low-cost, low-skilled labor across the border in Guangdong Province had not become available to these firms in the early 1980s, rapidly rising wages and recruiting problems in Hong Kong might well have blocked their path of growth. As things turned out, however, the opening of the Chinese economy made it possible for them to grow profitably along the OEM trajectory for much longer.

But yesterday's coherent and profitable strategy risks becoming today's trap. The task of upgrading products, processes, and business strategies will be impossible to achieve in the absence of skilled, motivated employees at each level of the firm. But as long as there is a perception among potential and actual employees that manufacturing firms remain committed to a business strategy offering few prospects for experimentation and innovation, the most talented of them are less likely to want to pursue careers in these firms. As one Hong Kong businessman, Michael Green, Chairman of Arnhold Holdings, expressed it:

> We are only now starting to talk about crafting competitive plans to attract the industries of tomorrow—years after Singapore—and as a result of this apathy, the quality of labour is going down because we are not receiving investment from value-added industries. If we want to create wealth and valuable jobs, we need to attract the kind of factories which employ five thousand high-salaried technicians, whether based in Hong Kong or Hong Kong-owned and operating in China.[9]

Employers with whom we spoke frequently complained that manufacturing had become an unattractive career destination for Hong Kong's best graduates. They attributed this to the widespread perception of manufacturing as a declining sector, and to the unwillingness of today's generation of graduates to 'get their hands dirty.' But it is actually difficult to believe that even an expanding manufacturing sector could successfully attract the most capable and ambitious young people to positions whose main purpose was to tend a low-cost, labor-intensive, technologically stagnant manufacturing engine.

We did find exceptions. Most of the foreign multinationals as well as the leading 'hongs' whom we interviewed offered significant training and career development possibilities to their employees. Significantly, they reported little or no difficulty in filling their positions with highly qualified people. One German multinational, employing 350 people in Hong Kong (of whom only eight were expatriates) described its human resources philosophy this way: 'Because of Hong Kong's high wage and land costs, it is better to have a smaller number of highly qualified people who can be more productive—it's better to have two people who are very capable than five who are not.' This firm conducts marketing, sales, distribution, maintenance, and product development activities in Hong Kong, and one-third of its staff are university graduates. Even some of its maintenance and installation technicians have university degrees. The company pays for its staff to pursue post-graduate degrees at night school, and has also worked with other German firms and the German Business Association in Hong Kong to develop a three-year apprenticeship program for vocational trainees based on the domestic German model. About 30 apprentices are enrolled in the program at any one time. Even though some of these trainees are lost to other Hong Kong firms, the company believes that the investment is worthwhile.

Large companies everywhere tend to devote more resources to training than do small and medium-sized firms, and often serve as a training ground for the latter. Hong Kong faces a particular problem in this regard because it has relatively few large employers, either home-grown or foreign. The small and medium-sized enterprise (SME) sector therefore derives fewer benefits from this source.

Primary and Secondary Education

The *Made By Hong Kong* team did not conduct an independent evaluation of the primary and secondary education sector, but we did hear again and again from interviewees who perceived a decline in the quality of Hong Kong's primary and secondary education, especially the inadequacy of English and to some extent also Chinese language skills among school leavers (graduates).[10] The issue of language proficiency is now a trilingual problem, with Putonghua (or Mandarin) joining English and Cantonese (the language spoken at home by 98 percent of Hong Kong's population) on the list of requirements. Almost everyone with whom we spoke emphasized the importance of multilingualism to Hong Kong's continuing ability to play the role of an East–West bridge and a window on the world for China. But many employers expressed dissatisfaction with the language skills of their recruits, and compared Hong Kong unfavorably on this score with other Asian countries, notably including Singapore but also, increasingly, China itself. Several Hong Kong-based representatives of Western multinationals commented that they had found a stronger commitment to mastering English in China than in Hong Kong. As one Western banker observed, 'if you want someone who writes good English, hire him from Beijing University, not Hong Kong U.'

The question of language instruction in the schools is a complex and controversial one. The current policy, recently reaffirmed by the Education Commission, is to encourage secondary schools to adopt Chinese as the medium of instruction.[11] One consequence of this policy has been to place more of the responsibility for English language education on Hong Kong's higher education institutions. These latter have introduced numerous language enhancement programs, and the government has allocated additional resources for this purpose. But many academics and others with whom we spoke expressed strong doubts that remedial language education at the tertiary level could be effective in offsetting what they consider to be the growing shortcomings of primary and secondary education in this regard.

The University Grants Committee, the senior body responsible for higher education in Hong Kong, took a generally optimistic view of the situation in its recent, comprehensive assessment of the higher education system:

> There may still be a long way to go before higher education in Hong Kong can truly claim to be providing bilingual or trilingual manpower, but at least the last ten years have seen the establishment of a language enhancement culture.[12]

But others are more pessimistic. As one observer commented, 'the claim that Hong Kong is a bilingual society is feeble, for most cannot function adequately in either language.'[13] The government recently announced that it would withhold funding of university places filled by students who were unable to meet published minimum standards of English language proficiency on entry. It is uncertain whether the primary and secondary education sector can come up with the necessary resources to respond, even though parents desire this and see it as useful for social mobility. To improve English language capabilities in Hong Kong will require strong political leadership. Paradoxically, the new government may be better placed to provide this than was the British colonial administration.

Links between Higher Education and Industry

Many of the industrialists we interviewed expressed dissatisfaction with Hong Kong's tertiary education institutions. Others in Hong Kong claimed that employers had only one significant complaint—about language proficiency—and that they were otherwise fairly happy with the quality of the disciplinary education that Hong Kong students were receiving. But a 1995 survey of manufacturers conducted by the Federation of Hong Kong Industries found that the great majority of the responding firms rated the overall quality of local graduates as either 'average' (59.5 percent) or 'low' (20.7 percent)—hardly a ringing endorsement of the *status quo*.[14] We tried to understand from our interviews whether these concerns went beyond the 'normal' criticisms of local educational institutions expressed by industrialists around the world. In certain areas—integrated circuit design, software engineering, and plastics engineering, especially—we heard concerns about the shortage of qualified engineering and managerial professionals.[15] But a more common complaint was that the universities hold themselves aloof from the industrial sector and do not tailor their teaching and research activities closely enough to its needs. (Here we will focus on education. We discuss the question of university research below, under the heading 'New Products, New Processes.')

According to the previously cited survey of Hong Kong manufacturers, local graduates are weakest in the area of management and human relations skills.[16] More than 80 percent of all graduates hired by Hong Kong manufacturers are in engineering, computer science, information technology, and other science subjects.[17] Some of the most frequent criticisms we heard concerned the lack of practical knowledge and the narrowness of the education received by these graduates. This comment from one of Hong Kong's leading software firms was typical:

> We used to favor Hong Kong-trained programmers, but now our programmers are predominantly from overseas. Hong Kong graduates are technically very good, but they have little understanding of the issues beyond that. For example, to develop a good user interface you have to understand more than the code, you have to understand what the customers are going to do.

Others cited the graduates' lack of accounting and financial skills.

Almost every employer who we asked expressed a strong preference for hiring graduates of North American and European universities over Hong Kong graduates. The former were seen as having broader, more practical knowledge and experience as well as an edge in creativity and initiative. On the other hand, the employers ranked Hong Kong graduates ahead of those from Chinese universities along these same dimensions. The head of one leading electronics manufacturer reported that he preferred to hire Hong Kong engineers (even though their salaries are higher) over their Chinese counterparts because 'they think and react faster.' But others described Chinese engineers as more loyal, hard-working, and exhibiting stronger theoretical backgrounds. These factors, when coupled with their lower costs, made Mainland engineers attractive hires. Another leading Hong Kong electronics firm reported doing much of its design work in China, where engineers 'are better and you can hire six or seven of them for every one from Hong Kong, who is quite likely to move into sales and marketing in a short time anyway.'[18]

Industry clearly bears some of the responsibility for the fragile relationship with the tertiary institutions. Its strategic choices and human resource practices have helped to reduce the attractiveness of industry as a career destination for college graduates. Moreover, many among the older generation of industrialists do not themselves have a university education, and are seen as having little interest in upgrading the skills of the workforce. But even new industries seem to excite little enthusiasm among university students. An informal survey of computer science undergraduates in their final term revealed that more than 80 percent had never heard of Hong Kong's leading established software developers, much less the kind of start-up and early-stage software ventures whose names are typically well known among their counterparts in the United States. This can be explained partly by the low profile of the software industry ('one of Hong Kong's best kept secrets,' according to the *Made By Hong Kong* Information Technology Subgroup), but it also reflects an academic environment with few links to local industry.

Our interviews with industrialists also revealed concerns about the state of vocational education and training in Hong Kong. Many felt that the vocational training system has lost its way. The rapid expansion of the higher education sector and the dramatic decline in the number of manual manufacturing jobs in Hong Kong add to the perception among both trainees and employers that vocational training is a dead end. Our study coincided with a major review of the Vocational Training Council (VTC), the main organization in Hong Kong responsible for vocational education and training. We therefore decided not to undertake an independent assessment of this critical question. The consultant's report, published in August 1996, emphasized recommendations designed to improve the efficiency and effectiveness of the Vocational Training Council.[19] While many of these recommendations are concerned with the Council's management and organizational structure, some focus on strengthening the role of employers in the design of training strategies for different sectors of the economy. Other proposals would increase the provision of training and skills-upgrading for people already in the workforce (and who even today account for nearly two thirds of the VTC's students and trainees.)

The scale of the vocational training system is large, and its offerings highly diverse. Today over 100,000 people in both full and part-time courses are receiving job-related education and training from VTC institutions (compared with 40,000 on full-time, first-degree university courses.) About 37,000 of these are school leavers and first-time entrants to the labor market. The courses range from full-time, three-year higher diploma courses at one of the VTC's two Technical Colleges to short evening courses at its Industrial Training Centers designed to impart specific new skills to people already in the workforce.[20] The central challenge for the vocational training system is to link its offerings to the rapidly changing needs of the Hong Kong economy. In the absence of a flexible, vibrant vocational training sector, even the best primary, secondary, and tertiary educational institutions will not enable Hong Kong to realize its aspirations for knowledge-intensive, higher-value-added economic growth.

New Products, New Processes

Hong Kong's manufacturing industries have come a long way since the days of cheap wigs and plastic flowers. The typical 'Made by Hong Kong' product today has achieved a level of sophistication that few could have imagined two decades ago. Even so, only a handful of Hong Kong-based firms are competing at or close to the technological or brand frontier in their product-market segments. Firms like VTech in educational electronic toys and cordless phones, Gold Peak in batteries and electronic products, Chen Hsong in manufacturing equipment for the plastics industry, Varitronix in liquid crystal display (LCD) products, and Johnson Electric in electric motors are international leaders in their industries. But the majority of Hong Kong manufacturers have pursued a different approach. Despite moving up-market they have continued more or less as they began, making mature, market-tested products via OEM or subcontracting relationships with local trading companies and foreign buyers.[21] As detailed previously, their main competitive advantage has been the speed and agility with which they are able to shift from one product line to another in response to rapid changes in the market, coupled with their ready access to low-cost labor, originally in Hong Kong itself but more recently in China and elsewhere. They have typically avoided making large investments in new technology or in the development of brand identity, preferring instead to use their flexibility as OEM suppliers and subcontractors to exploit fast-developing and often short-lived niches behind the frontier of rapidly changing markets. A few have approached their OEM relationships strategically, as a low-cost way to monitor the technological frontier. Thus, for example, Gold Peak's decade-long relationships with its large Japanese customers and partners, who are leaders in battery technology, have given it a privileged window on the latest technological developments which, in turn, has allowed it to pursue a more focused technology acquisition strategy. But most Hong Kong manufacturers have been less strategic about this. They have simply followed their customers' specifications for products that have already found acceptance in the marketplace. End-product manufacturers have also generally opted to import the most technology-intensive parts and components, rather than investing in the development of local sources of supply. (Thus, Hong Kong's watch manufacturers have concentrated on designing and manufacturing the watch cases and bands, while importing most watch movements.) This basic pattern of production is broadly confirmed by the latest survey of Hong Kong manufacturers carried out by the Industry Department. According to the results of this survey, of those factories that intend to expand production in Hong Kong (7 percent of the total) less than a third expect to develop any new products, and only 16 percent are planning to introduce new production processes.[22]

For many Hong Kong firms, contract manufacturing has remained a lucrative as well as low-risk strategy for considerably longer than anticipated two decades ago.[23] But one result has been that Hong Kong manufacturing industries tend, on the whole, to be less technologically sophisticated than their counterparts elsewhere. A recent survey of clothing and electronics manufacturers in Hong Kong and Singapore found, for example, that in both industries the Hong Kong manufacturers were significantly less likely to have invested in new technology and labor-saving machinery.[24] Another study of the Hong Kong textiles and clothing industry found that Hong Kong companies were lagging behind other Asian firms in the field of electronic commerce—an increasingly important technology for this industry as retailers put more and more emphasis on reducing ordering and delivery cycle times.[25] Our own researchers reported finding only one Hong Kong firm that was involved in EDI (Electronic Data Interchange) programs with foreign retailers. They also found little interest in Hong Kong in new textiles and clothing products around which high-end producers in the United States and Europe are building highly profitable businesses, such as new fabrics for industrial and office use and 'mass-customized' garments.

It should therefore come as no surprise that Hong Kong industry has hired relatively few technically trained university graduates in the past, that it has been generally disinclined to pursue collaborations with university research groups, and that it ranks close to the bottom of the pack in R&D spending.[26] The Federation of Hong Kong Industries recently reported that less than 30 percent of its members had actually carried out any R&D, and that most of those had spent very little on it.[27] (In the Federation's survey, 'R&D' was defined liberally to include design and even the adaptation of existing products. But even using this generous definition, nearly 85 percent of R&D-conducting firms reported spending less than US$700,000 on such activities in total.)[28]

This 'low-tech' pattern of industrial development has been reinforced by a wide range of supporting policies and practices. First, the government until recently did little R&D funding for upgrading industry. In recent years, it has become more active. The Research Grants Council was established in 1991 to distribute research grants to the universities on a competitive basis, and since then the volume of university research funding has increased sharply.[29] The government has also introduced new technology transfer and applied R&D initiatives directed at industry. The Hong Kong Industrial Technology Centre Corporation was created in 1993 to advance new technology. The Applied Research Council operates two applied R&D schemes, one of which encourages local companies to access the technological resources of the Mainland. The funding for both schemes takes the form of equity participation or an interest-bearing loan at below-market rates for individual firms. The working capital for these two schemes is HK$250 million, and as of early 1996 about a dozen projects had been funded.[30] Since 1994 the government has also funded the Industrial Support Fund at a level of about HK$250 million per year; this provides financial support for initiatives, including applied R&D projects, that are broadly beneficial to industry in Hong Kong. In addition to these new programs, the Hong Kong Productivity Council (HKPC), supported in part by an annual government subvention of about HK$150 million, has for many years provided a range of industrial consultancy, training, and technical assistance services. In recent years the Council has been playing a more active role in developing and introducing new manufacturing technologies to industry. Table 6.1 lists some of the main government-funded initiatives in industrial technology development and transfer today.

Even with the latest infusion of resources, however, Hong Kong's rate of spending on research and development continues to be very low by world standards (see Table 6.2), and the government remains little engaged in strategies that might favor particular firms and sectors.

Second, the universities have in the past matched industry's disinclination to exploit their research resources with their own lack of interest in seeking out industrial challenges on which to work. The situation here is changing. Mainly as a result of infusions of government funds, the overall volume of research activity on university campuses increased fourfold between 1991 and 1995, as did the number of research students,[31] and entrepreneurial university staff and administrators are energetically seeking out new ways to interact with industry.[32] Even so, the vast majority of research on campus is not directly relevant to the practical needs of industry. According to one well-informed source, no more than 5 percent of the R&D funds flowing to the universities goes toward applied research. Another interviewee reported that government policy in this area continues to be strongly influenced by the view that 'research is for the good of the researchers.' Attitudes towards industrially relevant research on campus remain ambivalent. One leading Chinese University researcher involved in three government-supported Industrial Support Fund projects in the information technology field acknowledged that these projects had considerable educational value for his students and helped them find better jobs. He added, however, that for him they were very much a spare time activity— something quite distinct from his research and, unless carefully managed, a hindrance to it. The University Grants Committee (UGC), which together with the affiliated Research Grants Council allocates almost all of the public funds for university research, has called for a symbiosis in research between higher education institutions and industrial and commercial partners; according to the UGC, the universities should not conduct '"ivory tower" activity with the rest of the community passively looking on and reluctantly footing the bill.'[33] But many of the university research administrators we interviewed acknowledged that attitudes in the universities are slow to change. As one senior official put it, 'I don't think the universities are prepared mentally or structurally to help the business and industrial community. Everyone says they support this. But I don't see a real commitment.' Asked to explain why, this official cited as the main reason the criteria used by the UGC and the RGC to allocate research funds, and the premium these place on academic, publishable research. Many others echoed this view.

The practices of Hong Kong's financial sector have been a third contributor to Hong Kong's low-tech pattern of industrial development. Banks have been heavily predisposed towards providing short-term trade credit and working capital, while longer term loans for R&D and capital investment have been relatively scarce, even for larger firms.[34] Nor has equity financing played a major role in industrial investment. The stock market has not valued industrial investments highly, and industrial stocks have tended to underperform relative to the market as a whole.[35] Industrial firms have historically been underrepresented on the Hong Kong stock exchange, and today no industrial company figures among the top 20 listed firms.[36] Finally, as we will discuss in more detail below, private venture capital has not played a significant role in financing early-stage, technology-based enterprises in Hong Kong. These firms have therefore often been obliged to resort to self-financing for longer-term investments in technological upgrading.

A fourth factor has been the comparatively small role played by foreign multinationals in Hong Kong's manufacturing sector. (They do have major activities in banking, insurance, trade, and other services.) In Singapore especially, but also in other Asian economies, the presence of large concentrations of multinationals has created channels for inward investment in new technology and automation that have been largely absent in Hong Kong.

TABLE 6.1: Government-Funded Industrial Technology Upgrading Initiatives

INDUSTRY	INITIATIVE	AFFILIATION	PURPOSE
Clothing	Clothing Technology Development Center	HKPC* + Clothing Industry Training Authority	Demonstrates cost-effectiveness of advanced manufacturing techniques and promotes adoption by industry
Clothing	Quick Response Center	HKPC	Collects and maintains information on technologies and services for quick response; Also conducts research and demonstrates specific technologies as well as provides training and education
Electronics	Electronic Design Automation Center	City U.	Provides technical support and consultancy services on ASIC, field programmable gate array, electronic design automation, and rapid prototyping of electronic products
Electronics	SMT Laboratory	HKPC	Prototyping, testing and measuring facilities for developing SMT-based products; Consultancy services
Electronics	Tape-automated Bonding Center	HKPC	Demonstrates and facilitates transfer of TAB technology to local manufacturers
Electronics	Wireless Design Engineering Group	HKPC	Provides assistance in RF design and evaluation
Electronics	Telecom Technology Center	HKPC	Identifies and transfers relevant technologies to the local telecommunications equipment sector for application in product design and development
Electronics	Center for Display Research	HKUST	Conducts research on new LCD technologies, provides prototyping facilities for local manufacturers to develop new LCD products, and offers training opportunities for students and engineers
Electronics	RF Product Characterization and Training Center	HKPC	Founded April 1996; Goal: Practical, hands-on training programs for RF engineers; Also, provides RF measurement facilities to industry

TABLE 6.1, *Continued*

INDUSTRY	INITIATIVE	AFFILIATION	PURPOSE
Electronics	Signal Processing Technology Center	City U.	Develops signal processing techniques for low-cost DSPs, microcontrollers, or ASICs; Also delivers demonstrable DSP prototypes
Electronics	EMC Compliance Engineering Center	HKPC (funding approved)	Will provide testing and consultation services to industry to support compliance with European Union's Electro-Magnetic Compatibility Directive
Electronics	Study on the Impact of the Development and Manufacturing Technology of Smart Card Products	HKPC (funding approved)	Will collect information on smart card applications, industry standards, and technological development for dissemination to manufacturers
Watches and Clocks	Various	HKPC	Develops new production technologies for the industry
Watches and Clocks	Watch and Clock Technology Center	HKPC	Monitors technology and design trends, transfers technologies and provides support services to the industry
Watches and Clocks	Feasibility Study on Wireless Controlled Timepieces	Hong Kong Watch Manufacturers Association	Will explore feasibility of developing a manufacturing capability for wireless watches
Food and Beverages	Food Packaging Technology Center		Helps manufacturers upgrade packaging technology
Metal Products	Various Projects	HKPC Hong Kong Polytechnic U. Hong Kong U.	Develops metal injection moulding, die casting, photochemical machining, fine blanking tooling, laser cutting, selective laser sintering, and provides technical support services to manufacturers
Plastics	Hong Kong Plastics Technology Center		Introduces advanced technologies to plastics industry; Provides training on advanced processing equipment and demonstration of new processing techniques
Plastics	Rapid Prototyping Technology Center	HKPC + City U.	Introduces rapid product development technologies to local industry and provides technical support services

TABLE 6.1, *Continued*

INDUSTRY	INITIATIVE	AFFILIATION	PURPOSE
Pharma-ceuticals	Good Manufacturing Practices Infor-mation Center	City U.	Provides information on Good Manufacturing Practices and related regulations
Pharma-ceuticals	Good Manu-facturing Practice Support Services Unit	Hong Kong Institute of Technology	Provides technical consultan-cy and support services and organizes training workshops for local manufacturers
Photographic and optical goods	Ultra-Precision Machining Center	Hong Kong Polytechnic University	Provides testing facilities and technical backup to local manufacturers
Photographic and optical goods	Various pro-jects	HKPC	Develops advanced plastic lens design and manufactur-ing technology
Jewellery	Jewellery Industry Technology Center	HKPC	Helps manufacturers shorten product development time; Assists in evaluation of gold assaying analysis; Monitors manufacturing technology development worldwide.
General	Standards and Calibration Laboratory	Industry Department	Maintains measurement standards
General	Product Standards Information Bureau	Industry Department	Provides information on international standards to manufacturers

* Hong Kong Productivity Council

Source: Hong Kong Government Industry Department, *1996 Hong Kong's Manufacturing Industries.*

Table 6.2
Total Spending on Research and Development as a
Percentage of GDP (1994)

Japan	2.88
US	2.44
South Korea	2.29
Taiwan	1.80
Singapore	1.18
China	0.50
Hong Kong	(0.10)*

Source: International Institute for Management Development,
The World Competitiveness Yearbook 1996, Lausanne, 1996, p. 524

*No data provided in IMD report. Figure in parentheses is authors'
estimate based on data provided by government and industry
sources.

Last but by no means least, a widespread tendency to discount the value of intellectual property has acted to discourage corporations and individual entrepreneurs from developing proprietary knowledge or importing it into Hong Kong.
As one leading Hong Kong industrialist acknowledged, intellectual property is 'the one area I really lose sleep over.' His
concerns extend to his customers' proprietary knowledge, to
which his own firm necessarily has access. This industrialist
worries that his customers may come to believe that their
intellectual property is at risk in Hong Kong; if this occurs, he
will be forced to move his operations elsewhere to retain their
trust and their business.

The problem of intellectual property protection is particularly acute in the software field. Hong Kong, despite having
some of the world's toughest legal restrictions, continues to
suffer from some of the most egregious public violations of
the law. A recent government-sponsored study of Hong
Kong's software industry identified intellectual property as
'the single most important factor currently inhibiting the
market for software in Hong Kong and the Asian region, and
the most important market factor that must be addressed for
Hong Kong to realize success in the packaged software mar-

ket.'[37] And as recently as late 1996, two of the world's largest software vendors identified Hong Kong as the easiest location in Asia for software counterfeiters to operate.[38] As our information technology research team observed, a particularly destructive long-term consequence of this problem is the toll it exacts on Hong Kong's young would-be software innovators, who realize they may lose the fruits of their creativity.

Today these issues are more likely to be raised by multinationals than home-grown Hong Kong firms, only a few of which appear to identify intellectual property as a critical part of their assets and competitive strategies. But it is these firms that are Hong Kong's best hope for creating high-value-added growth, and they are less likely to develop new products and processes in Hong Kong if they expect their intellectual property to be better protected elsewhere.

Despite these obstacles, Hong Kong does have its home-grown successes in innovation. In addition to the companies mentioned at the beginning of this section, our team learned of other significant new technology-intensive products and services that had originated in Hong Kong, including:

- the line of Chinese-language pagers and paging services developed by Champion Technologies, a publicly listed company founded in 1987 by former employees of a Cable & Wireless subsidiary;

- the line of hand-held Chinese–English electronic dictionaries and translators developed by Group Sense, a company founded in 1988 by two Hong Kong electronic engineering graduates;

- the automatic cash deposit machine developed jointly by the Hongkong and Shanghai Bank (HSBC) and the Hong Kong unit of Siemens Co. to meet the needs of small Hong Kong store owners in Hong Kong who stay open long after banking hours; the machine allows customers to deposit bank notes in all major currencies and have it immediately credited to their savings accounts;

- the hand-held wireless betting device developed for the Hong Kong Jockey Club by Varitronix, a publicly listed Hong Kong company founded in 1978, that allows users to place bets and obtain race results from any location in Hong Kong;

- the line of color CAD/CAM packaged software systems for garment manufacturers developed by Prima Design Systems, a Hong Kong company founded in 1985 that is today the world's third largest supplier of these systems;

- the early introduction of new telecommunications services, such as Hong Kong calling-number-displayed (CND) and video-on-demand (VOD) services, delivered over one of the world's first all-digital telecommunications networks, and New T&T's Intelligent Network software platform, one of the first to allow customers to change operators without changing phone numbers;

- the introduction of advanced information technologies that have helped transportation operators like Hong Kong Air Cargo Terminals, Ltd. (HACTL), the Mass Transit Railway Corporation, and Hong Kong International Terminals, Ltd. (HIT) in sea cargo to achieve world-class standards of efficiency, speed, and reliability.

Each one of these innovations was the product of unique circumstances, but they did share certain common features.

1. *The importance of the Hong Kong market.* Each of the products and services cited above was originally developed for the local market. Some who doubt Hong Kong's potential as a center of innovation observe that the Hong Kong market is not large enough to sustain innovative products on its own. But although most leading products are eventually exported, the preceding examples all illustrate that the Hong Kong market has special characteristics that favor early innovation. In some cases it was the presence of large individual users or clusters of users that stimulated the innovation. Prima Design, for example, developed its CAD software initially for Hong Kong's textiles and clothing firms, while Varitronix was able to establish an early position in the market for liquid crystal display (LCD) products through sales to Hong Kong's big watch industry. Similarly, the presence of a strong financial services industry was instrumental in the emergence of local firms like ABC Data and TA Consultants as suppliers of

internationally competitive brokerage and investment banking software. More generally, Hong Kong's software firms, to a significantly greater degree than their counterparts in Singapore and Taiwan, have been able to benefit from the local presence of large, sophisticated end users in the service sector.

In other cases the presence of an affluent, technologically sophisticated, fashion- and brand-conscious consumer base has also been a key factor. The high receptivity of Hong Kong consumers to new information technology products helps to account for the success of the Hong Kong Jockey Club's personal wireless betting device, the rapid penetration of Chinese-language pagers, and the fact overall that the usage density of pager and cellular phone service in Hong Kong is among the highest in the world. The healthy appetite of Hong Kong consumers for wireless products and services, coupled with an enlightened regulatory environment, has stimulated a succession of innovative applications, including: the region's first digital wireless telephone network; the world's first commercial application of Code Division Multiple Access (CDMA) technology for digital wireless service; the first implementation of Motorola's wireless data services (including fax and on-line financial data) anywhere in the world; and the development in Hong Kong of innovative products like digital cellular phones, long-range cordless phones, and wireless PDAs. And today the presence of Hong Kong's sophisticated base of consumers, coupled with its advanced telecommunications infrastructure, is making the territory a fertile testbed for experimenting with new interactive multimedia services such as video-on-demand, home banking, and home shopping.

2. *Locally developed product and process innovations typically do not depend on locally developed technological 'breakthroughs'.* Most of the innovations cited here have drawn heavily on technological advances that were made elsewhere, rather than in Hong Kong itself. Moreover, the key technologies have almost never been at the forefront of the field. The critical contributions made by the Hong Kong firms have been to identify new markets and new commercial opportunities for these advances, to adapt them to these target markets, and to integrate them into marketable products or services. Group

Sense, for example, licensed the digital signal processors for its electronic translators from US companies, and Chinese character recognition and text translation software from the Chinese Academy of Sciences' Institute for Computing Technology in Beijing. The software systems developed by HACTL and HIT combined locally developed and imported technologies. A key feature of the HSBC/Siemens cash deposit machine—its multiple-currency banknote counter/validator unit—was originally developed by a Swiss concern.

A few Hong Kong firms have developed sophisticated networks for monitoring technological developments around the world. One of the best-known examples is Johnson Electric, which has positioned technical groups and individual specialists close to key customers in the US, Europe, and Japan, and also at important centers of technological excellence in Europe and America that are most relevant to its core electric motor business. (Johnson also closely monitors developments in China and Eastern Europe, and has acquired significant new technical capabilities this way.) VTech locates 10 percent of its R&D personnel close to key centers of technological expertise in North America and Europe. Gold Peak uses its OEM relationships as an important window on new technological developments, especially in Japan. In other cases close relationships with large multinational corporations in Hong Kong have opened up important channels for technology transfer. Both Champion and Group Sense, for example, incorporated into their products the 'DragonBall' application-specific integrated circuit (ASIC) designed and produced by Motorola in Hong Kong.

Even when the basic technological advances were made elsewhere, however, the innovating companies in all cases have drawn on deep technological resources in-house to adapt them for useful products or services. Group Sense, for example, employs over 100 engineers in Hong Kong, while Johnson Electric employs several hundred.

3. *Sensitivity to market differences.* Hong Kong firms in consumer product industries such as clothing and consumer electronics have long demonstrated an ability to respond rapidly to changing market needs and fashions and to understand the significance of cultural and other differences between markets. These same capabilities have also been applied in

technology-intensive product areas. Firms like Gold Peak and Group Sense have moved quickly to enter smaller markets ahead of their big US and Japanese rivals, who typically have focused first on the larger countries. Group Sense, for example, has enjoyed success in the segmented markets of Southeast Asia, where language, educational levels, and cultural habits vary considerably and are important to the acceptance of its electronic products. Gold Peak, though deliberately focusing on products that do not change very rapidly from a technical perspective, has been successful in entering medium-sized emerging markets in Asia and Eastern Europe ahead of its larger rivals, often through the formation of strategic partnerships.

Family Firms

The history of Hong Kong industry is a history of family enterprises.[39] As we described above, this form has been successful because it harnesses entrepreneurship, a willingness to make long-term investments for the sake of future generations, and an extended network of trusted relationships in the service of business expansion. These characteristics, particularly in an environment like that of the emerging Asian markets, are valuable substitutes for the social, political, and legal institutions that buttress market and property relations in advanced countries. These informal kinship networks substitute as well for the historical values and attitudes that produce reliable economic behavior among strangers in advanced societies. The classic dilemmas of family firms are the same everywhere—above all, how to manage the issue of succession.

For Hong Kong companies that are trying to advance on a path involving larger investments in research, development, and design for new products and processes, family ownership adds yet another set of challenges. First, there may be incompatibilities between financing higher levels of investment and family control. Families tend to resist the kinds of outside scrutiny required to raise funds from banks or on the stock exchange. Indeed, only 2 percent of Hong Kong companies have an audit committee, the Hong Kong Society of Accountants reports.[40] When raising funds, ethnic-Chinese family firms seem to opt for solutions least likely to reduce the owner's control.[41]

Second, the organizational structures of family-owned businesses may discourage expansion into higher-value-added areas. One strong feature of these structures is their centralization and the concentration of decisionmaking power in the hands of a few at the top of the company. A large body of management literature on innovative and complex manufacturing emphasizes the importance of decentralized authority in order to promote easy and rapid communication among those working on problems, yet this cuts against the grain in the family businesses.[42] A recent major study of overseas Chinese businesses finds that these enterprises avoid areas where decentralization is necessary, such as complex manufacturing and service industries.[43]

Third, the concentration of family member control at the top tends to make it difficult to recruit and retain outstanding non-family managers. Seeing their opportunities for advance in the company blocked at the top, such managers are always looking for the best time to defect—either to join other firms, or to start their own. Particularly when companies need to recruit technologists with expertise that family members do not possess and to invest heavily in training them to manage the transformation of new ideas into commercial products, the failure to keep the best young managers will be very damaging. The effects of the concentration of authority in the hands of family managers at the top are visible in the thinness of the layers of management in the middle of the organization. The companies we visited during our research often seemed to lack the broad strata of middle-level managers and technicians we have found in companies making similar products elsewhere. The Hong Kong companies often could be described by one of the two patterns identified by Chu and MacMurray as characteristic forms of Chinese enterprise: 'management "spokes" around a powerful founder "hub," or a management structure of just two layers.'[44]

Studies of family enterprises tend to come up with more or less the same list of recommendations for overcoming their weaknesses: opening up senior management to non-family members; enlarging the role of outside owners; exposing the company to more outside monitoring; offering incentives in the form of profit-sharing or stock acquisition to promising young managers.[45] In Hong Kong as elsewhere, however, the question is how to advance this set of desirable changes, given that the choices involve closely held family matters outside the public realm. Here the most promising avenue for change lies in diffusing the experiences of a small number of pioneering Hong Kong firms that are experimenting with mixed forms of family–outsider management. Li & Fung, for example, is described in a Harvard Business School case (Case Study Nos. N1-396-107, Part A and N1-396-140, Part B) as going public to resolve issues of family control. The materials quote William Fung on the public listing of the company in 1973: 'It was a classic case of a family company in transition. Despite having 35 cousins, most were not interested in the business.' The case writer comments: 'With the business in need of professional-ization, Li & Fung saw going public as the only equitable solu-tion to divide the familial spoils among the extended family members.' The limited character of the shift was evident in the fact that the company was privatized again in 1989; then taken public again in 1992 with the sale of 25 percent of the shares. Li & Fung also innovated in promoting non-family members to top managerial roles and providing a profit-sharing scheme with very large rewards in order to retain the best people with-in the firm. Gold Peak, too, has brought non-family members into the top managerial posts. Most recently, when the founder of a very large garment company retired, he chose a Western banker as his successor as general manager. The mixed pattern that emerges from these experiments allows a blend of the old strengths with new inputs. Diffusing knowledge about these cases and stimulating debate over their relevance to a larger number of family firms is an objective that professional and trade organizations could facilitate.

Forming New Technology-Based Enterprises

The importance of new business formation to the growth of high-technology industries in the United States and else-where is widely recognized. Especially in software and other parts of the information technology sector, individual entrepreneurship has been a critical mechanism for promoting innovation and the diffusion of new ideas.

With more than 470,000 locally registered firms, Hong Kong enjoys an international reputation as a booming center of entrepreneurial activity and as one of the easiest places in the world to register a new company. Stories of self-made businessmen accumulating fabulous fortunes circulate widely, and starting one's own business is a popular option for many Hong Kong residents.

Very few of these new businesses have had a strong technology focus, however. The technology-intensive, home-grown firms discussed earlier in this book are the exception. Hong Kong's record in this domain may not be worse than that of others in the region, and the number of technology entrepreneurs may be on the rise.[46] Even so, the low level of high-tech start-up activity is striking, especially in the context of Hong Kong's generally entrepreneurial business environment. If this persists, it will surely be harmful to Hong Kong's efforts to upgrade its industries.

There are several interrelated causes of the problem: the absence until recently of a sizeable engineering and scientific research community at the universities; the relatively small number of multinationals conducting R&D and product development activities in Hong Kong (although Singapore's considerably larger contingent of such firms does not appear to have spawned many home-grown start-ups there to date); the shortage (at least by comparison with Taiwan) of foreign-educated 'techno-entrepreneurs' returning from abroad; and a lack of financing.

Finance is a special puzzle, for Hong Kong's financial markets are among the world's largest and most sophisticated. Hong Kong today is the world's fifth largest banking center, in terms of external financial transactions, and the Hong Kong stock exchange is now the world's seventh largest.[47] Moreover, the latest IMD *World Competitiveness Yearbook* ranks Hong Kong second only to the United States in the ready availability of venture capital for business development.[48] Yet our research has shown that almost no venture capital is flowing to start-up or early-stage firms trying to develop new products or processes (a more comprehensive account of this research can be found in Chapter 13 of this book.) The companies that call themselves venture capital firms—there are today nearly 90 members of the Hong Kong Venture Capital Association—are almost exclusively providing capital for established businesses that are seeking to expand (a form of investing often referred to as 'mezzanine' financing.) The time horizon of these investments typically ranges from five to seven years, and can be longer still, thus refuting the well-known stereotype of the short-term-driven Hong Kong investor. But very few of these so-called venture capital firms are actually making true venture investments—that is, equity investments in firms that have yet to sell their first product. They look for businesses with tangible assets such as factories or proven product lines in which to invest. And today there are no examples of venture funds in Hong Kong with a pure focus on technology.

Medium or longer-term bank financing has also been generally unavailable to early-stage companies, and practically all of Hong Kong's home-grown manufacturing and technology-intensive firms have relied on personal or family funds to get started. Firms with a flow of revenues from the outset of their operations have sometimes been able to obtain very short-term loans to finance expansion and capital expenditures. But for other firms engaged in new product development and lacking early revenues, even very short-term credit has been impossible to find. Only a few firms have succeeded in attracting longer-term bank financing, and these have already achieved a substantial track record of profitability.

One explanation for the absence of technology-oriented venture financing in Hong Kong is a lack of attractive investment opportunities. (In fact, the two problems have fed upon each other. Potential entrepreneurs in Hong Kong, knowing the difficulty of raising long-term capital, have been more inclined to consider other locations or other kinds of ventures.) Another reason, already implied above, is the strong preference for investing in businesses with tangible assets. But two additional factors have also weighed against technology-based technology investing in Hong Kong: first, the availability of alternative investment vehicles offering higher returns at perceived lower risk, especially in property development, but also more recently in infrastructure projects and manufacturing plants in China; and second, the lack of an attractive exit strategy for technology venture investors.

For Hong Kong's venture capital firms, as for venture investors everywhere, the availability of a viable exit route is a critical consideration. While a direct sale to a third party investor is always a possibility, a public stock offering is almost invariably the favored exit strategy. Hong Kong's venture funds are no exception, generally preferring to list their companies on the Hong Kong stock exchange. But to ensure the quality of listed companies and to build investor confidence, the Hong Kong exchange requires firms to have been profitable for three consecutive years prior to listing.[49] The practical effect of these requirements is to limit the range of companies seeking listing to relatively mature firms with established product lines and stable earnings. The possibility of listing is thus not really open to technology-based companies early in their life cycle, and for this reason venture funds are much less likely to see them as attractive investments. All of this is borne out by the current composition of the Hong Kong stock exchange. When the Exchange's Market Development Group recently counted how many high-technology firms are currently listed, they found just 15 out of a total of 542 listed companies, and even many of those were more accurately described as manufacturing firms with a rather limited technology focus.

The impact of the low level of venture investing can be seen in Hong Kong's software industry, which consists of about 500 independent software vendors employing 8,500 people. According to a recent government-sponsored consultancy study, the industry is severely undercapitalized, with an average start-up capitalization of about HK$1.6 million per firm, and current capitalization averaging under HK$3 million.[50] As the consultants note, 'software is not a capital intensive business, [but] independent software vendors would be hard pressed to invest in product or market development from this low of a capital asset base.' Every one of the software firms we interviewed was self-financed at the outset, and none had subsequently received venture capital. Many financed themselves through consulting and the development of customized products. A typical pattern was for the firm subsequently to try to turn custom software into a 'packaged' product for a broader market, but often this was unsuccessful. Several commented on the difficulty of finding the funds necessary for new product development and for marketing packaged products in and outside Hong Kong. This picture of small software firms scraping by with barely adequate financing is hardly unique to Hong Kong, of course. Most US firms fit this description too, and the great majority never receive venture capital, let alone infusions of public equity. Nevertheless, the knowledge that such financing is potentially available has an important bearing on the business decisions and strategies of these firms, and is an important difference between the US and Hong Kong today.

The implications of a lack of true venture capital activity in Hong Kong go well beyond the shortage of funds. The partners in the world's leading venture firms (most of them in the United States) also play a vital managerial role for the young and typically inexperienced companies in which they invest; they provide important marketing and strategic advice and draw on their extensive business networks to help recruit key personnel and to develop contacts with potential customers and suppliers. This critical tutoring function is almost completely absent in Hong Kong.

Government's Technological Capabilities

The work of upgrading Hong Kong's technological capabilities will be carried out primarily by its private firms and its educational institutions. But a corresponding upgrading of the government's capabilities in science and technology will also be needed. More and more of the issues facing the government have a significant technological component. Policies regarding trade, industrial development, intellectual property, economic regulation, education reform, and the recruitment of overseas technology companies to Hong Kong, to name only some, are frequently influenced by and sometimes turn on complex technological matters. The government's conduct of its own affairs—its internal administration, its delivery of public services—also increasingly depends on the application of sophisticated information technologies. Yet specialized technological knowledge is scarce within the public administration today. The government relies heavily on unpaid advisors and consultants for expert technical advice, and while this is a necessary and often effective strategy it is ultimately not a substitute for decisionmaking by responsible, technologically knowledgeable public officials. We believe that the government's in-house capabilities in this area should be considerably strengthened.

This issue is not a new one. It was raised at least as early as 1979, when the Governor's Advisory Committee on Diversification 'noticed a lack of knowledge and understanding within the Government Secretariat of matters within the field of applied science and technology.'[51] Since then, of course, the role of technology in public policy and in government administration has become much more pervasive, and the need for government to improve its understanding of the scientific and technological needs of both manufacturing and services industries has grown stronger.

High Labor, High Land

Finally, among the hurdles to a new future for Hong Kong industry, we need to mention the two factors that are the most frequently cited by Hong Kong industrialists and foreign investors: the high cost of labor and land. In the 1996 'Survey of Hong Kong's Manufacturing Environment,' of twelve factors affecting decisions on investment only two were judged negative by more than half the respondents: labor cost (68.1 percent) and cost of office and factory space (54.3 percent).[52] All industries except one small one (photographic goods) ranked labor costs as the most important investment factor; 85.8 percent of the respondents cited high labor costs as a problem and 34.8 percent described it as serious. More than half stated that the situation regarding labor costs was getting worse. Over a fifth of the respondents (and one-third of those in the clothing and electronics sectors) reported trouble filling vacancies.[53] Foreign investors as well see Hong Kong's labor costs as high relative to those in other comparable markets in the region. For example, the American Chamber of Commerce's comparison of the cost of doing business in Hong Kong versus Singapore concludes that compensation is 10–30 percent higher in Hong Kong and illustrates the point with the cases of the base salaries of senior secretaries (Hong Kong, US$25,376; Singapore, $17,059), heads of finance ($115,928 versus $92,291), and sales managers ($65,042 versus $45,230).[54] The report points out, however, that certain components of cost—notably taxes—are lower in Hong Kong than in Singapore. *The Hong Kong Advantage*, by Enright, Scott, and Dodwell presents an analysis of costs in Hong Kong, Singapore, Shanghai, Tokyo, and Sidney. The study concludes that the cost of labor and office space are very high in Hong Kong, but that when tax rates are factored in, the cost structure is comparable to the other major cities in the region.[55]

As Enright, Scott, and Dodwell emphasize, high wages and high rents are not necessarily bad if they result from rising productivity and profitability. Hong Kong's high standard of living corresponds to the aspirations and efforts of its people, and no one advocates the kinds of policies—massive labor importation, rent controls, regulating land prices—that in theory would lower these costs. But Hong Kong does need to address the problems that result from monopoly or quasi-monopoly situations and the absence of competition, or from restrictive policies that impose excessive burdens on one or another sector of society. And indeed, high land costs in Hong Kong not only reflect the fact that this is a small territory, but also that the Government owns all the land and disposes of it in ways that have particular consequences for rents. The 1996 Consumer Council report on property analyzes the role of two non-competitive factors in the land market in making land costs high by 'global standards': (a) 'the role of Government as monopoly provider of new land, and regulator of building development; and (b) the high market concentration of developers of private housing.' The report points to the concentration of property in the hands of relatively few developers and the difficulties for newcomers in entering this market.[56] The Consumer Council concludes with a set of recommendations that would open the market up and lower costs through more competition and through new Government policies that would make available lands that today are zoned to restrict new uses.

These issues obviously go far beyond the scope of the *Made By Hong Kong* research agenda, but they intersect it on two vital points: the immigration restrictions that limit new entrants to the Hong Kong economy; and the land prices that drive up the cost of facilities for new start-up activities and for housing for those whom Hong Kong seeks to attract from abroad to work in the new industries. With respect to the former, the challenge is to devise new rules that support industrial upgrading without opening the floodgates to an inpouring of workers willing to take any job at any wage. The current quota system for the admission and financial support of foreign (including PRC) students to Hong Kong's universities constitutes too narrow an aperture for the best and brightest students in the region, some of whom Hong Kong might well seek to recruit for work in Hong Kong after graduation. The immigration restrictions applying to PRC citizens make it very difficult for Hong Kong companies to bring them into their Hong Kong-based facilities. This is a serious obstacle to training programs that would develop new generations of managers for the 'Made By Hong Kong' production networks in China. It also blocks Hong Kong's access to scientists and technologists from strong university research laboratories in China who could contribute to new product innovation.

With respect to production workers, the current immigration policies also impose burdens on industry that may be too constraining. Even in advanced production facilities, there always are a certain number of positions for entry-level workers with lower skills. In most high-wage societies, these positions are staffed, in part at least, by young foreign workers who are less skilled and less educated than the natives, and for whom these entry-level jobs may constitute a first industrial experience. These foreign workers enter advanced societies through highly regulated and constraining immigration policies. Until 1996, Hong Kong, too, had such a policy; at its peak, about 20,000 non-permanent foreign workers entered legally. A new regulatory scheme has entered into effect in Hong Kong which requires such long and complex arrangements as to block effectively the legal entry of low-skilled workers. Over the next decade, if Hong Kong's population grows by family reunifications and other legal entrants from the PRC, some of the difficulties experienced by manufacturers trying to maintain or expand operations in Hong Kong may ease. But in the near term, this remains an issue.

The housing market, too, poses problems to the encouragement of new innovative industry in Hong Kong. For wooing back Hong Kong residents who have studied and worked abroad—or attracting others, perhaps ethnic Chinese seeking a prosperous and culturally familiar environment—the issue of affordable housing is paramount. Bringing international experts into Hong Kong industry and government for several-year stays requires attractive packages, and housing is a key element. Just as the Hong Kong universities have been able to bring in top-ranking faculty from around the world by offering housing, the new industrial activities may also require some housing support for particular categories of specialists being recruited from abroad. We have heard creative proposals to redesignate (and reconfigure) some buildings in the ring of industrial zones that lie within easy reach of the central parts of the city as residences for PRC technologists and managers on rotation in Hong Kong as part of their over-all training. It is clear that bringing new forms of expertise into Hong Kong and using Hong Kong as a training ground for the managers of Hong Kong-owned plants in China will require new solutions on the housing front.

To summarize: if Hong Kong is to move onto a new industrial trajectory, determined new efforts will be required in the following areas: building human resources; developing new products and processes; modifying company ownership structure and organizational hierarchies; forming new technology-based enterprises; strengthening government technologists' capabilities; and alleviating the burden of the high cost of land and labor. Each of these areas might be understood as a weakness in the existing system, or, as we suggest, as a challenge that must be met in order to move forward. In the section that follows, we outline a series of recommendations for how to advance on this route.

Notes

1 The data in this paragraph were obtained from the recent report by the University Grants Committee of Hong Kong, *Higher Education in Hong Kong,* October 1996.
2 Federation of Hong Kong Industries, Industry and Research Division, *1995 Survey on Manufacturers' Demand For Administrative and Technical Manpower,* 1996.
3 Ibid., p. 7.
4 Ibid., p. 18
5 Ibid.

6   IMD International, *The World Competitiveness Yearbook 1996,* Lausanne, 1996.

7   W.K. Chiu; K.C. Ho; Tai-lok Lui, *City-States in the Global Economy: Industrial Restructuring in Hong Kong and Singapore,* Boulder, Colo.: Westview Press, 1997, pp. 108–109.

8   Federation of Hong Kong Industries, *1995 Survey on Manufacturers' Demand for Administrative and Technical Manpower,* p. 10. The 8 percent estimate for the total Hong Kong labor force is based on data provided by the Hong Kong Government's Education and Manpower Branch, which recently reported that workers with a university education accounted for 6.3 percent of the labor force in 1991, and are expected to account for 10.3 percent in 2001. (See *Manpower 2001 Revisited,* Education and Manpower Branch, Government Secretariat, Hong Kong Government, 1994.)

9   *South China Morning Post,* 'Time to Halt the Territory's Certain Slide to Mediocrity,' September 23, 1996, Business, p. 10.

10 See, for example, the recent report of the University Grants Committee, *Higher Education in Hong Kong,* p. 43.

11 Education Commission, *Enhancing Language Proficiency: A Comprehensive Strategy,* Education Commission Report No. 6, December 1995.

12 University Grants Committee, *Higher Education in Hong Kong,* p. 75.

13 G.C.L. Mak, 'Primary and Secondary Education,' in Nyaw Mee-kau and Li Si-ming (eds.), The Other Hong Kong—1996, Hong Kong: The Chinese University Press, 1996, p. 395.

14 Federation of Hong Kong Industries, *1995 Survey on Manufacturers' Demand For Administrative and Technical Manpower,* p. 11.

15 According to the Hong Kong Government Industry Department's latest survey of Hong Kong manufacturers, a majority of the respondents (56 percent) viewed the availability of technical and professional skills as a positive aspect of the business environment in Hong Kong. (See Hong Kong Government Industry Department, *1996 Hong Kong's Manufacturing Industries,* p. 282.)

16 Federation of Hong Kong Industries, *1995 Survey on Manufacturers' Demand for Administrative and Technical Manpower,* p. 11.

17 Ibid., p. 13.

18 However, still another leading Hong Kong industrialist with engineering operations in both Hong Kong and South China reported paying his China-based engineers at Hong Kong rates.

19 *Strategic and Organizational Review of the Vocational Training Council: A Final Report to the Secretary for Education and Manpower,* Segal Quince Wicksteed (Asia) Limited, August 1996 (2 vols.).

20 The VTC also administers a scheme providing matching funds to companies wishing to train their employees in new technologies that would benefit Hong Kong. This program, known as the 'New Technology Training Scheme' is financed by income generated from a capital fund of HK$105 million set up by the government.

21 Chiu *et al.*, *City-States in the Global Economy*, p. 39.

22 Hong Kong Government Industry Department, *1996 Hong Kong's Manufacturing Industries*, Table 17.14, p. 297

23 Indeed, the formation of the Advisory Committee on Diversification by the government in 1977 was motivated in significant part by the belief that the days of low-cost, labor-intensive manufacturing in Hong Kong were numbered.

24 Chiu *et al.*, *City-States in the Global Economy*, p. 109

25 Kurt Salmon Associates, for Hong Kong Government Industry Department, *1995 Techno-Economic and Market Research Study on Hong Kong's Textiles and Clothing Industries*, Hong Kong, July 1996, Vol. I, p. 68.

26 See IMD International, *The World Competitiveness Yearbook 1996*, p. 524.

27 Federation of Hong Kong Industries, Industry and Research Division, *Investment in China: 1994 Survey of Members of the Federation of Hong Kong Industries*, March 1995, pp. 29–35.

28 Ibid., p. 31.

29 In commenting on this development, the University Grants Committee noted that it had recommended the establishment of a mechanism for disbursing government research funds to tertiary institutions on a competitive basis as early as 1983, but that the government of the day had not acted on the recommendation, 'it is believed because officials regarded university research as potentially very costly and also felt that private industry would unaided make the right decisions about R&D in market terms.' *(Higher Education in Hong Kong*, p. 21.)

30 Some interviewees complained that the funding available for individual projects is too small, that the application process is very lengthy (a year or more), and that the rule preventing candidates from applying more than once discourages interest.

31 The data on university research activity is from University Grants Committee, *Higher Education in Hong Kong*, p. 20.

32 A case in point is the current proposal to establish a polymer processing and engineering center at the Hong Kong University of Science and Technology.

33 University Grants Committee, *Higher Education in Hong Kong*, p. 159.

34 See Chiu *et al.*, *City-States in the Global Economy*, p. 134.

35 Ibid., p. 138.

36 Ibid.

37 Hong Kong Government Industry Department, *Consultancy Study on Hong Kong's Software Industry, 1994–95*, Vol. 3, Market and Technology Trends Analysis, pp. 8–57.

38 *South China Morning Post,* 'Giants of Software Name Hong Kong as Piracy Capital,' December 12, 1996, p. 1.

39 See Wong Siu-lun, *Emigrant Entrepreneurs: Shanghai Industrialists in Hong Kong,* Hong Kong: Oxford University Press, 1988; and M. Weidenbaum and S. Hughes, *The Bamboo Network,* New York: Free Press, 1996, Chapter 2.

40 Cited in *South China Morning Post,* Weekly Edition, January 25, 1997, Business, p. 2.

41 East Asia Analytical Unit, Department of Foreign Affairs and Trade, Australia, *Overseas Chinese Business Networks in Asia,* Canberra: AGPS Press, 1995, p. 134.

42 See for example the pioneering work of Joan Woodward, *Industrial Organization: Theory and Practice,* 2nd edn., Oxford: Oxford University Press, 1980

43 Department of Foreign Affairs and Trade, Australia, *Overseas Chinese Business Networks,* p. 133.

44 T. C. Chu and T. MacMurray, 'The Road Ahead for Asia's Leading Conglomerates,' *The McKinsey Quarterly,* 3 (1993). The authors cite a survey of over 150 ethnic Chinese entrepreneurs which found that 70 percent still operated around one of these two simple structures.

45 See 'The Road Ahead for Asia's Leading Conglomerates,' by Chu and MacMurray, and *Overseas Chinese Business Networks,* cited above.

46 Hard data on this topic are hard to come by, but impressionistic evidence suggests that technology-focused start-ups are even rarer in Singapore. In Taiwan, on the other hand, the level of new high-tech business formation appears to be significantly greater.

47 The Honourable Donald Tsang, Financial Secretary, 'Hong Kong 1997 Economic Outlook,' February 27, 1997 (text of speech available at www.info.gov.hk).

48 IMD International, *The World Competitiveness Yearbook 1996,* p. 455.

49 The profit level in the year prior to listing must be HK$20 million, and at least HK$30 million over the two years before that.

50 Hong Kong Government Industry Department, *Consultancy Study on Hong Kong's Software Industry: 1994–95,* p. ES-2.

51 Advisory Committee on Diversification, C.P. Haddon-Cave, Chairman, 'Report of the Advisory Committee on Diversification,' Hong Kong, 1979, paragraph 562.

52 Hong Kong Government Industry Department, *1996 Hong Kong's Manufacturing Industries,* Chapter 17, pp. 274–6.

53 Ibid., p. 277.

54 American Chamber of Commerce, Hong Kong, 'The Hong Kong vs. Singapore Debate: The Costs of Doing Business,' August 1995.

55 M. Enright; E. Scott; and D. Dodwell, *The Hong Kong Advantage,* Hong Kong: Oxford University Press, 1997 (see especially Chapter 7).

56 Hong Kong Consumer Council, *How Competitive is the Private Residential Property Market?,* 1996.

7 Upgrading Hong Kong's Core Capabilities

This book began with a vision of Hong Kong on a trajectory of rapid innovation in service-enhanced manufactured products and the prediction that Hong Kong could emerge as a world leader in making these goods. To construct such a future, Hong Kong needs to build on the strengths it has acquired during 40 years of rapid expansion along a path of labor-intensive, low-cost manufacturing in Hong Kong and China, while addressing the challenges that we have identified as weaknesses in the current system. The human and capital resources accumulated from this historical experience have already served as inputs for a wholesale transfer of productive capabilities into China with a vast increase in their scope and output. This shift of manufacturing has been a great success. But can such a pattern of development be sustained over the long term? We believe that it cannot. Changes underway in China (such as rising labor costs, as discussed in Chapter 5) make it likely that attempts to repeat the same patterns of production in the Pearl River Delta—or to replicate these patterns further inland—will start to produce declining levels of reward. An equally compelling reason to consider new directions is that Hong Kong today is missing out on major new opportunities for strengthening 'Made in Hong Kong' operations and with them, strengthening the productive capabilities of the 'Made By Hong Kong' networks of production outside the territory.

What would it take to move the 'Made By Hong Kong' industrial system into the manufacture of innovative products and processes incorporating new information technologies and join them to Hong Kong firms' traditional skills as flexible, rapid manufacturers? How should this be accomplished? In this section we turn finally to our recommendations to Hong Kong companies, government, and universities.[1] With these proposals we hope to contribute to a vital debate for Hong Kong, one whose stakes ought not to be obscured by the momentous political transition of 1997.

Our general recommendations fall under eight broad headings:

- acquiring technological knowledge from outside;
- strengthening Hong Kong's R&D base;
- information technology for new products, services, and customers;
- upgrading original equipment manufacture (OEM);
- education, training, and human resource development;
- fostering home-grown, technology-based enterprises;
- strengthening government's technological capabilities;
- building a 'safe harbor' for industry.

The six sector studies in Part Two also offer a set of recommendations which the researchers conclude are vital to the future of these industries.

Acquiring Technology from Outside

The three most important ways to pull more innovation into Hong Kong from the outside are through new initiatives with multinational corporations, with PRC scientists and technologists, and with international experts from advanced countries. Promoting such initiatives requires lowering the barrier presented by Hong Kong's high-cost housing and barriers to entry into industry and research of skilled personnel from the PRC. *We specifically recommend (1) new institutes at Hong Kong universities to study PRC science, technology and market evolutions and to exchange personnel with PRC institutions; (2) more targeted efforts to recruit Hong Kong residents abroad, other ethnic Chinese, and international specialists for assignments in government and private industry; and (3) government–industry cost-sharing in the provision of affordable housing for foreign scientific and technical personnel recruited to work on short-term or longer assignments.* The objective of facilitating the flow of new ideas into Hong Kong is important; however, it is vital to pursue it in ways that build capabilities in local companies and draw in Hong Kong people at all levels. The goal is to provide new resources for local enterprise, not to supplant it.

The innovations that fuel new generations of products and processes grow both out of the new ideas that a society develops on its own and those it finds in other countries and adapts and develops for its own purposes. Even a country like the United States, where domestic institutions generate a large stream of basic and applied research and development to grow new products, still needs mechanisms to monitor science and technology in leading centers abroad and to pull the most promising new developments into its own industries. Hong Kong needs both to enhance those institutions that allow it to tap into the most promising technologies developed abroad, and to stimulate a much greater production of applied research and development and new ideas within its own laboratories and industries. These two goals are not mutually exclusive; indeed, they are interdependent. In this section we consider three ways in which Hong Kong might pull in a larger set of innovations from the outside world: attracting multinational corporations; collaborating with PRC scientists and technologists; and recruiting international experts with experiences in leading edge companies elsewhere. In the following sections, we discuss other ways to attract innovations from overseas, as well as changes that would enlarge Hong Kong's endogenous capabilities for generating new ideas, products, and processes.

Multinational Corporations

One of the major ways in which emerging countries upgrade the skills of their workforce and the range of their industries' capabilities has been to learn from multinational companies that establish plants in their societies. What are the mechanisms through which such learning takes place? First, the operation of a MNC facility triggers a set of processes that train locals in new skills and introduce them to a range of unfamiliar technologies. The political decision at the outset to make the local environment an attractive one for MNCs usually involves investment in new programs at local universities and technical schools in order to deepen the pool of resident talent that the MNCs can employ. Multinational companies do bring people with them from their home societies and cast a wide net in hiring around the world—Motorola in Hong Kong, for example, in 1994–5 recruited [20] Hong Kong citizens working abroad to return to Hong Kong, as well as 42 fresh graduates from local universities. But MNCs are unlikely to choose a site unless it can offer a fairly deep pool of excellent candidates for hire. Other inducements a country may offer cannot outweigh the absence of qualified personnel in suffi-cient quantity. Expatriate workers are simply too expensive a solution—and the number of different sites in different coun-tries vying to attract new MNC facilities is too great. The political decision to bring in MNCs usually involves new expenditures on education and training; and then, the actual experiences of workers, technicians, and managers within the MNCs also enhance the knowledge and skills of the local pop-ulation.

Second, a multinational company can contribute to the upgrading of activities in a region through relationships with its suppliers; the MNC demands new levels of quality and capabilities for technological learning and also provides the tutelage that enables the suppliers to improve. Third, MNCs may spark a process of innovation in regions by spinning off new activities in new ventures. The employees of the MNC are well positioned for seeing the ways in which the tech-nologies and competencies of the MNC might be developed to produce new products—particularly those with special fea-tures that address particular needs and preferences in the region. For example, two Hong Kong high-tech companies, Group Sense and ACL, each have products whose origins trace back to innovations and people at Motorola.

For all these reasons, Hong Kong would seem to have much to gain from a determined effort to induce more MNCs to establish activities within Hong Kong. Yet we would argue that attracting MNCs to locate high-tech operations in Hong Kong should not be the centerpiece, but only one component among others in a coordinated set of public and private ini-tiatives to induce more rapid development of higher-value-added and innovative activities in Hong Kong. Singapore pro-vides an excellent example of the potential advantages and disadvantages of prioritizing this vehicle for bringing in exter-nal technological learning.[2] One caveat suggested by Singapore's experience is that it has induced extreme depen-dence on foreign enterprises. As Lim explains: Singapore is dominated by foreign capital, with foreign firms accounting by 1990 for 60 percent of all employment, 76 percent of all output, and 86 percent of exports.[3] What are the risks of such dependence? One is that the very reasons which persuade MNCs to locate in your society may lead them to relocate elsewhere in the region. Particularly as China presses MNCs that wish to sell in the China market to locate manufacturing and R&D activities there, the MNCs may increasingly find it desirable to jump directly into the PRC.

Dependence on the foreign enterprises carries with it another kind of vulnerability: that it may fail to strengthen, or may even weaken a society's own local companies. The Singapore government's strategy of providing multiple incentives to bring in MNCs with advanced technology has succeeded in attracting a set of activities that have upgraded the skills of Singaporean citizens and their standard of living. This strategy has helped to link Singapore's societal capabilities to those of some of the most dynamic and innovative technological enterprises in the world. But at the same time, there has been rather little spillover into the small and medium-sized Singaporean firms. Chiu, Ho, and Lui observe that 'in spite of Singapore's successful move into more sophisticated levels of production, the fact remains that Singapore has very little home-grown high-technology manufacturing and remains very much dependent on the production technology of MNCs.'[4] Lim does note a few cases of dynamic local high-tech entrepreneurship, but there are distinctly fewer than in a country like Taiwan, where government has provided incentives for technological upgrading but has not relied heavily on bringing in MNCs in order to achieve this objective.

There are various explanations for the failure of major spin-offs into Singaporean small and medium-sized enterprises; these tend to focus on lack of entrepreneurial traditions. One that seems particularly important for Hong Kong to consider, however, is the role of the MNCs themselves. As Hatch and Yamamura show, the Japanese MNCs bring along with them their own trusted Japanese suppliers, whom they (and the Japanese government) assist in relocation.[5] The challenging forms of collaboration in new product development are undertaken with these familiar suppliers, while the relationships between the Japanese MNCs and local suppliers are more short-term and focused on products that involve little real upgrading. When people in Hong Kong debate whether or not to try to encourage more MNCs to locate in the territory, discussion usually focuses on the break with government's traditional noninterventionism. We think the more important issue, in fact, is whether MNCs would interact with Hong Kong's vibrant universe of entrepreneurial enterprises in ways that would upgrade their capabilities and products. The existence of these local companies constitutes the strongest asset in Hong Kong's industrial future, and the best strategy for upgrading will be one that promises strong links between the new technological and human inputs and the local companies. The Singapore experience, successful though it has been on many levels, does not suggest that such dynamic connections have played a significant role. Rather, the Singapore story continues to be one of enlightened bureaucrats, an attractive local context, global partnerships, and a population with rising skills and incomes.

Collaboration with PRC Scientists, Technologists, and Enterprises

One of the great hopes we heard expressed throughout our project was that Hong Kong enterprises could team with centers of scientific and technological advance in the PRC. In this vision, the PRC partners would contribute their scientific or technological innovations; the Hong Kong partners would use their greater commercial and manufacturing skills to make the idea into a desirable product; and mutual learning would raise the capabilities of both sides. The Report of the Committee on Diversification in 1979 had already raised the importance of China–Hong Kong collaborations in technology and suggested that Hong Kong could serve as a '"laboratory" within which China's trading, banking and other organisations can both derive continuing experience not only of conducting business in a market environment, but also of facilitating the transfer of technology from advanced economies to China, particularly in respect of its export-oriented industries.'[6] Many of us on the MIT *Made By Hong Kong* research team have had the opportunity to visit laboratories in the PRC's outstanding universities—in particular, Tsinghua, Fudan, Beijing, and Shanghai Jiaotong Universities—and to observe work in the laboratories at the Academies of Science. We came away convinced that over the next few decades these laboratories will emerge as strong centers of innovation and technological advance, and that it is important for us and for our students to be closely involved with these research activities because of their rapidly growing capabilities and results.[7] Hong Kong people involved in research and development, whether in industry or in the universities, equally have such an interest, and it is important to create institutions that can promote and generalize these relationships.

In the near to medium term, however, a scenario that counts on using Mainland Chinese R&D as a major input for upgrading Hong Kong activities seems to us unrealistic. We were unable to locate more than one or two examples of a Chinese technological advance that had served as the basis for a new Hong Kong product. Hong Kong entrepreneurs have made some efforts to discover such possibilities—for example, through a fair in Hong Kong and through visits to technology centers in China, both at the universities and in centers of advanced industries like Xi'an. But these efforts, too, have not been very productive.

We see fruitful collaboration between PRC science and technology and Hong Kong industry as a long-term endeavor, and not a short-term fix. It will require mutual learning: on Hong Kong's part, to develop the institutional capabilities to monitor systematically the activities in outstanding PRC university, industrial, and academy laboratories on a continuing basis; on the part of PRC scientists, technologists, and managers, to understand through participation in Hong Kong how the relationships among manufacturers, customers, and suppliers pull into new research to create new generations of products. *To promote such learning, one or more 'observatories' for the study of science and technology in East Asia should be established within Hong Kong universities.* These observatories would bring together core groups of researchers who would: systematically monitor invention and innovation in the region; coordinate and carry out research on the links between research in industry and research in university, academy, and government laboratories in the region; and create databases on researchers and projects in East Asia that could be accessed electronically. *We further recommend that the immigration regulations that today constrain Hong Kong manufacturers who wish to bring even highly trained experts from the PRC be eased to facilitate Hong Kong rotations. Some sectors also need entry-level imported labor; recommendations for textiles and clothing are in Chapter 9.*

International Expertise

In the new areas of high technology in which Hong Kong firms wish to advance, they would have much to gain by recruiting international experts with experiences in leading-edge firms. Hong Kong's large resident international community suggests that its urban environment is attractive to talented people from many countries. There may be an advantage in trying to attract ethnic Chinese now resident in Western countries, whether Hong Kong citizens or others, for familiarity with culture and language is an additional appeal. The role that returning Taiwanese scientists and technologists have played in building new enterprises in Taiwan has been significant, and variants of this model should be considered in Hong Kong.

Housing is one of the most highly charged issues in Hong Kong. As a group of outside researchers with no special competence in the housing field, our recommendation can only be a general one. *We underscore that providing housing options for PRC managers and technologists on training stays in Hong Kong, and for international experts from whom Hong Kong industry hopes to gain access to cutting-edge innovation developed elsewhere, is a matter of societal interest and not just private benefit.* We cannot judge whether the imaginative proposals—one of which would convert some adjacent buildings within old industrially zoned land into executive residential dormitories for PRC personnel—are the right way to reach a target of several thousand units of high-tech personnel housing. But we believe it is urgent for representatives from industry associations, planners, and representatives from the Industry Department to convene to develop alternative options. Just as the universities have found it legitimate to provide housing on reasonable terms to attract distinguished foreign scholars, so, too, must Hong Kong industry and government develop creative solutions to this hurdle. The large majority of companies we interviewed identified the problem of high-cost housing as an obstacle to progress that companies could not remove on their own.

Strengthening the R&D Base

Government and private firms in Hong Kong should increase their investments in R&D. There is no formula that dictates how much an economy should spend on research and development in order to innovate in products and processes, but most advanced countries allocate somewhere between 1 and 3 percent of GDP for this purpose. Hong Kong's current level of R&D spending is far below even the low end of this range. Unless both government and industry increase their R&D investments significantly, it is unlikely that Hong Kong will be able to sustain a healthy rate of product and process innovation in the long run.

For a relatively small economy like that of Hong Kong, externally generated ideas will always play a more important role as sources of innovation than home-grown inventions. What is most critical is the capacity to incorporate new knowledge rapidly into new products, services, and processes, whatever the source. As discussed above, this underlines the importance of strengthening the links between firms and public research institutions in Hong Kong and technological centers elsewhere. The balance of R&D activity within Hong Kong needs to tilt more towards the monitoring and evaluation of externally developed knowledge and towards technology development and implementation relative to fundamental research.

We believe that industry must take the lead in promoting these activities. A large fraction of the investment decisions require a knowledge of the marketplace that only private firms can provide. In many cases, the resulting knowledge can be fully appropriated by individual sponsoring firms. But even where collective funding arrangements are necessary, it is the private firms, rather than the government or independent research institutions, which should be taking the lead in setting spending priorities and research agendas.

While manufacturing firms should be doing much more in this area, much of the action will need to take place within Hong Kong's large service industries—banking, transportation, trading, telecommunications, and the like. In every other advanced economy manufacturers have accounted for almost all private R&D activity in the past, and still dominate today even though their share of total output is declining (in the United States, for example, manufacturing firms are responsible for more than 90 percent of all private R&D spending.) But in Hong Kong the need is to create a significant base of R&D activity that cuts across the traditional boundaries between manufacturing and services, and that seeks to apply new information technologies to the development of service-enhanced products. Hong Kong's service firms will therefore share the responsibility for shaping the territory's R&D infrastructure—a responsibility that service firms elsewhere have not previously been called upon to shoulder.

Our specific recommendations are as follows:

1. *The government should increase the volume of funding that is available for R&D in support of industry.* The funds should be provided as much as possible on a matching basis, that is, they should be made contingent on the availability of private funds in comparable amounts. The government should give priority to cooperative industry–university projects. Where necessary, the scope of existing government programs should be expanded to encompass R&D in support of service industries.

2. *The procedures for allocating government research funds to the universities should be revised to bring university research into closer alignment with the needs of industry.* The method used by the University Grants Committee to determine the size of the research component of the block grant to UGC institutions should be modified to take account of the contributions university researchers are making to the advancement of industrial practice. Additionally, the share of funds disbursed by the Research Grants Council (RGC) that is allocated to cooperative university–industry research should be increased, and additional industry input into the resource allocation decisions should be sought. The committee structure of the RGC should also be reviewed to ensure that new fields of technology of particular relevance to Hong Kong industry, in services as well as manufacturing, are adequately represented. Finally, the government and the UGC should continue to look for ways to increase the proportion of public funds for university R&D that is allocated on a competitive basis.

Changes like these at the governmental level are the pre-requisites for equally important internal changes within Hong Kong's tertiary institutions. The most important of these would modify career structures so as to strengthen the incentives for individual researchers to conduct applied R&D that will be relevant to industry's needs.

3. *The government should establish a system of industrial sabbaticals for university faculty.* The purpose of this program would be to allow university faculty to spend significant blocks of time working in companies in Hong Kong or elsewhere to update their knowledge of industry and its problems. The pace of change in the tools and techniques used in industry is such that an active strategy must be adopted to ensure that faculty keep abreast of industrial developments and continually incorporate this new knowledge in their curricula.

4. *The government should provide base funding for two new applied research institutes.* A new institute dedicated to the study of the Chinese economy should be established, with a particular focus on the dynamics of consumption patterns and the development of marketing and distribution networks in China. The institute should be affiliated with one of Hong Kong's business schools. A second institute should be created to study the technical and institutional problems associated with the integration of multiple information services over Hong Kong's advanced telecommunication networks. This institute would provide a forum for different service providers to resolve standards and other integration issues, develop technical strategies and solutions for specific problems, conduct pilot studies and demonstrations of advanced concepts, and monitor important new technical developments around the world. Membership would be open to all information service providers and information technology suppliers active in Hong Kong, both domestic and international.

In both cases the goal should be to build research institutions with a worldwide reputation. In each case Hong Kong offers specific assets—to the former the knowledge of Chinese consumer markets that its entrepreneurs are rapidly accumulating; and to the latter, the wide variety of commercial broadband multimedia services its sophisticated telecommunications network is capable of supporting. We feel, therefore, that the goals of creating a world-class research institution and of attracting leading scholars and practitioners from around the world are realistic and attainable.

Information Technology for New Products, New Services, New Customers

The importance of information technology to Hong Kong's efforts to raise industrial productivity and performance has been a pervasive theme of this report. We have commented on the central role of information technology in the design, manufacture, and delivery of the service-enhanced products of the future. We have also stressed the importance of information technology to upgrading the performance of Hong Kong's service industries, including transportation, trade, telecommunications, and financial services, the fortunes of which are intimately tied to the production networks of 'Made By Hong Kong.' We have reported on Hong Kong-based enterprises that have emerged as internationally competitive suppliers of electronic end-products and components, of software, and of integrated systems for information generation and delivery. (Had we chosen to cast our net wider, we could also have cited strong Hong Kong companies in the domain of information 'content', that is, newspaper publishing, television programming, and motion picture production.) And we have noted Hong Kong's advantages as a testbed for demonstrating new information services—its advanced, all-digital telecommunications infrastructure, an affluent consumer base that is among the world's most technologically sophisticated and receptive, the wide range of services and service providers that customers can already choose from, and Hong Kong's proximity to and affinity with the emerging China market.

All of this leads us to see great promise in Hong Kong as a center of wealth creation through the exploitation of the new technologies of information generation, storage, and delivery. For Hong Kong's information technology sector to flourish and fulfill its potential, three conditions are indispensable: (1) the continued absence of restrictions on the flow of information; (2) stronger protection of intellectual property rights, and (3) a continuing commitment to regulatory liberalization and open competition in telecommunications and multi-media markets.

Beyond these three policy requirements, there is a critical need to build up Hong Kong's capabilities in the software sector. A strong software industry will allow Hong Kong to accelerate its transition from its primary role today as a user of information technology to a role of utilization *and* innovation. Relative to its counterparts elsewhere in East Asia, Hong Kong's software industry enjoys the advantage of proximity to large, sophisticated software users, especially in the telecommunications, transportation, trade, finance, and entertainment sectors; already today these exert a powerful 'pull' for new applications. It also benefits from a sizeable domestic population of sophisticated end users—an especially important requirement for the fast-growing home entertainment and education software market.

But Hong Kong's software sector is still small and uneven in its performance, with strengths in certain custom markets, yet little track record in the development and distribution of packaged products. The two most important requirements are risk capital and a larger base of skilled, high-quality professionals. Detailed recommendations in both areas are presented elsewhere in this section. Other recommendations are given in Chapter 11 on the information technology industry.

We have not sought to recommend particular product and technology markets. However, we do strongly encourage active exploration of opportunities in the burgeoning field of business-to-business electronic commerce. Electronic commerce, in addition to offering new business opportunities for software developers and information service providers, will rapidly become the *sine qua non* for Hong Kong's large population of small and medium-sized enterprises to compete effectively in global markets for service-enhanced products. (A 1994 survey found that more than 60 percent of Hong Kong's small and medium-sized firms did not own computers at all.[8]) These technologies can facilitate manufacturers' efforts to service customers in diverse national markets, and to pinpoint new product development opportunities. Our researchers identified specific opportunities in industries from clothing to biotechnology, and these are discussed in subsequent chapters. The Hong Kong Trade Development Council's formidable database of trade-related information, now being made available to an on-line audience, provides another valuable focus for private initiatives in this area. More generally, there are likely to be significant opportunities for Hong Kong software firms to partner with international vendors in electronic-commerce-related fields, and these should be vigorously explored.

Upgrading OEM

More Hong Kong companies should invest in balancing or replacing OEM with brand-name production, original design manufacturing (ODM), or high-tech manufacturing-process contracting. Most Hong Kong firms have moved along the industrial learning curve by mastering original equipment manufacture (OEM) under the tutelage of some of the world's leading manufacturers, who then market Hong Kong products under their own labels. In the majority of our interviews in the electronics, plastics, optics, and textiles and clothing sectors, senior managers described learning how to make products well with help from their early customers and then improving their products by selling to ever more demanding buyers. A company's capabilities as a manufacturer are proven in effect by its clientele; in the garment industry, for example, selling to Donna Karan may be worth it, even if quantities and profit margins are not high, because the firm learns how to produce top quality and uses the buyer's label to demonstrate firm capabilities to other potential customers. The fact remains, however, that in this common Hong Kong scenario, the manufacturer captures relatively little of the final price of the good, remains at the beck and call of the buyer, and faces competition from other OEM companies who threaten to take the business away.

For Hong Kong companies today, moving away from old-style OEM is a precondition for enhancing the value they create through new product and process innovation and for protecting their share of the market against competitors. One route to this objective is acquiring or creating a brand and selling some or all of the firm's production under the brand name. There are outstanding success stories among Hong

Kong firms that have developed brands for affluent Western markets as well as for the China market, yet they remain a distinct minority.[9] The principal reasons advanced for not taking such an initiative are: the difficulties that brand-name manufacturers face in reassuring their OEM customers about their proprietary interests; the high costs of advertising; and the risk of 'putting all one's eggs in a single basket' with a brand. Yet there are examples—such as VTech, Gold Peak and Fang Brothers/Episode—of companies which successfully manage OEM and brand production together. And high budgets for advertising are hardly uncommon in Hong Kong: Hong Kong's per capita advertising expenditures rank it third in the world.[10] Here again, driving the low-cost manufacturing engine into China-based production provided a strategy for expansion that seemed more familiar and less risky than facing the unknown challenges of building brand names.

Brand names, however, are not the only route out of old-style OEM towards higher value production. Firms like Gold Peak and Johnson Electric that are involved in original design manufacturing (ODM) are still making products that will be resold under another label, but in these instances, the uniqueness of the design and functionality of the products command higher prices and erect a set of barriers to the entry of competitors. ODM, as the examples of the best Hong Kong companies show, requires far higher expenditures on design and applied R&D than most Hong Kong firms are making today. This is also true of yet another development that might have real promise for Hong Kong companies: turnkey contract manufacturing. Under these arrangements a contractor specializes in process-specific technologies that allow him or her to provide production for a number of customers at levels of quality and price superior to those the brand-name firms can provide for themselves.[11] Developing the new manufacturing processes that make the contractor a valuable and difficult-to-replace partner for customer firms again requires substantial R&D expenditure. In short, there are a number of ways that firms can balance or replace OEM production with new higher-value activities. All of them require larger investment.

Education, Training, and Human Resource Development

No other factors are as important to the performance of Hong Kong's existing firms, or to its ability to create and attract new enterprises, as the quality and skills of the Hong Kong workforce. This fact is widely recognized in the territory. But the effort to upgrade the level of education and training, though considerable, has been uneven; significant gaps remain. In this regard, we have previously commented on the problem of English-language education at the primary and secondary level, as well as a variety of problems in vocational and tertiary education. Most important, however, the process of upgrading is unending. There is no threshold of adequacy. For Hong Kong, as for all advanced societies, there is a direct relationship between productivity and skills. If Hong Kong is to strengthen its capabilities for product and process innovation, it will need to invest more in upgrading the skills of its workforce. Our first recommendation in this area is directed to the universities:

University education in the sciences and engineering should be attuned more closely to the needs of the economy and industry. To prepare students to play productive roles in the enterprises of tomorrow, they should be sensitized to real-world problems of productivity and of developing, applying, and using technology as they pursue their studies of science and engineering. This means moving beyond a narrow disciplinary focus, at both the undergraduate and the graduate levels.

Undergraduate education in the sciences and engineering should be broadened so as to educate students in the practical problems of developing and applying technology in business enterprises. Students should be able to operate effectively beyond the confines of a single discipline and to combine sound knowledge of scientific and engineering fundamentals with practical, real-world knowledge, hands-on experience, and a basic understanding of the fundamentals of operating a business. We, as educators ourselves, are aware of the risks of broadening undergraduate education in this way. There is a real danger of students being lightly exposed to multiple fields and of consequent professional weakness. We doubt that the goal of broadening can be accomplished satisfactorily within the confines of today's three-year undergraduate curriculum. *We therefore recommend a fourth year of university education for selected undergraduate engineering students who wish to add management training, or a second disciplinary focus.*

The University Grants Committee (UGC) and the government recently reaffirmed their long-standing opposition to extending the normal undergraduate curriculum partly on grounds of cost, although the UGC in its most recent report declares that it is 'not unsympathetic' to the argument that undergraduates would be better rounded and more useful employees if their courses were longer and embraced more than one discipline. We believe that an intellectually compelling case can be made for adding a year to the undergraduate curriculum, even if only for honors students who wish to obtain a double major in a technical discipline and business studies, or alternatively in two technical disciplines.

There is a particular need to develop new capabilities in design and product and process development. Senior managers in almost all of the industries we studied, including electronics, software, textiles, clothing, and optical goods, lamented the lack of a critical mass of talented designers and product development managers in Hong Kong. The most valuable contributors to these activities are typically those who combine technical and business skills. Employers attest equally to the importance of engineers with an appreciation for marketing and other business issues and managers who have an understanding of how to bring technological concepts through the innovation process to the marketplace. *The universities should work with industry to create a new cadre of students and faculty in engineering and business studies with the ability to work in teams creating and designing new products, processes, and systems.* New Masters-level programs should be developed to train a new generation of engineers and managers who will be skilled in applying forefront engineering and managerial knowledge to product and process development and design.

More generally, as more Hong Kong firms recognize the need to be involved in developing, adopting, and using new technologies, the management of technology will assume an increasingly central role in general management practice.

While it is not necessary for every manager to have a degree in science or engineering, knowledge of the fundamentals of the innovation process, of how technology relates to firm strategy, and of how to evaluate alternative technologies and investment choices is becoming an increasingly important part of general management education. *Hong Kong's tertiary institutions should explore ways to expand the treatment of technology management issues in undergraduate and graduate-level business curricula.*

These new educational initiatives will be stronger if industry actively participates in planning and curriculum design. We found few, if any examples of this sort of interaction in our research. Relations between academics and industrialists in Hong Kong seemed, on the contrary, to be fairly distant. Closer collaboration between the universities and industry on education as well as research is highly desirable. Overcoming the mutual skepticism will require leadership on both sides.

Beyond closer involvement with educational institutions, *Hong Kong employers should review their internal human resource policies to bring them in line with business strategies based more heavily on innovation.* The great majority of Hong Kong firms are far from the frontier of best practice with respect to human resource management. The traditional model of the family-run company, with authority and initiative concentrated in the hands of a few family members at the top, is a far cry from the modern, knowledge-driven enterprise, with new ideas for product innovation and productivity improvement coming from all levels of the firm. Hong Kong firms must do much more, not only to invest in developing their employees' skills, but also to provide career development and financial incentives for their employees to stay and contribute their ideas to the stock of intellectual capital. At the level of production workers, new forms of training and incentive pay are needed to encourage 'multi-skilling.'

Design and product development skills should be enhanced by giving professionals in these areas wider exposure to new markets and customers. Designers should be encouraged to spend time in Chinese and Japanese cities. The rotation of managers to the Pearl River Delta needs to be balanced with opportunities to visit customers in Western markets. These managers also need the chance to meet with and come to understand customers in China's large urban communities. Many of the older Hong Kong managers have had more contact with foreign buyers than the younger generation, who are busy establishing and supervising new production sites in the relatively isolated and less urban settings of the Delta.

Fostering Home-Grown, Technology-Based Enterprises

Hong Kong's record as a center of entrepreneurial activity is well known, but few of its small and medium-sized firms derive much competitive advantage from the creative use of technology. *Hong Kong must increase the rate of formation of new technology-based enterprises.* We have two main recommendations in this area.

First, the range of exit options for venture investors should be broadened. There is a critical need to promote more true venture investing activity in Hong Kong, that is, direct equity investment in new enterprises that have yet to sell their first product. Today exit strategies for venture investors are limited to listing on the Hong Kong stock exchange or selling to another company, and the former is not feasible for most new technology firms because of the Exchange's strict listing requirements. One approach already under consideration is to set up a NASDAQ-style second stock exchange in Hong Kong. We recommend the continued exploration of this possibility. Moreover, because the establishment of such an exchange may be difficult in the short run due to the small number of technology companies in Hong Kong at present, *we further recommend consideration of the creation of a new class of technology shares, or 'T-shares,' to be traded on the Hong Kong stock exchange.* The new type of shares would have more flexible listing requirements, including reduced restrictions on current profitability and lower initial capitalization. To encourage increased outside supervision and external expertise, these companies would be required to float a greater fraction of their equity than is typical of currently listed companies. The separate 'T-share' designation would protect the reputation of currently listed companies and the Hong Kong stock exchange.

Second, the government's proposed plan to build a large science park should be accelerated by creating a decentralized, 'virtual' science park for startup, early-stage, and small technology-based enterprises. Access to affordable space in a suitable location is an important consideration for any business enterprise; for new or early-stage ventures it may spell the difference between success and failure. New technology-based businesses require proximity to important customers, to key suppliers, to the computing, testing, and library resources and intellectual stimulation of universities, and to other small firms working in related fields. Hong Kong, with its high rents and still small population of home-grown, technology-based businesses needs to make suitable space available in sufficient quantities to house new enterprises of this kind.

We recommend the creation of an electronically linked network of relatively small-scale sites at several locations around Hong Kong, each capable of housing and supporting a cluster of early-stage, technology-based enterprises. This 'virtual' science park approach is well suited to densely populated Hong Kong, where large land parcels are difficult to assemble and where several desirable locations for such sites can already be identified. Furthermore, the territory's highly developed digital telecommunications infrastructure can support the establishment of an ultra-high bandwidth communications network linking the sites at only a modest incremental cost. Since at least some, and perhaps all of these enterprise clusters could be housed in existing buildings, the network could be made operational relatively quickly and inexpensively. An important goal would be to create in each cluster a collaborative environment that would attract technology companies and foster networking and the easy exchange of ideas. The virtual science park would have the following characteristics:

1. Location:

The individual sites should be located either adjacent to university campuses or on industrial estates. Old industrial or office buildings could also be converted for this purpose. Many small technology-based companies see advantages in being close to university campuses. This is obviously true of companies founded by university researchers who wish to work with their companies while remaining on the university staff. But it is also true of companies without formal links to universities, who value the easy access to library and technical resources, intellectual stimulation, and potential employees and collaborators. (Many high-technology companies in the Kendall Square area close to MIT have no formal connection to the Institute.) One advantage to locating these sites on industrial estates or in old, rehabilitated industrial buildings is the greater space availability. In the latter case, revisions to existing zoning regulations might be necessary.

2. Scale:

The minimum scale for a site would be 20,000–40,000 feet, large enough for a cluster of 10–20 early stage businesses. Location in multistory office buildings is possible. Larger clusters could be created at industrial locations.

3. Organization and Management:

In principle, individual sites could be owned and operated by a public entity (such as the Industrial Estates Corporation, or the Industrial Technology Center, or the proposed Science Park Corporation), by one or more universities, or by private property developers. We favor a primarily private sector approach. Specifically, we recommend for consideration a scheme under which private property developers would acquire, develop and manage space that would be dedicated to early-stage or small technology-based enterprises (most likely in existing buildings). The developers would enter into agreements with the Industrial Technology Center Corporation for the provision of 'incubation' services to their tenants (such as management and marketing support, conference and seminar services) similar to those the ITCC now provides to its own occupants. Some of these services could be delivered over dedicated ultra-high bandwidth communication links. (The necessary optical fiber backbone is already installed throughout Hong Kong, unused capacity is available, and a dedicated network could be established at low cost.) The ITCC would condition its participation on commitments by the facility managers to meet specified standards of tenant type, building quality, and services appropriate to think of the firms that are providing technical, logistical, advertising, quality control, and other kinds of services to manufacturers in Hong Kong or elsewhere. To be sure, these firms are not actually involved in the physical handling or processing of manufactured goods. But many of them are no less dependent on the market for these goods than are the firms that actually make them in their factories.

A more meaningful breakdown of the economy is shown in Figure 3.1. Here we distinguish between *consumer* services (tourism, restaurants, retail trade, retail banking, health care, and so on) and *producer* services (services that are intermediate inputs to production chains). With respect to producer services we further distinguish among three kinds of companies:

(1) firms whose services are used exclusively to enhance manufactured products (such as trading firms, design and product development houses, freight forwarders, and environmental testing laboratories);

(2) firms whose services are exclusively used to enhance other services (hospital caterers, medical testing services, and real estate lawyers); and

(3) firms providing services that are used by both manufacturers and service providers (banks, telecommunications firms, electric utilities, and advertisers, among others).

Certainly some and perhaps all of these different populations of service firms have been expanding in Hong Kong. Unfortunately the economic statistics do not keep track of them, so we can only guess at what has been happening. But if we take 'Made in Hong Kong' in this larger sense to include manufacturing-related service firms (groups 1 and 3 above) as well as the narrowly defined group of firms that are formally classified as manufacturers, the current level of manufacturing activity is very much larger than is suggested by the official statistics, and may even be expanding. In any event, a complete understanding of the changing role of manufacturing industry in the Hong Kong economy is not possible without taking an integrated view of manufacturing itself.

high-technology occupancy. Prospective tenants would thus be assured of a suitable environment and the availability of valuable services. The ITCC would in effect be creating satellite 'franchises' for the delivery of its services around Hong Kong. However, because the sites would be privately owned and operated, there would be greater flexibility to tailor lease terms to tenants' particular needs (regarding, for example, lease duration and expansion options) than is possible at the Industrial Technology Center itself.

4. Relationship to the Proposed Tai Po Science Park:

The decentralized 'virtual' science park we are recommending here is not a substitute for the large science park now being planned for the Tai Po area. The latter can provide useful benefits to Hong Kong in the longer run, especially if it succeeds in attracting the applied research, development, and design activities of multinational corporations, and if some part of the allocated space is devoted to meeting the housing needs of the occupants. The virtual science park, on the other hand, is directed at start-up, early-stage, or otherwise small home-grown, technology-intensive enterprises—a different group of firms from those that will likely be targeted by the large science park. Unlike the latter, the virtual science park could be implemented almost immediately, and with very modest public expenditures. If it succeeds in its objectives, it is likely to improve the chances of success for the large science park. A visible, public–private initiative of the type we are recommending here, which would help create significant new concentrations of early-stage, high-technology activity, could only enhance the prospects for attracting the larger scale R&D and manufacturing activities that will be the main focus of the big Hong Kong science park proposal.

In addition to our two main proposals for encouraging a higher rate of new technology-based enterprise formation, *we recommend a review of the intellectual property and technology licensing policies of Hong Kong's tertiary institutions.* This review should examine current policies and practices in light of the goal of maximizing the contribution of university research to Hong Kong's economic growth and social welfare, while recognizing the nature of the universities as publicly funded institutions. The review should take account of the growing body of knowledge about the effectiveness of alternative policies and practices that is accumulating at universities around the world. One important consideration is the degree to which the coordination of faculty entrepreneurial and consulting activity is centralized within university administrations. In general, a combination of maximum autonomy for individual researchers with clear policies regarding the allocation of intellectual property rights is likely to be most effective in fostering the useful application of university-developed knowledge.

Finally, we note that a variety of other recommendations made elsewhere in this book, especially regarding housing, immigration, and the enforcement of intellectual property laws and regulations, will also encourage the formation of new technology-based enterprises in Hong Kong.

Strengthening Government's Technological Capabilities

The government's ability to support the technological upgrading of Hong Kong's economy is presently limited by internal organizational and human resource constraints. *The government should take steps to strengthen its internal technological capabilities.* As is the case for company managers, it is not necessary for every government official to have a degree in science or engineering. But they do need to understand how new scientific and technical concepts are brought to the marketplace, and how private firms evaluate alternative technological and investment choices. Government officials must have an overall sense of the evolving technical needs and possibilities in key sectors of the Hong Kong economy. The effective adoption and use of technology is also becoming increasingly important to the success of the government's own performance.

To increase its access to specialized technological knowledge, *the government should allow specialists from industry and academia to serve in government positions on a full-time basis for periods of one to two years.* The government should consider inviting international experts with ties to Hong Kong to serve temporarily in this capacity.

With respect to government organization, a review of the current structure of technology-related functions within the government administration is needed. We did not conduct a study of this question and have no specific recommendations to propose. Throughout this study, however, we have argued that the traditional separation of manufacturing and services is becoming increasingly outdated. We also have drawn attention to the growing importance of new technologies, especially information technologies, in a wide range of service sectors. We note that the current government organization preserves the old distinction between manufacturing and services, and is not well suited to the broader view of service-enhanced manufacturing that we advocate in this report. *More generally, we believe that government policymaking would benefit from an integrated, economy-wide perspective on technology-related issues within the administration, and that the responsibility for developing this perspective should be assigned and exercised at a senior level within the government.*

Building a 'Safe Harbor' for Industry

Our principal recommendations in this area are to the Hong Kong Government. Specifically, the government should:

- *Strengthen the institutions that make Hong Kong a 'safe harbor' for innovation and investment in technology-based activities;*

- *Support the protection of intellectual property with new resources for enforcement and new public education programs;*

- *Protect Hong Kong's reputation for compliance with international trade rules by tightening enforcement, thereby preserving Hong Kong's autonomous membership in international economic organizations;*

- *Create new regulatory agencies to ensure the purity, reliability, and origin of new Hong Kong products, like those of a future biotechnology industry.*

Hong Kong's public institutions are among its greatest assets as a free society for they not only protect individual rights under rule of law, but they also afford a large measure of protection to innovators and investors. As we have discussed in Chapter 4 (under 'Public Institutions'), Hong Kong's traditions of strong, honest, and impartial civil servants, and success in eliminating corruption have built an international reputation which has made Hong Kong a haven for international companies operating in the region. If Hong Kong firms are to evolve as major manufacturers of service-enhanced goods, however, more needs to be done to convince local firms and international companies considering new investments in the region that Hong Kong offers a particularly safe setting for innovation. Hong Kong needs to enlarge its international reputation as a *safe harbor* in which investors find: rule of law; transparent relations with government; a public opinion convinced that intellectual property violations are criminal and socially harmful; and rigorous enforcement of laws on intellectual property, country of origin, and other trade conventions. If Hong Kong succeeds in this, it will be able to attract innovative activities that MNCs and others still today hesitate to locate directly in China. The autonomy of Hong Kong, if the 'one country, two systems' approach is closely followed, will qualify Hong Kong to receive technologies, processes, and personnel from the United States that under current legislation cannot be sent into China proper. Even beyond the regulatory constraints imposed by US rules, Hong Kong autonomy would reassure international investors from around the world that within Hong Kong they could have unparalleled access to China as well as a reliable regulatory regime and a familiar legal framework.

   Today, the challenge is to build on the foundations of existing laws and practices to reinforce Hong Kong as a safe harbor. Within the safe harbor, public opinion would condemn violations of international trade and property norms and public officials would efficiently and rigorously enforce the law. The starting point is to recognize that intellectual property protection is a matter of vital concern, not only for international vendors, but for local innovators. One leading industrialist told us, 'We need to distinguish Hong Kong as a shining example of a code of values about intellectual property: to protect who and what we are. What we're selling in

Hong Kong is a culture that needs to be defended by a code of conduct. Intellectual property is a deeper issue than patent protection: if my customers start saying I can't talk to you in Hong Kong, we'll need to move our main people out. . . . Hong Kong has to change. Government has to come down hard on those who do wrong. We're at a fork in the road.' Major foreign software producers also are loudly voicing concerns about intellectual property, charging that software piracy in Hong Kong is second only to that in China. The 'Golden Arcade' (in Shamshuipo, Kowloon) is known worldwide as a place to buy such software. And counterfeited trademark goods are visibly for sale on many street corners in Hong Kong. The issue of transshipment of textiles and garments sparked a major trade conflict between the United States and Hong Kong in 1996, with serious consequences for Hong Kong businesses.

The paradox of intellectual property protection and customs enforcement of trade rules in Hong Kong is that Hong Kong has laws and an enforcement system that are international models, but nonetheless has an internationally unacceptable level of violations. The issues involved are complex. These range from: difficulties in gaining convictions due to complicated standards of evidence (requiring time-consuming research on CD-ROM source codes); to a shortage of officers available for enforcing the law on the border and within Hong Kong proper; to lax public attitudes towards those who make and buy pirated goods; to coordinating enforcement with China, where many of the factories turning out pirated products are located. Hong Kong has greatly stepped up its efforts in recent years. For example, penalties for intellectual property violations were increased in 1996, and 144 individuals received jail sentences, whereas prior to 1994–5 no one had gone to jail for such violations.[12] The Customs Bureau has had a major increase in personnel; and the level of seizures of illegal goods has risen—in the case of pirated music compact discs, for example, from 10,117 in 1992 to 216,991 in 1995.[13] Hong Kong—under pressure from US Customs, and from the Committee on Implementation of Textile Agreements (CITA) which has relayed Congressional concerns about the origin of textiles and garment imports—has markedly toughened its enforcement of textiles and clothing trade rules. It had previously added new pre-shipment notification procedures requiring domestic manufacturers to declare when they are about to begin making the goods that will be certified for Hong Kong origin and exported.

Could more be done? Virtually everyone we interviewed in Hong Kong—even those most energetic in defending the current system and pointing to its recent advancement—agreed that more could indeed be done. The major areas for improvement are: more resources for enforcement, both within Hong Kong and at the borders; accelerating the shift to Electronic Data Interchange (EDI) transmissions of customs documents; and above all, greatly increasing the resources devoted to changing public attitudes in these areas. The ICAC public outreach programs (including community presentations, the effective use of public advertising spots on television, and the development of a special television series) demonstrate that it is possible to affect public attitudes towards even 'victimless' crimes like bribery. In the areas of intellectual property violations, the current programs to educate the public seem to be underfunded, ill coordinated with enforcement, and do not compare well to the ICAC media products. Beyond even the issue of implementing the law, these programs need to demonstrate to the public the links between protection of ideas and innovation and the economic future of creative endeavor within Hong Kong. Such efforts to make Hong Kong a safe harbor are the necessary foundation of future development.

Finally, Hong Kong, as part of its safe harbor agenda, could use its well-established regulatory agencies, and the new ones it would create in the same mould, to certify and guarantee the quality of new generations of products coming out of Hong Kong industry. Consumers of such products as Traditional Chinese Medicines, food products, toys, and consumer electronics want and are willing to pay more for the assurance that these products are pure, unharmful, contain only listed ingredients, and conform to relevant regulations. Some, like the Japanese and the US markets, are particularly demanding in this regard. But it is likely that trends worldwide are moving in this direction. The 1995 Gallop Poll of Chinese consumers found urban consumers in China willing to pay substantially more for quality goods from known provenance. Hong Kong is well positioned to benefit from this trend.

Summary of Recommendations

For the reader's convenience, we restate here in summary form our principal recommendations to Hong Kong government, industry, and educational institutions:

Acquiring Technical Knowledge From Elsewhere

- Establish one or more 'observatories' at Hong Kong universities for the study of science and technology in the PRC and to exchange personnel with PRC institutions.

- Launch more targeted efforts to recruit Hong Kong residents abroad, other ethnic Chinese, and international specialists for assignments in government and private industry.

- Ease immigration regulations to facilitate rotations of highly trained PRC experts through Hong Kong laboratories and offices. Address labor import needs of various sectors.

- Government and industry should share the costs of a program to provide affordable housing for foreign scientific and technical personnel recruited to work on short-term or longer assignments.

Strengthening Hong Kong's R&D Base

- Increase the level of government funding for R&D in support of industry.

- Increase the rate of investment in R&D by private firms in Hong Kong.

- Revise the procedures for allocating public research funding to bring university research into closer alignment with the needs of industry.

- Strengthen incentives for individual university researchers to conduct applied R&D relevant to industry's needs.

- Establish a system of industrial sabbaticals for university faculty.

- Establish new applied research institutes at Hong Kong universities to focus academic research efforts on key problem areas for Hong Kong industry, including Chinese retailing and distribution, and information service integration in Hong Kong.

Strengthening Hong Kong's Capabilities in Information Technology

- Develop Hong Kong as a testbed for the demonstration of new information services and technologies.

- Continue to liberalize the regulation of telecommunications and multimedia markets.

- Enlarge the base of skilled, high-quality software professionals.

- Focus on new opportunities for developing and implementing business-to-business electronic commerce technologies.

- Prevent restrictions on the flow of information.

Upgrading OEM

- Hong Kong companies should invest more heavily in balancing or replacing OEM with brand-name production, original design manufacturing (ODM), or high-technology manufacturing-process contracting.

Upgrading Hong Kong's Human Resources

- Attune university education in the sciences and engineering more closely to the needs of the economy and industry.

- Broaden undergraduate education in the sciences and engineering to expose students to practical problems of developing and applying technology in business enterprises.

- Add a fourth year to the undergraduate curriculum for honors students in engineering who wish to obtain a double major in a technical discipline and business studies or in two engineering disciplines.

- Expand the treatment of technology management issues in undergraduate and graduate-level business curricula.

- Develop new interdisciplinary educational capabilities in design and product and process development.

- The universities and industry should work together to create a new cadre of students and faculty in engineering and business studies with the ability to work in teams creating and designing new products, processes, and systems.

- Hong Kong firms should review their internal human resource policies for consistency with innovation-based business strategies and move towards the frontier of international best practice in human resource management.

Fostering Home-Grown, Technology-Based Enterprises

- Broaden the range of exit strategies for venture investors.

- Consider creating a new class of technology shares (or 'T-shares') with more flexible listing requirements to be traded on the Hong Kong stock exchange.

- Accelerate the government's plan for a large science park by creating a decentralized, 'virtual' science park for start-up, early-stage, and small technology-based enterprises.

- Review and strengthen the intellectual property and technology licensing policies of Hong Kong's tertiary institutions.

Strengthening the Technological Capabilities of Government

- Enable specialists from industry and academia to serve in responsible government positions on a full-time basis for periods of one or two years.

- Review the current organizational structure of government with a view toward raising the profile of technology-related policy issues and developing an integrated, economy-wide policy perspective that cuts across the traditional boundary between manufacturing and services.

Building a 'Safe Harbor'

- Strengthen the institutions that make Hong Kong a 'safe harbor' for innovation and investment in technology-based activities.

- Support the protection of intellectual property with new resources for enforcement and new public education programs.

- Protect Hong Kong's reputation for compliance with international trade rules by tightening enforcement and thereby preserve Hong Kong's autonomous membership in international economic organizations.

- Create new regulatory agencies to ensure the purity, reliability, and origin of new Hong Kong products, like those of a future biotechnology industry.

Notes

1   We wish to acknowledge our debt to three pioneering studies of Hong Kong tackling similar issues, the analyses and recommendations of which have taught and encouraged us: C. K. Kao and K. Young (eds.), *Technology Road Maps for Hong Kong*, Hong Kong: The Chinese University of Hong Kong, 1991; Business and Professionals Federation of Hong Kong, *Hong Kong 21*, Hong Kong, May 1993; and M. Enright; E. Scott; and D. Dodwell, *The Hong Kong Advantage*, Hong Kong: Oxford University Press, 1997.
2   See S.W.K. Chiu; K.C. Ho; T.L. Lui, *City-States in the Global Economy: Industrial Restructuring in Hong Kong and Singapore*, Transitions: Asia and Asian America, Boulder, Colo.: Westview Press, 1997, especially Chapters 4, 5, and 7; L. Lim, 'Foreign Investment, the State and Industrial Policy in Singapore,' in H. Stein (ed.), *Asian Industrialisation and Africa*, New York: St. Martin's Press, 1995; L. Lim, 'Technology Policy and Export Development: The Case of the Electronics Industry in Singapore and Malaysia,' unpublished paper, April 1993. The text also draws on notes from L. Lim's lecture at the Producing in Asia seminar at the Industrial Performance Center, MIT, April 2, 1996.

3   Lim, 'Foreign Investment, the State and Industrial Policy in Singapore,' p. 219.

4   Ibid., p. 105.

5   W. Hatch and K. Yamamura, *Asia in Japan's Embrace,* Cambridge: Cambridge University Press, 1996, p. 166.

6   Advisory Committee on Diversification, C.P. Haddon-Cave, Chairman, 'Report of the Advisory Committee on Diversification,' Hong Kong, 1979, p. 156.

7   See United States National Science Foundation, *Asia's New High-Tech Competitors,* NSF 95-309, Arlington, VA., 1995. For a review of China's programs to spur high-tech development, see A. M. Segal, 'High Time for High Tech? China's Program for an Indigenous High-Technology Capability,' *Journal of Northeast Asian Studies* (Summer 1993).

8   Hong Kong Government Industry Department, *Consultancy Study on Hong Kong's Software Industry: 1994–95,* Vol. 2, pp. 3–27.

9   Top US firms also combine brand-name and OEM production. Thus, for example a recent Bose music systems catalogue advertised Bose OEM systems specially designed for the acoustics of particular car models.

10 After Switzerland and Japan. (IMD International, *The World Competitiveness Yearbook 1996,* Lausanne, 1996, p. 369.)

11 For an important analysis of the dynamics and strengths of this pattern, see T. J. Sturgeon, 'Turnkey Production Networks: A New American Model of Industrial Organization?' unpublished paper, March 4, 1997.

12 Interviews with senior Intellectual Property Investigation Bureau Customs officials, December 18, 1996 and January 8, 1997. The MIT team also interviewed senior officers in Trade and Industry with responsibility for intellectual property policy, senior officers in the Intellectual Property Department, customs officers operating along the border inspecting vehicles, and customs officers inspecting shops within Hong Kong, as well as managers from international firms with special interest in this area.

13 Hong Kong Customs and Excise Department, 'Seizure Statistics on Pirated Compact Discs,' 1992, 1993, 1994, 1995, & 1996.

8   Lessons for US Industry

At the end of a study of Hong Kong industry, we return to the question with which we started in Chapter 1: are there any lessons for others to be learned from Hong Kong's nearly 20 years of experience in extending production networks into China and in developing products for sale to China's new consumers? As US firms consider global strategies for expanding production at home and abroad and for locating research, development, design, and production capabilities, the example of Hong Kong, one of the world's first and most rapid globalizers, offers a wide range of experiences to observe. Hong Kong's trial-and-error learning in global production involves not only industries such as toys and clothing, but lines of new service-enhanced products as well.

For Americans confronting the challenges of adapting to an increasingly open international economy with low-cost producers on their doorstep, Hong Kong reads as a cautionary tale of rapid transformation in response to the opening of a nearby low-cost labor market. Over the decade 1984–1994, industrial employment within Hong Kong fell by more than half. In the United States, too, much low-skilled, low-cost manufacturing has disappeared and more will follow. What does this mean for the employment opportunities and standard of living in the United States?

The future we make in American manufacturing must rest on the development of human resources and technological capabilities that deliver highly valued products at reasonable cost. These are the activities that can generate high wages and profits. The future of industry, this study suggests, is one in which old boundaries between manufacturing and services are vanishing. New generations of goods combine services and manufacturing capabilities in products that respond to the new desires of customers around the world. Service-enhanced products are in high demand, not only in the affluent markets of the West, but also in emerging markets—as demonstrated by the success in China of Motorola pagers; or of Hong Kong's Goldlion brand neckties; or of Gold Peak's home theatre audio systems. The old debates over whether the United States is a 'post-industrial' society ought to give way, we believe, to discussions over the kinds of investment in education and research that would enable all of our work-

force to acquire the capacities to participate in the transformed economy that is emerging out of new consumer
demands and new industrial possibilities.

In the course of this Hong Kong study, we have observed
once again that the products of the future emerge in 'old'
industries as well as in new ones. Companies can innovate
and carve out new markets not only by creating wholly
unprecedented products, but also by bundling new characteristics with old products, and by using new technologies to
produce them. The products of Traditional Chinese Medicine,
for example, will acquire new value, our colleagues have
argued, when their properties are catalogued with the help of
large, electronic databases; when their purity is guaranteed by
a regulatory agency with an international reputation for
integrity; and when their manufacture takes place in certified
facilities. Blue jeans become a new business when new technologies transform the character of the garment. Research
and development serve, then, not only to invent new products and markets, but to enhance the value of old commodities, making these businesses into new ones that can prosper
in countries with high standards of living. For societies that
can both upgrade old industries and innovate in the development of new service-enhanced products, the future of manufacturing is bright.

Our research in Hong Kong also led us to think more about
our basic assumptions about government and the economy.
For the MIT researchers coming from the United States, a
country in which debates continue to rage over the appropriate role for government in support of industry, Hong Kong's
growth experience provides an interesting test case of industrial development without industrial policy. Here is a society
with a noninterventionist government, which has experienced very rapid growth over 40 years. Its small and medium-
sized firms have proved remarkably adaptive to changes in the
world economy as well as to new opportunities in their own
region. There is no way to discount the differences between a
city-state and the world's largest economic and military
power, and in particular, for the large US defense role and the
large US domestic market. Still, we wondered what we could
learn about the behavior of industrialists in an environment
that is freer of heavy tax or regulatory burdens and government industrial interventions than any other we know.

At the end of our study, we are struck by two facts. First, in a society with a broad consensus on the principles of *laissez-faire* government, government still has played a very major role through its provision of collective goods like public housing, health services, education, and the allocation of land. In some sense this bedrock of social provision appears to constitute the foundation of an economy characterized by dynamic entrepreneurship, and a labor market without minimum wages, collective bargaining, or job security. The question of whether the particular social policies the Hong Kong government has pursued are optimal for the economy was not within our purview; but the fact that some such set of policies emerge as the counterweight to the absence of other political and social constraints on local capitalists does suggest that even *laissez-faire* government needs a minimal social agenda.

The second observation about Hong Kong's noninterventionism does, however, come closer to the heart of our own inquiry. Absent a set of government policies for incentives or direct supports to encourage research and development, what kinds of efforts do private actors undertake? Here the results are striking: Hong Kong's companies have devoted less to R&D in all forms than virtually any other society at Hong Kong's level of economic advance. Historically Hong Kong firms have been able to exploit opportunities other than technological upgrading for expansion and transformation—above all, extending their production networks into China, as that country opened. But today, as we have argued, labor costs are rising, even in China. There are more competitors who have learned how to excel at labor-intensive manufacturing. For Hong Kong firms to do well in the future, they need to push towards a higher-value-added trajectory, and for this, higher levels of individual and societal R&D expenditure are essential. Individual entrepreneurial responses to changing market opportunities may well not trigger the level of investments that would build capabilities for designing and making the new generations of products and services in the 'Made By Hong Kong' system. The lesson seems clear: that higher levels of public expenditures on education, training, research and development will produce better outcomes, both for individual companies and for the society as a whole, than would be attained without a governmental role in promoting industrial upgrading.

The second set of lessons that is suggested by the Hong Kong experience has to do with the advantages companies derive from shifting production to low-cost labor markets. We were surprised to discover in our observations of Hong Kong-owned and managed plants in Guangdong that products of reasonable complexity and acceptable quality can be made by low-skilled workers, working in factories for as little as a year or two. Our previous research in plants in the United States, Japan, and Europe had not prepared us for the range of capabilities possible in factories operating with a very rapid turnover of inexperienced, low-skilled workers. The possibilities of such plants have obvious implications for the future of industry in the advanced countries with high standards of living. If complex and high-quality products can readily be made by workers with little training and wages that are less than one-tenth of Western wages, it is hard to imagine that significant manufacturing would remain in the United States or in other high-wage countries. But as we began to explore the requirements and limitations of low-cost labor production systems in China, a more complicated picture emerged.

As we observed the production sites of Hong Kong-owned and managed plants in Guangdong, we discovered that making such factories perform well takes a specific set of expensive resources. These plants are established in zones with poorly developed physical and legal infrastructure but a very heavy politico-bureaucratic presence. To operate in such a realm requires not only deep cultural and linguistic competence, but a network of relationships that substitute for the guarantees that rule of law, a secure system of property rights, and a neutral administration provide elsewhere but that are lacking here. The success of the overseas Chinese networks in extending production systems into China derives precisely from their ability to provide alternative forms of social and material capital for building stable relationships in this legal no man's land. For American firms starting out in these regions, it may be essential at least at first to set up joint ventures with partners who have this kind of local expertise. But in order to limit dependence on one's partners and to develop over time the capability for independent decisions, firms need to consider how to accelerate their own learning and autonomy on this difficult terrain. The range of options for doing so is fairly wide. The Japanese, for example, bring along their own suppliers and so reduce the levels of uncertainty in their dealings with some part of the foreign environment. The Singaporeans have established a special protected zone at Suzhou, within which the physical and social infrastructure is all regulated by Singaporean standards, thus producing a more familiar and manageable environment; joint ventures with overseas Chinese are a frequently used vehicle; bringing in US expatriate managers with Chinese language and cultural skills is yet another.

The common element in all these solutions insofar as they attempt to profit from the low cost of labor is that they require very large managerial inputs from the outside. Factories with inexperienced workers that turn over too rapidly to permit the consolidation of stable patterns of socialization, cooperation, and learning need to have large numbers of active managers. Managers of low-skilled labor operations need a very different set of skills from those of a manager in an advanced production site in the United States or Europe or Japan. The issues which loom large in the best factories of the advanced countries include: skills in teaching; in eliciting a group's best efforts in order to improve the performance of the whole; in negotiating and resolving conflicts; in rotating workers through a variety of assignments in order to produce versatility for team production and rapid changes in the system; in upgrading the skills of the workforce in pace with the introduction of new technologies. Yet all of these issues barely appear in these low-cost labor plants. Here, rather, the priorities are: to coordinate and stockpile a quantity of supplies that permit the plant to operate without shutdowns; to supervise recruitment of new workers and rapidly train them to an adequate level of skill; to jump in as needed to rebalance the line, to repair machines, to replace workers, to arbitrate in workplace conflicts; to shield the plant and the workforce against intrusions from the local community and local officials; and to interpret the orders coming in from headquarters and buyers too distant for face-to-face discussions. These tasks are difficult enough that, as we noted in our discussion of the Hong Kong plants, even after five years, the top positions still tend to be held by trusted and experienced managers brought in from the outside. It takes years to train locals to perform these functions, and this is true, not only in Hong Kong-owned and managed plants, but in foreign firms in China more generally.

Like Hong Kong companies, American corporations that shift manufacturing operations out into plants with low-skilled, low-cost workers need to be prepared over the long term to compensate for the weakness of the workforce and the general instability of the workplace with high (and expensive) inputs of managerial resources from the outside. They also need to recognize that in this game there is a lot of competition, and that Americans have no special comparative advantage. What are the alternatives? One set of options is reflected in the strategies of Japanese corporations in Southeast Asia and China and the German companies in Central and Eastern Europe. Both kinds of companies are investing massively in training for the production workers, technicians, and managers.[1] But these strategies work only if wages rise substantially, in order both to provide incentives for the new learning and to ward off attempts by other companies in the region to poach the workers the firm has trained.

As wages rise in the low-cost labor market, as competition grows in the local market, the next range of solutions involve in one way or another developing a set of capabilities for upgrading and producing higher-value-added products. In a sense this is what our report is about: an analysis of the difficulties of upgrading the 'Made By Hong Kong' production network and a set of recommendations for enhancing the 'Made in Hong Kong' inputs in order to drive the production networks that Hong Kong controls higher up the technology ladder. US firms are far more likely than Hong Kong firms to have the R&D facilities in-house that could enable them to upgrade their overseas operations. Their puzzle, however, is to decide whether these R&D activities should remain within home territory or be shifted closer to the production sites.[2] Multiple factors are involved here: the availability of skilled technical personnel; the proximity of university laboratories with relevant applied research activities; the absorptive capacity of the local production facility. Moreover, foreign corporations confront a demand from governments in a number of countries that they transfer technology as a condition of gaining market access.

To these well-recognized dilemmas, our observations in the Hong Kong plants add yet another: that removing some subset of R&D activities from home territory and relocating them close to these low-cost labor sites means taking them out of easy interaction with a company's most sophisticated end users and suppliers. The customers and suppliers of even rather 'low-tech' apparel firms go out to visit the China-based plants in which their garments are being manufactured only rarely and with reluctance. The absence of a dense fabric of connections among suppliers, buyers, industrialists, technicians, researchers, and equipment salespersons out in the 'greenfields' of new industrial development in East Asia—in contrast to the vibrant communities in, for example, the Emilia-Romagna in Italy, Baden-Wurttemberg in Germany, Silicon Valley, or the industrial heartland of Michigan—means that firms can transfer researchers, but not the environment in which they become most productive.

As advanced manufacturing becomes the production of goods with attributes supplied by new information technologies and other services, the true competitive edge will be held by those able rapidly to identify new customers in large and differentiated markets and satisfy their desires with new generations of goods. The markets for these new products are not niches, but large segments that cut across nations (although they require some measure of mass-customization to fit national tastes). The challenge—as Hong Kong firms are discovering—is to be close enough to the customers in the new markets to discover their preferences, yet maintain the firm's assets for innovation in proximity to the sources that can nourish, renew, and enlarge them.

For US firms preparing to tap the enormous potential of emerging markets in Asia, Latin America, and elsewhere around the world, the problem of globalization emerges in a new light. Added to the task of organizing the physical network of production facilities, product flows, and transportation links is the challenge of creating a parallel network of knowledge-capturing and knowledge-generating activities. The sources of new knowledge are widely dispersed. The value of each discovery is multiplied when firms have the capacity to absorb and use the new knowledge elsewhere. Among the most important lessons taught by the production networks of 'Made By Hong Kong' is the complementarity of investments in new knowledge creation at home and abroad. As US firms chart the course of globalization, they need both to strengthen their home-based capabilities for innovation and their abilities to monitor, understand, and learn abroad. What is 'Made in America' makes possible what is 'Made By America'; so, too, what is 'Made By America' may benefit 'Made in America.'

Notes

1   See especially W. Hatch and K. Yamamura, *Asia in Japan's Embrace,* Cambridge: Cambridge University Press, 1996, Chapter 7.
2   See the early findings of the University of California/San Diego study of globalization in the hard disk drive industry in P. Gourevitch; R. E. Bohn; and D. McKendrick, 'Who Is Us? The Nationality Problem in Globalization of Production,' the Data Storage Industry Globalization Project, University of California, San Diego, Report 96-01, December 1996.

Part Two
Industry Studies

9   Textiles and Clothing in Hong Kong

Suzanne Berger with David Gartner
and Kevin Karty

The Questions

In every advanced society with a high standard of living, the future of the core manufacturing industries raises major debates. Can the mass-manufacturing industries that fueled growth in the first stages of industrialization remain strong, once the cutting edge of technological advance moves to other sectors and wages rise? Can the core industries continue to provide good jobs, contribute to productivity growth, and promote social well-being? Or does their survival in an economy of emerging low-cost producers depend on the protection of tariffs and quotas? Are these 'sunset industries' destined to disappear? Should they be speeded on their way out? The textiles and clothing activities of all advanced industrial countries confront such questions and doubts about the future. For Hong Kong—with its small domestic market, geographical, cultural and political access to low-cost labor in China, and unparalleled experience in transferring and coordinating production in its vast hinterland—these issues arise with even more force.

In the near term at least, the prosperity of Hong Kong textile and clothing companies remains very important to the domestic economy. In this report we discuss textiles and clothing together as one industry, although Hong Kong statistical categories separate clothing and textiles, and, in reality, these labels cover a wide set of different activities, from fiber production, spinning, weaving, dyeing, finishing, knitting, linking, assembling, cutting, pattern-making, sample-making, sewing, packaging, to buying, trading, and wholesale and retail trade. Together they make up the largest manufacturing sector within Hong Kong proper, comprising 40 percent of manufacturing employment. In 1994, 173,241 persons had manufacturing jobs in this industry and another

150,723 were employed in retail sales and trading companies linked to it. Almost 40 percent of domestic exports, a quarter of Hong Kong's re-export trade, and a third of total industrial output derives from this sector. In 1993, Hong Kong was the world's largest exporter of clothing with sales of US$21 billion, out of a world total of US$153 billion; that year it was the second largest exporter of textiles (after Germany).[1]

The overarching issue, however—for Hong Kong industry and government, and for this research project—is that of future prospects. Here we suggest several ways to address the key questions of: whether the textiles and clothing industry in Hong Kong can remain strong in the economy of the twenty-first century; whether some parts of the manufacturing activities in this sector need to remain in the Hong Kong Special Administrative Region (SAR)—that is, in Hong Kong proper; and finally, whether there are steps that companies and government ought to take to enhance future strength. We start by challenging the view that textiles and clothing are a 'sunset' industry in other high-wage countries. Next, we present findings from the MIT firm-level analysis of companies in textiles and clothing. Third, on the basis of these findings, we identify which manufacturing and manufacturing-linked services need to remain in the future SAR in order to sustain the production activities outside of Hong Kong. Finally, this chapter offers recommendations for industry and government.

Lessons from Other Countries

The notion that textiles and clothing is a sunset industry in high-wage economies is a myth, if by 'sunset' we mean marginal, unprofitable, or destined to disappear. In the United States, this sector continues to rank among the top four industries in the country in employment (12 percent of the manufacturing workforce in 1992—the largest group in manufacturing); in sales (the largest sales for consumer durables or nondurable goods); in productivity increases in recent years, and in contribution to manufacturing GDP (larger than autos, paper, petroleum refining, or primary metals). Even in New York City, which like Hong Kong is a high-wage economy, the garment industry employs over 100,000 production workers, about two thirds of them unionized workers with wages starting at US$6.50 (plus a 25-percent benefit package). Many of these workers are newcomers to the country and to the economy, and these jobs represent a valuable point of entry to industrial experience. On the base of these production workers rests a pyramid of tightly linked and well-paying professional opportunities for technicians, designers, showroom employees, models, buyers, salesmen, fashion media specialists, and others in the business—almost equal in numbers to the production workers.[2] Nor is this a unique New York story: garments is the fastest growing industry in Los Angeles. On the front of research and development, the American Textile Partnership (Amtex), a three-year-old collaborative endeavor among industry, professional associations, and the national laboratories under the Department of Energy have laid out a varied menu of research activities to bring technologies from the cutting edge into the industry. Much of this effort has yet to show its relevance to industrial practice, but already one of the by-products—the National Sourcing Database—is being heavily used: since August 1995, the Apparel Exchange Website had 2.64 million accesses.

The clothing and textiles industry in Western Europe over the past decade has been battered by multiple problems: a persistent recession has depressed consumer spending; currency fluctuations have allowed some states in the European Union to gain market share at the expense of others; a growing concentration of retailers has put pressure on prices; and the end of Communism has opened Eastern Europe for foreign direct investment and trade. No country has been more hard hit by these events than Germany, where employment in apparel-making over the decade 1986–1996 declined by more than half, with many companies going bankrupt and others moving east. And yet the picture that emerges from interviews in a number of leading firms shows a remarkable adaptation to new circumstances, and the reorganization of production in ways that promise real strength in the future. There are new product lines and new technologies for linking companies from fiber to retailers. The new patterns of production redistribute activities between Germany and low-wage Central European plants. What remain in Germany— and are often expanded in Germany—are logistics centers, design and sample facilities, cutting, development of new fabrics, the development and maintenance of Electronic Data Interchange (EDI) systems, and at a minimum about 20 percent of production for product innovation. These activities provide high-paying and interesting jobs. In the plants run by German managers in the Czech Republic, Hungary, and elsewhere, major expenditures are being made for long-term training, apprenticeships, and the continuing education of the workforce, as well as for modernizing capital equipment. Textiles and apparel in Germany proper will be a smaller industry, but still a major employer, a major exporter, and a sector with profitable and innovative firms.[3]

Hong Kong Textile and Clothing Companies: The View from the Company

In Hong Kong, as in the United States, Western Europe, and Japan, the numbers employed in textiles and clothing manufacturing have declined rapidly over the past decade. For both clothing and textiles, 1980 was the year of peak employment in Hong Kong. Clothing dropped from 301,545 that year to 137,287 in 1994; textiles, from 88,812 to 35,854 over the same period.[4] But as in the United States and Germany, the real question for the future is about the strength, dynamism, and adaptive capabilities of the companies and activities that remain. Even in its reduced dimensions, this sector continues to be very important—both as the largest component of Hong Kong manufacturing, and as the coordinating hub of production networks that carry a high volume of business into and out of China and beyond. The Hong Kong companies own and manage many plants outside the future SAR, mainly in the Pearl River Delta of Guangdong Province. The viability and performance of these factories depend in critical measure on inputs from the Hong Kong firms.[5]

The principal methodology of the MIT research on Hong Kong textiles and clothing was firm-level analysis, drawing on long interviews and factory visits in Hong Kong, the Pearl River Delta, and elsewhere in the People's Republic of China. We spoke with chief corporate leaders and senior managers in 31 companies. Of these, five were primarily textile producers;

26 were mainly clothing manufacturers; and nine had major retail operations as parts of their business. We also interviewed ten buyers for very large US and European companies and five individuals who are consultants to the industry. We visited nine public institutions that provide services to this sector. Finally, because of the importance of trade and trade regulations to this industry and its future in Hong Kong, we interviewed about a dozen trade officials in Hong Kong and Washington, DC.

The group of companies that form the basis for our findings and conclusions are far from a random sample of Hong Kong's 5,628 clothing establishments (which employ an average of 24 workers in the territory) or its 2,482 textile establishments (with an average of 13).[6] Rather, we tried to identify some of the best and most successful companies as judged and recommended by their professional peers. Our reasoning was that these firms might provide models of some of the most promising and innovative ways of responding to new challenges; their problems and weaknesses might illustrate more general difficulties. To offer an initial snapshot: these companies are far larger than the average, with only three of them employing fewer than 100 persons in Hong Kong; eight of them employing between 100 and 300; four, employing 400–500; and four employing more than 800 in Hong Kong. A number of these companies have very large PRC operations: five employ fewer than 1,000 workers in China; four, 1,000–3,000; four, 3,000–4,000; and one, a labor force of more than 8,000.[7] Only three of these firms produce in Hong Kong and nowhere else. Four have only headquarters activities in Hong Kong. The others have some mix of production in Hong Kong, China, and in far-scattered foreign sites from the United States to Burma (Myanmar). In all of these companies, control and management remain squarely in the hands of the founder or the founder's family. Even in the firms that have gone public, the senior family figure, as far as we could judge, has dominant influence. The markets these companies target are increasingly diverse, but the United States is still the principal market for 21 of them. Eighteen of them do substantial or even principal business with Europe; seven have significant markets in Japan. For five, the local Hong Kong market is a major part of their business. Eight of them are making major efforts to sell in China. Almost all of these companies sell original equipment manufacture (OEM), which is then resold by another firm under its own label; but ten of the companies we interviewed have also developed their own brands.

The Findings: Hong Kong's Strengths

The key point that emerges from the plant visits and from our long interviews with corporate leaders and managers, and with the buyers and industry consultants is the existence of world-class performers among the Hong Kong companies. These outstanding Hong Kong companies are manufacturing products that incorporate such highly valued attributes as: speedy delivery; new technologically engineered fabric properties; greater sensitivity to the diverse demands of customers in such markets as Japan and China; consistency of quality and image embodied in a brand name. And they are doing so at a reasonable cost, even while using many of the high-priced inputs of Hong Kong society. As we discuss in Part One of this book, manufacturing performance in advanced societies today means the production of goods with special attributes often derived from activities that have conventionally been identified as services (from new information technologies, for example). In this sense the old boundary between manufacturing and services has disappeared; producing goods that satisfy the demands of an increasingly diverse universe of mass consumers requires that manufacturing be joined to services technologies and to other societal capabilities. (Monitoring to eliminate azo-dyes, which have been banned by Germany in textiles sold in its market, is but one example.)

Manufacturers seeking high returns in high-wage societies need to deliver not simply a carefully sewn pair of jeans in a sturdy denim at a reasonable price, for example, but jeans that must be delivered rapidly to retailers and restocked quickly in time to catch a seasonal fashion trend; jeans made for diverse new customers located through new electronic technologies, with materials located through new electronic databases; jeans custom-cut to a consumer's individual measurements that have been electronically transmitted to the production site; jeans laundered with a fabric finish that requires laboratory monitoring and adjustments to be communicated among all involved in making them; jeans with a label that—because of corporate reputation enhanced by advertising—allows consumers to make purchases that express their social and environmental preferences, as well as their desire for fashionable reliable goods. We found outstanding companies among those we interviewed that excel in producing textiles and clothing with such attributes.[8] Some of them produce only in Hong Kong; the majority distribute their activities between Hong Kong and low-cost labor sites. All of them require significant Hong Kong inputs to produce these highly valued goods. These companies stand as examples of what is possible in Hong Kong and as a model starting point for the new flexible and innovative firms that the *Made By Hong Kong* report foresees.

What are the factors that enable the production of high-value-added goods in textiles and apparel in Hong Kong? The firm-level research discovered six common features as recurring themes in many of the success stories.

Flexibility in Production

Compared with excellent companies of similar size that we have studied in the United States and Europe, most of the Hong Kong businesses we visited displayed an unusual capacity to turn out a wide range of products and to switch their lines rapidly from one product to another. This flexibility has a number of dimensions. First, these companies are producing an increasing number of products within the same plants in order to satisfy demand for a greater array of goods. The chief executive of a sweater company with 200 employees described the firm's ability to work on 20 different styles at the same time and to provide customers (in Japan) with orders as small as 150–350 pieces.[9] The corporate head of one medium-sized denim manufacturer operating wholly within Hong Kong told us that over the past two decades his company had moved from making one to three items, to 300 different items, all within the same plant.[10] He laid out what this entails: warehousing larger quantities of stock so that orders for any of the 300 items can be filled rapidly; training for the workers that enables them to work on a larger array of products; developing information technology skills within the firm that facilitate fast communication with customers—in order to get early warning of what will be ordered. (In this case the founder's son received a degree in computer science and returned to work in the family business.)

The head of a spinning factory told us his cost structure was not far off Pakistani costs, because automation has driven down his labor costs and because mill management now involves smaller and smaller lots, and more variety in raw materials. Pakistan is one of the world's great cotton producers, with a rapidly growing textile industry; textile labor in Pakistan costs only 12 percent of the average textile wage in Hong Kong.[11] While Pakistani suppliers may be cheaper, it takes a month to get their yarns—whereas the local Hong Kong spinner provides the highest quality and is willing to entertain changes in orders from day to day.[12] The general manager of another spinning company observed that they have the same machinery and make the same products in their China plant and their Hong Kong plant, but the Hong Kong plant is capable of far greater diversity. In Hong Kong they can make 70 different kinds of yarn a month; in the China facility, they can only make eight different yarns a month. Anything can be done in China—but it takes longer. He explained this by Hong Kong's production planning capabilities and easier access to raw materials.[13]

In a plant in Guangdong, we observed jackets heading for Japan being inspected for stray needles (a Japanese safety requirement) on one cordoned-off part of the factory floor; Ellen Tracy jackets that would retail for US$300–400 being pressed in mid-production in another area; and blouses that would cost one-tenth of these jackets and sell in low- to mid-range stores being sewn in yet another area.[14] The chief executive of a knitting firm that works almost wholly with the European market told us: 'I do low-end, medium-end, and designer labels—but all of one quality!'[15] The head of one very large company described making garments for Bradlees, WalMart, Polo, Liz Claiborne, and Armani Jeans all in the same plant—albeit a far smaller and faster order in better fabric for Ralph Lauren.[16] In these companies and others we observed, the flexibility in production was being achieved within the same plant, but in other cases, the flexibility in company output derives from using multiple production sites and coordinating their efforts. The flexibility required in the above examples of production for diverse customer needs stands as a remarkable achievement.

Such flexibility requires not only the ability to work on a diversity of products at the same time and to shift the mix; it also requires the ability to move the products to the customers rapidly. We found only one company using the most advanced Quick Response Electronic Data Interchange (EDI) process to link manufacturing to retailers (in this case, linking its Taiwan-based shirt operations to a large-scale US retailer who provides point-of-sale information). Such Quick Response technologies greatly accelerate ordering, stocking, and replenishing merchandise and reduce both inventories and the wastage of products that have to be sold at the end of the season at a loss.

The manufacturer can have the goods custom-cleared in the retailer's warehouse within 30 to 33 days of receiving the order. The retailer has reduced the warehouse inventory to six weeks and is trying to bring it down to four weeks. The manufacturer now receives all of the retailer's orders in this line. The same manufacturer is doing 50-day replenishment for a Hong Kong-based retailer (with 550 stores in the region) that we interviewed.[17]

Although there are few cases today of EDI-coordinated production in Hong Kong (a point to which we return in the recommendations section below), many companies describe strategies to handle orders that arrive later and later in the season, as retailers try to hedge bets and reduce inventories. The majority of companies across all size categories and products mentioned a major trend toward faster production as a result of shorter lead times. Weavers told us of delivering four to six weeks after orders; a denim manufacturer reduced lead time from 45 days to only 30.[18]

The major obstacles to getting orders to customers much more rapidly are transportation times—since air freight remains very expensive—and availability of fabric—since much of it comes from China, Japan, or Europe. Retailer pressures for shorter intervals from order to delivery make the proximity of Mexican and Central American production to North American markets and the North American Free Trade Agreement (NAFTA) a major threat for Hong Kong manufacturers. Three of those we interviewed have responded by opening plants in that region. But NAFTA producers are even more hampered by the difficulties of obtaining fabric than are the Hong Kong manufacturers. The textile sector in Mexico and Central American is small and does not produce high-quality goods. US fiber and fabric is expensive, and certain goods are not available from the United States and need in any event to be brought from Southeast Asia or East Asia. One of the major European retail buyers explained: 'Fabric comes first. To go somewhere with no fabric availability—you're in trouble. Unless you are prepared to fly fabric in, as we are in Sri Lanka. The United States jumped head first into NAFTA without stopping to think about fabric—and it's been a real problem.'[19] Another major buyer reasoned that the real issues are pre-manufacturing lead time, the design and sample-making and the availability of piece goods: not manufacturing time. 'There isn't a factory in Asia that can't cut and sew in 30–45 days, drop and ship.'[20]

The costs associated with reducing transportation and the fabric constraints may simply be too high to make very fast customer response systems possible out of Hong Kong. Still, virtually all the companies we visited experience real pressure to compress their production cycles and the best among them have achieved good results. As a senior manager in a trading company noted, 'If the production is coming out of non-Hong Kong-controlled plants—even if they are no further away than Hong Kong-controlled plants—it'll still take about 70 percent longer to get the goods.'[21]

Understanding Customers in Different Markets

The second common characteristic of some, but not all of the strong Hong Kong firms is the ability to interpret and respond to the preferences of very diverse customer bases. For the majority, the American market dominates; indeed, since 1984 the domestic exports of Hong Kong clothing companies to the United States have hovered around the 50 percent mark and those to major European markets at about 21 percent.[22] But within these national markets the Hong Kong companies have over time changed the customers to whom they sell, adding new segments of the consumer market without giving up their old clients. Companies started in the American market in the 1960s and 1970s by selling to low-end market stores, such as K-Mart, moved up to department stores, then to major brand names such as Liz Claiborne, The Gap, Ralph Lauren 'Polo', DKNY, and Donna Karan. Over the past five years, the companies we studied not only changed their customers within the same national markets but also have made major efforts to add new national markets; today most of them sell at least 20 percent of their production to a second market other than their primary market.

What does it take to work in several different national markets at the same time? Over the long run there may be a trend towards an internationalization of tastes that makes it desirable to promote the same items in different countries. But today companies find extreme differences in the requirements of buyers in different markets. To grasp these requires: knowing foreign languages and cultures in some empathetic depth (here English language capabilities help); long stays and regular visits to foreign countries; and frequent and diverse contacts within one's own society with people of different ethnic and national groups. Hong Kong provides all of these opportunities, and its open international environment has served the industry well in its rise in the 1970s and 1980s.

Already in those years it was clear that European and American buyers had such different demands and ways of doing business that were so different that most Hong Kong companies tended to work with either one or the other market. The American buyers came with highly detailed specifications, emphasized price, and provided long runs and high-volume business. The European buyers solicited design ideas from the Hong Kong manufacturers, focused more on consistency and quality, and remained more loyal to their suppliers. As one large European buyer, with a US$1.5 billion mail order business and regional headquarters in Hong Kong explained, 'The US buyer looks for the basics and he has exactly what he's looking for and wants it to be copied. He also knows what price he wants. '"807" is a typical American buyer's idea.' ('807' garments are those produced under outward processing arrangements with US fabric, sewn in low-cost labor factories, then re-imported to the United States under legislative provisions that lower their duties.) 'Europe is not one market; it's more fragmented, with much smaller markets,' the buyer continued. 'One thousand dozen is small for the United States; 200 dozen is a good size for Europe.'[23] Companies that worked with Europe or the United States developed different sets of capabilities. Those working for Europe, for example, had higher labor costs, larger design capabilities, and made more frequent visits to the markets whose preferences they had to discern than those who sold to Americans and could work to the highly detailed specifications the American buyers brought with them to Hong Kong.

Today, the best of the companies we visited are trying to leverage the capabilities developed over the course of years of dealing with Americans or Europeans into capabilities to move into new markets. Japan and China are two markets with both great potential for Hong Kong and great difficulty of access—albeit different kinds of potentials and access difficulties. Japan has very affluent consumers, with extremely demanding standards of quality, a retail system dominated by small shops and department stores with counters controlled by individual brands. Unlike the United States and Europe, Japan does not have country of origin rules that limit imports of products made by Hong Kong companies within their China plants. Access to the Japanese market, however, virtually requires Japanese partners, and cultivating relationships with them is an indefinitely long process, over the course of which multiple small orders must be carefully filled. Only three of the companies we interviewed do more than 5–10 percent of their business in Japan; and they described an arduous and expensive process of convincing their Japanese interlocutors of their capabilities. As the CEO of a knitting firm explained, 'For Japanese, a small run is 150–300 sweaters, and we do about 30 percent of our business with them in that category. A middle-sized run is 1,000–2,000 and we do another 30 percent with them in that category. First, there are exhibition samples in August or September; then production samples, so you have to turn out 15 pieces before you can expect an order in October. Imagine if they want us to use European yarns! They expect delivery in December or January. We wait longer for an order, but actually it's not risky. The trading house balances what you can produce.'[24]

The companies trying to sell in the China market see a future of enormous promise, as well as some great, but surmountable difficulties. Retail sales have been growing at 12 percent per year in China, and there are a growing number of urban consumers willing and able to spend RMB100–500 on an item of clothing. These consumers are willing to pay more

for products identified as good quality by advertising or reputation.[25] Surveys of China's urban consumers find brand-
name recognition high, and those Hong Kong companies
that have brand-name strategies in China—Jeanswest and
Goldlion stand out—are doing well, despite the high costs of
advertising. Goldlion has doubled its turnover every year
since 1985/6. The main issues here are the absence or weakness of retail outlets, the regulations that make it difficult or
impossible for a Hong Kong business to establish its own
retail shops, and high rents.[26] The common solutions are selling through department stores and through franchise stores,
though increasingly companies are trying to open their own
shops. Six of the companies we studied have major retail businesses in China. In each case the companies have developed
extensive monitoring capabilities to assure that the products
they are promoting as high-quality goods in China are presented in ways that do not undermine their image (for example, are presented by competent and helpful sales personnel
in a clean and well-lighted setting).

Another issue in China is that the same brand name that
identifies a product as a desirable object is a tempting target
for copying. One company in our sample that does most of its
business in China through retail franchise stores and department store counters, described pirating of goods as a huge
problem. Two hundred cases last year—and only 1–2 percent
of the cases were really fixed. But the fact is that those at the
top of the income scale who buy our product won't buy these
copies, so the pirated goods probably are not cutting into our
market, though they damage our image.'

Coordinating Production

The third common strength that emerges in the companies
we studied is an unparalleled ability to coordinate production
at home in Hong Kong and in diverse foreign sites. Most of
their foreign-located plants are in the Pearl River Delta, within a two- to four-hour trip from Hong Kong.[27] But others are
in distant parts of China, like Xinjiang, in Taiwan, the
Philippines, Indonesia, Burma (Myanmar), Cambodia, India,
Sri Lanka, Bangladesh, the United States, Mexico, Dominican
Republic, Mauritius, and Malaysia.

Coordinating production among various sites means, first, choosing among plants in various locations. These decisions are driven to some extent by the quality of the workforce in different locales. In dyeing and finishing plants, for example, the need for care and consistency at every step of the process means that the most complex jobs and those requiring the highest quality are likely to be carried out in Hong Kong. In garment-making and sweaters, however, many of the companies reported that they can achieve equal quality in any of their plants after about one year.

Some parts of the process need to be carried out in specific locales and then combined with the inputs of plants in other regions. The international trade regulations for textiles and clothing are major drivers of location decisions, for Hong Kong has a relatively large quota, hence Hong Kong manufacturers try to carry out those parts of the process that confer origin in Hong Kong and transfer other parts of production to lower cost labor sites. Until July 1, 1996, a sweater manufacturer in Hong Kong who wished to have garments enter the United States under Hong Kong quota had to knit the panels in Hong Kong, but might then truck the panels to a PRC plant for assembly and finishing, then back to Hong Kong to send abroad. For Europe, the rules of origin were different: the site of assembly conferred origin, so clothes destined for European markets would be knitted in China, trucked to Hong Kong for linking, then sent back to China for finishing and packing, then back to Hong Kong to be shipped out. Each shift in the arcane and complex set of foreign national rules governing quota and rules of origin—and there have been many changes over the years—determined shifts in the manufacturers' locational decisions and required exceptional organizational capabilities for coordinating fragmented activities. When, for example, in 1984 the United States changed the rules of origin to require that knitted goods destined for the US market under the Hong Kong quota must actually be knitted (instead of only assembled) in Hong Kong, the Hong Kong manufacturers had to rapidly build up their knitting capacities. Unable to find enough workers or enough knitting machines from the usual European machine-makers, they finally located a Japanese automated knitting machine manufacturer on the verge of bankruptcy, and bought so heavily from him that today Shimaseiki is the world leader in computerized knitting machinery. A change in the rules of origin thus drove locational and technological shifts that produced a massive expansion of Hong Kong's production and capabilities.

Coordination also demands combining activities that might be carried out in any one of a number of different sites with those that cannot be moved (or that cannot readily be moved) to other locales. For example, foreign buyers want to remain in Hong Kong and are reluctant to operate in the PRC. Thus approval of designs, sample garments, colors, and printing usually takes place in Hong Kong, and the rest of the production process has to be geared to that fact. The General Manager of a large finishing and dyeing company explained that his company needed to keep some yarn dyeing in Hong Kong because it had a knitting factory next door, and for complex stripe patterns, it required excellent communication between the two operations. The company needs to keep printing in Hong Kong because the buyers come in to monitor the final results before fabric enters into full production. A problem in dyeing can always be refinished, but printing mistakes are irreparable, so they are not likely to move printing operations to their Pearl River Delta plants.[28]

Managers and Performance in Network Production Systems

Of all the coordination problems that Hong Kong companies master, the most demanding is the provision and allocation of managerial resources for the plants established outside of Hong Kong. Solving this problem has been one of Hong Kong's greatest accomplishments. Most of the offshore plants are located in the Pearl River Delta where Hong Kong companies employ several million workers. There are many difficulties in operating in this environment, among them: poor infrastructure; nonexistent banking services; changing and uncertain customs regulations about the importation of machinery and supplies; and the need to obtain licenses from government officials that too often are arbitrary or corrupt. Perhaps the most intractable of all the issues which require high levels of managerial inputs, however, are the problems presented by the characteristics of the workforce.

ing their new workforce, our interviews found very minimal training programs in the Pearl River Delta plants.

What is extraordinary under these circumstances is that Hong Kong's Pearl River Delta plants manage to turn out goods of a quality high enough to be acceptable to most buyers in all markets. 'Company Alpha' makes clothing sold under Ellen Tracy, Escada, and other top-of-the-line, ready-wear brands. Many of the other senior managers described similar quality achievements. What makes high performance standards possible with inexperienced and low-skill employees are the managers, upon whom rests the enormous burden of making these factories outside Hong Kong operate well. In the absence of a stable workforce (with the natural habits of cooperation, group leaders, and professional standards that develop over years of working together) a company needs an unusually large managerial presence to coordinate the plant, balance the line, and produce consistent results in quality and productivity.

Four decades of extraordinary success and expansion of manufacturing in textiles and clothing in Hong Kong has created a large reservoir of managerial talent in the territory. The managers' skills derive from university education in engineering and science in Hong Kong and abroad; years of work in Hong Kong in plants with skilled workforces; multiple close contacts with demanding and sophisticated buyers in Hong Kong and abroad; a high level of understanding of international markets; and varied experiences in a number of Hong Kong companies, across different parts of the industry. These irreplaceable managerial assets have now been turned to the task of replicating the performance of Hong Kong's best plants in settings that lack many of the basic ingredients of the Hong Kong setting: workers with long experience and varied skills; the cosmopolitan environment; the intensity of interactions with others in the industry; frequent contacts with buyers and suppliers. For an outsider it is striking how well the Hong Kong managers succeed. But whatever the process of institutional learning at work in the Pearl River Delta plants, the extreme dependence of these plants on Hong Kong managers is not likely to be reduced in the near or medium term.

One-Stop Shopping

Some of the most highly valued attributes that are bundled with Hong Kong products derive from the characteristics of the city itself. Buyers who locate in Hong Kong find within easy reach companies that can meet virtually any requirement and do it rapidly and reliably at low cost. Hong Kong firms specialize in matching up the requirements of foreign markets and the capabilities of manufacturers who may or may not be located in the city proper, but belong to production networks that can be rapidly activated from their Hong Kong centers. All of the buyers interviewed for the study emphasized this advantage of locating regional headquarters in the city. Most of them concluded that this asset was so great that Hong Kong would never be supplanted as the center of the region's great textiles and clothing production networks.

Hong Kong's role as a one-stop shopping center, as with New York City, depends on the concentration of activities within a small territory and on having a comprehensive industry with all its parts readily accessible from within the city. As the managing director of one very large Hong Kong company explained: 'Even though the United States is so big, all the buyers go to New York because there's a market there, a concentration of activities and knowledge. All the infrastructure of fashion is there. It's the same in Hong Kong: we manage the whole chain. Everyone wants to come here and see what others are doing—to look at our samples and at other people's projects. I don't see this business being dispersed into 20 different centers or cities. All the sales are in Hong Kong; the factories are controlled and financed by Hong Kong people; and the profit comes to Hong Kong. It is "Made by Hong Kong". Hong Kong is the nerve center of global manufacturing.'[32]

In Hong Kong buyers can find any specialties they may need; here they can choose fabric; verify colors and patterns; check production samples; meet with the company designers or merchandisers; monitor the quality of the production. Looking at—touching—samples remains especially important for the buyers; even the biggest among them do not yet rely on electronic transmission of images in lieu of direct inspection of samples. Moreover—unlike New York—Hong Kong abounds with people good at interpreting the requirements and preferences of foreign societies into manufacturing specifications.

Public Institutions

The strengths of the best Hong Kong companies depend not only on their own efforts, but on public institutions that provide an environment in many respects unique in the region. The superior infrastructure of Hong Kong transportation, telecommunications, and cargo services are obviously a great boon to businesses. But even more important, the transparency of administration, honest and competent civil servants, limited government, and rule of law create a framework supportive of business and sustain Hong Kong's full and independent membership in international economic institutions. As we argued in the sections on 'safe harbor' in Part One of this book, the same capabilities of Hong Kong's public institutions that have produced a civil service with low levels of corruption might be enhanced and turned to other purposes vital for the society.

The public and parapublic institutions designed to support the textiles and clothing industries also have developed a set of capabilities that might well support major new initiatives. In the course of our research, we had the opportunity to learn about programs for the industry at the Hong Kong Productivity Council (HKPC), and the Hong Kong Trade Development Council (HKTDC), the Clothing Technology Demonstration Centre (CTDC), the Clothing Industry Training Authority (CITA), Kwai Chung Technical Institute, and the Hong Kong Polytechnic University's Institute of Textiles and Clothing. Large-scale public investment in these institutions is evident from their magnificent facilities; a broad support from private companies is demonstrated by the active participation of industrialists on their boards, as well as by the special customs levy that supports the training programs of CITA. Since 1976, a 0.03 percent levy on garment exports has been channeled into the educational activities. These institutional resources could be reorganized as a platform for new activities in support of the industry's efforts. .

Challenges for Hong Kong Industry

Our firm-level investigation of Hong Kong's clothing and tex-tiles industry has discovered strengths that cut across the industry, appearing in companies with different products, sizes, and markets; at the same time, however, we have iden-tified nine areas of serious vulnerability. The company heads with whom we spoke often raised these issues with us and urged us to lay them out for public discussion in a clear and frank manner. We regard these as challenges, responses to which can be constructed on the foundations of Hong Kong's prior experiences and traditions.

Lock into Low-Wage Manufacturing

The opening of China from 1978 on provided an extraordi-nary set of opportunities to overcome labor shortages and the high cost of Hong Kong land by shifting labor- and space-intensive activities into Guangdong Province. With this opening, a vast zone that previously had seemed no more than 'white space on the map north of the New Territories,' in the words of one of Hong Kong's industrial leaders, became a territory to be organized for industrial production. The results were an extraordinary rate of growth in production and of living standards in Guangdong, and for the Hong Kong entrepreneurs who mastered the organizational and coordination skills required to maximize network produc-tion—an enormous expansion of activities and profitability. The Kurt Salmon 1995 study of the industry (see Note 1) esti-mates that 55 percent of Hong Kong's clothing and textiles firms have overseas production capacities. Just four of the 31 companies we visited produce only in Hong Kong. The oth-ers, who all have some production in China, list access to low-wage labor and to cheaper inputs of land and water as the major factors driving their move. This pattern of network pro-duction has been so successful that many in the industry today see no reason to alter the pattern of development, but seek, rather to extend the networks deeper into China and even into Hong Kong itself, by locating a processing zone within Hong Kong, adjacent to the Mainland border.

Why change? The essential vulnerability of this production system based on low-cost labor derives from three facts: first,

Hong Kong is not alone in the world in its ability to organize low-skilled cheap labor in ways that produce acceptable goods for affluent markets. New emerging countries in the region—Indonesia, Burma, Sri Lanka, India, and others—offer abundant opportunities to copy the pattern, and in these countries Hong Kong entrepreneurs have no special advantage. Further away, Mexico and South America loom as low-cost labor production sites with closer proximity to large American markets.

Secondly, the lock into low-cost labor has perverse effects on the industry's efforts to attract excellent managers, technicians, and production workers, and it has retarding effects on technological advance. In our discussions with managers in the plants in the Pearl River Delta and elsewhere in China, we observed the great hardships of difficult travel, absence from home, lack of professional community (and of community in all senses of the word for those residing in the isolated, encapsulated factories scattered across Guangdong Province), the dearth of opportunities for technical experimentation and product development. We doubt that the best and brightest of today's students in chemical engineering or management or electrical engineering will choose careers whose central mission would be running this low-cost labor production system.

Moreover, with respect to technological advance, the focus on maximizing the gains from low-cost, low-skilled labor rules out the adoption of many of the technologies that could offer real productivity gains. For example, if a garment is being produced in small or medium batches, the organizational changes on the factory floor required to implement a Quick Response system (reducing the length of time between orders and retail deliveries) work best when the factory changes from individual piecework and bundle production to team-based modular production.[33] The Clothing Technology Demonstration Centre tried for many years to promote such a system, even building a pilot factory within its own walls to demonstrate the feasibility and superiority of modular production. Modular production requires teamwork among multi-skilled workers. There were a number of Hong Kong companies that tried it out, but as one by one they moved their plants into China and shifted to the low-cost labor model, they abandoned their experiments, and today no one in Hong Kong is using modular production.[34] The need for well-trained workers and continuous upgrading of skills as a prerequisite for introducing new technologies in clothing and textiles is a dominant theme in US and European industry publications.

The third, and perhaps most intractable fact that makes Hong Kong's lock into low-wage manufacturing in Guangdong a growing source of vulnerability is the situation in Guangdong itself. Once a zone of low wages and an abundant workforce, Guangdong wages and land costs have been rising rapidly.[35] As costs go up, Hong Kong manufacturers who wish to retain the same system must move their facilities deeper and deeper inland into China. In so doing, they will once again encounter the bad roads, inadequate water and power systems, and lack of commercial infrastructure that made operating in Guangdong so difficult for so long. As they move inland, however, the problem of providing an adequate supply of Hong Kong managers to produce good results out of the factories is likely to become acute. Commuting will be more and more difficult as the distances become longer, and the supplies that need to be brought in from Hong Kong will traverse longer, slower distances. There are, of course, already examples of companies replicating the Pearl River Delta pattern further inland. Having learned the details of several of these experiences—and having observed firsthand the managerial costs of running the plants in the Delta—we seriously doubt that the Delta pattern can be generalized on a large scale further inland. Rather, as we explain in Part One of this book, the most promising path for the future is upgrading operations in the Guangdong plants by feeding upgraded inputs from Hong Kong into the entire dispersed production system. By raising the technological and skilled components of the stream of products designed in Hong Kong—as well as the range of competencies needed to make them—and driving these through the plants that Hong Kong owns and manages in Guangdong and elsewhere, 'Made in Hong Kong' inputs can generate a transformation of 'Made By Hong Kong' production.

Reproducing the Supply of Hong Kong Managers

The second serious vulnerability of the Hong Kong textiles and clothing situation lies in the extreme dependence of the plants outside Hong Kong on an abundant supply of Hong Kong-trained managers. For 15 of the companies in our sample, we were able to obtain detailed information on the managers in their China plants. In twelve of them, the top position(s) in the China factory (ies) is held by a manager from Hong Kong (or Taiwan). In many of the plants, even those established over five years ago, the presence of Hong Kong managers quite far down the authority ladder is pronounced. The case of a textile plant is quite typical (although the size of its workforce is larger than even the average of our sample): the plant was set up in Guangdong in 1984 with 388 workers and today has 4,035. The general manager and three deputy general managers are from Hong Kong; one deputy general manager is a local. Of the foremen, supervisors and mid-level managers (600 persons), 15 percent are from Hong Kong. The workers come from the PRC—about 80 percent of them, from outside the Delta.[36] Another example is provided by a company that has since 1978 opened 17 factories in China, 15 of which are joint ventures. All the general managers come from Hong Kong. Among the 100 persons next to the top in the organizational structure (assistant general managers, supervisors), 30 percent are from Hong Kong; of the foremen, 100 percent are Mainland Chinese. Even in the two cases where the China plants are headed by local general managers, the role of Hong Kong people in everyday management is critical. In one of the plants (with 200 workers) located in the company founder's home town in 1984, a Hong Kong manager goes once a month to check that scheduling, maintenance and the general factory environment are kept up.[37] In another of the cases where the China plant is headed by PRC managers, the foreign sales and design of the product remain so firmly in the hands of the Hong Kong side that the local vice president for sales could not come up with the name of a single retailer of the garments they make for sale in the United States, Europe, and Japan.[38]

There are various ways of understanding the role of the Hong Kong-trained managers in the China plants—and the relatively low profile of the PRC personnel in top management positions. What Hong Kong-trained means is work experience in mature industrial settings with skilled workers; direct contacts with the sophisticated consumers who buy the company's products; intimate knowledge of foreign ways of doing business, of foreign life styles; as well as university education and management courses. The latter can be provided in China and increasingly are being provided. The former is not now available in the PRC, nor will it be in the foreseeable future. The evidence we collected in interviews with well-educated PRC managers of Hong Kong-owned companies suggested that even they lack the feel for international markets that is vital in this business.

This picture, taken together with the extremely heavy dependence of plants with inexperienced and rapidly changing workers on managerial inputs, suggests, first, that while replacing Hong Kong managers with PRC managers will happen eventually, it will be a lengthy process and one requiring Hong Kong companies to involve their PRC personnel more deeply than they do today in all their operations in Hong Kong and abroad. Second, extending the Guangdong pattern deeper into China without Hong Kong managers is not likely to be successful in the near term. Finally, maintaining, reproducing, and enhancing the quantity and quality of Hong Kong managers is a key challenge for the future. Without such a supply of managerial resources, the capacity of the China plants to work as well as they do today would be severely jeopardized.

The Future of the Quota System

Many of our respondents told us that the main reason that clothing and textiles manufacturing remains in Hong Kong is the quota system and that without it, and without the restrictions on the access of China-made goods to the large markets of the West, all manufacturing would shift into China. The agreements reached in the final stages of the Uruguay Round trade negotiations do, in fact, set a date for the final phase-out of the Multi-Fibre Arrangement which regulates the trade of textiles and clothing in the world and is the basis for today's system of quotas and rules of origin restrictions. According to the new Agreement on Textiles and Clothing (ATC), these barriers to trade are to be gradually lowered over a ten-year period and to disappear completely by 2005. Whether or not a world without textiles and clothing trade restrictions would be 'good' for Hong Kong may be disputed. Many of our respondents argued that it would be; one consultant insisted that quotas were a kind of drug that doped up the Hong Kong economy and that Hong Kong should 'just kick the habit.'[39] The Hong Kong Government has consistently and energetically advocated free trade and the abolition of the quota system.

Whatever the future of the quota system, at least for the next eight years the Hong Kong quotas represent Hong Kong manufacturers' widest route of access into mass consumer markets in Europe and the United States. Moreover it is highly likely— if the majority of experts on trade whom we interviewed in Washington, DC and in Hong Kong are to be believed—that the quota system will not disappear in 2005. Rather the current restrictions may well live on under other labels because of the pressure of powerful interests in advanced industrial countries. There is, moreover, a rising sentiment in public opinion in the United States and Europe against allowing foreign goods produced under conditions of extreme hardship for workers to compete in the market with domestic goods on the basis of low price—and the conviction that emerging countries contain many such workplaces. Whether for the next eight years or for an indefinitely long period, then, the quota system and rules of country origin will still be around. The issue for Hong Kong is how to maximize its companies' access to international markets under this system.

The vulnerability arises from the growing perception in the United States and Europe that Hong Kong producers are not respecting the rules, and the view that large quantities of the goods imported into Western markets under Hong Kong quota have been transshipped from China. Our research did not attempt to verify these charges. In any event, the serious consequences of the perception were demonstrated in 1996 by the controversies over inspection and transshipment that put Hong Kong and American governments into a deeper trade conflict than any they have previously experienced. These conflicts, occurring on the eve of Hong Kong's return to Chinese sovereignty, reveal but a fraction of the dangers posed by a conclusion on the part of the international community that the boundaries between Hong Kong and China are too porous to allow Hong Kong's independent status in the international trade organizations that regulate global commerce. We discuss how this situation might be mitigated in the sections on 'safe harbor' in Part One.

Opening New Markets for Hong Kong Manufacturers

Within the group of Hong Kong companies we studied, a number of pioneers have made outstanding efforts to sell goods in China. But this is not the case for the vast majority of Hong Kong firms, for whom the difficulties of gaining access to Chinese consumers—and the habits of mind and patterns of production associated with the long dependence on selling to the United States—combine as obstacles to moving into this vast new market. The 1994 Federation of Hong Kong Industries survey on investment in China found that 72 percent of the textiles and apparel companies producing in China did not sell in China; those who did sold less than 20 percent.[40] With respect to Japan—which offers the unique opportunity of affluent consumers and low trade barriers—most Hong Kong companies have neither made a large effort, nor are they prepared to do so. For different reasons, both Japan and China today represent 'green field' opportunities for reasonably priced, mid-quality consumer products. If Hong Kong firms miss the opportunity today to establish their brands and reputations, they may in the future find the field occupied by others.

Training: A Sunset Concern?

As manufacturing jobs in textiles and clothing have disappeared in Hong Kong and plants have migrated into China, the resources devoted to training workers and managers have gone down even more precipitously. The evidence of training efforts in the industry in the past suggests a serious decline in the level of attention to training at all levels: of managers, technicians, and production workers. The Shanghai cotton spinners who emigrated to Hong Kong after 1949 brought along with them, not only leading-edge cotton spinning technology[41] but also highly educated managers and a commitment to vocational training for their workers and to development of technicians.[42] These industrialists also understood the strengths of an experienced and stable workforce and, as

Wong Siu-lun relates in his study of the Shanghai emigrant textile manufacturers, instituted benefits programs in order to retain their best workers. More recently, programs at the Clothing Industry Training Authority, which in its heyday in 1987 trained 6,000–8,000 sewing operators a year, have entered a steep decline. Today CITA turns out 180 students a year with one- or two-year certificates and runs a number of other short-term programs.

We found that in-firm training usually consists of no more than watching one's coworker perform a task. And there are few employer-supported opportunities to take classes outside the company. The level of textiles and apparel companies' in-house training for workers and staff is low relative to Hong Kong industry in general. A 1995 survey found that in-house training was provided by 40.4 percent of all industrial firms, but by only 16.7 percent of the apparel firms, and 23.5 percent of the textile firms.[43] The two Hong Kong companies we visited in Xinjiang Province appeared to have stronger training opportunities both in-house and out-of-company (with foreign stays) than any we visited in Hong Kong or the Pearl River Delta.

The decline of attention to education stands in stark contrast with the situation in other countries undergoing similar processes of restructuring in textile and apparel. Both in the United States and Germany—and as earlier noted, in Germany's Central East European plants—a rising level of resources are going to training production workers and managers. The paucity in this sector of careers that offer opportunities to learn how to maintain one's personal abilities at the cutting edge of industry practice, combined with other factors, makes the industry an unattractive employer for talented, capable, and ambitious young people. Indeed the 1995 survey of all manufacturing industry in Hong Kong found that 36 percent of all companies employed one or more university graduates but only 23 percent of textile companies and 13.3 percent of clothing companies.[44] Managers of firms whose most valued future products will be service-enhanced need an education that includes solid grounding in both information technologies and the management of technology. Without such education, however strong the Hong Kong managers may be in running plants in diverse locations with low-cost, low-skilled workers, they will not be able to manage plants which require informed and plant-specific applications of information technology for the integration of production and links to suppliers and customers.

Design

Among the unfilled training needs of Hong Kong's textiles and clothing industry, the education of designers merits special attention. Many respondents noted the peculiar situation of design and designers in Hong Kong. On one hand, Hong Kong has an abundant pool of merchandisers (sometimes called designers) who help to interpret the requirements and preferences of foreign buyers for Hong Kong manufacturers. At the other extreme, Hong Kong has a tiny group of couture designers, whose originality and craftsmanship assure them a small niche market of wealthy customers, but who have little impact in establishing more general fashion trends.[45] In between, however, there is an absence of the class of designers who form so large a part of the fashion scene in New York or Milan or Paris. None of the companies we visited that have developed brands for Western markets are using Hong Kong designers; rather their design offices are located in Europe or New York City. Even some firms selling primarily in Asian markets use US or European designers. The weakness of these design skills represents a major lost opportunity in Hong Kong—a hole in the panoply of services that 'one-stop shopping' promises to provide. It also will be a problem for developing brand names in the region.

New Products, New Processes

Certain promising areas in product development and new technologies are barely represented in Hong Kong today. *The 1996 Survey of Hong Kong's Manufacturing Environment* reported that in response to a question about future areas of expansion, none of the clothing manufacturers planned new products and only one (7 percent) planned to introduce a new process; in textiles, 23 percent were projecting new products and 7 percent, new processes.[46] On the textile side, for example, fabrics for wall-covering and furniture for industrial and office use have come to be highly profitable businesses in the United States and Europe, yet these opportunities have not been explored in Hong Kong. In apparel, the new programs in customized mass-garments appear to have major possibilities for Hong Kong companies, both for Hong Kong customers and for affluent customers in Japan and the rest of the region. Levis in the United States, for example, can take a customer's measurements, transmit them by EDI to the sewing factory, and deliver the custom-made jeans within two weeks. On the technology side—with the exception of one outstanding pioneer—we found no companies involved in Quick Response/ EDI programs with foreign retailers. The 1995 Kurt Salmon report also noted that 'Hong Kong is lagging other Asian competitors in this [electronic commerce] area. EDI is a technological enabler that facilitates import and export transactions and thus reduces lead times.'[47] Given the great challenge of meeting retailers' demands for shorter cycles—and the growing competition from NAFTA producers who are closer to US markets, but still quite slow—Hong Kong companies have a major stake in developing and using these information technologies.

Fabric

A recurring theme in our interviews was the importance of fabric. The common factor which underlies success in the clothing industry is the timely supply, quality, and availability of fabric. It was the buyers who insisted on this point, far more heavily than did the manufacturers; and it was the buyers who pressed on us Hong Kong's advantage relative to NAFTA countries of closer proximity to good fabric suppliers. How this advantage can be maintained and enhanced is a topic which receives too little attention in Hong Kong.[48]

Family Firms

Finally, the sixth major area of vulnerability posing a major challenge to the future vitality of Hong Kong textile and clothing companies, in our view, is the ownership structure and distribution of authority within the typical firm. [In Part One, we have discussed the great strengths that Hong Kong industrialization drew from the family enterprise.] As noted above, every one of the companies we studied remains under the direct control of the founder or the founder's family members. Only a few had non-family members in top positions. The classical issue for family firms everywhere is that of succession and of finding strong leadership in the second and third generation. In the Hong Kong companies this universal dilemma is compounded by the traditional patterns of distributing ownership and control among male siblings, with the senior brother assuming overall control of the group as well as direct control of some segment of the business and other brothers (or male relatives) carving out distinct businesses within the family company as well as direct control of some segment of the business.[49] On one hand, this leads to a fragmentation of the business; on the other, it makes it even harder to overcome the obstacles to introducing outsiders into the business.

This latter difficulty, we believe, is a major problem in many of the companies we visited, where comments from mid- to senior-level non-family managers indicated that they felt that had no chance of rising to the top of the company because they were not family. This perception that the professional ambitions of the best and brightest managers cannot be satisfied within the company, leads many of these potential leaders to look for opportunities to 'jump,' and, if possible, to set up their own companies. One has only to look at the long tenure in a single company of the ablest managers in Japan or Germany or even the United States to appreciate that no 'natural' imperative drives the best managers to leave. Family control at the top combined with the absence of clear career ladders creates the sense that advance through the ranks to the top is impossible, and departure the only avenue to success.

A separate organizational issue is that of the thinness of the layer of middle-level managers, technicians, skilled machinists, and maintenance personnel. At the base of these organizations are production workers whose skills are aging (in the case of the Hong Kong plants) or narrow (in the China plants); at the top, there is group of senior managers dominated by family members; in between, we found a relative dearth of the skilled and responsible personnel who play so vital a role in the stability and performance of industrial workplaces. In US and European factories today the most severe job cuts have taken place in these middle levels of authority, but in those countries the thinning of the ranks of the middle has been compensated, to some extent at least, by providing those lower down in the system with more training and more responsibility. No such transfer has taken place in Hong Kong (or in its China plants). Thus these firms remain unusually dependent on strong control from the top. Beyond the founder's generation, dynamic leadership cannot be taken for granted.

Recommendations

The vision of a textiles and clothing industry for the Hong Kong economy of the twenty-first century must first and foremost identify new generations of products that consumers in the mass markets of the advanced and emerging countries will desire. The MIT researchers of the 'Made By Hong Kong' project see these high-value-added products—like the blue jeans that served as our example at the beginning of this chapter—as manufactured goods with special attributes provided by services and specific societal capabilities. These new products are not niche markets, but, we believe, the mass consumer markets of the coming decades. These markets build on long-term trends in retail structures in advanced countries, in consumer preferences, and in technology. The future of good jobs and profitable companies in the textiles and clothing industry in countries with high wages and standards of living depends on the ability to nurture multiple competencies for manufacturing that bundles together production capabilities, new information technologies, and certain public goods.

What will it take to make these new goods in the networks of 'Made By Hong Kong'? Today there are already some outstanding Hong Kong companies that have made major strides towards this new industrial system. They have done so despite the temptation to turn their factories into lucrative property developments or to concentrate their efforts on harvesting the 'low-hanging fruit' of profits from low-cost labor production of standard goods. They have introduced product and process innovations in an environment that has been generally discouraging for such risk taking. These companies stand as examples of what is possible in Hong Kong as first steps in the right direction. But the real question is how to facilitate a much wider adaptation to the new economic challenges of global production, so that success with the new technologies need not remain a story only of a select few. Even in the best of companies that we visited, much remains to be done—particularly to develop human resources and to acquire new technological capabilities.

How can the entire system of production that extends from a hub in Hong Kong into production sites in China and beyond be upgraded in the coming years? The firm-level analysis above suggests that over the next decade the key inputs for maintaining and enhancing the value of 'Made By Hong Kong' production will be inputs that are 'Made in Hong Kong'. Our recommendations aim at upgrading, broadening and pushing to the frontier of industry practice the 'Made in Hong Kong' inputs that feed into the stream of production of both Hong Kong-based activities and those beyond Hong Kong. These inputs include: managerial skills; new technologies, particularly information technologies; design; advertising; sophisticated sample-making and pattern-making; advanced manufacturing sites, and public institutions that can protect brand names, repress fraud, certify conformance with environmental or social standards.

Manufacturing as an Input to Service-Enhanced Production

Of all the recommendations for ways to strengthen and improve the 'Made By Hong Kong' production system, perhaps the most controversial is the idea of supporting and enhancing some advanced manufacturing within Hong Kong proper. We list it first, not because it has highest priority— indeed no single input can affect outcomes, absent a coherent and interdependent set of changes—but because it is the most difficult to defend, given its implications for labor and land. Many now believe that textile and garment manufacturing has no future within Hong Kong, and that sooner or later— depending on the future of quota—all manufacturing will and should shift to China or other low-cost labor markets. Our observations of the conditions of these PRC plants, however, suggest that they lack the experienced and skilled workforce and technicians, and managers knowledgeable both about technologies and customer preferences and about how to integrate them flexibly into a production system. Over the next decade, these plants are not likely to become fertile sites for experimentation with a new system of production of service-enhanced products. The upgrading of these plants (the upgrading of 'Made By Hong Kong') will continue to depend on a flow of inputs from Hong Kong itself. The advanced training of the PRC managers themselves—often talented individuals with degrees from very good tertiary institutions—will depend on their opportunities to participating in and rotate through Hong Kong-based advanced production sites.

The key rationale for manufacturing activities within Hong Kong, then, is the learning that takes place in the creation of service-enhanced products when innovation and production are co-located. We believe that innovations emerge when technologists and managers deal directly with customers and can anticipate their future needs and preferences. To achieve this, it is critical to have customers and the people in production in close contact and communication. Such a process of innovation will be driven by major opportunities in product development, new markets, and quick response that are the obvious targets of advance towards higher-value-added options in textiles and clothing. But to realize them over the next decade will require production facilities in Hong Kong.

Two difficult questions should be squarely addressed. First, how can we be sure that if manufacturing remains in Hong Kong it will indeed support a process of upgrading and transformation and not simply feed off low-cost labor (whether those groups in the Hong Kong population who are too old or too uneducated to find alternative employment, or immigrant laborers who might be brought in)? Our analysis suggests that there is no 'silver bullet': no *single* solution or policy whose adoption would shift Hong Kong textile and garment activities onto a different trajectory. The solutions lie in an integrated set of recommendations, none of which, taken alone, would suffice to make a significant difference for the future of the industry. Without the whole package of change, maintaining manufacturing in Hong Kong might indeed do no more than provide rather bad jobs at bad pay.

Secondly, what kinds of jobs would be provided by the manufacturing plants one would ideally envisage in Hong Kong—which could drive a process of innovation to upgrade the entire 'Made By Hong Kong' chain of production? In contrast with today's realities, in which jobs in textiles and garments earn less than the average wage in manufacturing in Hong Kong, would many more of the jobs in such plants be high-paying jobs held by technicians, managers, and highly skilled workers?

Table 9.1
Real Daily Wages for Craftsmen and Other Operatives

	1984	1985	1988	1989	1990	1991	1992	1993	1994
Garments	103.8	108.6	105.2	104	105.7	102.5	100	7.8	97.3
All manuf.	90.8	92.2	98.2	98.2	99.3	101.5	100	101.1	99

Source: 'Report on Half-yearly Survey of Wages, Salaries and Employee Benefits,' Hong Kong Census and Statistics Department, 1995

If a new generation of products and inputs to the products of 'Made By Hong Kong' are to emerge, creating these new careers and recruiting capable people will be essential. But with manufacturing activity of any scale there will inevitably be some entry-level jobs that are relatively less skilled and less well paid than the average in the society. Does the reality of such a stratum of production workers in the textile and garment industry condemn the project? It does not, we would argue, so long as these entry-level production jobs are part of a comprehensive and progressing industry. If, as in New York City, the existence of manufacturing activities within the city supports a comprehensive industry—with interesting and high-paying jobs in design, information technology, management, media, tourism, and retail, as an integral part of the whole—then it is desirable for Hong Kong's future. If entry-level production jobs are an integral part of a process of upgrading and developing of new products, and are themselves improved by this change, then they are jobs that Hong Kong needs to fill. If the industry were indeed to shift to a trajectory of product and process innovation, the chances for mobility out of the bottom rungs of skill in the factories would be significant, and starting jobs for production workers could serve once again, as they did in earlier periods, as first steps in industrial experience, and not as dead ends. Should Hong Kong's population grow to 7.5 million or even to 8.1 million by 2011, as the *Territorial Development Strategy Review*

'96 has projected, (this is expected, in part, to result from family reunifications after Hong Kong's return to China), then the new residents will need jobs (or else, social welfare payments).[50] Textiles and clothing manufacturing provides an array of relatively well-paying jobs that are a good entry point to the economy for those who have not been employed in industry previously.

Third, what are the human resource requirements for transforming Hong Kong's existing manufacturing plants into beta sites for the new production system? Can these requirements be satisfied by the existing workforce? At each level of the workforce, the new production system will require substantial changes in personnel. To acquire managers with appropriate skills in technology and the management of technology, the industry must significantly raise its current low level of recruitment of tertiary institution graduates. In the middle ranks of technicians, repair mechanics, designers, and information technologists, today's companies look weak and understaffed. Finally, although the plants that move onto the trajectory of upgraded production will have many fewer semi-skilled jobs than today's factories, they still will need some. There has been rather little progress in the automation of garment-making anywhere, and for the foreseeable future, a comprehensive manufacturing site will still need a stratum of relatively young and agile entry-level workers, with some education, even if not advanced training. Every one of the senior managers we interviewed has insisted that moving onto a higher-value-added track is impossible without access to some new young recruits to the production workforce. The aging of the current production workers, the perceived failure of retraining schemes in Hong Kong, as in other countries, and the tight labor market all make it unlikely that this problem can be solved without recourse to new immigrants to Hong Kong prepared to enter the workforce, or to temporary foreign labor.

Recommendations for Public Policies and Company Strategies to Support Higher-Value-Added Manufacturing

In Part One of this book, the MIT research team has laid out eight clusters of recommendations to encourage the development of service-enhanced manufacturing capabilities. Each of these recommendations requires special implementation within the context of the textiles and clothing industry. Here we distinguish between those recommendations for which the Hong Kong government needs to take the lead and those for which companies will have to assume the largest part of the agenda. This separation is somewhat artificial, for on virtually every item the efforts of both public authorities and private entrepreneurs would need to be mutually reinforcing to attain the desired outcome.

Our research findings strongly suggest that the priority areas for action should be those requirements for a shift toward higher-value-added production. As newcomers to the Hong Kong scene, we believe our most useful contribution will be to stimulate discussion of possible policies and vehicles for attaining the desired objectives, rather than to attempt to prescribe in detail concrete steps for achieving this goal. The core capabilities that Hong Kong should strive for, however, would (1) upgrade products and processes, (2) strengthen those public institutions that create a 'safe harbor' environment in which innovators and investors feel secure to bring new products and processes; (3) enhance government's role as an 'intelligent technology agent,' skilled at promoting the flows of information and resources that facilitate change; (4) augment resources for education and training; (5) maintain Hong Kong's internationalism; (6) promote new technology-based enterprises; and (7) collaborate with PRC scientists, engineers, and managers. The suggestions which follow are intended to illustrate possible vehicles for developing these capabilities in some of the most important dimensions of the textiles and clothing sector.

Upgrading

Government: The central objectives for public policy in this area are to promote larger efforts in applied research and development for textiles and clothing in universities, in institutions like the ITDC, the CTDC, the HKPC and in a future science park. Some of the new products and processes in this industry will come out of the experimentation of individual companies. But given the small scale of most companies in this industry—and the generic nature of the information technologies required for upgrading their products—it is clear that public action is necessary and legitimate. The development of Quick Response/EDI, and database-driven systems are so costly that even in the United States, where the drivers in this movement have been large-scale retailers and textile manufacturers, it still has been necessary to mobilize public and professional resources (TC 2, Amtex, the national Department of Energy laboratories) to make advances in this area.

How to assure that new funding for research and development generates a stream of useful products and processes for industry and not simply a stream of academic publications? However essential and valuable fundamental research is in and of itself, it does not spontaneously generate commercializable ideas and products. The incentives for advance in basic research are provided by an academic promotion system, by peer-reviewed publications, and by peer-selection in research funding. The incentives for developing a large stream of applied research and development (R&D) relevant to industry's needs remain to be set into place in Hong Kong's tertiary institutions. The mechanisms that might provoke such a transformation are discussed in Part One of this book. They rely largely on tightening links among government, industry and university and bringing industrialists into the process of evaluating and co-funding of research.

The Profession: How to produce a larger stream of activity and results from the R&D activities that take place within the professional organizations of the industry? How to diffuse the results more broadly to smaller firms within the industry? How to bring in expertise from home or abroad that could accelerate the adaptation of the latest information technologies? Given the clear limitations of short-term consultants, how to make such expertise resident within the R&D labs of the professional organizations? These are the issues that need new thinking within the organizations that serve the textiles and clothing industry. Our interviews revealed a significant measure of dissatisfaction with the current level of outreach and accomplishment of these organizations' R&D programs. If industry leaders were to champion a new vision of Hong Kong's future in textiles and clothing, these R&D activities could be identified as critical components. Today—to far too many—they seem marginal and exotic activities, without practical consequences. Our concrete recommendation is that industry leaders of the HKPC, CTDC, ITDC, and the university-based centers of textile research should meet to critically evaluate their own current research programs and jointly determine how to acquire the technological and human capabilities in areas of information technology, management of technology, and new product and process design that today are visibly lacking. Industry leadership and championship are the key first steps.

The Companies: A focus on new technologies for higher-value-added manufacturing was rare among the companies we visited, but the existence of some successful pioneers on this road shows what may be possible. Five areas seem the most promising to explore. The first is new fiber and fabric treatments—for denim finishes, wrinkle-free clothing, and properties such as breathability, non-flammability, and soft hand, among others; for new uses of new fibers—like Tencel; and for more environment-friendly products and processes. The resources for experimentation along these lines seem well within the means of individual companies—since a number of them are already doing it with good results. Second, a major effort should be devoted to technology for new links with customers. Information technologies can facilitate the development of databases with the distinctive size, color, fit preferences of different national markets; they can identify new customer bases; they can allow systematic tracking of fashion trends. They can facilitate a manufacturer's ability to service customer bases as diverse as China and Japan. They can enable a more detailed satisfaction of customer preferences. One of the most exciting developments in this area is customized mass production, which, as mentioned above, enables a retail-

er to offer a customer a garment made to individual specifications at cost far below that of tailored clothing (Levis new custom-made jeans, for example). Third, technology for EDI and
Quick Response links with retailers should have high priority
within companies. The rapid transformation of retail structures in the United States and Europe, the stagnation of retail
prices, the unwillingness of retailers to hold inventory, or to
make timely commitments for purchases—all these changes
mean that manufacturers who have mastered the new information technologies that enable Quick Response will have
great advantages. Fourth, new sample-making technologies
deserve special attention, for they can support Hong Kong's
role as a coordinating center of the entire 'Made By Hong
Kong' production system. A fifth and vital area to explore
toward higher-value-added manufacturing, is a shift from
company strategies based on OEM manufacturing to brand-
name production strategies. Brand-name products are a specific kind of service-enhanced product: to the manufactured
good are added the attributes of advertising, company reputation, design, and the public protection of brand name. There
are outstanding industry leaders in the development of brand
names in Hong Kong, including those firms which have developed their own brands (such as Glorious Sun's Jeanswest,
Goldlion, Fang Brothers' Episode, Tse, and Giordano) and
those that have licensed and nurtured existing labels (like
Nordica and Tommy Hilfiger). The difficulties of building
these labels are great: they take large advertising budgets;
require compartmentalizing the activities related to OEM
design and production, in order to reassure OEM customers;
they need large outlays for design staff both in Hong Kong and
abroad; and above all, they depend on corporate strategies to
cultivate the label's image.

Why make so costly and risky a shift when good profits are
still to be made out of OEM production? The examples of the
industry leaders suggest that the rewards of brand-name production are very high. Brand names require initially heavy
investments, but the very scale of the investment creates a
barrier to entry and competition which enables higher profitability. As more and more of Hong Kong's competitors
improve their performance in low-cost manufacturing of garments, competition on price alone will become a losing game

for Hong Kong firms. Balancing the company's efforts between brand-name and OEM production will, for most companies be an essential component of success over the next decade.

Focus on New Markets

Companies: Historically Hong Kong industries have been heavily oriented toward the markets of United States, and, secondarily, Europe. Today, the largest growing markets are in Asia. As we have mentioned, a few companies are making new and successful efforts to enter the Japanese market and to reach the emerging China market. Here, one can only point to the gap between the pioneers and the others and ask how industry-wide and public efforts could narrow the difference between best and average practices. One approach would emphasize the potential in databases that could be developed in professional bodies like the CTDC or the HKTDC to enable small and medium-sized firms to gain better information on the preferences and requirements of customers in new markets and to identify these new customers. The TDC-backed Trade Mart in Panyu (in Guangdong Province, within an hour and a half by boat from Hong Kong) is another approach, one that focuses on the difficulties small companies face in linking up to retail distribution in China. This project is still in the early stages and thus it is too early to evaluate its potential for generalization.

Safe Harbor

Government: Part One laid out the vital importance to Hong Kong's industrial future of enhancing the government's abilities to make Hong Kong an environment with a strong international reputation for rule of law, transparent and honest administration, speedy and effective prosecution of intellectual property violations, and strong enforcement of international agreements on quota and rules of origin. The textiles and clothing industry has a special stake in the 'safe harbor' issues, for its access to the markets of the United States and Europe is determined by these international rules. Whatever one may think of regulating international trade by quotas and rules of country origin—and both the Hong Kong government and industry have attacked it and advocated free trade—still, today the system represents the freest possible entry for Hong Kong-made goods into Western markets. In fact, many believe that a restrictive regime for textile and apparel trade will survive its projected end in 2005, in one form or another. To endanger or undermine the channel of entry provided by Hong Kong's quotas would, therefore, inflict real and lasting damage on the industry, and not simply hasten an inevitable outcome. Even the threat to narrow the access to US markets last year created a massive crisis of confidence among Hong Kong's buyers that required major efforts to overcome.

Industrialists investing heavily in the high-value-added capabilities of new technologies, brand names and education and training will continue to desire the fullest possible access to the world's most affluent consumers. For this, maintaining Hong Kong's quotas—as long as this remains the widest route into international markets—is worthwhile. Thus for the textile and apparel industry—as well as for Hong Kong's overall international reputation—it is important to strengthen the customs enforcement capabilities of Hong Kong to reduce real and perceived levels of transshipments.

Because of the centrality of the 'safe harbor' issues, we have devoted significant research efforts to interviews and site visits in the Hong Kong Government Trade Department and various branches of the Customs services as well as to their counterparts in Washington, DC. In thinking of institutional changes that could enhance enforcement capabilities, we believe much can be learned from the example of the Independent Commission Against Corruption (ICAC), which combines enforcement, public outreach, and preventive measures. It may be that the particular history of the ICAC makes it a hard model to copy in all details. But we recommend exploring institutional models that, like the ICAC, bring responsibilities for enforcement, public outreach, and prevention together in a single coordinated effort.

Human Resource Development

Government: As Part One underscores, the thinness of the links between tertiary institutions and industry is a major weakness for the education of new generations of engineers and managers for all industries. The programs of research opportunities for students, a fourth year of university training for engineering students who wish to add management training, or a second disciplinary focus, the redirection of some university resources towards more applied research activities—all of these general recommendations would serve needs that have been identified in the textiles and clothing sector. The industry's chances of attracting the new generations of engineer-managers or engineer-information technologists will, however, depend on making textile and clothing companies locales for product and process innovation, on rewarding through promotion and through pay those who have acquired additional education and who demonstrate an ability to bring new forms of knowledge to fruition in a new stream of products within companies.

Companies: As we have emphasized throughout this book, the striking lack of attention to education and training in industry will be a crippling handicap for Hong Kong industry if it moves to a new trajectory of high valued-added production. The most important areas to be addressed are: (1) to enhance the training and foreign exposure of designers and merchandisers; (2) to bring PRC personnel of Hong Kong-owned and managed companies into the Hong Kong plants, sample rooms, and headquarters on rotations, as well as into Hong Kong offices abroad, in order to widen international experience; (3) to support training of production workers, both in-firm to develop more multi-skilled workers and out-of-firm in new programs such as maintenance, software, and statistically based quality inspection. Local tertiary institutions, the technical institutes, and CITA need to develop new programs in these areas. (4) Recently, Hong Kong's vocational education system has been under review. As a follow-on to this effort, existing vocational education options for textiles and clothing should be expanded to include more fully new information technologies. (5) If a large new wave of immigration follows the return of Hong Kong to Chinese sovereignty, the new entrants will be potential recruits for factory work. To educate these workers for a twenty-first century factory may well require companies to plan and implement new programs in language, technology, machine maintenance and repair, together with local educational institutions.

Alleviate the Burdens of Existing Public Policies

Government: The current legislation of Hong Kong raises significant barriers to the entry of foreign participants to the workforce. In the universities, restrictive quotas limit the number of foreign undergraduates. At the level of technicians and managers, there are major difficulties in rotating into Hong Kong the PRC personnel that are being prepared for major positions of responsibilities within Hong Kong-owned and controlled businesses. At the level of production workers, a new, complex, and highly restrictive set of regulations went into effect in early 1996. Three months into the new system, only 130 authorizations had been granted. In effect, the import of labor had been stopped. At its peak, about 19,000 legal imported workers were employed at one time within Hong Kong factories. The objections that animated the union-led movement to halt these labor flows focused heavily on abuses in the system, the vulnerability of these workers to exploitation, and the fears of growing unemployment among Hong Kong permanent residents.

The MIT research did not attempt to adjudicate between these charges of abuse and the industrialists' insistence on the need to preserve the industry by returning to labor import levels approximating those of the old system. We wish only to underscore one central possibility here: that grounds for compromise exist which would respect the major objectives of all sides. Virtually all advanced industrial countries authorize a certain limited, regulated entry of foreign workers for entry-level positions that locals are uninterested in holding. A large body of research on these countries concludes that, because of segmented labor markets, the presence of limited numbers of foreign workers does not contribute to unemployment and sending them home does not create more jobs for locals. Nor does the inability to fill these positions usually lead to upgrading them or automating them. Often, as in

Hong Kong, it seems simply to accelerate a shift of the activity out of domestic territory. Of 110 clothing industry respondents in a 1996 survey, one-third reported difficulties in filling job vacancies. Forty-five percent of them offered higher wages; another 25 percent offered higher benefits; others subcontracted locally (20 percent) or transferred work outside of Hong Kong (31 percent relocated production; 25 percent subcontracted to China). Sixteen per cent hired expatriate or imported labor.[51]

Is it necessarily undesirable to bring in low-skilled workers for jobs that are relatively low-paying? This is the question we have attempted to answer above. The justification of a certain limited and regulated import of foreign labor lies in its contribution to maintaining the stratum of workers necessary for building a comprehensive and upgraded production site. The production facilities that ought to be in Hong Kong are those directly engaged in the process of product and process innovation, in moving towards new generations of service-enhanced products, in providing inputs to upgrading the 'Made By Hong Kong' production networks. The only justification for bringing in new foreign recruits to the low-paying, less skilled entry rungs of the production system is the contribution this group can make to the viability of an industry which is rapidly moving towards a higher-value-added trajectory. To bring in new recruits simply to cheapen the cost of labor within Hong Kong would reinforce a lock into low-cost manufacturing that would be damaging to the future of this industry. The forms of labor inspection needed to ensure against the abuses of individual workers lie within the normal competence of government. If inadequate in the past, they can be enhanced. A more novel approach (but possible, we believe), would be to condition approval for labor import requests on the company's overall engagement in a process of upgrading its activities in Hong Kong.

In Hong Kong's future as a great industrial power, we foresee major possibilities for textiles and clothing—two of the oldest activities in the territory—to transform themselves into manufacturers of the kinds of products that consumers in the affluent West and in the emerging markets will desire most. These products increasingly involve attributes that advanced technologies and services provide. To make them will require using 'Made in Hong Kong' inputs of skills, technologies, and public capabilities to upgrade 'Made By Hong Kong' production. The foundational strengths of this industry are there. The leadership and determination to shape these choices of direction and commitment will make the difference.

Notes

1 Hong Kong Government Industry Department, *1995 Hong Kong's Manufacturing Industries,* December 1995, pp. 41–42, 75–77. This volume presents the most current overview of the clothing and textiles industries in Chapters 3 (Clothing) and 4 (Textiles). See also Kurt Salmon Associates, *1995 Techno-Economic and Market Research Study on Hong Kong's Textiles and Clothing Industries,* Vols. I, II, Hong Kong: Hong Kong Government Industry Department, July 1996. For an historical view of these industries in Hong Kong, see T. L. Lui and S. Chiu, 'A Tale of Two Industries: The Restructuring of Hong Kong's Garment-Making and Electronics Industries,' *Environment and Planning,* 26 (1994): 53–70.

2 Interviews with Bruce Herman, President, Garment Industry Development Corporation, New York City; Earl Andrews Jr., New York Commissioner of Business; Gerald Scupp, Deputy Manager, Fashion Center Business Improvement District, October 5, 1996.

3 Interviews with German apparel and textile firms were carried out for the Industrial Performance Center's ongoing research on globalization and the relocation of production by Suzanne Berger in 1993 and by Brian Hanson in 1996.

4 Hong Kong Government Industry Department, *1995 Hong Kong Manufacturing Industries,* Table 2.12, p. 31.

5 See Federation of Hong Kong Industries, *Hong Kong's Industrial Investment in the Pearl River Delta: 1991 Survey among the Members of the Federation of Hong Kong Industries,* Hong Kong, 1992, especially Chapters 3 and 9; and more generally on Hong Kong industry in Guangdong, Sung Yun-Wing; Pak-Wai Liu; R. Wong Yue-Chin; and Lau Pui-King, *The Fifth Dragon: The Emergence of the Pearl River Delta,* Singapore: Addison Wesley, 1995.

6 Hong Kong Government Industry Department, *1995 Hong Kong Manufacturing Industries,* pp. 51, 84.

7 We have greatly benefited from the survey presented in the Kurt Salmon Associates *1995 Techno-Economic Study,* which drew its 64 textile and clothing companies with a procedure that sampled by firm size and employment, value of exports, and by

industry segment. Private communication, December 24, 1996, from Richard K. Y. Liu, Hong Kong Government Industry Department.

8   We could not measure exactly the success of those companies that are considered to be industry leaders, since most of them are privately held and we did not ask for—nor did they volunteer—detailed and systematic information on profits or return on investment.

9   Company 22. To preserve confidentiality, as we promised those we interviewed, firms will not be identified by name. To enable readers to check whether a firm mentioned is or is not one previously cited, each company has been assigned a number, and each citation and example will be attributed to the relevant company by number.

10 Company 17.

11 Kurt Salmon Associates, *1995 Techno-Economic Study*, Vol. II, p. 77.

12 Company 10.

13 Company 3.

14 Company 27.

15 Company 16.

16 Company 29.

17 Companies 23 and 11.

18 Companies 5 and 20.

19 Buyer 4.

20 Buyer 1.

21 Company 15.

22 Hong Kong Government Industry Department, *1995 Hong Kong Manufacturing Industries*, p. 56.

23 Buyer 5.

24 Company 22.

25 Companies 12 and 13. 1995 Gallup Poll of China Consumers.

26 For valuable information on the retail trade in China we are grateful for the explanations of Mary Wong and Joyce Hui in the Trade Development Council and for the chance to visit the new trade mart at Panyu in Guangdong Province.

27 One of the managers who accompanied us on a plant visit to Huizhou—a trip of under three hours from Hong Kong—told us that three years earlier the road had been so bad that some days it took eleven hours to go 100 kilometers.

28 Company 10.

29 Indeed, local rules discourage integration of the newcomers, requiring, for example, that the internal passports of children born to marriages between newcomers and locals show the same place of origin as their out-of-province mothers, thus making the children ineligible for attendance in local schools.

30   Company 27.
31   Federation of Hong Kong Industries, Industry and Research Division, *1995 Survey on Manufacturers' Demand for Administrative and Technical Manpower,* 1996, p. 14.
32   Company 18.
33   P. Berg; E. Appelbaum; T. Bailey; and A. Kalleberg, 'The Performance Effects of Modular Production in the Apparel Industry,' in *Industrial Relations,* 1995.
34   Interviews with Dr. Kenneth Wang and Mr. Alan Li, Clothing Technology Demonstration Centre.
35   See the evidence on changes in labor markets and property markets presented in Sung, *et al., The Fifth Dragon,* Chapters 6 and 8.
36   Company 10.
37   Company 13.
38   Company 25.
39   Consultant 2.
40   Federation of Hong Kong Industries, Industry and Research Division, *Investment in China: 1994 Survey of the Federation of Hong Kong Industries,* 1995, p. 49.
41   Wong Siu-lun, *Emigrant Entrepreneurs: Shanghai Industrialists in Hong Kong,* Hong Kong: Oxford University Press, 1988, pp. 46–48.
42   Ibid., pp. 63–72.
43   Federation of Hong Kong Industries, *1995 Survey on Manufacturers' Demand,* p. 18.
44   Ibid., p. 10.
45   Company 2.
46   Hong Kong Government Industry Department, *The 1996 Survey of Hong Kong's Manufacturing Industries,* p. 297.
47   Kurt Salmon Associates, *1995 Techno-Economic Study,* Vol. I, p. 68.
48   Note that it is briefly mentioned in the recommendations of the Kurt Salmon Associates *1995 Techno-Economic Study,* Vol. I, p. 64.
49   See the very interesting discussion of this traditional pattern in the Shanghai region from which many of the great Hong Kong textile companies originated in Wong Siu-lun, *Emigrant Entrepreneurs: Shanghai Industrialists in Hong Kong,* Hong Kong: Oxford University Press, 1988.
50   Hong Kong Government, Planning, Environment and Lands Branch, *A Consultative Digest Territorial Development Strategy Review '96,* p. 15.
51   Hong Kong Government Industry Department, *The 1996 Survey of Hong Kong's Manufacturing Industries,* pp. 286–7. Respondents could give more than one reply, thus the numbers total more than 100 percent.

10   The Hong Kong Electronics Industry

Rafael Reif and Charles G. Sodini

The electronics industry is one of the top manufacturing industries in Hong Kong. In 1994, even though electronics accounted for only 3.5 percent of all manufacturing establishments in Hong Kong, it employed 10.5 percent of all Hong Kong manufacturing labor, and contributed 26.2 percent of the total domestic exports of Hong Kong.[1] In order for the electronics industry in Hong Kong to grow at a rate of approximately 5 percent per year [the annual growth rate of Hong Kong's real gross domestic product (GDP)], one or more of the following scenarios should occur:

- the size of the present companies in Hong Kong must continuously increase; and/or

- the number of Hong Kong-based companies must continuously increase; and/or

- the number of multinational corporations in Hong Kong needs to continuously increase.

This chapter offers recommendations addressing these scenarios. In preparing this report, our team visited a total of 33 companies with operations both in Hong Kong and Guangdong and interviewed their leaders. Small, medium-sized, and large companies (with revenues of up to HK$500 million; between HK$500–2,000 million; and HK$2,000 million and above, respectively) were included.[2] We also visited several universities and interviewed their faculty. Our site visits also included several organizations in Hong Kong as well as several companies with operations in Shanghai, and interviews with their leaders.

The next section of this chapter summarizes our assessment of the current status of Hong Kong's electronics industry. Following that, we present our vision for the expansion and growth of the electronics sector in Hong Kong, which relies heavily on the manufacture of products early in their life cycles. We then analyze why this vision is important to Hong

Kong and why it exists today only in a limited way. Finally, we offer recommendations as to how to implement this vision.

The Electronics sector is defined here as that sector which manufactures electronic components and/or products containing electronic components. Examples of electronic components are application-specific integrated circuits (ASICs), batteries, and precision electro-mechanical components. Products containing electronic components include such items as electronic toys, consumer audio equipment, and telephones.

Below are definitions of a range of electronic products ranked by innovative content from highest to lowest.

'Silver-Bullet' Products

Silver-bullet products are those which create a new market. Among them are consumer items which require technology innovation, such as the Compact Disc player. Some (such as the Walkman) do not require technology innovation, but do require product innovation. Silver-bullet products that involve technology innovation are derived, by and large, from research and development (R&D) activities within the company. Those which build on product innovation, on the other hand, require a talented product engineering/product design team that works closely with a marketing operation that thoroughly understands the market. It also takes a corporate structure willing to risk product introduction—for example, a corporate structure willing to be the first to introduce an untested (from the marketing point of view) product.

Novel Products

Novel products are those which begin a new product life cycle. Pagers that display Chinese characters, for example, enjoy a premium profit margin over conventional pagers, due to their additional utility for a large market. Significant technology innovation was required to make this product possible. Novel products and the electronic components (such as the nickel metal hydride battery) required to make them point the direction for the future Hong Kong electronics industry.

Enhanced Products

Enhanced products add value to an existing product line by using product design to customize items for a particular market. The customization may take the form of added features— such as advanced telephones with call forwarding, conference call capability—or it could remove some features to enhance the product's price competitiveness. In both cases, product design skills are necessary.

Original Equipment Manufacture (OEM) Products
OEM products are requested and very often designed by a customer company, usually foreign, which normally owns a brand name. These products are, by and large mature, and in comparison with other categories much less risky.

The Current Status of Hong Kong's Electronics Industry

Product Types

Hong Kong electronics companies predominantly serve the OEM market. Under the current model, companies manufacture mature products when prices have eroded to the point where the original producers can no longer make an acceptable profit margin. Since Hong Kong companies can quickly ramp up lower cost manufacturing of these products, they can enjoy a higher profit margin. Through continuous improvement of their manufacturing techniques Hong Kong companies can significantly extend the time over which an acceptable profit margin can be achieved. After the product price erodes beyond an acceptable profit margin the companies find new mature products to begin the cycle again. Figure 10.1 illustrates this point.[3]

The electronic products manufactured today by Hong Kong companies fall into two categories:

1. Electronic end-products, including sound producing and recording products and audio equipment in general (cassette tape recorders, all varieties of radio receivers, including car radios, and others), communication equipment (telephones, for example), electronic watches and clocks, and so forth;

2. Electronic components, including batteries, printed circuit boards (PCBs), liquid crystal displays (LCDs), and different types of semiconductor device components.

Figure 10.1
Typical Electronics Product Profit Margin vs. Time,
Describing Hong Kong's Current OEM Electronic Business
Practice

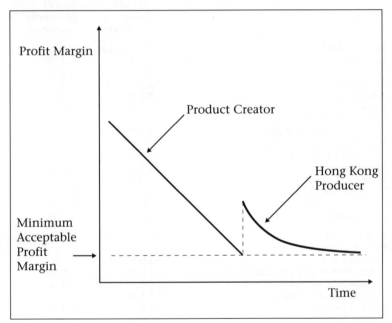

Table 10.1 summarizes Hong Kong's exports in electronics in 1995 as a percentage of the total, and domestic electronic exports, which was HK$379.3 billion.[4] The exports are categorized by end-products and components.

Table 10.1
Hong Kong's Percentage of Total and Domestic Exports of Electronic End-Products and Components in 1995

Examples	SHARE (total exports)	SHARE (domestic exports)
End-Product	**53.1 percent**	**28.2 percent**
Calculators	1.2 %	0.3 %
Photocopying apparatus	1.2 %	4.2 %
Computers	3.6 %	2.3 %
Television receivers	3.1 %	0.4 %
Radios	9.3 %	0.3 %
Video recording or reproducing apparatus	1.1 %t	
Sound reproducing and recording apparatus	2.2 %	
Telephone sets	1.4 %	0.2 %
Hi-Fi equipment	2.0 %	
Transmission apparatus	3.0 %	1.0 %
Electronic watches	7.0 %	10.8 %
Electronic toys	8.2 %	2.1 %
Components	**46.9 percent**	**71.8 percent**
Parts & accessories for		
computers	12.0 %	16.7 %
telephones & telegraphic apparatus	1.0 %	1.5 %
radio telecommunications	5.6 %	8.4 %
all kinds of recorders	3.1 %	3.5 %
Static converters	1.8 %	2.1 %
Printed circuits	1.6 %	5.3 %
Color TV picture tubes, cathode ray	1.2 %	
Transistors (excl. photosensitive)	1.3 %	3.4 %
Digital monolithic integrated circuits	7.3 %	10.6 %
Non-digital monolithic integrated circuits	3.4 %	9.3 %

Source: Data from Hong Kong Trade Development Council, 'International Exhibitions in Electronics and Electrical Products,' July 1996.

The workers recruited for the Hong Kong-owned and managed textile and clothing plants in the Pearl River Delta are rarely natives of the region; most come from China's inland provinces, and provincial labor offices have organized their employment and transportation to the plant site. Many are young women in their late teens or early twenties who are working at their first industrial job. The women are housed eight to twelve to a room in dormitories provided by the companies. They eat in company cafeterias. Their excursions off company grounds—typically surrounded by fences and security personnel—are regulated. The dorms, food, supervisory personnel, sanitary conditions, and wages may be good or bad—but in either case, the workers regard their time in the plant as temporary. They have come to earn some money—for marriage, for taking care of old relatives, for setting up a little business back home—and plan to return, typically at Spring Festival. This is a workforce with so little contact with the local population, that inevitably ties to the home town remain strong.[29] In many of the plants we visited, workers stayed only a year or two.

One Hong Kong-owned garment plant in the Pearl River Delta that employs about 5,000 workers—let us call it 'Company Alpha'— tracked its worker and staff turnover on a monthly basis through the first eight months of 1996 and found worker turnover was about 80 percent.[30] Staff turnover was close to 30 percent—three times the rate of staff turnover in Hong Kong garment factories.[31] We heard about similar turnover rates at other plants we visited in Guangdong Province. With such short stays in the factory, the level of training of the workforce is necessarily low, for few of the workers have been around long enough to acquire more than a few basic skills and or even the fundamental abilities to cooperate with others in a factory setting, to solve simple problems as they arise, or to repair simple machine breakdowns. The flow of new workers through these plants means a continuous process of teaching rapidly passing generations of workers the same basic skills and socialization for factory life. The possibilities of upgrading the skills of such workers—and the incentives to do so—are very low. Indeed, in contrast to the major efforts of German manufacturers operating new plants in Eastern Europe who devote major resources to train-

Electronic Industry Activities

The activities critical to success in the electronics industry are identified in Table 10.2, which describes the level of intensity practiced by the Hong Kong electronics industry, as well as the specific location of the activity (Hong Kong or Guangdong Province, for example).[5]

Table 10.2
Activities in the Hong Kong Electronics Industry

Activity	Intensity	Location
Technology Innovation	Low	Hong Kong
Product Innovation	Low	Hong Kong
Product Design	Medium	Hong Kong
Manufacturing	High	Guangdong/ Hong Kong
Marketing		
OEM Companies	Low	Hong Kong
Brand-name Companies	High	Hong Kong
Distribution		
OEM Companies	Low	Hong Kong
Brand-name Companies	High	Hong Kong

Source: Authors' interviews.

One important activity—*technology innovation*—is usually carried out within a company's research and development (R&D) section.[6] The intensity of technology innovation in Hong Kong companies is relatively low; when it does occur, it usually takes place within Hong Kong. Gold Peak, a large brand-name producer of batteries and other electronic products, is one example of a company that has used significant technology innovation (in its case, to develop state-of-the-art rechargeable batteries). *Product Innovation,* another key activity, also has low intensity in Hong Kong companies and mainly takes place within Hong Kong. VTech, a large manufacturer of electronic toys, computer peripherals, and telephones is one example of a company with significant product innovation, especially in electronic toys and advanced cordless telephones.

The next activity, *product design,* is required for customizing a product for a specific market and improving the manufacturability of a product, as well as its packaging, aesthetics, and other aspects.[7] Product design mostly occurs in Hong Kong, and its level of intensity in Hong Kong companies is higher than those of technology innovation and product innovation. The next activity is *manufacturing,* which Hong Kong companies carry out with a high level of intensity, both in Hong Kong and Guangdong. Hong Kong companies are very strong in low-cost manufacturing, timeliness, quality, and flexibility. The final two activities, *marketing and distribution,* take place by and large within Hong Kong. Original equipment manufacture companies are relatively weak in marketing and distribution. Their level of intensity in these two activities is relatively low because most OEM companies deliver products to customers who manage their own distribution channels to reach the final consumer. Brand-name companies, on the other hand, are relatively strong in these two areas.

Table 10.3 illustrates the level of activity (high 'H'; medium 'M'; and low 'L') in a sample of Hong Kong companies.[8] The activities included are technology innovation (TI), product innovation (PI), product design (PD), manufacturing (Mfg), and Marketing and Distribution (Mkt/Dist.). The table also includes ISO certification, whether the company is listed on the stock market (in Hong Kong or elsewhere), and the company size.

Table 10.4 identifies, for the purpose of this discussion, production factors and requirements. The factors include *cost, quality, timeliness,* and *flexibility.* Production requirements include *raw materials, labor, space,* and *infrastructure* (electricity, water, transportation, communications, among others). The major reason for a company to keep its manufacturing activity in a given location is to optimize overall production. The manufacturer does so by studying the interaction between the production requirements and the production factors in a given location. For example, as illustrated in Table 10.4, all production requirements affect cost. Some, such as raw materials and labor, affect not just cost but also quality. Optimizing production means that the manufacturer studies not just how a particular location may be more cost-efficient (by offering cheaper labor for instance), but also how that particular location affects the quality of the product, its timeliness, and so forth.

TABLE 10.3.
Level of Activities in a Sample of Hong Kong Electronics Companies

Company	TI	PI	PD	Mfg	Mkt/Dist	ISO	Listed	Size
#1	L	L	M	M	OBM	9002	N	M
#2	L	M	M	M	OEM	-	Y	L
#3	L	L	M	H	OEM	-	Y	L
#4	H	H	H	M/H	OBM	9001	Y	M
#5	L	L	L	M	OEM	-	N	S
#6	L	L	L	L	OBM	9002	Y	M
#7	L	M	M	M	OBM	9002	Y	M
#8	L	L	L	H	OBM	9002	Y (Japan)	L
#9	M	H	M	H	OBM	-	Y	L
#10	M	M	H	H	OBM	9002	Y	M
#11	L	L	L	M	OEM	9002	Y	M
#12	M	M	M	H	OBM	9002	Y (Japan)	L
#13	L	M	M	M	OBM	-	N	M
#14	H	H	H	H	OBM	9002	Y (US)	L
#15	L	L	L	L	OBM	9002	Y	L
#16	M	M	H	H	OBM	9001	Y (Neth)	L
#17	L	L	L	M	OEM	-	N	S
#18	H	M	H	M	OBM	9002	Y	L
#19	L	M	H	M	OE/BM	9001	N	S
#20	M	H	H	H	OE/BM	9001	Y	M
#21	L	L	L	M	OE/BM	-	N	S
#22	M	M	H	H	OBM	9001	Y	M
#23	L	L	L	L	OE/BM	-	N	M
#24	M	H	H	H	OE/BM	9002	Y	M
#25	L	L	M	M	OE/BM	9002	N	S
#26	M	M	M	H	OBM	9002	Y	L

TI: technology innovation (low, L; middle, M; high, H)
PI: product innovation (L, M, H)
PD: product design (L, M, H)
Mfg: manufacturing capability (L, M, H)
Mkt/Dist: marketing/distribution (OBM: original brand-name manufacturer; OEM: original equipment manufacturer)
ISO: quality certification (9001, 9002)
Listed: whether listed on the Hong Kong stock market or (elsewhere)
Size: company size (small, S, revenues <HK$500M; middle, M, revenues between HK$501–2,000M; large, L, revenues>HK$2001)

Sources: TI, PI, PD, Mfg, Mkt/Dist, based on authors' interviews and research; ISO based on *Directory of ISO 9000 Certified Companies in Hong Kong,* Hong Kong Trade Development Council, 1996. Data listed and sized based on interviews by authors and *The Thornton Guide to Hong Kong Companies,* Hong Kong: Edinburgh Financial Publishing, 1996.

Table 10.4.
Interaction between Production Factors and Production
Requirements

Production Requirements Production Factors	Cost	Quality	Timeliness	Flexibility
Raw materials	x	x	x	x
Labor	x	x		x
Space	x			
Infrastructure	x			x

Source: Authors' research.

Table 10.5 illustrates some of the reasons behind decisions to locate the manufacturing activity of a particular product type in a given location (for example, Hong Kong versus Guangdong).[9] Most of the assembly of consumer electronics end-products is carried out in Guangdong, for this activity requires a significant amount of raw materials, and it is labor intensive. Its space demands are relatively low, and it does not require a significant infrastructure. Guangdong offers access to raw materials at a reasonable price and with a reasonable degree of quality and timeliness. Moreover, Guangdong offers cheap labor which is capable of delivering a quality product. Consequently, Hong Kong companies have been moving this type of manufacturing operation to Guangdong. Near the other end of the spectrum, however, the manufacture of high-end printed circuit boards (PCBs) requires relatively fewer raw materials and is less labor intensive since it is more automated. Companies with higher automation have relatively higher space demands and infrastructure needs (such as a stable supply of electricity). Consequently, Hong Kong has been a very attractive location for the manufacture of high-end PCB products.

To develop a picture of the choice of manufacturing sites across a profile of companies, Table 10.6 provides examples of electronics producers and breakdown of their employees in Hong Kong and the Pearl River Delta.

Table 10.5
Location of Manufacturing as a Function of Production
Requirements

Example	Dominant Location	Raw Mat.	Labor	Space	Infra-structure
Consumer Electron. End Products	Guangdong	High	High	Low	Low
Semiconductors	Hong Kong	Low	Low	Med	High
PCB (High End)	Hong Kong	Low	Low	Med	Med

Source: Authors' interviews and research.

Table 10.6
Number of Total Employees in Hong Kong and the Pearl
River Delta for Some Hong Kong companies

Company	Employees in Hong Kong	Employees in PRD	OBM[a]/OEM[b]
Cons. Electron. End Products			
D	250	3000	OEM
E	1400	14000	OEM
F	25	300	OEM
G	500	4250	OBM
Semiconductors			
H	800	0	OBM
I	210	0	OBM
PCB (Low & High End)			
A (Hi)	350	0	OBM
B (Hi/Lo)	670	2100	OBM
C (Hi/Lo)	700	1040	OBM

[a]OBM = Original Brand-name Manufacturer

[b]OEM = Original Equipment Manufacturer

Sources: Employee figures for companies D, E, F, G, I, A, B are from
1996 Directory of Hong Kong Electronics Industries Ltd., Hong Kong
Electronics Industries Association, Inc., 1996. Employee data on C
and H are from company annual reports and authors' research.
OBM/OEM data from authors' own research and interviews.

Hong Kong's Competitive Advantages

Hong Kong has numerous competitive advantages that make it an attractive location for specific kinds of electronics manufacturing activities. These are:

1. *The Hong Kong people.* The people in Hong Kong are extremely flexible and adaptable, qualities which make them an ideal match for industries manufacturing products characterized by short life cycles. Hong Kong manufacturing can also pride itself on being able to respond quickly to market needs. Hong Kong people also enjoy a strong reputation as managers, and possess excellent professional and technical skills;

2. *Proximity to relatively inexpensive labor and land in Guangdong.* The Pearl River Delta region of Southern China has been developed for low-cost manufacturing over the last ten years, giving it a head start over other low-cost regions. As indicated in Table 10.2, land and labor are important cost components of manufacturing activities for quite a few electronic products;

3. *An understanding of the culture and systems of mainland China.* This is a major asset that enables Hong Kong to take advantage of its proximity to China for manufacturing as well as product design. Hong Kong is well positioned to market and distribute products in China;

4. *Availability of suppliers, both in Hong Kong and Guangdong.* As indicated in Table 10.2, the ready supply of materials for production is another important cost component of manufacturing activities for many products;

5. *Excellent infrastructure.* Hong Kong's excellent infrastructure includes stable electricity, communications networks, airport, shipping, legal system, and financial strength;

6. *International nature.* The international and cosmopolitan nature of Hong Kong allows Hong Kong companies to understand customer needs. Hong Kong has relatively easy access to updated technological information and market trends.

Hong Kong's Competitive Disadvantages

Among the disadvantages to electronics companies are the following:

1. *Labor costs.* The relatively high cost of labor in Hong Kong has forced companies that manufacture labor-intensive products to move to Guangdong Province to stay competitive;

2. *Technology/product innovation.* There is relatively little technology and/or product innovation taking place in Hong Kong today. As we discuss later, these activities are essential, if as we recommend, Hong Kong is to move its electronics sector toward products which are earlier in their life cycles.

A Vision for the Hong Kong Electronics Sector

Our vision for this sector is a Hong Kong-based electronics industry which conceives, designs, manufactures, and distributes end-products and their components. We believe that the growth opportunities in the electronics sector will come with the introduction of products earlier in their life cycles— products with increasing innovation content which also take advantage of Hong Kong's strength as a low-cost, high-quality, flexible and timely manufacturing engine. This vision expands the current business model, which predominantly serves only the OEM market.

We considered targeting specific products within the electronics sector, so that Hong Kong could concentrate its resources toward becoming a world-class manufacturer of these specific products. Significant resources from the government could then be applied to 'jump-start' the industry. But we discounted this strategy, since it does not take advantage of Hong Kong's unique, flexible, low-cost manufacturing engine or its excellent understanding of the 'tastes' of a variety of end users. Rather, we are recommending that the individual companies focus on the specific products in which they possess or can deliver the required design/innovation activities.

Although the electronics sector has been growing at a healthy pace under the existing practice, keeping to this road is a risky strategy in that other low-cost manufacturing countries could begin to chip away at Hong Kong's advantage. Regions in China such as Shanghai offer cheaper labor than Guangdong, as well as a more stable workforce, since most companies there do not use migrant workers. Moreover, they enjoy access to relatively skilled labor, as well as a very competitive transportation infrastructure (shipping ports and roads). Even if Hong Kong electronics manufacturers adopted a strategy to improve significantly their production processes, this strategy would not allow the industry to reach its full potential (defined here as a much higher rate of growth than they would achieve otherwise). Rather, we are advocating an increased emphasis on the conception of products to strengthen Hong Kong's overall position in innovative electronics.

It is important to emphasize that we are *not* advocating a complete, rapid transformation of Hong Kong manufacturers from largely OEM to brand-name production. Although we do see a risk in maintaining a dominant OEM-based manufacturing structure, we do recognize that Hong Kong manufacturers are extremely capable and flexible enough to know how to compete successfully. We are suggesting that some OEM companies will need to add more innovative content to their product portfolios to reach their full potential in terms of rates of growth and expansion.

The formation of new companies is important for the expansion of the electronics sector into new areas. The new companies we envision should be based on product/technology innovation which results in novel end-products or components, such as the latest personal digital assistants and their associated electronic components. These companies will be more competitive in the future if they start as innovation companies as opposed to OEM companies producing mature products. Issues regarding start-up financing are addressed in Chapter 13 ('Capital Markets').

A question often posed is how can small and medium-sized enterprises and newly formed companies obtain the resources to add the required activities such as R&D, marketing, and distribution. The key is partnering with other companies with complementary strengths. A small, new, end-product producer, for example, may distribute and market its products by establishing joint ventures with enterprises in China. It could also partner with a multinational company to make use of its brand name and/or its distribution channels. A producer of novel components may partner with local end-product makers and optimize the relationship to give the end-product manufacturer an advantage. Other examples of partnering can be constructed, but the most important point is that partnering can reduce the need for extensive resources.

The Activities Required to Implement this Vision

The dominant activities required to build a successful innovative electronics industry map directly onto many of Hong Kong's strengths. The most important activity is the *low-cost, flexible manufacturing* of quality products. Flexible manufacturing is the key ingredient for innovative electronics, since most of these products have extremely short product life cycles.

The degree of automation present in an electronics factory is driven by conflicting requirements for flexibility, low cost, and quality. In a highly automated factory, one can ensure a high level of quality due to the repeatability of the process. The cost of the capital investment can often cause products to be higher priced compared with those manufactured by low-cost labor. By and large, highly automated plants do not possess the flexibility needed to respond quickly to changing products. Labor-intensive manufacturing plants, by contrast, can be extremely flexible and are low cost, provided a sufficient supply of inexpensive labor is available, as in China. Quality often suffers, however, when products are manufactured by a low-skilled, low-wage labor force. Hong Kong-based companies manufacturing in Guangdong such as ALCO (a large manufacturer of consumer audio equipment) have been striking an excellent balance between automated and labor-intensive manufacturing and are producing a variety of quality products in a cost-competitive environment. This delicate balance is continually monitored and improved by the manufacturer, which makes Hong Kong, coupled with Guangdong, one of the most dynamic low-cost manufacturing engines for electronic products in the world.

The efficient *distribution of products* is another essential activity for the innovative electronics industry. Hong Kong, with its excellent infrastructure and variety of partners, has historically been successful in carrying out this activity. In addition, Hong Kong is in a unique position to access the tremendous and growing demand for these types of products in China. Hong Kong companies can form joint ventures with MNCs for the use of brand names, or joint ventures with enterprises in China, to carry out this activity more efficiently.

Another activity required for this industry is *marketing*. By this term, we mean the ability to sift through the vast array of electronic products and determine which of those are most needed in the targeted market. Hong Kong has an excellent understanding of the China market, which gives it a competitive advantage in this activity over other nations. This provides opportunities for partnering with MNCs to provide product definition for the China market.

Hong Kong engineers are able to perform routine electronic *product design* given a set of specifications from a larger company. Hong Kong engineers often redesign products with low-cost manufacturing in mind. This activity predominantly takes place in Hong Kong, where prototype manufacturing of a new product design occurs. This activity must be strengthened in order to generate enhanced products with increased profit margin. An example of product customization in the electronic component industry is the vast array of miniaturized electric motors from Johnson Electric.

Hong Kong's strengths in low-cost, flexible manufacturing of quality products has allowed Hong Kong to build a significant electronics industry as original equipment manufacturers. In order for Hong Kong to reach its full potential in this industry, however, significant improvements in the activity of *product innovation* are necessary. Strength in this activity forms the seeds for new, innovative electronic companies, as well as expansion of existing ones. Product innovation is a necessary requirement to begin the process of building brand-name recognition in electronic products. One example of product innovation is the use of cellular telephone technology to make portable home phones capable of clear reception over a larger range.

Technology innovation is an activity which can provide new or improved components for the end-products. Manufac-

turers which own unique technologies can maintain significant control of their product in the marketplace. Examples of
technology innovation are precision mechanisms made for
cassette recorders and application-specific integrated circuits
such as the Dragon Ball chip manufactured by Motorola. This
chip, developed for personal digital assistants (PDAs), is the
key component for a variety of Chinese translation products.

The innovative electronics vision presented can only be
achieved in a limited way without product/technology innovation. We are advocating that Hong Kong companies develop innovation and name recognition to complement OEM
electronics products. Product/technology innovation activities strengthen existing companies by helping increase the
barrier of entry for their competitors. It also stimulates the
creation of new companies based on new product ideas. We
are also advocating increased emphasis on product design. In
particular, moving from OEM to ODM (original design manufacturing) will give small and medium-sized enterprises
higher-value-added products.

Opportunities for Growth

There are countless ideas for new and innovative end-products such as pagers with text, digital cellular phones, personal digital assistants, portable CD players. It is not our intention to advocate any one of these products over others, since
it is our assessment that the individual companies, through
their strength in the activity of understanding markets, can
choose the right products.

Small and medium-sized companies can participate in this
vision by focusing on a particular product area and developing the expertise within their company to understand the key
technologies required by that area. The expertise allows a
company to improve its product design and to enter the marketplace at a higher profit margin. For example, a twin CD
changer was designed at ALCO and sold to selected multinational companies to perform marketing and distribution. The
product sold over 600,000 units in the first six months after
introduction. This business model requires high-quality manufacturing capability coupled with a keen understanding of
the key technologies in a specific area.

In the area of components, a relatively new company, Valence Semiconductor, specializes in integrated circuit design. This company helps capture product differentiation through the design of application-specific integrated circuits (ASICs). An example of technology innovation for components was found in battery products at Gold Peak, which developed its own technology for rechargeable nickel metal hydride batteries.

In short, innovative electronic products and components offer the Hong Kong electronics sector a high-growth area, which is well matched to many of its current activities and strengths.

The Hurdles to Achieving Full Growth Potential

There are some existing, but surmountable barriers that are limiting the ability of the Hong Kong electronics sector to reach its full potential. We discuss these challenges below.

The Success of the Existing Business Model

Most electronic companies in Hong Kong have exploited the low-cost, flexible manufacturing engine. This is true for both end-product and component manufacturers. The emphasis has been on producing electronic products which have already been created and accepted by the market, and doing so with lower manufacturing costs. At some point in the product life cycle, the creators of these products, which usually have higher manufacturing costs, no longer earn what they consider to be an acceptable profit margin. The market demand for the products, however, remains. At this point, Hong Kong companies, with their low-cost, flexible manufacturing can quickly fill the gap and produce these products at a higher profit margin. Of course, over time, this profit margin continues to erode even for the Hong Kong companies. At that point, the Hong Kong companies quickly begin producing other products with acceptable profit margins, and the cycle goes on.

This business model has been extremely successful in Hong Kong. Its success, however, has played a role in maintaining the *status quo* and slowing a move toward innovative products. Sole dependence on the current business model is risky in that other low-cost manufacturing countries can begin to copy this model due to its relatively low entry barrier. The vision which we presented expands the current electronics sector and offers the benefit of raising the barrier of entry for its competitors.

Weak Product/Technology Innovation and Product Design

The activities which appear relatively weak today in Hong Kong, as we have mentioned above, are product design and product/technology innovation. These activities are essential if end-product and component manufacturers are to expand their product base by conceiving and/or developing value-added products and components for the electronics area.

Fortunately, Hong Kong has some examples of companies which are strong enough in product and technology innovation to offer proof that it is possible to develop and manufacture brand-name products to expand business. VTech is one example of a company manufacturing mass-market electronic end-products that has successfully demonstrated this strategy. This company has been continually innovative in the area of electronic toys. It has recently introduced high-frequency (900MHz) cordless phones by using the technology developed for the cellular phone market. VTech has successfully demonstrated that the activity of product innovation can occur in the Hong Kong electronics sector.

Several key elements that have led to VTech's success in the activity of product innovation are given here.[10] It has established and is focusing on specific areas of excellence such as ASIC design, microprocessor applications, and educational software. The company has built a global R&D team that places a fraction (roughly 10 percent) of its engineers in the location where the technology is best understood. It has an ASIC design center in Canada and telecommunications engineering in the United Kingdom. Partnerships with major suppliers such as semiconductor manufacturers help VTech access expensive integrated circuit technology. Interactions with universities help the company bring new technology in specific areas to the marketplace. It runs continuous training programs to update employees' skills so that they have an understanding of the new technologies available. The success of VTech's commitment to product innovation is shown in its R&D output—65 new products per year.

Gold Peak is one example of a component manufacturer which has successfully demonstrated technology innovation. The company's development of state-of-the-art nickel metal hydride batteries is offering a significant challenge to larger established multinational battery producers. Just as in the case of VTech, Gold Peak focused on specific areas of excellence (batteries, in this case), and committed and built a strong R&D team and laboratory. Although a single specific recipe for improving product and technology innovation is not possible, one common theme among all of the success stories is the commitment to these activities by senior management.

Lack of Initial Capital for New Companies

The formation of new companies in the electronics sector will require access to capital at the outset, and help with the distribution of their products. Although in the past significant money was available for start-up companies in the industry, these were by and large unsuccessful, partly because of weak product and technology innovation. (It is also true that the investment system in Hong Kong does not allow an investor an exit strategy that would make the investment more appealing. See Chapter 13, 'Capital Markets'.) Today, new ventures are normally created by family funding, which in turn limits the pool of people who can start these new companies. Those with strength in product and technology innovation who wish to start a new enterprise, but lack family funding find themselves in a difficult position.

Little R&D/Design by Multinational Corporations in Hong Kong

Multinational corporations (MNCs) can serve three very useful roles in economies such as that of Hong Kong. One of the most obvious advantages is their ability to give individuals practical experience and know-how not usually available from other sources. There are numerous examples in the United States of individuals starting new companies after gaining experience in large multinational corporations. This same model could be applied to the Hong Kong electronics sector. Second, they can serve as a customer for the local industry. Small manufacturers need customers with well-specified requirements and the MNCs need quick response, high-quality suppliers. Third, MNCs can bring expensive, capital-intensive technology (such as that of the semiconductor industry) to Hong Kong. Even though there are approximately 486 manufacturing MNCs present in Hong Kong today (there are a total of 1,583 MNCs in Hong Kong in all industries),[11] very few are practicing R&D, design, or manufacturing in the electronics sector.

Recommendations for Implementing the Vision

As identified above, Hong Kong electronics manufacturers' relative lack of product/technology innovation and weakness in product design activities have impeded the industry from realizing its full potential in innovative electronics. The most important point is the need to attract the 'right' people, that is, human resources familiar with these activities. In this section, we offer recommendations for strengthening and integrating these activities into existing companies, and for making them the basis for the formation of new companies. We also suggest a strategy to attract MNCs.

Strengthening Product/Technology Innovation and Product Design

The best short-term solution for strengthening the activities of product/technology innovation and product design, is to bring international experts to Hong Kong. These experts should possess a deep knowledge of worldwide markets, as well as experience in product innovation and design, or the research and development skills required to bring new technological capabilities to Hong Kong.

To identify the appropriate international experts, several strategies could be employed, including the following:

(i) There are many Hong Kong-born experts with the right experience living abroad. An effort should be made to encourage them to participate in this expansion of the Hong Kong electronics sector;[12]

(ii) Hong Kong companies can identify experts in countries where they have branch offices containing small engineering groups;

(iii) A technique used by several American high-tech companies is to form technical advisory boards. These boards are comprised of business leaders in non-competitive segments of the market, university professors with research experience in the company's product area, and private consultants with a track record of product and technology innovation;

(iv) With the completion of the Hong Kong Convention Center Extension, Hong Kong is becoming a trade fair and exhibition center in Asia. The Hong Kong Government Industry Department could play a role by sponsoring international conferences with a focus on new products and technology for innovative electronics. Conferences, panel discussions and workshops on current and future products could discuss the technology required for innovative electronics. Such forums offer an excellent opportunity for electronics industry leaders to network with international experts.

Identifying international experts is the first step in this short-term solution. These experts are very well remunerated in their home countries, however, and would have to be better remunerated still to attract them to Hong Kong. In addition, housing in Hong Kong equivalent to what these experts have in their home country is extremely expensive. To reduce the barrier of high-cost housing, we suggest that a system similar to that found in universities be implemented. Universities have been extremely successful in bringing international experts to teach, perform research, and share ideas by offering subsidized housing on the university campus. As a result, internationally recognized faculty, who would otherwise find Hong Kong prohibitively expensive, have come to Hong Kong and have increased the international reputation of Hong Kong universities. Perhaps a similar model should be established to make it possible for industrialists, entrepreneurs, and international experts to come to Hong Kong for a period of time, and to live in relatively comfortable housing.

It is beyond the scope of this sector report to detail a plan for subsidized housing. It should be possible, however, to establish a distributed network of technology parks which could be located close to universities either to utilize some of the housing found on these campuses, or to construct new housing located in the technology parks. It is important to locate these technology parks close to university campuses so that the new generation of Hong Kong industrialists have early access to the experts and their ideas.

Importing international experts to Hong Kong offers a way to begin the process of strengthening the activities of product/technology innovation and product design. However, in order for the innovative electronics vision to become a reality, Hong Kong must develop its own experts. Two recommendations to accomplish this goal are first, to evolve the educational system toward developing individuals with the necessary creativity to become product/technology innovation experts. Second, in order to attract the best and brightest individuals, the industry should wage an active campaign to transform the image of engineers from implementors and problem solvers to product creators.

Several university professors with experience in highly industrialized countries, told us that Hong Kong students entering the university system possess the necessary math and science skills, but have learned the material only through memorization. They have difficulty applying fundamental concepts to areas in which they are not familiar. This situation should be explored carefully in order to find ways to evolve secondary school education from memorization toward emphasizing the creative process. This examination is already taking place in other countries in Asia such as Singapore.[13]

During our research we visited several universities and examined their curricula and research efforts. In general, most universities stressed the engineering science model, which concentrates on fundamental physical and mathematical concepts with the goal of generating new knowledge. This type of education is excellent at generating future academicians, but is unfortunately mismatched to the needs of Hong Kong's electronics industry. Rather than developing new knowledge through fundamentals, we recommend that a significant fraction of the research undertaken by faculty should be geared toward understanding the fundamentals in an applied context. No one would recommend ignoring fundamentals and just teaching the technology of the day, but fundamentals can be used to understand the technology and electronic products practiced by the electronics industry. Integrated circuit design, for example, is an extremely important discipline which has the ability to capture product ideas. The world's best IC designers have a fundamental understanding of the physics of semiconductor devices and their application to analog and digital circuits. Another example is the design of precision mechanical components for mass marketing electronic products. A strong background in materials and mechanical engineering is necessary to lead in this field.

At MIT we recognize that it is our students who help us continue to sustain our reputation. With this fact in mind, Hong Kong universities should move toward increasing their international student population at both the undergraduate and post-graduate level. By enlarging the pool of students considered for admission, the overall student quality will increase.

In order to attract the best and brightest local students toward a career in product/technology innovation, Hong Kong should begin a campaign to transform the image of engineers from implementors to creators. A similar image-building issue was identified in the *Made in America* study for manufacturing engineers.[14] This campaign could be orchestrated by the Hong Kong Government Industry Department working closely with companies that have demonstrated successful product/technology innovation. The success stories of the founders of large and small companies should be highly publicized through the media. Product and technology innovation projects should be funded at local universities with the goal of seeing the products enter the marketplace. Successes should be highly publicized and monetary rewards given through technology licensing.

We have given some examples of ways to strengthen the activities of production/technology innovation and product design through education and transforming the image of the engineer. We are convinced that, with the commitment of the Hong Kong Industry Department, the local electronics industries and academia, a variety of other ideas will quickly be generated.

Integrating Product/Technology Innovation and Product Design into Local Industry

We are *not* suggesting that a large fraction of the existing electronics companies must add product/technology innovation to their current expertise. In fact, the sector would benefit if a number of companies continue to practice a modified version of the current business model. These companies should focus on improving their product design expertise to move from OEM to ODM production. The design content will add value to pay for the investment in designers. These ODM companies must continually improve the flexible, low-cost manufacturing engine in order to stay competitive. This improvement will benefit the entire innovative electronics sector through the ability to flexibly manufacture high-quality products at low cost.

A few companies may choose not just to move from OEM of mature products to ODM of products early in their life cycle, but may choose to go all the way and become brand-name manufacturers for some markets. These companies must be prepared to invest significantly in their own research and development to obtain the financial rewards. This investment should take the form of both money and time commitment. There may be ways to lower the cost of carrying this out. One would be to bring engineers and scientists from China to Hong Kong to spend a year or two as visiting professionals in Hong Kong companies and then return to China. This would require an examination of the immigration policies between China and Hong Kong. The main point is the commitment from existing companies to carry out R&D.[15]

Universities could also carry out a larger fraction of applied R&D as partners with the local industry. The funding for these efforts should come from the government, and the interaction with researchers and their results, from the industry. It has been our experience in American universities that industrial involvement in research projects funded by the government has provided an excellent matching of academics to industrial needs. In general, those companies that spend the time necessary to mentor these programs, reap the benefits of well-trained engineers prepared for an industrial career, as well as their innovations. Attracting graduates from these programs is the first step toward acquiring expertise in product/technology innovation. It will be necessary to make significant investments to retain these individuals through substantial rewards for their innovation. Stock options, bonuses, and other methods of remuneration are commonplace in the US high-technology sector and should be considered by Hong Kong industries.

In addition to commitment to R&D, the marketing and distribution of brand-name products must be strengthened. We recommend that China be viewed as a key market for brand-name products, and to establish joint ventures with enterprises in China to get initial help in distribution and marketing. The proposed research institute on chinese retailing and distribution in part one can help with this challenging task. The distribution of innovative end-products can also be accelerated by establishing joint ventures with MNCs that want to enter the China market. Hong Kong's tremendous understanding of this market's needs and culture of doing business should help make this possible in a relatively short time.

Another key to expanding the electronics sector is the formation of new companies. We strongly recommend that new companies start through product/technology innovation as this activity will define the future character of the company culture. As Hong Kong develops its own experts in product/technology innovation, several of these experts would be candidates to form new companies based around a product or technology idea in the innovative electronics sector. The distribution channels for these products can be accessed through partnering with established companies in China, the West, or both.

Assuming an increase in technology/product innovation experts, the major barrier to the formation of new companies will be their initial funding. In the past, companies started with a small investment and began manufacturing low-end-products. They financed growth by borrowing against future sales. This financial model makes it difficult to invest significantly in product/technology innovation. Another initial funding model which we saw is the use of family finances. This model severely limits the pool of 'founders,' however, since these individuals must have both an innovative product idea and sufficient family resources to form the new venture.

We recommend that Hong Kong work to broaden the pool of potential founders with venture money. If Hong Kong is successful in strengthening the activities of product and technology innovation, venture money could reap significant benefits. We recognize that this will require changes in the capital markets to provide an adequate exit strategy. This point is elaborated in Chapter 13.

Attracting Multinational Corporations

We have pointed out above that attracting multinational corporations to Hong Kong offers major benefits to the local electronics industry. Furthermore, large semiconductor manufacturers offer an additional benefit, since it is generally agreed that semiconductor technology is the heart of most electronic products. One strategy for obtaining the technology locally is to attract multinationals to practice it in Hong Kong. Since the semiconductor industry requires few raw materials, has low labor content, and needs only moderate space, Hong Kong with its excellent infrastructure should be a perfect place to house this industry. Why has it not happened? Simply put, additional economic incentives must be seen by these multinational semiconductor corporations.

One of the major reasons why multinationals come to Asia is to gain access, not only to relatively inexpensive labor, but also to expanding markets. No market is more promising than that of China. If a multinational company wants to access the growing market in China, it certainly views establishing a presence there much more favorably than anywhere else, including Hong Kong. At present, Hong Kong is at a disadvantage when competing for multinational presence with other countries in Asia, which are offering significant advantages such as a tax holiday, reduced land prices, and reasonable housing costs.

Some industry people who we interviewed pointed out that if selected products manufactured in Hong Kong could be sold into China as if they were manufactured in China (with no import tax), the excellent infrastructure of Hong Kong and other advantages already noted would be sufficient to attract MNCs, especially from the semiconductor industry. In addition, the policy of a 'safe harbor,' as outlined in Part One of this book, could protect investments and maintain Hong Kong's ability to access state-of-the-art equipment without import restrictions. We recommend that this idea be explored further, since the location of MNCs in Hong Kong is important to the long-term health of its electronics industry.

In Summary

The current electronics industry in Hong Kong enjoys one of the most dynamic low-cost manufacturing engines for electronic products in the world. The present Hong Kong business model is to produce mature products that have been tested in the marketplace with their low-cost manufacturing capability at an acceptable profit margin. We mentioned that continuing the existing practice is risky, as other countries including China will compete fiercely for this market.

We presented a vision for this sector: a Hong Kong-based electronics industry that conceives, designs, manufactures, and distributes innovative end-products and their components. We have identified the activities of product/technology innovation as a major weakness to achieving this vision. We found examples of Hong Kong companies that possess either product or technology innovation. They enjoy higher profit margins by introducing products earlier in their life cycles. These companies are proof of the potential of this new business model.

Some existing companies, in particular small and medium-sized companies, should consider introducing products earlier in their life cycles by improving product design capabilities. This requires that they focus on a particular product segment and develop expertise in the available technology and its applications for that product segment. The products can then be marketed and distributed by multinationals. Other companies, in particular those larger companies with more resources, may choose to expand by introducing brand-name products. We recommend that these companies view their initial primary market as China, and join enterprises in China for help with marketing and distribution, or form joint ventures with MNCs that want a presence in the China market.

New companies, in our view, should include innovation from their start-up phase, and consider introducing products early in their life cycles, preferably brand-name products.

A summary of our conclusions and recommendations follow:

1. Bring international experts to Hong Kong as a short-term solution, to strengthen technology/product innovation.

   a. In particular, recruit Hong Kong-born experts.

   b. Reduce the barrier of high-cost housing for these experts by implementing a system similar to that found currently in Hong Kong universities.

2. Create distributed science parks located near universities as recommended in Part One of this book. These parks could serve the function of offering lower cost housing for the experts and low-cost space for product development. They also offer a direct link to university faculty and students.

3. Develop local expertise in technology/product innovation.

   a. Examine a possible evolution of secondary school education from memorization-based to creative learning.

   b. University research should have a significant component of applied R&D that exercises the fundamentals. These projects should have significant industrial input.

   c. To attract the brightest students, transform the image of the engineer by publicizing success stories of current innovators.

4. In general, the current electronics industry should move toward the introduction of products earlier in their life cycles.

a. Small and medium-sized companies should add investment in the people who understand the latest available technology for a select set of products and who could improve their product design.

b. Medium-sized and large companies should add investment in the people necessary to acquire technology/product innovation to develop brand-name products, with China viewed as a key market.

c. To lower the cost of this investment, engineers and scientists from China could spend one to two years in industry. This requires easing somewhat the restrictions on immigration to Hong Kong.

5. New companies should be started through product/technology innovation.

a. These start-ups will require low-cost space.

b. The university research shift toward applied R&D can offer seeds for new products.

c. Venture capital must be available (see Chapter 13, 'Capital Markets').

We believe that Hong Kong's electronic sector has a very bright future if a significant fraction of its manufacturing moves towards early product introduction and towards viewing China and MNCs as partners, particularly in the key activities of marketing and distribution of innovative products.

Acknowledgements: The authors gratefully acknowledge the many contributions by Kheng Leong Cheah, who helped tremendously as a research assistant for this project.

Notes

1   C. Tuan and L.F.Y. Ng, 'Evolution of Hong Kong's Electronics Industry under a Passive Industrial Policy,' *Managerial and Decision Economics*, 16, 6 (1995): 509–523. See also Hong Kong Government Industry Department, *1995 Hong Kong's*

Manufacturing Industries, 1995, pp. 60–74; and M. W. Liu, 'Discussion on Hong Kong High-Technology Manufacturing Development and the Role of Government,' provided by the Hong Kong Electronics Traders Association and the Chinese Manufacturers Association

2   Interviews by MIT researchers; see Hong Kong Trade Development Council, *Directory of ISO 9000 Certified Companies in Hong Kong*, 1996; *The Thornton Guide to Hong Kong Companies*, Hong Kong: Edinburgh Financial Publishing (Asia) Limited, 1996.

3   Ping K. Ko (Dean of Engineering at Hong Kong University of Science and Technology) and York Liao (Executive Director, Varitronix Ltd.), private communications.

4   Hong Kong Trade Development Council, 'International Exhibitions in Electronics and Electrical Products,' July 1996, pp. 103–114.

5   Interviews by MIT researchers.

6   Hong Kong Government Industry Department, 'Drivers of Competitive Advantage,' Chapter 6 in *Techno-Economic and Market Research Study on Hong Kong's Electronic Industry 1993–1994*, Vol. 2, 1994, pp. 100–127.

7   Ibid.

8   Interviews by MIT researchers; Hong Kong Trade Development Council, *Directory of ISO 9000 Certified Companies in Hong Kong*.

9   Hong Kong Trade Development Council, *Directory of ISO 9000 Certified Companies in Hong Kong*.

10 A. Wong, 'Competitive Elements in Establishing and Managing a High-Tech Company,' presented at Business & Technology Exchange Forum on Catalysts for Success in High Tech, Hong Kong, January 7, 1997.

11 Hong Kong Government Industry Department, *Report on the 1995 Survey of Regional Representation by Overseas Companies in Hong Kong*, December 1995, pp. 11–13.

12 V. Davies, 'Building Our Future with High Technology,' *South China Morning Post*, December 3, 1996.

13 From 'Time for a Reality Check in Asia, *Business Week* (December 2, 1996): 58–67.

14 M. L. Dertouzos; R. K. Lester; and R. M. Solow, *Made in America*, Cambridge, Mass: The MIT Press, 1989, pp. 77–80.

15 B. Gilley, 'New Model,' *Far Eastern Economic Review* (December 21, 1995): 50–52.

11   Information Technology in Hong Kong

Victor Zue, Helen Meng, Jake Seid, David Tennenhouse, and Trudy Wilcox

Our daily lives increasingly are touched and shaped by the information surrounding us—from education (learning a new language, conducting a science project, or writing a paper) and nourishment and health (finding a restaurant, maintaining fitness, or diagnosing an illness), to traveling (planning a trip, buying a ticket, or selecting a hotel), commerce (purchasing products, managing finances, or paying bills), and entertainment (watching a movie, reading a novel, or betting at a racetrack). The technologies underlying the creation, manipulation, and delivery of this information, therefore, are playing an ever-broadening role in a region such as Hong Kong, both in the lives of its citizens and the overall economy.[1]

Three comments should be made at the beginning of this chapter. First, information technology (hereafter 'IT') is an industry in and of itself which is well suited for real growth in Hong Kong. This is particularly true, we believe, in the areas of telecommunications and software. At the same time, IT provides the backbone to support all areas of the local economy, from manufacturing (factory automation, for example) to services (such as banking). Its impact cannot be measured strictly in terms of the jobs created or the goods sold in the IT industry alone. In fact, IT will be covered in other chapters of this book either explicitly (the manufacturing of 900MHz telephones in the electronics sector, for example) or implicitly (the use of IT to improve the efficiency of garment manufacturing). Second, the IT industry encompasses the manufacturing of equipment that enables information creation and access (such as computers and telecommunication devices), the transporting mechanisms for the information (telecommunications), and the information itself (in media such as newspapers and television programs). As a result, the dichotomy of manufacturing versus service may not always be appropriate for this sector. Finally, we are in the midst of the digital revolution, whereby information is increasingly captured in the form of bits, whether text or image, data or voice. We have thus focused our examination of the future of the IT industry within the digital realm, realizing that this focus may have prevented us from examining some fruitful areas (such as motion picture production).

For the study presented in this chapter, the IT team (consisting of researchers from the MIT Laboratory for Computer Science, the Industrial Performance Center, and the Sloan School of Management) made twelve person-trips to Hong Kong for a total of 60 working days. In addition, a graduate research assistant stayed in Hong Kong for one semester, and another worked at MIT for two. We have conducted more than 100 interviews, covering traditional IT industries (such as telecommunications) and industries where IT plays a major role (such as banking). A list of the companies, government and private organizations, and universities can be found at the end of this chapter.

The State of Information Technology in Hong Kong

Our overall opinion about the prospect of IT in Hong Kong is very positive—the present state of affairs in IT is healthy, and there are potential opportunities for real growth. The current success can be attributed to several key factors. First, we found many examples of the manufacturing of IT products in niche markets. Some of these products are the direct result of companies leveraging the symbiotic relationship between Hong Kong and China, and the multilingual nature of the Hong Kong culture. For example, the Dragonball chip produced by Motorola in Hong Kong for two-way Chinese pagers utilizes technology originally developed at Tsinghua University in Beijing, thus enabling Hong Kong to achieve world dominance in Chinese-language paging. Similarly, the hand-held, Chinese–English translating personal digital assistant (PDA) produced by Group Sense licenses its underlying language technology from the Institute of Computing Technology, Chinese Academy of Science.

Second, Hong Kong enjoys a world-class, all-digital telecommunications infrastructure that delivers flexible and high-bandwidth services to all sectors of the economy. (Hong Kong's telecommunications infrastructure will be dealt with in the telecommunications section below.) This is clearly one of Hong Kong's competitive advantages that needs to be exploited, nurtured, and expanded.

Third, the Hong Kong IT industry is very good at creating innovative solutions to real-world applications by *integrating* IT products and services, and it often leads the rest of the world in this regard. These successful IT activities are often the result of 'application pull,' rather than 'technology push.' In other words, the identified need of an application serves as the driving force behind the integration of the technologies necessary to fulfill that need. In fact, there is very little of the 'not invented here' (NIH) syndrome in Hong Kong; it makes little difference to the developers whether the technologies are developed locally or abroad, as long as they are the best available. Examples can be found in: Hong Kong Bank's development and deployment of the first cash *deposit* ATM (which is still not available in the United States); Motorola and Champion Technology's development of the Chinese-language pager; Hong Kong Jockey Club's telebetting PDA; Dah Sing Bank's and Star Paging's joint development of the DNA Alert system (which can instantaneously alert a customer of credit card usage through a pager); and Hongkong Telecom's platform combining movies-on-demand and Internet services via Java. Pushed to an extreme, such an approach may limit the technology horizon in that basic technologies would not be developed with enough foresight. Thus far Hong Kong seems to have benefited from such an approach, more than it has been hurt by it.

Last but not least, Hong Kong possesses a consumer base that is among the world's most technologically sophisticated and receptive. Hong Kong's density of cellular and pager usage, for example, is among the highest worldwide (see the discussion under 'Telecommunications' below). People are eager to adopt new IT technologies and services, as long they can derive demonstrable benefits by using them. A related competitive advantage, as mentioned elsewhere in this book, is that Hong Kong is truly a bilingual society in which both the Chinese and English languages are used extensively. Moreover, citizens of Hong Kong are very cosmopolitan; they are knowledgeable about, and comfortable with Western culture and practices while preserving Chinese values and traditions. As a result, Hong Kong stands unique at the crossroads of China and the Western world. On the one hand, the territory can serve as the beachhead for multinationals seeking entry to the China market, due to the Hong Kong people's intimate familiarity with China and Chinese cultural norms. On the other hand, Hong Kong is the logical gateway for China to gain access to the Western world, due to its long experience with Western business practices and laws.

A General Information Technology Strategy for Hong Kong

Information is fast becoming *the* commodity that will empower companies and countries alike, and will further widen the gap between the 'haves' and the 'have-nots.' Hong Kong must be vigilant to capitalize on her assets and make plans to expand her horizons, lest she be overtaken by her competitors in the Asia–Pacific region, including Singapore and Taiwan. Hong Kong needs to recognize that IT offers a competitive edge that the territory must learn to exploit and can ill afford to lose. Our first general recommendation, therefore, is that Hong Kong should transform IT into a 'core competence' industry. Hong Kong should aggressively expand beyond the mere use and deployment of IT to include IT development, so that the region can chart its own destiny with less reliance on outside help.

The barrier to achieving these goals has less to do with capability than with attitude. Students in the universities do not perceive a career in the IT industry to be as attractive as other alternatives that will lead to quicker and greater financial gain. Even those working in the IT area tend to focus on opportunities within the region, rather than in China and the rest of the world. Actions are needed to raise awareness, both within the industry and among the Hong Kong populace, of the importance of IT and the opportunities it can provide. The government and the IT industry must promote the growth of IT and to create the institutional framework required to accelerate the transformation into a core competent industry. Government can help to promote an understanding on such issues as intellectual property rights and information security. It should also seek to influence the mindsets of the next generation, and prepare its citizens through education reform.

Our second general recommendation stems from our observation of pockets of excellence in a number of areas contributing to manufacturing and trade, such as telecommunications, transport, and banking. We see the opportunity for these seemingly separate activities to be integrated to provide a 'virtual total solution' to the customer.[2] Thus, for example, a potential buyer of watches can browse through an electronic database to find an appropriate manufacturer, order the product, and deal with subsequent shipping, clearance, and settlement, all in one integrated step. Similarly, the needs of a tenant in a high-rise apartment complex, ranging from telecommunications and utilities to shopping and entertainment, can all be satisfied by a single virtual provider. To enable such activities, the service provider need not be engaged in all of the activities. In fact, it need not even be involved in *any* of the activities. Such a capability is enabled by enhanced sharing of infrastructure and extensive utilization of IT to reduce the transaction overhead across sectors. Hong Kong may be uniquely suited to attain this higher level of productivity and better service because of its existing strengths in all the sectors, enabled by advanced utilization of IT.

Our interviews during the course of the study covered a wide range of IT activities. We have chosen, however, to focus our chapter on four subsectors: telecommunications, transport, electronic banking and commerce, and software. The first three are chosen because IT has helped create competitive advantages that Hong Kong currently enjoys in these subsectors. Taken together, these three subsectors can help elevate Hong Kong up to the next level of manufacturing and services through the concept of total solution provision mentioned above. The fourth subsector—software—is included because of the crucial role it plays in IT development, and the potential industry of 'process-specific' software that Hong Kong can create.

In the remainder of this chapter, we present our findings and specific recommendations by subsector. We conclude with our comments on the roles that the government can play in this crucial and fast-moving industry.

Telecommunications

One cannot overestimate the critical role of telecommunications in a country's economic growth and development. During the last two decades, telecommunications has evolved from a social want to an economic necessity. Today it supports a range of industries—from finance, to transportation, to textiles—and is a major common determinant of a society's success in the growing global marketplace.

By current world standards, the telecommunications infrastructure in Hong Kong is first-rate. Hong Kong implemented a digital network in 1993, becoming one of the first societies worldwide to boast a 100 percent digital backbone. The domestic network is fiber; regional and international calls are transmitted using fiber, microwave, and satellite. The fiber-based infrastructure provides high bandwidth (which allows the transmission of video and high-speed data over the regular telephone network) and supports a number of value-added services [such as video-on-demand (VOD)]. Telephone density hovers at 60 percent, and mobile penetration is 16 percent, the highest in Asia.

The telecommunications industry in Hong Kong is also highly competitive. Since 1995, four companies[3] have competed to provide local telephony service in Hong Kong. (An exception to the competitive environment is the monopoly in international telephone service, the ramifications of which will be addressed below.) Cellular service is provided by two companies and two consortia, and six Personal Communications System (PCS) licenses were awarded in July 1996. There are approximately 110 Internet Service Providers (ISPs) in Hong Kong. A major ISP is the Hong Kong Supernet, which emerged from Internet development at the Hong Kong University of Science and Technology (HKUST). The Hong Kong Internet Exchange, which is coordinated and operated at the Chinese University of Hong Kong (CUHK), is the prime interconnecting node routing intra-Hong Kong Internet traffic.

The greatest strength of Hong Kong's telecommunications sector lies in its fully digital fiber network. The available bandwidth alone allows the rapid implementation and deployment of new technologies to respond quickly to customer preferences. Moreover, the sophisticated network permits the easy adaptation of new services such as calling-number-displayed (CND) and video-on-demand (VOD). According to International Telecommunication Union (ITU) statistics, Hong Kong's multimedia-ready infrastructure ranks 15th in the world, and second in Asia, based on the three criteria of telephone, television, and PC density.[4]

Hong Kong's affluent and technically adroit customer base helps to drive technical innovation in telecommunications. Users are not afraid of cutting-edge technology, but readily express interest in and embrace new services. The wide use and popularity of two-way, bilingual pagers, and telebetting devices at the race courses of the Hong Kong Jockey Club are but two examples. Additionally, Hong Kong telecommunications providers are quick to respond to the tremendous 'demand pull' posed by its consumer market. Hongkong Telecom, for example, in offering calling-number-displayed also introduced text-to-speech caller announcement and detailed call logging for saving the duration, date and time of manually dialed calls.[5]

As indicated above, Hong Kong provides a rich environment for training local telecommunications professionals, both managerial and technical, and for building up a wealth of operational experience and expertise to accelerate Hong Kong's technological progression into the twenty-first century. Furthermore, Hong Kong has the opportunity to take these specialized skills and exploit them offshore.

The Hong Kong telecommunications industry is not without some weaknesses. At a time when many of the world's largest telecommunications companies are actively pursuing global opportunities, Hong Kong companies tend to think locally or regionally, despite the fact that they are at the forefront of the information revolution with their high levels of technical expertise and experience. This may be a consequence of the recent deregulation in the local market together with the monopoly held by Hongkong Telecom in international telephony. Nevertheless, this outlook curtails growth and limits future opportunities. Two exceptions are Hutchison's investment in the wireless service, Orange, in Britain, and Hongkong Telecom's venture into Thailand's cellular service.

Hongkong Telecom International Ltd. (HKTI) has been granted an exclusive license in international telephony until

2006. This monopoly has limited the lowering of international calling rates, and encouraged the growth of call-back operators and exacerbated uneven traffic flows. According to the US Federal Communications Commission (FCC), there are seven US-to-Hong Kong calls for every one call from Hong Kong to the United States, and 20 percent of the US-to-Hong Kong traffic is attributed to call-back operators.[6] Restricted competition slows growth and innovation in telecommunications and keeps rates artificially high; the successful liberalization of local telephone service in 1995 stands as an illustration of the principle.

Recommendations for the Telecommunications Arena

In the digital revolution, where technology changes rapidly, innovation should take a 'customer-first' approach, and markets should look beyond parochialism, in order to expand the telecommunications industry. Below we offer a few specific recommendations.

Develop a 'virtual total solution'. Given the existing infrastructure of fiber and cable connectivity—and the nascent competitive environment in local telephony, wireless, Internet services, and cable television—Hong Kong is well positioned to provide a 'one-stop shop' for a wide range of telecommunications services. Hong Kong telephone companies are faring quite well in targeting the goal of 'total solution provision'—a single company can offer a variety of services including fixed-network, mobile, paging, Internet service, as do Hongkong Telecom, Hutchison Communications, and others. However, as technological advancements bring new services, a total solution provider will have no choice but to keep up by way of expansion. This may become increasingly difficult as a single company has finite resources at any given time. A company that manages to keep abreast of the situation may dominate the market and ultimately monopolize, because by then there will almost be an insurmountable barrier towards entry into the industry. However, the emergence of a monopoly may also suggest that inhibition by a regulatory authority is imminent, and this may stymie innovation within the company.

The 'Made By Hong Kong' strategy for telecommunications is one of 'virtual total solution provision,' emphasizing a decentralized, customer-first approach. No single company needs to provide all services. Instead, telecommunications companies providing specialized service(s) should form market alliances. In this way, the industry will be able to select the appropriate handful of market alliances to provide a *virtual* total solution tailored to the particular needs of a customer. Market segmentation can be extremely efficient, as service packages thus devised can minimize any payments by the customer for unwanted elements. Moreover, the proposed configuration for the industry could accommodate competition at every service sector, thereby dismissing the undesirable aspects of a monopoly. The ultimate goal is to create an efficient industry which would grow through a shared infrastructure of alliances. Some fixed marketing arrangements between telecommunications companies do exist. New T&T, for example, is leasing fixed telephone network access from Hongkong Telecom. Progression from the *status quo* towards a virtual total solution will probably take place in lockstep with technologies supporting electronic commerce. As it becomes easier to form market alliances dynamically and quickly, service providers may develop a virtual total solution which evolves flexibly and rapidly with the changing needs of the customer. The service providers would readily be able to incorporate new, innovative services. This would induce market growth and, in turn, produces greater revenues for all the players in the industry.

Promote comprehensive customer care. Another added benefit of the 'virtual total solution provision' framework is the availability of 'one-stop shops' for the customer. Once a selection is made, the customer would have the convenience of a single point of contact for a large collection of services, such as sales and marketing, handling customer inquiries and complaints, and billing, among others. Comprehensive customer care is conducive to securing loyal customers and inducing market growth. A 'one-stop shop' for customer care may again be a 'virtual integration' of distributed parties under a single brand name. Each party may specialize in specific types of customer service. Some examples include the rapid turn-up and deployment of new services, meeting target due dates, minimizing circuit downtime, and the establishment of an 'institutionalized' feedback loop from the customer back to the service provider. Customer feedback is regarded as an indispensable element in guiding improvements in service. The industry could take a proactive stance in encouraging competition, and give freedom to the customer to switch freely from one branded arrangement to another without any service interruption. An emphasis in comprehensive customer care, set in the framework of virtual total solution provision, would distinguish Hong Kong both as a bellwether in technical innovation and as a leader in responsiveness to the consumer.

Broaden the definition of customer. Hong Kong telecommunications firms can broaden the definition of customer to include foreign telecommunications companies. With the opening of telecommunications markets worldwide, it is inevitable that foreign multinational companies would be eager to enter one another's domestic markets. Once Hong Kong's international services are liberalized, domestic and foreign firms alike will jump into the competitive fray. The new local telephony service providers should establish a firm foothold in the region, and then work proactively with potential foreign entrants, perhaps by leasing trunk capacity and switch access to them. This 'condominium' approach to network access and service provision has several advantages. It becomes unnecessary for foreign companies to build parallel networks, thus lessening the social disruptions associated with installing multiple infrastructures. This keeps network control firmly in the hands of Hong Kong firms. Moreover, local and foreign firms could collaborate in developing and deploying new value-added services, especially those which involve an incubation period and a lag time for dismissing risks and securing steady revenue. This approach would ensure that Hong Kong stays at the forefront of telecommunications technological evolution by allowing all parties (both local and foreign) to seize technical opportunities that perhaps none would pursue individually. This would position Hong Kong well to become a technology showcase, and a leading global participant and collaborator in telecommunications.

Exploit technology showcase opportunities. The fiber-based infrastructure, small physical size, and knowledgeable and receptive consumer base all contribute towards Hong Kong's role as a 'technology showcase' in telecommunications. Hong Kong has repeatedly demonstrated its ability to identify new telecommunications and IT trends and rapidly execute new ideas within the region. For example, New T&T's Intelligent Network software platform is one of the world's first to provide number portability in commercial operations, which allow customers freely to change operators without changing phone numbers.[7] Hongkong Telecom will also be the first to launch the VOD service,[8] showcasing the advanced technology territory-wide. Hutchison Telephone Co. Ltd. launched the world's first commercial digital network based on Code Division Multiple Access (CDMA)[9] technology in Hong Kong during 1995. It is encouraging to see the telecommunications industry in Hong Kong strive continually to exploit technology showcase opportunities and conduct real experiments with its superior infrastructure. Hong Kong should capitalize on the extra transmission capacity of the existing fiber backbone. One possibility would be to establish 'virtual parks' such as the 'virtual science park' proposed in Part One of this book, where a distributed 'network' of research, development and industrial sites are connected via telecommunications linkages. The speed and bandwidth of fiber access to the general consumer should also be increased. Increasing information flow may generate more revenue from the use of the fiber, provided that appropriate pricing policies are developed and implemented.

Move beyond territorial borders. Hong Kong has focused primarily on developing and exploiting local and regional telecommunications opportunities. But many other profitable ventures are located outside the neighboring region, and Hong Kong expertise also is well suited to capitalize on these opportunities. Though some broadcasting companies are already looking outward, the trend for telecommunications firms has been to concentrate on the new competitive atmosphere in domestic wireline and wireless telephony. One way to develop a global vision is by joining up with existing global alliances or creating new ones. These consortia are positioned to compete with local telephone companies in foreign markets and would allow Hong Kong to establish a global presence in communications.

Establish an alliance with China. China's intended investment to develop its telephone infrastructure is well known;
the government has set a teledensity target of 8 percent by
the year 2000. Hong Kong, with its operational expertise in
wireless systems (CT2,[10] analog and digital cellular, and paging), is a prime candidate to contribute towards China's construction and operation of second and third networks, by
employing 'air loops'[11] off of the fiber inter-exchange network. Wireless local loop technology is a viable alternative to
wireline service to the customer, saving both time and
expense not only in building a parallel infrastructure but also
in realizing China's overall telephony penetration goal. Hong
Kong, with its métier in wireless technology and fluency in
both English and Chinese, is well suited to assist China in
aligning its telecommunications policies with emerging global liberalization. Furthermore, Hong Kong could help to engineer one of the world's most ambitious communications
build-outs in the next five years. Hong Kong's experience in
cutting-edge technology and application could allow China
to leapfrog over older technology. For example, the new
interexchange networks could be designed and built to
accommodate bundled services from the start, thereby allowing the introduction of basic telephony, Internet access, e-
mail and VOD, and other services, over the same infrastructure. The combination of China's telecommunications expansion, Hong Kong's successful telecommunications sector—in
terms of teledensity, the wide range of services for customers
to choose from, and the competitive environment for fixed
local telephony and wireless communications—and the 'one
country, two systems' rule promises to create a symbiosis
between Hong Kong and its hinterland. This would allow
Hong Kong to expand greatly its communications industry
and China to meet its own telecommunications goal for the
next decade.

Maintain government–industry partnership. There are several steps the government can take to grow the Hong Kong
telecommunications industry. First, the government can continue aggressively to create a pro-competitive environment in
international telephony. Currently, there is tremendous
growth in call-back services, which allow local telecommunications firms to sidestep the one company exclusivity rule,

and generate revenues that must be shared with foreign (primarily US) long-distance companies. Although this call-back arrangement allows the local service providers to build up their customer base, much of the revenue is siphoned off by their foreign carrier partners. This affects the growth of the local service providers since long distance revenue could be used to finance the construction of additional infrastructures in Hong Kong, as well as the development of new value-added services in the territory and beyond. Second, with the phenomenal growth in wireless systems, the occurrence of the fraudulent use of mobile phones is likely to rise, as it has in other countries.[12] The government could take a proactive role in working with the wireless operators to create and organize a territory-wide 'authentication' center to reduce such usage. The pooled intellectual and financial resources of the service operators and the government would enable Hong Kong to stand at the technological forefront of wireless security by promoting a cross-company and government alliance to ensure consumer and firm fraud protection. Last, the government could nurture and promote Hong Kong as an international hub by encouraging multinational companies and global consortia to locate headquarters in Hong Kong.

Transport and Information Technology

Some may be surprised to see the issue of transport being addressed in this chapter on IT. Our findings indicate that IT has become an indispensable enabler in Hong Kong's superior transport infrastructure, which supports a thriving entrepôt economy. The region has attained leading global positions in the transport of cargo (both air and sea), and people (both on the ground and in the air). The Hong Kong Air Cargo Terminals Limited (HACTL)[13], the sole air-cargo handling organization for the region, has the highest cargo throughput for a single enterprise, some 1.5 million tons per annum, along with a world record low rate of consignment mishandling (1 in 28,000) which is several orders of magnitude better than the global average (1 in 24). Hong Kong has the world's busiest container port, measured in terms of vessel arrivals/departures and passenger throughput, as well as the global record in sea cargo throughput—12.5 million TEUs (twenty-foot equivalent units) per annum.[14] The Mass Transit Railway (MTR),[15] one of the first subway systems in Asia, commenced operation in 1978 under the management of the Mass Transit Railway Corporation (MTRC). The operation leads railway systems of major cities in Europe and the United States, according to international benchmarks such as passenger density, train reliability, staff efficiency, cost efficiency, asset allocation and equipment performance.[16] Currently, the MTR is carrying 2.4 million passengers over a 19-hour day of uninterrupted service. Hong Kong's Kai Tak Airport is one of the world's busiest airports, ranking second and fourth in terms of freight and passenger transport respectively. It has served Hong Kong's economy very well over the past decades. Meanwhile, the new Chek Lap Kok Airport,[17] when it commences operations in 1998, will feature a plethora of new technologies and strengthen Hong Kong's role as an aviation hub in Asia. Despite these successes, Hong Kong continually strives to improve its leading transportation infrastructure to maintain its role as a transport hub in the Pacific Rim, and to prepare for and promote rapid future growth in the trading economies of both Hong Kong proper and South China.

Much of the success in the transport subsector can be attributed to deep IT penetration in streamlining operations, improving efficiency, and enhancing effectiveness. Processes are carefully designed and engineered, and involve heavy investments in IT systems, including software development, database administration, and telecommunications networking for information sharing. In air cargo transport, a key contributing factor to HACTL's success is the tight synchronization between the movement of shipping information and the movement of air cargo. The company has developed computer systems for the real-time, economic allocation of resources (such as truck docks), logistics control (for cargo buildup and breakdown), and for initiating 'electronic actions' which are translated into 'mechanical cargo movements.' All this helps reduce human error, shorten dwell time (the length of time cargo sits in the terminal), and increase throughput (the flow of cargo through the terminal). This impressive performance also includes many convenient services for shippers and consignees—cargo tracking through the Internet, pre-arrival customs information and up-to-the-second cargo information. In sea cargo transport, Hutchison International Terminals Ltd. (HIT) also employs extensive automation in processes like terminal management, ship planning, tractor traffic control, and cargo tracking, among others. It has developed fully networked computer systems, the electronic linkage for which is progressively extended to HIT's customers to provide convenient communication and services. HIT's IT-enabled operations enjoy a high degree of real-time optimizations for cargo handling and storage. Its world record in 'container throughput per hectare' is achieved by the optimization of cargo stacking, within the constraints of incoming and outgoing cargo schedules, and the limited amount of land space available at the terminal. In passenger transport, MTRC has continuously partaken in major efforts of IT integration, sometimes reaching beyond the realm of transportation for the sole purpose of satisfying customers' needs. For example, a merger of the MTR systems with telecommunications supports seamless mobile phone services; and the Airport Express Railway under construction will support luggage check-in facilities at the central business districts. A particularly noteworthy example is the experimentation with a 'Contactless Smart Card,' a ticket which a consumer will be able to use across a spectrum of transportation modalities—railways, buses and ferries. The new Chek Lap Kok airport has centralized fiber backbone for communication, and its IT design stresses connectivity, integration, and interoperability across the various cutting-edge computer systems. These include a state-of-the-art security system, a high-speed baggage handling system, an advanced telecommunications network for telephone and mobile radio, as well as fully integrated flight information, terminal management, and business systems.

These success stories have all been 'Made in Hong Kong.' In the case of HACTL and HIT, the conceptual design of the cargo handling process, project management and software development were all accomplished locally. For MTRC and Hong Kong's aviation, we see the assimilation of imported technologies, and their subsequent and future coordination and integration by local talents. The end-product in each of these cases is the creation of a winning process by international standards, and from it grows a wealth of operational and managerial expertise. This expertise is potentially highly marketable, and its dissemination may transform the various 'Made in Hong Kong' phenomena into 'Made By Hong Kong' phenomena.

Recommendations for the Transport Arena

Our observations within the transport arena prompt the following recommendations.

Expand winning operations. With the construction of the Chek Lap Kok Airport and the massive Container Terminal Nine in Hong Kong, many of the aforementioned transport operations will be magnified to larger scales. As the transport processes are redefined and re-engineered, constant effort needs to be devoted to research and the use of technology in order to create new competitive edges. This may be done by identifying process bottlenecks and other hindrances towards improvements, and seeking bypass solutions through collaborative efforts and strategic partnerships. For example, many of the logistics management problems encountered in transportation activities (such as optimizing cargo utilization) are of major interest to operations researchers in engineering institutions. A number of companies are making headway in areas of electronic commerce related to transport. For example, Federal Express is distributing software to its customers for the automatic generation of shipping documents, and integrating electronic order entry with merchandise delivery.

It is also worthwhile to investigate how the successes brought on by extensive process-specific automation may be spread to other subsectors, especially software. HACTL, for example, needs to magnify its current software capabilities in anticipation of Chek Lap Kok's demands. The company has begun outsourcing partial software development to a local software firm. The firm develops process-specific custom applications for HACTL, with the intention of packaging and reselling the software in the future. In this way, HACTL's superior transport process, as well as its expansion, is helping fuel the local software industry.

Disseminate operational know-how. Hong Kong could provide fertile training ground for the dissemination of its operational know-how. Knowledge and technology can be transferred through consultancy or other contractual arrangements, across company divisions, companies, industries, regions or countries. While isolated examples of such activities have been found, such as MTRC's training programs for Guangzhou Metro in China,[18] and the localization of HIT's operation to Shanghai and other ports in the region, we feel that many more possibilities may be pursued. IT may also be used to raise the marketability of know-how diffusion, e.g., running multimedia simulations, and distance learning programs. The reach, range and speed of knowledge transferrals may thus be effectively increased to spread the 'Made By Hong Kong' phenomena around the world.

Develop a 'virtual total solution'. We would like to recapitulate our recommendation for the pursuit of a virtual total solution. We have seen individual fiefdoms of eminence in the various modes of transportation. It would be highly desirable to bring them into alliance by crossing the modality boundaries. Process chains in each mode of cargo transport may be desegregated electronically. The 'cross-modal systems integrators' can become the 'one-stop shops' for consumers in providing end-to-end, multimodal transportation services. A garment manufacturer who wants to move his products from South China to New York, first by rail, then via shipping followed by trucking, for example, may make the entire arrangements through a single point of contact. Cross-modality integration also opens up opportunities for optimizing logistics at the modality boundaries (the breakdown of a sea cargo container for loading onto a freight train, for example). In addition, a virtual total solution in transport may provide streamlining solutions with trade-related procedures in clearing customs, issuing bills of lading, and others. In this regard, we have observed initiatives in Electronic Data Interchange (EDI) for example, in the TradeLink[19] and EZ*Trade[20] projects. The territory's ability to select promising pilot programs, and implement them quickly and successfully, continues to be vital in sustaining Hong Kong's competitive edge and its role as the transport hub in the Pacific Rim.

Electronic Banking and Commerce

Despite its small size of 400 square miles and population of 6.3 million, Hong Kong ranks eighth in the world among the largest trading entities, and has a distinguished presence in banking and finance. The Stock Exchange of Hong Kong (SEHK) is the eighth largest stock market in the world in terms of capitalization, ranked after New York, London, Tokyo, Paris, Frankfurt, Switzerland and Toronto. Hong Kong's banking industry ranks fifth in the world in terms of external transactions. The territory houses a significant and diversified representation of international banks, including 85 of the world's 100 largest banks (ranked by assets).

With the onset of the information age, success in trade and finance is increasingly reliant on the sound management of information. In this regard, Hong Kong's trade and financial community is extremely 'IT savvy.' We observed numerous instances of the use of IT during our visits to the various financial institutions.

The Hong Kong Trade Development Council (HKTDC)[21] promotes Hong Kong's goods and services by serving as an information broker and matchmaker among traders, exporters, manufacturers, buyers, and service providers. It has a vast proprietary data bank of business information, including company listings and market and industry profiles, accumulated over 30 years. The HKTDC's matchmaking function is amplified worldwide by its global network of 51 offices which collect information from international buyers, promote Hong Kong products and services, and locate Hong Kong contacts for overseas businesses. Traditionally, the organization has distributed trading information by mailing its 17 trade publications to their respective subscribers. With the advent of the World Wide Web, the HKTDC introduced a host of electronic advertising and publishing activities to take advantage of the Web's instantaneous, low-cost information distribution to a wide on-line audience. The HKTDC homepage offers hypertext links to: the Hong Kong Trader, a monthly newspaper of market information; the Hong Kong Enterprise Internet, an on-line product catalog which supports rapid retrieval of homepages describing companies or products; and TDC-link, a real-time trade inquiry service which handles over 420,000 queries per year.

In the financial markets, the Stock Exchange of Hong Kong (SEHK)[22] boosted its efficiency in 1993 by introducing a computerized trading system, the Automatic Order Matching and Execution System (AMS). AMS bypasses floor traders' over-the-phone negotiations with an instant matching algorithm, thereby economizing response times and allowing transactions to be completed within seconds rather than minutes. Last year the SEHK introduced the AMS Second Terminal System to support remote, off-the-floor trading, and doubled trading capacity while maintaining fast transaction rates over a high-speed network.

In monetary affairs, the Hong Kong Monetary Authority (HKMA), Hong Kong's central bank, launched the Real Time Gross Settlement (RTGS) system at the end of 1996. This interbank payment system replaces end-of-the-day settlement with real-time settlement, and hence significantly reduces payment and settlement risks. IT has also intensified cost savings and convenience in the banking industry. An electronic banking transaction costs about 30 times less than a transaction conducted by a bank teller, prompting some banks to open a 'tellerless branch.' Automatic teller machines (ATM) are ubiquitous. Many banks have joined a debit network linking to the point-of-sale, and in some cases the connectivity extends to Guangdong, China. There are also other innovative banking services, such as the cash deposit ATMs, and DNA Alert as mentioned earlier in the chapter.

Hong Kong's distinguished presence in global trade and finance has been established with the help of a superior infrastructure—its rule of law, taxation policy, human capital, and increasingly, the use of information technology. Information technology applications will continue to bring about evolutionary and revolutionary changes, which are important to maintain Hong Kong's role as an international center of trade and finance in a new political, economic and technological epoch.

Recommendations for Electronic Banking and Commerce

All entities engaged in trade, monetary affairs, banking and finance flourish with information. Therefore, it is important that access to information continuously be made faster, cheaper, more reliable, and free of time or geographical constraints. Below we present three general directions for IT which would help improve Hong Kong's infrastructure for trade and finance. The furnished examples serve to illustrate our conceptual thinking, and are by no means exhaustive.

Install an 'electronic information exchange'. Widely accessible trade and finance information will empower and benefit both institutions and investors alike—from multinational corporations to local small and medium-sized enterprises, and from institutional to individual investors. We would like to generalize the model of the HKTDC in trade information provision, and propose the establishment of an 'electronic information exchange' (EIE) for trade and finance. We envisage the EIE to be a repository of trade and finance information. It should consist of a trusted party which could guarantee the truthfulness of its information through digital authentication. This process would be facilitated by a 'centralized' repository, or more appropriately, a 'virtually centralized' repository with software coordination across a cluster of physically distributed repositories. For example, one of the repositories should be a backup for EIE as a defensive mechanism (to guard against information warfare and accidental failures). The information should be made widely available through inexpensive means to subscribers or the general public. Therefore, the EIE should preferably be accessible from the Internet, and its information should conform to open standards. Such a high-volume information flow would need to be supported, and in this regard Hong Kong's telecommunications infrastructure should surely suffice. The EIE should also ensure that the content delivered to the consumer is timely, accurate and reliable. This would necessitate a suite of technological underpinnings, such as encryption, audit-tracking, and data integrity verification.

The EIE would be enriched by an increase in the disclosure of trade and finance information. The 1996 assessment of

Hong Kong's economic performance by the International Monetary Fund (IMF) Mission welcomes HKMA's initiative in 'enhancing disclosure requirements for banks, which will improve transparency and bank soundness.'[23] One precedent for the disclosure of bank information is the Institutional Directory (ID) System implemented by the US Federal Deposit Insurance Corporation (FDIC), which enables Web access to demographic data and financial profiles of each FDIC-insured depository institution. Another example is the US Securities and Exchange Commission (SEC), which ensures that investors have access to disclosed information concerning all publicly traded securities. This EDGAR (Electronic Data Gathering, Analysis and Retrieval) database is also accessible through the Web. A similar system for Hong Kong's financial markets may help promote market transparency and investor confidence. In addition, easily accessible filings for a small cap market (such as the 'T-shares' as proposed in the Chapter 13) may help increase the visibility of small and medium-sized enterprises and high-tech start-ups. It is worthwhile to point out that the concept of an EIE is not limited to trade and finance, but may also be ported to other sectors such as tourism, healthcare, and airline safety, among others.

Emphasize software development for content creation and retrieval. To manage a centralized electronic information exchange, one must ensure that the solution can scale up and be extended as the quantity of information continues to grow. This requires software tools for content capture, management, retrieval, as well as presentation for the end user. Providing a set of 'authoring tools' to the content contributors may alleviate the burden of information creation off the exchange. Meanwhile, control over the stored information could still be maintained at the exchange with a set of 'management tools'—for authenticating the information sources, confirming that the information is up-to-date, and incorporating it into the central repository. Additionally, a set of 'interface tools' would be most useful for real-time information repackaging into formats tailored to the preferences and needs of the end user. For example, a consumer may be interested in retrieving on-line information with spoken requests over the telephone, comparing different computer vendors based on price listings, performing graphical analyses of recent stock market trends, or viewing information from an English Web site in Chinese. These are examples of potential value-added services which may be provided by a third party between the information exchange and the end user. The first example calls for speech recognition and understanding software, while the last example calls for 'translingual' software for automatic translation between English and Chinese. It is worthwhile to note that bridging the English–Chinese language gap is extremely important for electronic information access, especially since English is currently the *lingua franca* of the World Wide Web, and Chinese is the predominant language of the burgeoning Asian economy. Hong Kong's bilingual populace should have a distinct advantage in undertaking the task of developing translingual software. Other issues concerning software development will be further addressed in the software subsection of this chapter.

Promote a 'virtual total solution' in electronic commerce. Commerce involves a legion of activities, including interpersonal communication, references to trade information, transfer of business documents, advertising and marketing, banking and investments, and bill payments. All of these activities may be distilled into the transferal of information 'bits' along a 'bit-way.' Therefore, electronic automation expedites many of the trading and financial transactions. The use of Electronic Data Interchange (EDI) in EZ*trade, for example, is enabling rapid communication between trading parties, and the RTGS system mentioned previously is lowering interbank payment risks tremendously. Existing examples of automation are plenty, albeit fragmented. Efforts should be devoted to further the extent of automation. For instance, RTGS is currently integrated with the Central Money-market Unit (CMU) for automated book-entry, bond clearing, and settlement. CMU, in turn, is linked across continents with London-based Euroclear and Cedel. This electronic channel for capital flow may be extended to the cash management systems in banks for their corporate and retail customers. As Hong Kong returns to Chinese sovereignty in 1997, there may be an increasing number of companies that choose to list on the Hong Kong stock exchange as well as other exchanges in the region. It would be advantageous to form better communication linkages among the stock exchanges to promote market transparency.

We recommend the development of a 'virtual total solution' to support the large assortment of activities in electronic commerce. Since abundant information is necessary for many of these activities, an EIE should be an integral part of the virtual total solution. Furthermore, the virtual total solution would require a high degree of connectivity and interoperability. A densely connected network would provide the 'couriers' of information to reach as many commercial parties as possible, and would permit all trading parties to interact with one another dynamically and freely. A common set of protocols and standards should be widely embraced by all commercial parties, so that the information is packaged in a way that is readily understood by everyone. This would achieve interoperability, and dispense with the costs of overcoming interface incompatibilities whenever a new trading relationship is formed. The Internet has hitherto served as an inexpensive substrate for worldwide communication; EDI standards are used in many value-added networks (VANs) for reliable communication of business information; and the World Wide Web standards are widely adopted for multimedia on the Internet. Technologies and standards continue to emerge to create a promising future for electronic commerce. One example is RSA cryptography[24] which can secure e-mail, Web sessions, payment card transactions, and more. The current snapshot leads one to posit that the convergence of Internet, EDI, and the World Wide Web through virtual integration may well bring electronic commerce to new horizons.

Software

There are some 500 independent software venders (ISVs) in Hong Kong,[25] about 60 percent of whom are engaged in custom software, as opposed to packaged software development.[26] These ISVs focus their business on supporting industries such as manufacturing and finance. In fact, these mainstay customers create pockets of excellence within Hong Kong's software industry. The demand-pull generated by sophisticated customers in specific industries forces software companies focusing on these industries to develop exceptionally competitive products. It is Hong Kong's strong financial sector, for example, that has allowed local software companies like ABC Data and TA Consultants to develop world-class broker and investment banking software. The pull from Hong Kong's vibrant textile industry drove local software company Prima Design Systems to become one of the earliest pioneers in utilizing color CAD systems for textile and garment design. Today, they are one of the top software companies in the world in that area.

Within the realm of custom software, some of Hong Kong's leading software vendors are capable of producing world-class products to support local and foreign industries. The industry is one of the best kept secrets of Hong Kong. The growth of the industry, however, has been stunted by several significant barriers. First, there is the problem with human resources. Throughout our interviews, we frequently heard the remark that the Hong Kong university system does not produce an adequate pool of local talent for the software industry. Of the talented individuals, more find themselves working in Management Information Systems (MIS) departments than in software development houses. In the United States, computer science students can identify the hot software start-ups, as well as the established firms. In Hong Kong, our survey shows that over 80 percent of computer science students in their final term of college have never heard of Hong Kong's established software developers, much less the start-up ones. This is partly due to the fact that the small ISVs cannot present themselves as attractive alternatives when faced with stiff competition, such as the MIS departments of large financial corporations, which can spend more time and money marketing themselves to students, offer enticing benefits like low-interest home loans, and foster the perception of stable jobs with better prospects for advancement.

Second, the value of software is poorly understood by the populace. Within the industry, the ISVs do not always recognize their software as a product in its own right. Instead, they often view themselves as their customers' MIS department. Software produced locally is more often than not customized to suit the needs of an individual client with little regard towards standardizing and leveraging. It is not unusual for a client to withhold payment and demand additional services and modifications even after the original product has been delivered and certified. The problem also permeates the populace at large. Despite the fact that Hong Kong has among the toughest laws and enforcement concerning intellectual property rights, the territory continues to suffer from some of the most persistent public violations of these laws. While the debate continues regarding explanations for such a paradox—ranging from the lack of intellectual property laws in China and the porous border between the Mainland and Hong Kong, to resources and coordination for enforcement—the consequences of such visible and rampant piracy are lost revenue for the software vendors like Microsoft and Electronic Arts. Perhaps more importantly, it also takes its toll on the indigenous software industry in ways that extend far beyond lost profit. One of the most damaging effects is in the way it shapes the attitudes of the younger generation—Hong Kong's software innovators of the future. They never learn that expressing creativity and innovation through the development of software can be a worthwhile and profitable career.

Third, there is a lack of a coordinated promotional effort from the software industry, the universities, and the government to ensure the long-term growth and stability of the industry. While there are a number of initiatives among the universities designed to nurture and promote the software industry (the Sino-Software Center and the Cyber Space Center at HKUST, for example, and similar activities at the Chinese University and Polytechnic University), none of the ISVs we interviewed acknowledged that they actively used these services. In fact, most were unaware that such programs existed. Lack of coordination between the Hong Kong government and industry has also presented a barrier to the industry's growth. One of the biggest local consumers of IT is the Hong Kong government, with an annual IT budget of HK$1 billion. Working on government software projects represents an excellent opportunity for local companies to hone their expertise while generating revenue. The Hong Kong Government's IT procurement, however, favors a 'system integrator' approach on large projects such as the Chek Lap Kok airport. This makes it difficult for local ISVs to compete with multinationals such as EDS, Anderson Consulting, and IBM, because they lack adequate experience in system integration.

On smaller IT projects, the government is likely to employ temporary consultants directly from 'Information Technology Professional Services' (ITPS), often referred to in the industry as 'body shops,' rather than working with the local ISVs. In either case, the local ISVs are not afforded a level playing field when it comes to government IT projects.

Finally, several ISVs have mentioned during our interviews that financing high-tech start-ups in Hong Kong is difficult, presumably due to a lack of a viable exit strategy for investors. This topic is covered in greater detail in Chapter 13, which deals with capital markets, and a near-term solution has been proposed until a NASDAQ-like mechanism can be established.

Recommendations for the Software Arena

Software is an environmentally friendly, high-value-added industry, the growth of which is being fueled by advances in computing and information technology, multimedia, and the Internet. Our analysis suggests that software may be an ideal high-tech industry for Hong Kong to promote. In contrast with other high-tech industries, software development needs little investment in land and other infrastructure. In many ways, we share the opinions expressed in the software consultancy report produced for the Hong Kong government in 1995. However, we do not believe the present climate in Hong Kong is conducive to *packaged* software development for the reasons outlined above. Removing those barriers will take time and effort. In the meantime, we believe the *custom* software industry can significantly expand its contribution to the Hong Kong economy. To develop this industry fully, however, the Hong Kong government and industry must take a number of actions, as recommended below. We will not address the issue of creating a capital market in this section, as the topic is covered in Chapter 13.

Develop 'process-specific' software products. Much of the custom software in Hong Kong is developed to satisfy individual clients, and there is often a strong demand for customization.[27] To fulfill such needs effectively, the ISVs must apply sound software engineering principles to ensure interoperability and ease of maintenance. To achieve software reuse and reap economies of scale, they must also move from custom software to 'process-specific' software by abstracting from the expressed needs of the clients the process that is common to all, and developing the necessary tools for rapid customization. This way, the software product will be able to serve the needs of specific industries, rather than only an individual client. Examples of such very successful development of process-specific software abound worldwide.[28] In the case of manufacturing, for example, the same software system can be used by one company to manage the production of aircraft and another for the production of automobiles. In the case of financial management, the same product can potentially be used by a company, a bank, or a university. Because of the strong presence of industries in Hong Kong such as telecommunications, transport, and finance, the software industry may be ideally suited for growth in this area.

Pursue niche markets for packaged software. In the area of packaged software, we recommend that Hong Kong pursue niche markets, building on its past success and leveraging off its competitive edge. Hong Kong has been successful, for example, in developing firmware for a number of consumer electronic devices such as hand-held telebetting devices and dictionary/thesaurus personal digital assistants. Such symbiosis between the electronic and software sectors can and should be nourished. Two other niche markets that leverage the unique cultural expertise of Hong Kong are localization of Western software for Asian Chinese markets (both within and outside the region) and the development of bilingual software.

Form strategic partnerships. Hong Kong's software firms are relatively inexperienced in packaging and distributing software. They may seek to form strategic alliances with branded firms so as to leverage off their marketing experiences and channels, while building up their own branded images. As a quid pro quo, Hong Kong may seek to establish distribution networks in the Chinese or regional markets, for both local and foreign software products.

Establish an industry presence. We see a real need for Hong Kong's software industry to establish a more visible presence. The industry must be able to promote itself to students in secondary and tertiary educational institutions so that they will begin to consider a software-related career. It should work with the universities to influence their curricula, so as to properly prepare the students for the profession. It should also explore developing internship and technology transfer opportunities with the students and the faculty. Finally, it must present a unified voice to government, and work with the government to ensure that intellectual property laws are maximally enforced. To achieve these goals the industry may have to create an entity to serve as its advocate, one that will play a broader and more proactive role than that of a mere professional organization such as the Hong Kong Computer Society.

The Role of the Government

Many of the strategies that we have proposed can be carried out within the private sector. However, certain actions can only be realized through government participation. In this section, we outline four general areas in which the Hong Kong Government must play a major role.

Identify and promote IT as a core competence industry. The importance of IT to the future prosperity of Hong Kong cannot be overstated. As a result, the Hong Kong government must identify and promote IT as a 'core competence' industry, serving as its mouthpiece. It must work with the IT industry to create a road map for technology development as well as use. The government must also serve as an advocate for small IT business, for example, by modifying its IT procurement approach to level the playing field. It must continue to invest in nurturing the IT industry through the appropriate allocation of start-up grants from the Applied Research Council, and perhaps by significantly expanding the Technology Incubation Program at the Hong Kong Industrial Technology Center (HKITC). Another key area that requires active government participation is that of intellectual property (IP) protection through tougher enforcement of IP laws by the IP Enforcement Bureau of the Customs and Excise Department.

Partner with industry in formulating infrastructure development strategy. The excellent telecommunications infrastructure that Hong Kong enjoys is the direct outcome of an industry monopoly. Without a monopoly, infrastructure development on a large scale can only be fulfilled with government's active participation. While the government need not, and perhaps should not, be involved with infrastructure development *per se*, it should partner with the industry to develop a strategy, and to ensure its proper implementation.[29] To increase the efficiency of trade and transport, for example, mechanisms must be established to standardize and make accessible information ranging from customs to settlement.

Educate Hong Kong citizens. In the area of education, the government can ensure that the universities' curricula will adequately prepare their students for a career in this area. It can help to promote better understanding of science and technology among the territories, through publication, science and technology competitions, and other media. Last but not least, it must promote an appreciation for the virtue of, and respect for intellectual property rights.

Improve and acquire IT expertise within the government. To carry out these responsibilities, the Hong Kong government must above all improve and/or acquire its own internal expertise in this technical area. Information technology is too important for the government to rely on occasional outside consultants to help her chart strategic directions. Instead, we recommend that the Hong Kong government consider forming an entity to deal specifically with IT, modeling after some similar organizations in other parts of the world. In the United States, for example, the Defense Advanced Research Projects Agency (DARPA) has been responsible for stimulating much of the IT innovations over the past three decades, including interactive computing, the Internet, and information security. Perhaps more important than the form of this entity is the requirement that it be staffed with technically savvy individuals who understand the technology deeply, and can identify future industrial needs. They must also be familiar with the local landscape in order to understand, strengthen, utilize and expand Hong Kong's assets and competitive edges. Most importantly, they must have the governing authority to push forth changes or programs, as well as catalyze their development and implementation.

APPENDIX 11.1: Companies, government and private organizations, and universities visited and interviewed by the Information Technology team.

Companies
Telecommunications:
AsiaNet
HK Net
Hongkong Telecom
Hongkong Telecom Interactive Multimedia Services
Hutchison Communications
New T&T Hong Kong Ltd.
P-Plus
Star Telecom
Wharf Cable
Transport:
Hong Kong Air Cargo Terminals Ltd.
Hong Kong Airport Authority
Hutchison International Terminals Ltd.
Kai Tak Airport
Mass Transit Railway
Trade and Finance:
AIA Investments
Dah Sing Bank
Hongkong Bank
IBM Greater China Group
Hong Kong stock exchange
Software:
ABC Data Communication
Creature House
Excel
FinaTech
Future Solutions Ltd
Integrated Solutions Ltd
MegaTrend Software
Microsoft
OnFlo Software
Prima Designs
Resource Technologies Ltd.
Software Industry Information Center
SuperLogic
TA Consultants
Unitech
Wing On Computer Systems Ltd.

Government and Private Organizations
> Hong Kong Article Number Association
> Hong Kong Civil Aviation Dept.
> Hong Kong Computer Society
> Hong Kong Customs IP Investigation Branch
> Hong Kong Department of Immigration
> Hong Kong Hospital Authority
> Hong Kong Intellectual Property Dept.
> Hong Kong Immigration Dept.
> Hong Kong Industrial Dept.
> Hong Kong Industrial Technology Center
> Hong Kong Productivity Council
> Hong Kong Secretariat Works Branch
> Hong Kong Trade Development Council
> Office of the Telecommunications Authority

Universities
> Hong Kong Baptist University
> City University of Hong Kong
> Chinese University of Hong Kong
> Hong Kong Polytechnic University
> Hong Kong University of Science and Technology
> Tsinghua University (China)

Others
Baker & McKenzie Law Firm
Gemstar, Pasadena
Gemstar, HK
Group Sense Ltd.
Jardine Fleming Holdings
Motorola
Hong Kong Jockey Club
South China Morning Post
Siemens
Television Broadcast Ltd.
Industrial Technology Research Institute (Taiwan)
Science Park (Taiwan)

Notes

1   For the purpose of the *Made By Hong Kong* study, we have adopted the definition proposed by the Hong Kong Government's Information Technology (IT) Committee in November 1992: 'IT deals with the capture, manipulation, extraction, and distribution of information in any form supported principally by elec-

tronics, computer and telecommunications technologies, including both hardware and software.'

2   The notion of providing a 'virtual total solution' is emerging around the world, brought on largely by the sharing of information infrastructure among the participants. For example, when flight reservation databases are shared by means of global alliances, a passenger can approach an airline counter, check in, and receive boarding passes for several flight segments on a number of airlines without dealing with a specific airline.

3   Hongkong Telecom (Hong Kong Telephone Co. Ltd.), Hutchison Communications Ltd., New T&T Hong Kong Ltd., and New World Telephone Ltd.

4   ITU World Telecommunication Indicators Database, 1994.

5   Asia–Pacific Telecommunications, November 1996.

6   Telecommunications Reports, October 21, 1996.

7   *South China Morning Post,* 'New T&T Brings In Portable Numbers,' January 21, 1997.

8   *South China Morning Post,* 'Telecom Eyes Optus Venture,' January 21, 1997.

9   CDMA is a terrestrial transmission technology that offers superior voice quality with an extremely efficient use of bandwidth.

10 Cordless Telephone 2 (CT2) is a digital technology which provides mobile one-way call out service.

11 An 'air loop' uses mobile radio technology, instead of the traditional copper or fiber media, for the last circuit link from the central office to the customer. It is an economical alternative to building basic telecommunications infrastructures in developing countries.

12 The 'fraudulent use of mobile phones' refers to the theft and illegal use of mobile users' phone numbers, codes, or calling card numbers, resulting in high phone charges. Some companies attempt to detect this fraud by monitoring customers' calling patterns and notifying them should any abnormal usage arise. The industry has not come up with a good strategy for preventing such fraud.

13 See the homepage of HACTL (http://www.hactl.com.hk).

14 Statistics from the Hong Kong Port Development Board, http://www.info.gov.hk/pdb

15 Mass Transit Railway Corporation, 'Mass Transit Railway Corporation Annual Report 1995.'

16 Mass Transit Railway Corporation, 'Performance Review 1995.'

17 See Hong Kong's new airport at Chek Lap Kok (http://www.hkairport.com)

18 The Guangzhou Metro in China has contracted with MTRC to learn the skills and knowledge to ensure high standards of management,

safety, and customer service. 'Mass Transit Railway Corporation Annual Report 1995.'

19 TradeLink, a service which allows businesses to submit trade-related documents electronically to the government. It will begin operations in 1997 in the textiles area.

20 EZ*Trade is a new service provided by the Hong Kong Article Numbering Association in partnership with IBM, to allow local businesses to connect with one another electronically.

21 See the homepage of the Hong Kong Trade Development Council (http://www.tdc.org).

22 The Stock Exchange of Hong Kong, 'Annual Report 1995.'

23 Hong Kong Monetary Authority, Press Release on December 18, 1996; see also '"Widely Held Confidence in Hong Kong" Prospects—IMF Says,' (http://www.info.gov/hkma/961218e.htm).

24 RSA is one of the most widely used public-key cryptosystems for both encryption and authentication. It was invented at the MIT Laboratory for Computer Science in 1977, by Ron Rivest, Adi Shamir, and Leonard Adelman (see http://www.rsa.com).

25 During the course of this study we visited 15 software developers, ranging in size from 3 to over 200 employees, with an average of 10 to 15. For a comprehensive report on the software industry, readers are referred to 'Consultancy Study on Hong Kong's Software Industry 1994–95 (Phase II Study—Market and Technology Trends Analysis),' commissioned by the Hong Kong Government Industry Department.

26 The development of packaged software relies heavily on significant R&D, a 'creative genius,' and marketing skills to move the products. Moreover, package software development is not location-based. In contrast, custom software development represents a partnership between the customer, who specifies the need, and the ISV, who attempts to satisfy it. Once the software is written and debugged, the work is essentially over; marketing skills come into play only minimally. What is important to custom software development is proximity to the customer, and familiarity with the customer's needs.

27 An independent software vendor mentioned that one of its clients, a popular franchise in Hong Kong, demanded that the software it orders be customized to each store.

28 See, for example, the homepages of Aspen Technology, Inc. (http://www.aspentech.com), SAP (http://www.sap.com), or Trilogy (http://www.trilogy.com).

29 This role, in the telecommunications area, is being admirably served by Office of the Telecommunications Authority, but government agencies must play similar roles in other IT areas.

12   Biotechnology and Hong Kong

Daniel I. C. Wang
James C. Leung
I-Ching Wu
Nicholas Gao

The field of biotechnology, or the application of biological systems and organisms to industrial processes, has grown to encompass extremely broad and diverse industrial sectors and a large number of products. The recent success of US biopharmaceutical companies specializing in recombinant DNA products—companies such as Amgen, Chiron, and Genentech, which together were valued at US$25 billion in 1996—has brought a great deal of attention to the industry and attracted investment in the development of biopharmaceuticals in the United States and elsewhere in the world.

Recombinant DNA technology has had a far greater impact on biotechnology than its original purpose—to produce proteins as therapeutics or diagnostic agents—two decades ago. When combined with other scientific tools, such as information technology and novel analytical techniques, it has created important breakthroughs in our understanding of various biological systems. In the United States and in Europe, the boundaries of the biotechnology industry, from a commercial perspective, have expanded rapidly to include areas such as genomic research, rational drug design, metabolic engineering, and combinatorial chemistry, among others. On the other hand, with much less fanfare, the traditional biotechnology industries—including pharmaceuticals, fine chemicals, food, and agriculture—have been embracing modern biological techniques as routine, essential tools for developing and improving their manufacturing processes and products.

The question we raise in this chapter is what future manufacturing role, if any, Hong Kong can play in the development and growth of this promising industry within Asia, and worldwide. Our goal, as part of the 'Made by Hong Kong' project, was to identify and evaluate potential areas of biotechnology manufacturing for Hong Kong. Our methods of study included: examining various publications; attending workshops and round-table discussions in the territory and in mainland China; and visiting with and interviewing government agencies, universities, and companies in the United States, Hong Kong, China and Taiwan.

The broad definition of biotechnology covers a wide range of industries and products well beyond the scope of this study. Since the aim of this book is to identify pursuits which could help significantly to strengthen Hong Kong's manufacturing sector as a whole, our study concentrates only on *high technology and high-value products* and industries. To further narrow our focus, we also evaluated what advantages and points of leverage the candidate industries could derive from location in Hong Kong, given its special assets, including its geopolitical position, private and public infrastructure, the quality of the workforce, bilingual capability, and formal and informal networks to neighboring markets. We also considered Hong Kong's potential constraints to industry, such as limited natural resources and the high cost of land.

With these criteria as the preliminary screen, we have focused our attention on biomedical products for human use, such as therapeutic compounds and diagnostic agents. We have selected three types of biotechnology products to evaluate for manufacturing in Hong Kong: Biopharmaceuticals (Recombinant DNA Proteins); Generic Pharmaceuticals (Antibiotics); and Traditional Chinese Medicine.[1]

There are other types of biotechnology research of social value to Asian countries—in areas such as agriculture and aquaculture—which we have excluded from our study based on our judgment that higher value overall could be attained in human biomedical products than in food products. Also, the markets for these food products are mostly restricted to certain geographical areas, thus limiting the potential to market them globally.

Hong Kong's own biotechnology sector is relatively low profile. Local pharmaceutical companies are small and engaged mainly in importing, repackaging and distributing bulk generic Western drugs or producing Traditional Chinese Medicine (TCM) products. Traditional Chinese Medicine is the most active area of research in Hong Kong—and potentially the most promising for manufacturing, in our view. While some research is conducted by Hong Kong universities on recombinant DNA technology similar to that carried out in the United States and Europe, no biopharmaceuticals (recombinant DNA proteins) have been developed in or are manufactured in the territory. Some of the recombinant DNA research by Hong Kong universities is directed uniquely to the future needs of the Asian region; one could envision future payoffs to Hong Kong from these research programs. The universities, however, will need research and development support if these activities are to flourish as commercial successes for the future.

The question of whether the industry can evolve in Hong Kong depends to an extent, but not solely on technological development and capabilities. Market-driven factors, independent of technology—such as demand, market size, profit margins, barriers to competition, and government policies and regulations—are of equal, and possibly greater importance in determining the feasibility of biotechnology manufacturing. For that reason, we examine both the technology-driven and the market-driven factors for potential biotechnology products.

Recognizing that Hong Kong's domestic market is small and local demand alone could not support a sizeable expansion of the industry, it is important to understand the current and potential markets available elsewhere. We have selected, on the basis of market size, sophistication, and maturity, three other regions for study: China; the Pacific Rim region; and the United States and Europe.

China represents both a large potential market for biotechnology products and a potential source of technical know-how in certain areas which complement abilities in Hong Kong. Furthermore, China is regarded by many multinational companies (MNCs) as a significant future market for their products and services. These companies represent an opportunity for collaboration with firms in Hong Kong, but also possible competition.

The rapid economic growth of many Pacific Rim countries in Hong Kong's backyard, represents another potentially important market for high-value products. At the same time, some of these countries also plan to become major players in biotechnology in the global market. Both of these factors are assessed in our study of the prospects for high-value biotechnology products made by Hong Kong.

Finally, all of the leading biotechnology companies, including the multinational pharmaceutical companies and the 'recombinant DNA' companies have originated in the United States and Europe. Even if these models are not suitable for Hong Kong to copy, it is important to benchmark the industries in Hong Kong and other Asian countries against the technology and market leaders in the biotechnology industry as a whole. This helps to identify Hong Kong's strengths and weaknesses as a potential player in markets for the biotechnology products targeted in this study.

Biopharmaceuticals (Recombinant Proteins)

The advances in recombinant DNA (hereafter 'rDNA') research in the 1970s have been the catalyst for the evolution of the modern biotechnology industry. The United States has emerged as the world leader in the development and the commercialization of modern biotechnology. In the early years, rDNA technology mainly offered the ability to mass-produce specific proteins otherwise unattainable by synthetic chemical syntheses or most product extractions from natural sources. The wide applicability of this technology to the various sectors of biotechnology industry stimulated the formation of many different start-up companies, ranging from fine chemicals, to bulk chemicals, to agricultural uses. Most companies, however, concentrated on developing human biomedical products, therapeutics, and diagnostics.

The development and marketing of these products as human therapeutics are overseen and regulated by government agencies—such as the US Food and Drug Administration (FDA) and similar agencies in Europe and Japan—in most markets worldwide. In general, existing pharmaceutical regulations apply to biopharmaceutical products. In some cases, augmented regulations have been established to address issues specific to rDNA methodologies in the manufacturing and analytical areas.

Pharmaceutical regulations in the major markets are established to safeguard consumers. Developers and manufacturers are required to supply results from pre-clinical studies (using laboratory and animal systems) and clinical studies (using human subjects) to demonstrate the safety and efficacy (or effectiveness) of their products. These studies, which need to be conducted according to the standards established by the regulatory agencies, usually require a long time to complete and are costly to the companies developing these products.[2] Thus, companies involved in the development of pharmaceutical products, including biopharmaceuticals, must plan to operate under the long product development cycle, which ranges from three to ten years. They must also be able to finance the high cost of developing a new drug, which has been reported to range from US$125 million to $500 million.[3]

Most biopharmaceutical products have been developed as proprietary products (not in the public domain) in the leading markets. Biopharmaceutical companies, given their need to operate under high costs and long lead times for product development, have sought to maximized the use of patents to protect the intellectual property rights to their products. In 1994, for example, there were up to approximately 4,000 biotechnology patents issued in the United States, of which 67 percent were granted to US inventors. More than 15,000 patent applications in biotechnology were submitted in 1995[4] The existence of enforceable patent protection systems in the leading markets has arguably been the cornerstone of the biotechnology industry, including the biopharmaceuticals sector.

The Global Biopharmaceuticals Industry

Market Players

Since the formation of some of the pioneering biopharmaceutical companies almost two decades ago, many more start-up companies have been formed in the United States, and some formed in other countries. The United States continues to be the world leader in the development and commercialization of modern biotechnology, including biopharmaceuticals. The industry is made up of a large number of players. (In 1994 close to half, or 42 percent, of the 1,311 US biotechnology companies belonged to the human health care biopharmaceutical industry. Among the 265 publicly traded biotechnology companies, the proportion involved in human therapeutics was even higher at 69 percent.) The major players, however, are the successful survivors of the first generation companies, such as Amgen, Biogen, and Genzyme, which are now independent and established companies with substantial resources and product revenues. Many of the multinational pharmaceutical companies, such as Roche, American Home Products, Bristol–Myers Squibb, Eli Lilly, Merck, Norvatis (Ciba–Geigy and Sandoz), SmithKline Beecham and Schering–Plough have also become major players in this field. They have used their financial, marketing strengths, and infrastructures to form strategic alliances with more innovative, smaller companies. Since the late 1980s, cash-rich multinational pharmaceutical companies have used mergers and acquisitions to acquire directly and quickly products, technology, and innovations.

Industry Performance

From an industry perspective, the performance of the biotechnology industry appears to be respectable; the 1995 market capitalization of all public companies in the industry was valued at US$51 billion. It is important to note, however, that a significant portion of this figure was accounted for by the capital valuation of a small number of the top-tier companies, which were operating with positive earnings. The rest of the valuation was based on the large number of companies operating with losses. In fact, in 1995, total losses to the industry amounted to US$4.6 billion.[5]

Though the financial performance of the top-tier companies in recent years has been excellent, the track record of product development by the industry as whole has not met the expectations of many investors. Of the thousands of products under development in the last two decades, so far only 35 have been approved and are available in major markets throughout the world. The combined worldwide sales revenue of the major biopharmaceutical firms was more than US$6.8 billion in 1996.[6]

The biopharmaceuticals industry, however, continues to attract investment with the potential it offers.[7] In 1996, for example, there were 127 human health care biopharmaceuticals reported in Phase III (the final phase) clinical trials.[8] Despite investor confidence, however, investment in the biotechnology industry (including biopharmaceutical companies) remains risky.

Elements of the Industry's Success

Technology Capability and Commercial Experience

The robustness of the US biopharmaceuticals industry and the spectacular performance by the top-tier companies were the results of a combination of critical factors. One of these factors was the US capability to develop the needed technology. Recombinant DNA technology was a product of the US research and development infrastructure embedded in its academic institutions, hospitals, and government organizations, such as the National Institutes of Health (NIH) and National Science Foundation (NSF). The research and development infrastructure in the United States has been strongly and continuously supported by the government and private sector for decades.

Though the technology was not originated by the industry, many of its pioneers came from academia; others from the established pharmaceutical industry joined the start-up biotechnology companies. These veterans brought the critical business and technical know-how enabling the survival and growth of the industry. For example, the ability to select the appropriate disease indications and market targets based on commercial experience is one of the strengths of the leading biopharmaceutical companies. The continuous migration of the workforce from the pharmaceutical industry to the growing biotechnology companies also has been a key factor in the successful development of the biotechnology industry.

Regulatory Environment

The development and the manufacturing of pharmaceuticals is a complex and technically sophisticated process requiring expertise from multiple scientific and technical disciplines. The successful supervision and regulation of such processes requires the same (or similar) levels of technical sophistication and know-how on the part of regulators as that of developers. In the major markets such as the United States and

Europe, the infrastructure of these regulatory agencies are structured to meet this requirement. The ability of the regulatory body to change and grow to deal with new and advanced technology is instrumental to the rapid adoption of new technology in the pharmaceuticals market. This is illustrated by the US FDA, which has worked closely with the US scientific community and the biopharmaceuticals industry in the formulation of practical policies and regulations toward the commercial application of the rDNA technology. By contrast, in Europe problems arose regarding the siting of facilities with rDNA research and development. The public policies in Germany that reflected public fears restricted commercial biotechnology activities there.

The Availability of Financial Resources

In the United States, where many of the capital-intensive biopharmaceutical companies are started, the availability of venture capital funding for high-technology industries is key to the existence of the industry today. There are many reasons for the availability of venture capital funding in the United States. One of the important factors is the existence of an enforceable intellectual property rights protection system. The protection by patent laws of the company's major assets, product inventions, and concepts, assures the investors of the potential value of the product and the company.

The multinational pharmaceutical companies also play important financial roles in the development of the biotechnology industry in the United States. In the early stages, these MNCs were investing in the smaller biotechnology firms through product-licensing agreements. As the biotechnology industry has evolved in recent years, however, the MNCs are increasing their financial roles significantly through merger and acquisition transactions.

The Biopharmaceutical Industry in Hong Kong

To obtain a general picture of the present status of the Hong Kong biopharmaceutical industry this team held a workshop attended by the Hong Kong pharmaceutical companies, universities, and government. We also interviewed the biotechnology community both at Hong Kong universities and within government. Lastly, we visited a number of Hong Kong pharmaceutical companies. These meetings inform our assessment of the status of biopharmaceutical research, development and manufacturing in Hong Kong and our recommendations as to what role Hong Kong could play in biopharmaceutical manufacturing.

Commercial Experience

Pharmaceutical companies in Hong Kong today are relatively small and number over 100.[9] All of these are involved in the sale of generic products. They do not manufacture bulk pharmaceuticals, but import generic products from elsewhere and their main functions are tableting (producing pills) and packaging. Furthermore, most of these products are over-the-counter remedies and, to a lesser extent, generic prescription drugs. Since most of these companies market their products locally and to the surrounding regions, their facilities and operations need only meet the local regulatory standards in Hong Kong.

The Hong Kong government is imposing gradually the requirements of Good Manufacturing Practices (GMP)[10] on pharmaceutical manufacturers in Hong Kong. It seemed evident from our discussion with local manufacturers and through our site visits, that some of the existing companies will not be able to fund the upgrade of their facilities and operations to meet these requirements. We did find, however, that the facility set-up, equipment, and operations of some of the leading companies would be able, with minimal additional effort, to meet the proposed GMP requirements, and possibly the more stringent international standards. We also found that while the technical and managerial leaders are usually trained abroad, most employees were local people educated in Hong Kong. Strong technical know-how, management skills, and a disciplined workforce are critical elements to a high standard in all pharmaceutical manufacturing activities, and our observations of the leading companies in Hong Kong suggested that a trainable and disciplined workforce exists in Hong Kong for pharmaceutical manufacturing. We conclude, however, that Hong Kong is facing many other hurdles to successful entry into biopharmaceutical manufacturing.

We did not find, through our workshop with government representatives, company visits, and research, any Hong Kong pharmaceutical companies involved in the sale of biopharmaceuticals (rDNA proteins). Nor did we find any research or development activities within the Hong Kong pharmaceutical companies. Therefore, one would not expect any drug discoveries or biopharmaceutical manufacturing to originate from the territory's industrial sector.

Research Activities

There have been some efforts in the last few years to initiate biotechnology activities in Hong Kong. Public funding, on the order of HK$300 million (US$39 million), allocated through the Royal Hong Kong Jockey Club, was put into the development of two separate institutes in Hong Kong: the Hong Kong Institute of Biotechnology (HKIB) and the Biotechnology Research Institute (BRI). While the BRI has been set up as a virtual center operating inside the Hong Kong University of Science and Technology (HKUST), the HKIB was set up as an independent institute with its own site and building located near the Chinese University of Hong Kong (CUHK). The funding was in the form of a one-time grant to these entities. Both the BRI and HKIB thus far have used the grant money mainly for procuring equipment or building construction, leaving little money left over for actual research and development work.

The biotechnology team for this study also visited a number of Hong Kong universities to assess their research in rDNA technology and found a number of them actively engaged in research in this area. Some of the projects, such as protein engineering, neuroscience, rational drug design, biosensor development, diagnostics development (monoclonal antibody-based and DNA-based) are similar to research activities in the United States and Europe, using modern molecular biology techniques. More intriguing is the research addressing diseases, such as thalassemias and malaria, most prevalent in Asia. From our visits in Hong Kong, however, we were not able to find any new products at the discovery stage which might be implemented immediately in Hong Kong. On the other hand, discoveries for some specific diseases in Asia could come in the foreseeable future.

Education and Training

The most positive and promising aspect for Hong Kong's future in biotechnology development and manufacturing is the potential of its educational and training programs. At the undergraduate level, the curricula—including biology, biochemistry, zoology and chemical engineering—compare well with Western countries. The combined student population enrolled in these curricula is substantial; in 1996 there were over 1,000 graduates and over 250 graduate students combined in three of the universities.[11] Since there is no pharmaceutical industry in Hong Kong, however, there is concern about the placement of these undergraduates. Although the research at the universities is conducted at the post-graduate level, we found the number of post-graduate candidates, especially doctoral students (who make up less than 15 percent of the post-graduate number) at best very minimal. Again, this is not too surprising, since there would be rather limited industrial opportunities for such graduates.

Regulatory Environment

The Hong Kong Department of Health oversees the manufacturing and marketing of pharmaceuticals in the territory. Market approval of pharmaceuticals in Hong Kong is administered by the Department of Health and it is based solely on previous approvals obtained in those foreign countries deemed to have adequate regulatory measures. Hong Kong has not approved any pharmaceuticals on its own. From our interview conducted with the Department of Health, we do not believe there are adequate regulations or technical abilities in Hong Kong's regulatory agency to review applications of pharmaceuticals not approved elsewhere. As stated above, the role of a technically sophisticated and pro-active regulatory agency, such as the US FDA, has been critical to the success and growth of the industry. The lack of a more sophisticated agency in Hong Kong, we believe, would be a major barrier to Hong Kong's entry into biopharmaceuticals manufacturing.

The establishment of a stronger and more technically savvy agency will be required, therefore, not only for the development, manufacture, and commercialization of biopharmaceuticals, but for other human drugs as well.

Experience in Financing the High-Risk, High-Technology Industry

We learned, through our investigations and meetings with investment companies and the business community in Hong Kong, that there has been little or no precedent for venture fund investment in biotechnology-based industry in Hong Kong. Biotechnology is generally viewed by many investors as a high-risk and relatively immature field of technology. (For more about capital markets, and venture capital and industry in Hong Kong, see Chapter 13.)

The Growing Biopharmaceuticals Industry in China

In contrast with Hong Kong, the biopharmaceutical industry in China appears to be rapidly expanding. We found evidence in the following areas of the promise of growth for this industry in China.

Government Commitment

Biotechnology development in China is centrally coordinated under the Chinese government's national policy, which we found to be relatively proactive and well defined. The State Science and Technology Commission (SSTC) is the national agency which oversees the research and development of biopharmaceuticals. The SSTC has implemented a program for China called the '1035 Project' intended for completion by the year 2000. The '10' refers to the goal of developing ten new drugs. The '3' and '5' refer to the goal of forming five establishments in each of three areas of expertise required for drug development. The three areas are: Good Laboratory Practice (GLP) laboratories; Good Clinical Practice (GCP) laboratories; and drug screening centers.

Under the auspices of the SSTC, the China National Center of Biotechnology Development (CNCBD) serves as the primary agency to initiate and develop rDNA technology. It selects and supports research and development by allocating government grants to the academic institutes, government institutes, and industry. The Shanghai Research Center of Biotechnology, for example, is such an enterprise supported by the China National Center for Biotechnology Development.

It is difficult to predict the outcome of the ambitious '1035' plan as stipulated by the SSTC, since there is no recent precedent for plans on a similar scale for pharmaceuticals in China. But the industry clearly has been growing rapidly, especially in the major industry areas such as Shanghai, Beijing, Shenzhen, and industrial activities are supported strongly by the city governments. Though the biopharmaceutical products made in China are mostly replicas of products originally developed elsewhere, the skills and knowledge developed today by the biopharmaceutical industry in China will contribute significantly toward the '1035' plan.

Commercial Activities

Since China did not recognize, and thus does not protect, international patents filed outside of China prior to January 1993, all of the rDNA proteins discovered in the United States or Europe are under research or development on the Mainland. These include alpha interferon, beta interferon, interleukin-2, erythropoeitin, C-GSF, hepatitis B vaccine and others. These activities are being conducted at universities, government institutes and private companies.

The number of companies involved in biopharmaceutical products has been increasing rapidly in recent years. While we were unable to obtain the most recent national statistics for the industry in China, there were over 20 companies in Shenzhen[12] alone engaging in the development and production of biological products, most of them based on rDNA technology. Most of these companies are located in the industrial park planned by the city government. We found a similar level of activities in research, development, and commercialization of rDNA-based products in Shanghai and Beijing. The State Pharmaceutical Administration of China (SPAC) revealed in our interview that at least ten companies have market approval for biopharmaceuticals in China. Of the many rDNA manufacturing plants in China, none has been inspected or approved by the US Food and Drug Administration or other foreign regulatory agencies.

The description below of two manufacturing facilities in China should help to give a picture of industry activities on the Mainland:

The largest biological protein production facility is the National Vaccine and Serum Institute located in Beijing, China. This Institute was established by the government in 1958. The total plant site is over one million square feet and the Institute employs 1,600 people. Their product portfolio includes more than 100 different protein biologics. The major biologics are derived from human blood such as human serum albumin, Factor VII, Factor IX and others. This Institute is also responsible for the manufacturing of all types of vaccines, recombinant and non-recombinant, used in China. The vaccine using rDNA technology produced at this Institute is Hepatitis B vaccine licensed from the Merck & Co. (USA). China produces about 60 million doses of Hepatitis B vaccine, of which one-third employs rDNA technology and two thirds is derived from blood plasma.

The Shenzhen Kangtai Bioproducts Co. Ltd., which was established in 1992 is partly state-owned and partly private. Its main product is recombinant Hepatitis B vaccine. There are 180 people employed at this manufacturing site. The license fee to Merck & Co. was reported to be US$7 million. The technology transfer was achieved by participation of the Chinese operating personnel at the Merck site in the United States. The process technology as well as the equipment, designed modularly, was transferred from the United States to Shenzhen. After the transfer, the manufacturing is operated independently by Kangtai Bioproducts' personnel. The price of the vaccine is government-regulated. The price for three doses was only RMB12.00 (US$1.50). In comparison, the cost of Hepatitis B vaccine in the United States is US$15 per dose.

The Regulatory Environment in China

It was clear from our visit to the State Science and Technology Commission (SSTC) and State Pharmaceutical Administration (SPAC) of China that the Chinese government recognizes the importance of China's ability to meet international regulatory standards for pharmaceuticals, including biopharmaceuticals. In the past few years, SPAC and other agencies have amended the regulations for pharmaceutical development and production, modeling them after some of the established standards outside of China. The government also recognizes that the standards of China's products and the standards of the regulation process can improve as these regulations are successfully implemented. At this time, their implementation is still very much in progress.

The promotion of the biopharmaceuticals industry by the government in recent years has resulted in the review of biopharmaceutical applications originating from Chinese biopharmaceutical companies. Though we were unable to obtain the total number of biopharmaceutical approvals in China, from individual visits with various companies, we learned that there were approvals for Hepatitis B vaccine, alpha interferon, and interleukin-2. These are replicas of biopharmaceuticals originally discovered outside of China and then developed and manufactured by local Chinese firms. Though details of the sophistication and rigor of the Chinese approval process were proprietary and thus unavailable to us, the very existence of a system and regulations on the books to deal with these kinds of products suggests a certain technical ability within the Chinese regulatory system which is lacking in Hong Kong.

Recommendations for Hong Kong

We evaluated several critical factors relevant to the biopharmaceuticals industry in Hong Kong and found that there is an absence of commercial experience, product development, manufacturing, sales and marketing. The regulatory ability in Hong Kong at present is not capable of supporting a more advanced pharmaceuticals industry employing sophisticated technology such as rDNA technology. Both commercial experience and regulatory ability in Hong Kong are not only behind that of the leading markets in the world, but they are behind that of China. Furthermore, we did not find in Hong Kong the requisite venture capital funding available for 'high-risk' enterprises. We have therefore concluded that Hong Kong should not consider biopharmaceutical development and manufacturing as a priority area for expansion at this time.

Generic Pharmaceuticals

Generic pharmaceuticals are products which contain the same active ingredients as brand name products and are used as substitutes for the original products. This industry is one area in which Hong Kong companies do play a role—not as bulk producers, but as local processors and marketers—and an area in which, as mentioned above, we feel Hong Kong could play a greater role in manufacturing.

Generic pharmaceuticals are sometimes referred to as 'multi-source pharmaceuticals,' since they are produced by many manufacturers in addition to the original developers. This can occur when the patents for the original brand name products expire. It can also be the result of differences in patent laws across countries.

There are two types of generic pharmaceuticals: over-the-counter (OTC) products and prescription (Rx) drugs. Although, OTC products made up a significant portion of total pharmaceutical sales. In 1994, of the US$227 billion worldwide pharmaceutical market, OTC product sales accounted for $38.9 billion (17 percent).[13] This ratio is relatively similar to the major pharmaceutical markets, for example, 22 percent in the United States.[14] We decided not to include the OTC products in our evaluation because they are of lower commercial value and thus reduced profit margins. Furthermore, the issues facing OTC products, which mainly related to marketing and sales concerns, are quite different from those for prescription products, .

The Impact of Regulations on Generic Pharmaceuticals

The regulatory regimes for pharmaceuticals in the United States and Europe are considered to be the most sophisticated in the world and serve as models elsewhere. As the exchange of goods and services between different regions in the world are increasing rapidly driven by business globalization, variations in pharmaceutical regulations across regions are diminishing rapidly, with the highest standards predominating. We focus here, therefore, on issues brought about by the US or European regulations on generics products.

The generic market in the United States has grown rapidly as a result of the 1984 legislation relaxing requirements on off-patent products. The Waxman–Hatch Act requires a manufacturer to demonstrate the chemical equivalency of a generic product to the original drug, including such aspects as active ingredients, dosage form, potency, and method of administration. The manufacturer must also demonstrate bioequivalency—measured as the rate and extent of absorption of the active ingredient—between the two products.

FDA approval of a generic drug depends heavily on the clinical testing data of the original, patented drug. It also depends on the ability of the manufacturer to meet the regulatory requirements for ensuring the maintenance of product quality standards. Thus, the regulations for generic drugs allow for a shortened product development cycle, especially in the area of clinical trials. While the typical development time for an original product ranges from five to ten years, the development time of a generic product could range from one and a half to three years.

Stringent requirements on manufacturing—in the areas of facilities, trained personnel, and operating procedures, among others—remain necessary to produce high-quality pharmaceuticals. The capital requirement for the development of a generic pharmaceutical, therefore, while substantially lower than for an original product, or New Chemical Entity (NCE), is still significant. The capital costs for most pharmaceutical plants, for example, are on the order of tens of millions of US dollars. Generics generally sell at 30 to 60 percent below their brand-name counterparts.[15] Lower pricing for these products makes lowering production costs, or cost of goods sold (COGS) more important. Since the cost of production depends on the sophistication of the technology and the ability to implement the technology efficiently, the role of manufacturing technology is of great importance in this industry.

Generic Pharmaceutical Market

Generic pharmaceuticals in the US and European markets are derived from brand name products after their patents expire. In China, pharmaceuticals protected by foreign patents which were not recognized by local patent laws can be manufactured and marketed freely. The 1994 GATT agreements attempt to harmonize the differences of the varying patent laws in many regions in the world. Still, many pharmaceuticals with foreign patents granted before 1993 are not protected and they can be replicated as generics by other manufacturers in China. Since the most available pharmaceuticals in China belong to this category, most Western pharmaceuticals used in China could be considered as generic products. While there are many common issues for the generic pharmaceutical industries in China and other regions outside of China, many issues are unique to the China market and these will have relevance to Hong Kong in any future collaboration in this sector.

Pharmaceutical Market in China

The pharmaceutical industry within China has been growing steadily in recent years. The turnover for Western pharmaceuticals increased from 35 billion to 59 billion RMB (at constant 1990 prices) between 1991 to 1994, with an annual growth rate of about 16 percent for the past two years in the period[16]—a small fraction of the overall pharmaceutical market worldwide. Since the products were produced as generics with prices much lower than the other major markets for comparable products, the unit volumes of pharmaceutical products produced and consumed are substantially larger than reflected by the dollar value of these products.

Of the many Western pharmaceuticals produced and sold, anti-infectives ranked first in production and usage in China. Antibiotics are the major products in this class. Six of the ten best selling Western medicines in China between 1991 and 1992 were antibiotics[17] In 1992, the top-ranking product was penicillin injection, sales of which amounted to RMB350 million (close to 1 percent of the overall pharmaceuticals market in China at that time).

The importance of antibiotics in China is reflected in the government emphasis on these products, since the production of pharmaceuticals in China until recently was centrally directed. In 1994 the top five bulk pharmaceuticals produced in China were antibiotics, including penicillin, streptomycin, chloramphenicol, tetracycline, and oxytetracycline. The combined output of these antibiotics topped 19,500 tons (metric) utilizing about 70 percent of the 27,500 tons capacity available in that year.[18] The large capacity for this class of products signifies the importance of these products and suggests that the Chinese industry will have to create new capacity and higher efficiency to support additional growth of the market.

Our research, including site visits and interviews with experts and authorities in China, suggests that the state of technology in the antibiotics industry—which has either been developed within China or was imported from Russia many years ago—is outdated. Before the economic reforms of the 1980s, the top objective for the manufacturer was producing quotas set by the state. With no market pressures, efficiency to yield lower manufacturing costs was not a major issue. Today, by contrast, state-owned pharmaceutical companies need to calculate their own profits and losses and to focus on process efficiency. Many of them are just beginning to improve their process performance; this creates a window of opportunity for newcomers, including Hong Kong, to play a role in this industry.

We visited three antibiotic manufacturing plants in China—the top producers of some antibiotics in China and representative of other pharmaceutical plants there—and found their facilities quite old and their process technology inefficient. There has been a lack of capital to update and retrofit these plants to world standards. The current situation offers an opportunity for the initiation of new manufacturing facilities which could compete on a global scale. We see this need for modern plants as one possible high-technology manufacturing opportunity for Hong Kong.

Another opportunity for improvement in the pharmaceutical industry in China is product quality. The government agencies, such as the State Pharmaceutical Administration of China (SPAC) under the Ministry of Health, have been developing new regulations for manufacturers. Many of these regulations are on the books but not yet implemented. Quality not only involves the safety and health of the consumers, it also affects the potential to export pharmaceuticals, bulk or finished, to major markets outside of China, such as the United States and Europe, where product quality standards may be more stringent. The regulatory standards for pharmaceutical products and the means to implement systems to meet them are fairly well established in other countries; Hong

Kong could well take the lead in introducing such standards and systems to the industry, first within the territory, and then to the other parts of China.

So far, multinational companies have not been active in the antibiotic business on the Mainland for various reasons. Foreign firms are restricted in investment or participation in ventures directly in competition with some of the existing capabilities in China. Foreign participation in the production of some of the antibiotics, such as penicillin or chloramphenicol, for example, was forbidden. MNCs have also been very cautious in introducing the more advanced and sophisticated technology into China, in part because of the difficulty of protection of proprietary information there. Thus, market penetration by the MNCs is still in the early stages.

Recommendations for Hong Kong

Hong Kong's second priority for biotechnology manufacturing, in our view, should be the production of generic pharmaceuticals, specifically, off-patent antibiotics which are produced by fermentation processes. Our research on generic antibiotics has found more rapid growth in the use of generic antibiotics in Asia, particularly in China, than in the United States and Europe. By the year 2001, roughly US$15 billion worth of drugs will come off-patent in the United States and $6.5 billion in Europe. These off-patent drugs represents new opportunities for Hong Kong, which could begin to manufacture them for the growing Asian market.

China today is a major producer of generic antibiotics and manufactures over 25,000 tons per year of these products. Our interviews and visits in China suggested there is a great opportunity to update the manufacturing technologies, if generic manufacturing is to become a target industry for Hong Kong.

The leading concerns for the production of generic pharmaceuticals, specifically for antibiotics in China are production efficiency and product quality. We believe Hong Kong can contribute directly to the improvement of production efficiency by acquiring the advanced technology through in-licensing from technology leaders outside of this region. More importantly, the impetus for this recommendation comes from the potential for producing high-quality products by means of the disciplined workforce and sophisticated management experience in Hong Kong.

At present there is no antibiotics manufacturing in Hong Kong. Hong Kong's Health Department plans gradually to introduce Good Manufacturing Practices (GMP). Many of the existing pharmaceutical companies will not be able to invest the capital required to upgrade their plants to GMP standards. This would mean an erosion of what little pharmaceutical manufacturing presently exists in Hong Kong. Hong Kong could help to prevent this erosion and create new opportunities by introducing more advanced technologies in generic antibiotic production.

A manufacturing facility for generic antibiotics in Hong Kong could be used as a 'beta site,' with technology transfer to China as the ultimate goal. Hong Kong could bring to bear the quality of its own workforce, manufacturing abilities, and product standards, in future collaborative efforts and joint ventures with China, and thus help to increase overall the manufacture of generics on the Mainland. In our view, efforts to raise equity capital to construct a modern world-class manufacturing sector would stand a much better chance of success in Hong Kong, than in China.

Since China would be the primary target market for generic pharmaceuticals from Hong Kong, and also a potential recipient of the manufacturing technologies from Hong Kong, China should be considered a critical part of the vision and original planning for such a venture.

Strategies for Pursuing Generic Antibiotic Manufacturing

Hong Kong should begin by considering the manufacture of generic beta lactam antibiotics—specifically penicillin and cephalosporine—with China as the initial target market. China, as mentioned, is a major producer of penicillin and the major portion of production is consumed domestically. We found that the present penicillin manufacturing technology is significantly behind that in the United States and Europe. Chinese manufacturers, for example, have not advanced to computerized control in either upstream or downstream practices to improve process performance. (The product titer in penicillin fermentations is only about 50 to 60 percent of what is obtained in the United States or Europe.) More recent advances in product purification, such as whole broth extraction, are not practiced in China, further increasing overall production costs.

The second beta lactam, cephalosporine, was selected because it is the major antibiotic that China imports from the West. China does not possess the manufacturing technology for this antibiotic. The use of cephalosporine, however, has been increasing in China in the past few years. The manufacturing know-how for production of this and other antibiotics could help China to meet its future needs and to become less dependent on imported material. Enterprises or individuals who might be interested in exploring opportunities toward this end need to coordinate closely with the Chinese authorities, such as the State Pharmaceutical Administration of China (SPAC), which monitors pharmaceutical demand in China, and the State Science and Technology Commission (SSTC), which assesses the technology status and needs of China.

To manufacture generic antibiotics, there are a number of hurdles which need to be surmounted. First, it is necessary to in-license these technologies from companies with prior manufacturing experience. The most probable licensers would be those companies which have been in the production of these antibiotics but no longer manufacturer them [for example, Eli Lilly & Company (cephalosporine)]. The second type of alliance would be an engineering and construction company which has had prior experience in the design and construction of antibiotic manufacturing plants. The incentives for such an organization to be a corporate partner are twofold. First, it would be guaranteed to be the prime contractor for the plant's construction. Second, and probably more important would be access to future plant constructions in Hong Kong, China and elsewhere in Asia.

Other than the need for adequate capital to initiate manufacturing, which will require the private sector in Hong Kong to play a major role, the success of pharmaceutical production relies on a disciplined and experienced workforce and the maintenance by manufacturers of high standards for product quality. These are areas where the Hong Kong government can play a significant role. While a continuous commitment to training and education programs by the government addresses the long-term need for qualified workers, we believe there should be few barriers to the access of personnel from outside of the region in the short term. We also believe that it will be important to update the local regulatory agency. A functional and self-reliant regulatory system not only projects a positive perception for the products manufactured locally, it also improves the effectiveness of the supervision and regulatory functions, which is essential to the maintenance of high standards for manufacturers and their products.

Since the patent system in Hong Kong was developed independently of the Chinese system and it is more in line with the standards of the major pharmaceutical markets outside of China, Hong Kong would be limited to producing those products which are off-patent in the major pharmaceutical markets. But the antibiotics which we recommend most highly for production in Hong Kong are already off-patent, as are most of the top-selling pharmaceuticals.

Traditional Chinese Medicine

Traditional Chinese Medicine (TCM) refers to the practice of health care which is based on empirical experiences accumulated over a thousand years or more in China and other Asian countries. TCM encompasses several areas of health care—disease prevention; disease diagnostics; medicinal treatment of disease; and non-medicinal treatment of disease.

For the purposes of this study, TCM refers to consumable products, including herbal-slice products and formulated compounds. Herbal-slice products are herbs cultured on farms or collected from the wild, which have undergone some low-value processing such as drying and packaging. These products usually require further preparation, such as cooking with other herbs and ingredients, by the consumer. Hong Kong has not been a producer of herbal-slice products because of its limited arable land and climate. Herbal-slice products, therefore, receive lower priority on our list of TCM products.

A large number of processed herbal TCM preparations are available as formulated compounds in the form of ointments, patches, powder, tablets, or liquids. Some of them are based on traditional prescriptions consisting of multiple herbs and ingredients; others may consist of compounds derived solely from a single type of herb.

Despite the long history of Traditional Chinese Medicine, the worldwide TCM industry and markets are not as well developed as those of other health care products, such as Western pharmaceuticals. Consequently, detailed market data on TCM products are scarce or unavailable in many regions. Since most TCM products are based on herbs and many of the herbal products available worldwide are TCM-related—and the two share common technology, regulations, and marketing issues—we used herbal product data interchangeably with TCM data.

The Market for Traditional Chinese Medicine

In many regions of the world, herbal medicine (including TCM) plays an important role in health care. The combined sales of herbal medicine products in major markets around the world was reported at greater than US$12 billion in 1994[19] (see Table 12.1). These figures were small in comparison with worldwide sales of pharmaceuticals for the similar period. (Global sales of pharmaceuticals in 1994 amounted to US$195–225 billion.)[20] The annual growth rates of herbal product markets were over 10 to 15 percent in most regions between 1985–1992.[21] In considering the potential growth of the herbal markets, it is useful to focus on the US/Europe and China markets, since they represent two very different situations and possibly different market trends.

Table 12.1
1994 Global Market for Herbal Medicine Products

Region	Annual Herbal Product Sales, in millions US $
Europe Union	6,000
Rest of Europe	500
Asia	2,300
Japan	2,100
N. America	1,500
Total	12,400

Source: (Adapted from Jörg Grünwald, 'The European Phytomedicines Market: Figures, Trends, Analyses.' *Herbalgram* 34, (1995): pp 60–65.)

The US and European Markets

The combined sales of conventional pharmaceuticals in the United States and Europe amount to about two thirds of the global pharmaceutical market. Herbal medicine, of course, plays a lesser role in these markets than established Western therapeutics, but this is slowly shifting. A recent study reported that as much as 34 percent of the US population used alternative therapies in 1990.[22] Herbal medicine, however, was only a small fraction of this total. Americans in 1990 spent an estimated US$13.7 billion on these therapies, which are used as adjuncts to (not substitutes for) conventional therapies. Despite the heavy reliance on reimbursement for health care in the United States, end users were responsible out-of-pocket for over US$10.3 billion of these expenses. Though these figures are of limited value in projecting the future US market for herbal products *per se,* they do suggest the growing acceptance of alternative medical treatments in the United States.

The acceptance of alternative medicines in Europe is more advanced than the US market, as indicated by its leading position in herbal product sales worldwide. In 1993, herbal product sales in Europe (US$6 billion worth) far exceeded sales in Asia (including Japan) where most of these herbal products originated.

While the sales figure in Europe was impressive, it still constituted a small fraction of total pharmaceutical expenses in that region. In Germany, the largest herbal product market in the European Union, herbal product sales (US$3 billion) were only 11 percent of the total pharmaceutical sales during the same period (1993). The comparable fraction for the US market was less than 3 percent. In both of these markets, due to regulations or marketing strategies, herbal products are usually sold as food supplements or OTC drugs at much lower prices than conventional pharmaceuticals. More consumers accept and use herbal products in these markets than is indicated by the sales dollar figures alone.

Despite the small sales volumes of herbal products in the United States and Europe markets, the growth trend is real and is supported by the growing acceptance and consumer demand. The large gap between sales of herbal products and conventional pharmaceuticals represents the potential for growth in these markets for herbal medicine and opportunities for Asian producers such as Hong Kong. The growth of herbal products in these markets depends on many factors, including the evolving regulatory environment in these markets, which will be discussed below; and, more importantly, the efficacy, safety, and quality of the products themselves.

The Market in China

As elsewhere, TCM and other alternative medical practices in China do not displace the role of Western, or conventional pharmaceuticals, but are used in a parallel and complementary fashion. Since the establishment of the People's Republic of China in 1949, the Chinese government has proactively promoted the coexistence of TCM and Western medicine. This policy has helped to make effective and affordable health care widely available and reduced reliance on Western pharmaceuticals, which are imported or more expensive to manufacture. The legacy of this policy is a healthy and increasing demand for TCM products, which made up more than one-third (37 percent) of the total medicine sales in China between 1991 and 1994. Sales of TCM products in China in 1993 were reported to be US$1.6 billion,[23] the largest herbal products sales in Asia outside of Japan.

Since health care expenditure is usually proportional to the overall economic growth of a region, pharmaceutical sales in general, and TCM products in particular, can be expected to increase with the growth of China's economy, and that of other Asian countries. The future growth of the TCM industry will also depend upon the provision of 'better' TCM products, products which are safer and more effective than existing pharmaceutical products, both TCM and Western. This represents a manufacturing opportunity for Hong Kong to exploit.

Traditional Chinese Medicine as a Source of Western Drugs

From a Western drug development perspective, one of the more promising aspects of TCM or herbal medicine, is the use of this knowledge for drug discovery. The wealth of information collected in the medical practices in China and Asia and the application of herbal preparations for health maintenance and disease treatment is well recognized and exploited in many cases by the pharmaceutical industry. Artemisinin, for example, which is also referred to as Qinghausau, was discovered from a TCM herb, Qinghao *(Artemisia annua L)*, and is used to treat malaria. A new oral anti-malarial, Cotecxin, an artemisinin derivative, was developed and granted production approval in China in 1996. (For a brief case study of its path of discovery and approval, see Notes.[24]) And, Taxol, which was approved for the treatment of breast and ovarian cancer was derived from a plant.

The use of plants and herbs as sources for new drugs is not a static endeavor. In China, as of 1992, about 200 drug products had been developed directly or indirectly from TCM plants.[25] In Western markets between 1980 and 1996 there were at least 60 drug candidates derived from natural sources, some of which became approved pharmaceuticals.[26] A recent successful example, was the US approval (in May of 1996) of topotecan for the treatment of advanced ovarian cancers. Topotecan is derived from the bark of a Chinese tree, *Camptotheca acuminata.*

The advances of other technological areas, such as computerized information management and automation technology, have made drug discovery from natural products more attractive than ever before. The application of these technologies could enhance significantly the ability to utilize the large, yet diverse and fragmented, collection of information on TCM products.

The Evolving Regulations for Traditional Chinese Medicine Products

One of the major hurdles to developing successful TCM, or herbal products in the major Western markets is the stringent regulatory environment for pharmaceuticals. The five-to-ten-year average lead time required to develop a pharmaceutical product, and the costs involved (from US$125–350 million) are major considerations.

Most of the regulatory agencies in these major markets, including the US FDA, are used to dealing with conventional pharmaceuticals, which usually consist of single active component, and the analytical techniques required for testing them. A product with two different active compounds would require two separate sets of preclinical and clinical testing: one for each compound. With the approval of the regulatory agency, a third set of clinical testing would then be conducted for the two active compounds combined. Thus the resources required to develop a single product combining two active ingredients may be as much as for three separate products.

Most TCM preparations are made up of multiple herbs and ingredients. The chemical complexity of the resulting mixture and the possible large number of active components within the mixture could be daunting from a drug development perspective. The regulatory obstacles in these major markets and the resources required to surmount them are the main reasons most TCM companies have chosen to market their medicines as food products. Regulations for food products in most Western markets, though relatively stringent in comparison with others, do allow the marketing of herbal products as food supplements. Manufacturers are required to clearly label their product, listing all of the contents, and are forbidden to make specific claims about the medicinal efficacy of their product.

The food supplement route for introducing TCM products to these major markets is a practical, short-term solution. In our view, however, this approach sacrifices the full potential of TCM products, or derivatives: the consumer may be only vaguely aware of the medicinal value of TCM products marketed as food supplements; and the manufacturer forgoes the greater returns brought by commercializing their products as mainstream pharmaceuticals in the most lucrative markets in the world.

Manufacturers in many industries regard the development of technology, product innovation, and the ability to meet regulatory requirements as major value additions. These hard-won abilities are also seen as barriers to competitors, thus enabling companies to retain the high value of product development. This is especially true in the pharmaceutical industry, as illustrated by some of the successful examples in bio-pharmaceuticals discussed earlier.

The commercial values of many pharmaceutical products are supported by health care systems in the US and EU markets which reimburse end users for the cost of medicines. Though in recent years, managed health care systems in these markets are striving to contain medical costs, the decision to reimburse medical treatments, including pharmaceuticals, is still mainly based on their effectiveness (as approved by the FDA or other regulatory bodies) and the availability of other comparable alternatives. Without FDA approval, reimbursement from the health care systems is unlikely. Furthermore, in the case of new pharmaceutical products, regulatory approval provides the added barrier to the availability of comparable products.

The success of the herbal product market in the European Union (the world leader in herbal product sales) in the last few years has benefited from the fact that Germany and France reimbursed 40 percent of all herbal products. The presence of a large number of reimbursable herbal products in Germany and France was due to the relatively relaxed regulation of herbal products before 1994. Herbal medicine will be regulated as drugs in line with newly adopted EU laws, and product registration will be based on quality, safety, and efficacy in the near future. Regulations will be unified across the EU market.[27] The impending changes in Europe further support the argument that TCM should be developed as pharmaceuticals for these major markets.

While changing regulations for herbal products are pushing the development of TCM as drugs, pharmaceutical regulations within the United States are also changing in a way that could make this route of development attractive. In the past few years, representatives from the FDA have been informing the industry of evolving attitudes within the agency toward the development of herbal products as drugs.[28] The clinical testing of well-defined, well-characterized 'single' components is no longer considered the only acceptable approach. The FDA is encouraging prospective companies to base the development of complex products, such as herbal products, on strong and scientific data in materials production, chemical analyses, and clinical protocol design. In fact, the existence of well-documented, clinical experience for some of these products in other markets is now treated as relevant to clinical testing in the United States. Clinical testing for at least one herbal product was allowed recently and several Investigation of New Drug (IND) applications for herbal products have been submitted to the FDA.

While the changing regulatory environment is a positive sign, it also signals the start of the race for the industry in this product category. Flexible and fast-moving companies may be able to take advantage of this new environment before other competitors, such as the MNCs who have more resources, increase the intensity of the competition.

Patent Protection for TCM Products is Difficult

The difficulty in securing patent protection has often been cited as the 'show-stopper' for many companies hoping to develop TCM-based pharmaceuticals. It is difficult to impossible to patent TCM products 'as is,' in areas such as composition of matter, use, and methods of preparation. These aspects are simply too well known to trained artisans in the field and are not considered proprietary knowledge in the Chinese cultural context.

If the development of TCM-derived pharmaceuticals is selected as an important manufacturing area for Hong Kong, as we recommend, it will be critical for the industry to maximize the use of patent protection. Many TCM products and the general principles behind them have been in existence for hundreds of years and have been available to the public-at-large. The empirical nature of their evolution, the large number of products, the complexity of their functions and their actions, have created a technical area which is not well understood in modern scientific terms. We believe that the possibilities for patent invention in the TCM field are enormous and real because knowledge in this area is increasing and could be improved further with directed efforts, which will lead to yet more discoveries. Most patent systems grant patents to herbal-based inventions and they are usually defended successfully, as evidenced by the cases of taxol, topetecan and others. The composition, use of, and manufacturing processes for these products are covered by patent protection.

Market Players

China

Of the many regions where TCM products are made and used, China, as one would expect, has the richest historical background, and most active centers of development. In general, TCM development is governed by rules and methods similar to Western medicine. While many pharmaceutical regulations are modeled after established regulations of high world standard, the implementation of these regulations is still in progress and the standards for product quality overall have not yet achieved international thresholds. Product quality, therefore, is still a concern for the TCM industry in China.

In the areas of product discovery and development, our impression from interviews and site visits was that China continues to rely on the exploration of hypotheses formed from manual research from modern and classical literature, and on intensive analyses of individual clinical cases. These methods, which mainly depend on the expertise of a limited number of people, are usually labor-intensive and relatively slow to achieve progress. Though some TCM concerns we visited told of plans and intentions to utilize modern technology, such as computer-based information management systems and advanced preclinical and clinical protocols, we were not able to see details of progress in this type of research in China.

Hong Kong

Sales of TCM products in Hong Kong are about equal to that of Western pharmaceutical sales in the territory. None of the 100 or so TCM pharmaceutical companies, however, engage in research and development activities. These companies are mostly sales and distribution organizations with some packaging capabilities for proprietary products, which are sold unregulated in Hong Kong and exported to regions outside of Hong Kong with significant ethnic Chinese populations. The academic community in Hong Kong is quite active in the area of TCM research; most of the various tertiary education institutions are engaged in some form of research in this field. One of the most common Traditional Chinese Medicine projects in Hong Kong is the construction of information databases. We learned of three such ventures, each distinctively different. The database at the Chinese University of Hong Kong, for example, is a compilation of scientific reports, including selected translations from Chinese sources and journal references; and the database at the Baptist University is aimed at providing a multimedia-type presentation of identification of Chinese herbs and methods for their preparation. Most of these projects are in the early development stages and thus it is difficult for us to foresee the outcome of these projects. Also, it is not obvious at this stage that whether and how these databases relate to each other.

We found, through our interviews, that a number of Hong Kong universities are actively planning research and develop programs to modernize TCM products, and some of these are underway. Many of the researchers at these universities have already begun to standardize and improve the quality of TCM products. In addition, they already are working to develop identifiable compounds from traditional products. Furthermore, Hong Kong universities are establishing networks and collaboration with research and development institutes in China. These recent developments certainly will enhance Hong Kong's overall capabilities for manufacturing 'modern' TCM products, should this become a priority area for development.

We did find some product development activities in Hong Kong. The most interesting example was a project which was originated by a university and is being developed in collaboration with an outside company. The dietary supplement product, which contains putative anti-oxidation activities, was discovered based on TCM knowledge. As far as we know, there are no development activities towards TCM-based pharmaceuticals in Hong Kong.

Hong Kong is in a unique position in this field of research. It is considered by many to be most progressive and successful in the application of information technology to a number of commercial activities. The Hong Kong scientific community's bilingual ability in English and Chinese is an important advantage. While Chinese language is important for collecting and interpreting information in a field mostly documented in Chinese, English is crucial for the exploitation of advanced information management and research techniques. English language ability is also important for bridging the understanding of information manipulation and research with current advances in Western medicine and biological science.

Europe and the United States

Europe is probably the strongest region in herbal medicine research and development outside of Asia, as evidenced by some of the research activities described in literature and conferences[29] and by the sales volumes of herbal products. The companies involved in the herbal product sales so far are smaller pharmaceutical companies such as Schwabe, Scotia Pharmaceuticals and others.

Herbal products in the United States, as mentioned above, are mainly sold as food supplements by sales and marketing organizations such as General Nutrition Corporation (GNC), whose sales in 1995 were over US$600 million for all food supplements. These companies have no research and development activities toward converting their product to drugs, or developing new drug products. Research activities in herbal medicine are scattered in both universities and government agencies, such as the National Cancer Institute (NCI). The efforts expended by the US scientific communities to this area amount to a small fraction of the overall national R&D effort in biological sciences.

Multinational pharmaceutical companies have not been actively involved in development of TCM products *per se*, but many, including American Home Products, Borehringer

Ingelheim, Pfizer, SmithKline and Beecham, Rhone–Poulenc Rorer and others, have entered markets through acquisitions of herbal medicine companies in Germany.[30] Published information from the MNCs indicates that these companies pay minimal attention to the development of herbal-based medicine. The reported MNC acquisition transactions in the herbal product market may position them to expand into this area quickly when they deem it appropriate in the future.

Recommendations for Hong Kong

We recommend that manufacturing in Traditional Chinese Medicine (TCM) become the highest priority for future consideration in Hong Kong. It should be stated emphatically, however, that we are not recommending the expansion of TCM manufacturing in the traditional areas of over-the-counter medicines or food supplements. What we are recommending is using Traditional Chinese Medicine as a base from which to embark upon new drug discovery leading to patent-protected products which will compete with Western drugs.

TCM, as described above, has a strong history in the prevention and treatment of a large number of diseases throughout Asia. Many TCM products, however, have not undergone the rigors of testing in comparison with Western pharmaceuticals; systematic toxicological and efficacy data—prerequisites for capturing key international markets—are as yet inadequate. But long, practical experience with various TCMs suggests a positive efficacy and the lack of toxicity. The cumulative, empirical knowledge of TCM offers a promising shortcut to the process of finding 'hits' for disease prevention and treatment. More scientific and systematic, data-based approaches are needed to improve further the probability of product success.

The second major reason why Hong Kong should make Traditional Chinese Medicine the top priority is the potential market size. China, and perhaps Hong Kong, in our view, represent the forefront leaders in the field. Hong Kong offers unique scientific/technological advantages to product development in this field. Extension into manufacturing could well allow Hong Kong to capture worldwide markets for some human health care products. Since time-to-market is the key to success in pharmaceutical ventures, actions toward commercialization should be taken immediately.

A third reason to explore TCMs in Hong Kong is the existence of a large library of compounds which have already been demonstrated as effective treatments for numerous ailments. Furthermore, these compounds of origin are well known (mushroom extract and *Gingko biloba,* for example) and thus avoid the problem of directed or random screening, practices used in modern drug discovery. These factors would reduce further the time for product development, which translates into reduced costs and earlier time-to-market. In addition, the availability of raw materials can be assessed *a priori* and reduce the burden of product sourcing which often plagues modern drug development. The large-scale production of Taxol is a successful case in point. Resource availability in a territory the size of Hong Kong, where most items for manufacture are imported, will always be a challenge; China will therefore be a critical player.

A fourth reason for Hong Kong to explore TCM manufacturing is that it is the strongest sector of biotechnology research and development within Hong Kong universities. It was quite apparent from our visits that these universities have had many years of research and development experience in Traditional Chinese Medicine. Furthermore, the academic community in Hong Kong already has established networks and cooperative ventures with TCM institutions in China.

A final reason to pursue this sector is the existing, indigenous TCM knowledge base. Many people in the Hong Kong medical research and health care community, as well as those pharmaceutical companies in Hong Kong which sell TCM products, are well familiar with the various types of herbal compounds and indications. This factor, coupled with the advanced information technology available in Hong Kong and its proximity and affinity with China, would present a formidable barrier to competition from the Western pharmaceutical companies considering joint development of herbal products in China. Here again, a close partnership with China is absolutely essential to the success of a TCM industry in Hong Kong. Through our interviews, we discovered that Hong Kong is well poised to develop this partnership; Hong Kong universities indicated that they have already established an excellent network leading to 20 to 25 centers of excellence in the TCM area in China. This further supports our recommendation that Hong Kong should make TCM-based pharmaceuticals a priority.

Technological Recommendations and Proposed Infrastructure

Proposed Infrastructure

Our conception of an infrastructure for establishing a TCM Company and strategical alliances in Hong Kong is shown in Figure 12.1. A private, for-profit, parent company would be established in Hong Kong. If a new structure for capital formation is established, such as the concept of 'technology shares,' this could offer investors an exit strategy for their private investments, and thus the confidence to commit their money to technology development companies. This Hong Kong company would establish the initial manufacturing facility in Hong Kong. The rights to product sales in the Asia region would be retained by the Hong Kong company, whereas the rights for manufacturing and sales to the United States and Europe could be licensed. The Hong Kong company would be responsible for research and development, as well as some of the other activities shown in Figure 12.1.

We also foresee needs from institutes in China, and from Hong Kong universities as part and parcel of the strategic alliance network in Hong Kong. These strategic alliances would take the form of collaborative research and development activities at the institutes and universities. Specifically, the Hong Kong company should negotiate contractual rights with these research programs through the financial support of these activities. At the same time, it is imperative that the Hong Kong company assist and guide the research activities to ensure their commercial relevancy.

Figure 12.1: A Conceptual Diagram of the Proposed
Traditional Chinese Medicine Company and Strategic
Network in Hong Kong

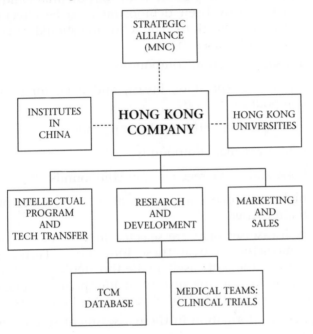

Other activities in Hong Kong should include the development of intellectual properties , marketing, and sales. Some of
the other activities of this Hong Kong company could include
the establishment of the databases, and the use of the databases to aid the medical team for product prioritization.
Lastly, we envision that clinical trials for potential products
be conducted either in Hong Kong or China.

Lastly, the establishment of 'virtual science parks' in Hong
Kong could offer the new Hong Kong company the required
space for its initial start-up and infrastructure. In addition,
the close proximity of the 'virtual science parks' possibly near
the universities, would be ideal for collaborations and technology exchanges.

Assessment on Existing Data

The first technological development towards TCM manufacturing is to assess the present status of potential candidates which have already been demonstrated to be effective in treating disease indications. The following should be considered for this initial assessment:

- anti-inflammation compounds
- anti-cancer (prostate, breast, and liver, for example) compounds
- anti-viral and anti-fungal compounds
- cardio-vascular compounds
- bone and nerve regeneration compounds
- high molecular compounds able to cross the blood–brain barrier

These disease sectors were selected in view of the lack of present medicine to treat these indications. Furthermore, since many of these diseases are life-threatening or have profound influences on the quality of life, pharmaceuticals to treat them represent ideal, high-value-added products.

The types of information in these assessment studies should include:

- past clinical data
- toxicological and safety profiles
- efficacy data

In addition, within the scope of these assessment analyses, the present status as to the availability of raw materials must be considered. Some of the criteria to be employed in these assessments should include:

- the location of the natural resources
- the seasonal availability of resources
- the availability of raw material (quantity)
- the cost of raw materials
- import and export regulations

Research and Development Recommendations

a. *Clinical Medicine Group*

Before any research and development is initiated, a 'Clinical Medicine Group' should first be established. This clinical medicine group would be part of the Hong Kong subsidiary company. This group must have representation from the medical communities of non-Asian regions (such as the United States and Europe). The other members of this group would be from the Traditional Chinese Medicines community but must also have a substantial knowledge of Western medicine. The Clinical Medicine Group would examine the potential of the existing TCMs with respect to efficacy on the various indications. The decisions from this group could be considered similar to those from modern drug development and discovery programs, where assignments on the probability for success of various TCMs are first generated.

b. *Research and Development Groups*

The research and development groups would also be part of the Hong Kong company and would focus their activities on the findings of initial assessments on the potential compounds which have already demonstrated some degree of efficacy and lack of toxicity. The research and development facilities and the personnel for this endeavor, however, must be of world standard. Their findings must withstand peer review in scientific journals, as well as pass the scrutiny of Western regulatory agencies (the US Food and Drug Administration and its equivalent in Europe).

The functions of the research and development activities would include:

- the chemical characterization of TCM compounds
- the standardization of product quality
- pharmacology and toxicology
- identifying mechanisms of action of TCM products
- in vivo and in vitro testing for safety and efficacy
- product and process development
- technical and economic feasibility studies

Prospects for Biotechnology Manufacturing in Hong Kong

After many months of research and analysis, we have concluded that Hong Kong could and should play an important role in the manufacture of biotechnology products. While competition is prevalent in most major markets for valuable goods worldwide, Hong Kong should focus on biotechnology products of high value with defined market targets. The selection of these markets should be based on their potential size, but more importantly the relative weakness of resistance to entry for competitors.

Specifically, we conclude that of the three product areas we evaluated in this chapter, new biopharmaceuticals should be the lowest priority for Hong Kong; fierce competition in the major markets for these products may be difficult to overcome given the current technical capabilities for biopharmaceuticals available in Hong Kong at this time.

The highest priority in our recommendations is the development and manufacturing of high-quality pharmaceuticals based on Traditional Chinese Medicine. TCM-derived products should be targeted to major pharmaceutical markets, including the United States and Europe, where these products are just emerging as potential health care products. Though competition in these markets is growing rapidly, it is not yet insurmountable and Hong Kong's knowledge of TCM products provides a slight edge over the competition.

The manufacture of selected generic pharmaceuticals should be the second priority among the candidates we evaluated for Hong Kong. The primary target markets for these products should be regions such as China, which are outside of the major pharmaceutical markets where competition is most fierce.

We consider these opportunities to be real and feasible. The successful exploitation of these opportunities will require the existence of many other elements: resources, the commitment of individuals and the business community, hard work by many people, innovation, perseverance, and possibly luck. We are convinced through our many contacts with people in Hong Kong that these are the exact elements which have been responsible for the success of Hong Kong, and their presence in Hong Kong, without a doubt, will continue.

Notes

1   Our study was broader than the material we have included for this chapter. The biotechnology team originally selected a fourth area of biotechnology to evaluate for Hong Kong manufacturing—medical diagnostic products. We have excluded this sector from our chapter due to space considerations and the fact that we concluded that this would not be a practical product option for Hong Kong. There is essentially no indigenous, medical diagnostic reagents industry in Hong Kong. There are a number of small companies in Hong Kong which are subsidiaries of US or European companies and they purchase or redistribute various products. The diagnostic industry is essentially absent from China as well. Most of the reagents from China are manufactured by small organizations and the product quality is quite poor. Furthermore, the market for diagnostic reagents in China, which would be the most likely sizeable target market for Hong Kong, is small when compared with that of the West. For example, a total of 30 million units of blood are tested annually in China and the number of assays annually is about 100 million. The average allowable cost for these assays is approximately US$0.25. Thus the diagnostic market in China for blood screening is rather insignificant at US$25 million, compared with the US market of $423 million. We found the diagnostic reagent market in China to be fragmented, and the cost structure will not support this industry as a potential manufacturing sector for Hong Kong. Furthermore, the business is not driven by high-technology manufacturing, but rather controlled by marketing, and offers little potential for strengthening Hong Kong's high-technology base. Those who seek a detailed report of our findings for this particular product sector, may contact the authors.

2   Safety and efficacy are the major criteria for the approval of market licenses for pharmaceuticals in the United States. These factors are established through a series of studies of each compound—first, in pre-clinical tests with model systems, such as *in vitro* and animal systems, and then in clinical trials using human subjects. The latter are conducted in multiple stages, usually progressing from small numbers of healthy volunteers to a larger number of subjects with the relevant health problems. There are three phases of clinical trials prior to the application of prod-

uct license for market, the objectives for which have been established clearly by the FDA. The emphasis in Phases I and II is on the demonstration of safety, and in Phase III on both the safety and efficacy of the product. These phases usually require years to complete. Phase I generally lasts an average of 15 and a half months; Phase II, 24 months, and Phase III, 36 months. The costs of clinical trials, especially Phase III, are quite high—in the tens of millions of US dollars. Phases I, II, and III are reported to cost on average US$4.1 million, $6.6 million and $17.3 million, respectively. (M. P. Mathieu (ed.), *Parexel's Pharmaceutical R&D Statistical Sourcebook 1995*, Boston: Parexel International Corp., 1995, p. 49.)

3 Mathieu, *Parexel's Pharmaceutical R&D Statistical Sourcebook*, p. 39.

4 Biotechnology Industry Organization (BIO), 1996. Figure published on the BIO Web page.

5 K. B. Lee and G. S. Burrill, *Biotech 96: Pursuing Sustainability: The Ernst & Young Tenth Annual Report on the Biotechnology Industry*, Palo Alto: Ernst & Young LLP, 1995, p. 30.

6 A. M. Thayer, 'Market, Investor Attitudes Challenge Developers of Biopharmaceuticals,' *Chemical & Engineering News*, 74, 31 (August 12, 1996): 13–21.

7 Between 1987 and 1995, a total of over US$11.6 billion of public and private equities has been placed into the biotechnology industry. ('Venture Investment on a Roll,' October 7, 1996, on Recombinant Capital Web site: http//www.recap.com/ in the Archive section.)

8 Lee and Burrill, *Biotech 96: Pursuing Sustainability*, p. 24.

9 Hong Kong Government Industry Department, *1996 Hong Kong's Manufacturing Industries*, p. 195. The drugs and medicines sector was the Hong Kong chemical industry's largest sector in terms of the number of establishments and total employment. In 1995, the sector accounted for 0.73 percent of the total number of all manufacturing establishments, and 0.65 percent of the total manufacturing employment in Hong Kong.

10 Good Manufacturing Practices are manufacturing and product regulations imposed by the US Food and Drug Administration on manufacturers of food and pharmaceutical products sold in the United States.

11 The Chinese University of Hong Kong (CUHK), The University of Hong Kong (HKU) and The Hong Kong University of Science and Technology (HKUST). These universities either have well-established programs in biological science because of their history, or have comprehensive curricula covering both science and engineering.

12 Conference proceedings: Shenzhen Biological Engineering, sponsored by Shenzhen Science and Technology Commission in December, 1995 in Shenzhen, China.

13 *Scrip's 1995 Yearbook,* S. Khan (ed.), Surrey: PJB Publications Ltd., 1995, pp. 75, 83.

14 S. C. Chappel, 'Where the Industry Is Today.' Paper presented at 'The Pharmaceutical Industry in the 21st Century' program sponsored by The Program on the Pharmaceutical Industry of MIT, Cambridge Mass., November 1995.

15 H. Grabowski and J. Vernon, 'Brand Loyalty, Entry and Price Competition in Pharmaceuticals after the 1984 Drug Act,' *Journal of Law and Economics,* 35, 2 (October 1990): 331–350.

16 *The Chinese Pharmaceutical Market Guide 1996,* Vol. 2, Yu Maozhang; Bi Chen; and Fang Ning (eds.), PJB Publications Ltd. (Surrey, UK) and State Pharmaceutical Administration of China (SPAC) Information Centre (Beijing), 1996, p. 2.

17 *The Chinese Pharmaceutical Market Guide 1996,* Vol. 2, p. 2.

18 Ibid., pp 9–12.

19 J. Grünwald, 'The European Phytomedicines Market: Figures, Trends, Analyses,' *Herbalgram,* 34 (Summer, 1995): 60–65.

20 *Scrip's 1995 Yearbook,* p. 83.

21 Grünwald, 'The European Phytomedicines Market,' p. 62.

22 D. M. Eisenberg; R. C. Kessler; C. Foster; F. E. Norlock; D. R. Calkins; and T. L. Delbanco, 'Unconventional Medicine in the United States: Prevalence, Costs, Patterns of Use,' *The New England Journal of Medicine,* 328, 4 (January 28, 1993): 246–52.

23 *The China Pharmaceutical Market Guide 1996,* Vol. 2, p. 2.

24 Cotecxin contains dihydro-artemisinin and has been found to have a rapid onset of activity and to cure most cases of malaria, with a low rate of recurrence and few side effects. It is the third artemisinin derivative to be developed for the treatment of malaria, following artemisinin succinate and artemisinin methylether.

Cotecxin or Qinghausau was developed by researchers at the Institute of Traditional Chinese Medicine (ITCM). This product represents a new pathway for drug development by combining TCM knowledge with modern drug discovery methods. In developing Cotecxin, ITCM reviewed existing databases to identify TCM raw materials with known properties traditionally used in treating malaria problems. The plant with the desired functionality was extracted and isolated in order to identify the lead compound. The long, arduous process of discovery followed the rigorous concept of Western drug development. Thus, Cotecxin, unlike the traditional TCM products, is a product with clear chemical structure, a high degree disease specificity, and clinical data on its efficacy and toxicology. Cotecxin has been licensed to Beijing Cotec New Technology Corporation and Beijing No. 6 Pharmaceutical Factory for manufacturing and marketing. Filings are planned for African countries such as Kenya, Sudan and India.

25   P. G. Xiao, 'Ethnopharmacological Investigation of Chinese Medicinal Plants,' in *Ethnobotany and the Search of New Drugs,* Ciba Foundation Symposium, Vol. 185, Chichester: Wiley, 1994, pp. 169–177.

26   Y. Shu, 'Natural products, Still an Unparalleled Source of Molecular Diversity to Drug R&D,' paper presented at the Society of Chinese BioScientists in America (SCBA), BioPharma Conference, November 1996, in New Haven, Connecticut.

27   Grünwald, 'The European Phytomedicines Market,' p. 62.

28   T. Chen, 'Clinical Development of Botanicals: New Regulatory Approaches,' paper presented at the conference 'Bio/Pharmaceuticals, from Laboratory to Market Place,' sponsored by Society of Chinese BioScientists in America (SCBA), May 1996, in Taipei, Taiwan.

29   R. Rawls, 'Europe's Strong Herbal Brew,' *Chemical & Engineering News,* 74, 39 (Sept. 23, 1996): 53–60.

30   Grünwald, 'The European Phytomedicines Market,' p. 64.

Capital Markets in Hong Kong

Andrew B. Bernard
Mary Hallward-Driemeier

An adequate and affordable supply of capital is a necessary ingredient for the development and growth of any industry, and particularly so for investment-intensive, high-technology sectors. This chapter looks at the factors shaping the nature of the capital markets in Hong Kong, focusing on the extent to which the existing structure meets the needs of Hong Kong industry. The reports by the technology experts in this book have tried to identify new potential opportunities, but the viability of such projects still depends on whether or not these firms can get adequate financial backing. Understanding the capital markets is important both from the perspective of new start-up companies seeking financial backing and from that of members of the financial community so that they can be positioned to take advantage of opportunities as they arise. The conclusion of this study is that while there is plenty of capital available in Hong Kong, it is striking how little of it is directed into start-up firms or into funding technological upgrades. In addition, surprisingly few institutional investors have such investments as a focus of their strategy.

While Hong Kong serves as a financial center for Southeast Asia, the sophistication of its services are rarely extended to local Hong Kong firms. There is little or no venture capital as it is understood in the United States; start-up firms need to rely on family finances or rolled over trade credit. Companies that do call themselves venture capital firms are largely providing funds for expansion to proven companies. Technology upgrades, let alone new technology firms, are not a focus for investors in Hong Kong. Determining whether such investment opportunities exist would only offer a partial explanation of this phenomenon. What must also be understood is how the dynamics of the investment community in Hong Kong contributes to this pattern. The importance of property as a source of wealth, the opportunities for mass production in China and the feasibility of different exit strategies have provided little incentive for firms to investigate the higher risk opportunities associated with investments in technology.

Hong Kong has many advantages that account for its role as a major financial center in the region. Importantly, many of these attributes are likely to remain in place over the next decade; Hong Kong is not likely to be displaced in the near future by another city rivaling it for its position. Hong Kong's infrastructure is universally praised both by investors and by manufacturing and technology enterprises. The low tax rate is seen as a critical reason underlying Hong Kong as a financial center, not only the low capital gains tax, but also the flat personal income tax. The lack of withholding taxes also increases the role of Hong Kong as a regional financial center compared with its neighbors. Other contributing factors to Hong Kong's success include the rule of law, certainty of property rights and the relative absence of corruption. The lack of government intervention is seen as a benefit for companies looking to raise capital through investments or loans. Hong Kong is also centrally located, adding to its attractiveness as a regional financial center. Hong Kong is also seen as a reasonably outward oriented economy; there is easy communication with the United States, Japan, and Europe. The standard of living is high; virtually no foreign banker or fund manager whom we interviewed was interested in living anywhere else in the region.

Another major advantage for Hong Kong comes through its link with China, as Hong Kong is a natural gateway into China. Its bilingual nature greatly facilitates communication between Chinese business people and North American, European, and even Japanese investors who often use English as the language of commerce. Coupled with the knowledge of English and Cantonese is a familiarity with Chinese customs and a greater ease in navigating the bureaucratic requirements associated with doing business in China. In making investments in China, a local Hong Kong business partner is often seen as a crucial component of a successful deal. While manufacturing sites are moving out of Hong Kong into China, the headquarters and regional offices often remain in Hong Kong. From the financial community's perspective, proximity to the manufacturing sector is not particularly relevant, but close interaction with representatives from the headquarters is a definite advantage that Hong Kong continues to offer. Shanghai may become a rival over the next decade or two, but there is a significant degree of deregulation in the Chinese banking sector that must be accomplished first. And, it is not unreasonable that by that time China could warrant two financial centers serving its economy.

Despite all the advantages of locating in Hong Kong, there are still obstacles hindering the development of Hong Kong's financial services. Some of them stem from the existence, or the lack thereof, of investment opportunities. Others lie in the dynamics of the local investment community's priorities and preferred methods of operation. This chapter is particularly interested in investigating these dynamics and understanding how they present challenges that must be met for Hong Kong to continue to evolve and maintain its position as a financial center for Southeast Asia.

To examine the interaction of capital markets and investment opportunities we interviewed 146 people in 83 institutions offering a range of financial instruments as well as firms involved in manufacturing and technology. On the financial side, these included foreign and domestic banks, both commercial and retail, large investment banks, smaller venture capital or direct investment firms, leasing companies, and the Hong Kong stock exchange. The collection of interviews covers a wide variety of financial instruments, types of clients, and investment strategies. To be sure we would understand both strategic and tactical issues we conducted interviews both with senior managers and operational personnel directly involved with the evaluation and monitoring of the investments or loans. Equally important to developing a complete picture of the flow of funds to Hong Kong companies is the perspective of the current and prospective recipients of the funds. To this end we conducted extensive interviews with managers and owners of Hong Kong companies involved in manufacturing in both Hong Kong and China, as well as with participants in technology-intensive industries. In the rest of this chapter we provide profiles of typical participants in the investor–banking community as well as of the producing firms themselves. We start, however, by discussing the overall investment opportunities available to firms. In concluding, we consider what can be done to stimulate investment in start-up firms, and in high-technology sectors in particular in Hong Kong.

Overall Investment Opportunities

At present, there is little question that there is a gap in the financial market; there is virtually no medium or long-term financing for start-up firms in manufacturing or technology-intensive fields.[1] In addition, even viable ongoing firms in these areas obtain little or no medium-term financing. Some debate whether it is because of a lack of demand from the firms' side, or a lack of supply from the financial community unwilling to make longer term financing available. What is true is that the existence of traditionally higher return opportunities in property development and, more recently, in investments in China, continue to divert funds away from Hong Kong industry.[2]

Businessmen in Hong Kong, whether they run financial, manufacturing, or technology firms, are often criticized for focusing excessively on short-term gains and having a short-time horizon. Implicit in such criticism is that these individuals are missing important and lucrative long-term opportunities through their focus on the short term and, more importantly, that both their companies and Hong Kong would be better off if they could change their behavior. Producing firms claim that this is driven by the financial community through the structure of loans and investments which is disproportionately focused on the short run; investors and bankers argue that all Hong Kong producers eschew long-term projects for activities with quick payoffs. Whatever the causes, the current situation in the provision of capital to Hong Kong companies is that few activities in the financial markets focus on the medium and long run. In fact, when interviewed, leading figures in both commercial and investment banks initially protested this characterization of a missing set of financial instruments for local producers. These same individuals—strategic policymakers for their financial firms—eventually conceded, however, that they could name few examples of intermediate-term loans or investments in technology in Hong Kong companies by their own firms. This concentration of resources on short-run activities is neither irrational nor inappropriate from the perspective of both the investors or the producers given the alternatives that are available. However, as discussed elsewhere in this book, there may be unintended consequences for the set of activities that emerges in Hong Kong in the years to come. In the remainder of this section, we discuss the two most important alternatives to investments in local manufacturing or technology start-ups, namely investments in property and in China.

Property underlies an enormous share of the wealth in Hong Kong. The success of the richest individuals and many of the largest companies is based on property investments and property development. Well-known success stories such as Li Ka-shing, for example, and the late Sir Y. K. Pao, started out in other industries (plastics and shipping, respectively) but built the preponderance of their wealth in the property market. Property remains the destination of choice for investment funds both in Hong Kong and in China. The continued high returns on such investments combined with the desire to own land, and the continued government policy of restricting new land for development have maintained property development as an attractive investment. The dominance of property over manufacturing -related investments is so great that many former manufacturers who acquired their factories over a decade ago have moved their manufacturing activities to China and have become real estate developers in Hong Kong. They are able to earn substantially more money redeveloping their land and buildings than by running their plants. With such high returns in property, many investment companies see little reason to devote many resources exploring other investment opportunities.[3]

An interesting recent development that has been given less attention in discussions of property is that many of the largest companies and wealthiest individuals have been diversifying their portfolios substantially to include non-property investments. However, this trend has not necessarily been pursued by the average Hong Kong citizen who still sees property as the most desirable form of holding wealth and puts any extra funds into paying off his or her mortgage.

The second major channel for money that is seen to promise large rewards is investing in China. With the potential for such an enormous market and the abundant supply of cheap labor and land, many Hong Kong manufacturers have moved their operations into China in the last decade. The lower costs of production in China meant that Hong Kong businesses could continue to rely on large-volume, small value-added processes that could earn them a reasonable profit. There was no need to seek new technology or new lines of business; they could relocate and continue to do business as they formerly had in Hong Kong. The existence of so much 'low hanging fruit' in China, kept alive the prospects for Hong Kong manufacturers as production costs rose in Hong Kong itself, but it also kept their horizons low. To continue to make money in manufacturing, they did not need to move up the technology ladder or to improve their efficiency.[4] The strategy has worked reasonably well in the short run; but it may have just postponed many of the challenges that Hong Kong faces as a more developed economy.

Opportunities in property and opportunities in China, either manufacturing or property, remain attractive due to the expectation of continued high returns. The lack of investment in start-up companies in Hong Kong and, especially, in high-technology companies is less surprising in the presence of these appealing alternative investments. However, to understand why there is a lack of financial instruments for new firms in technology related activities and to consider the future of such activities, we must understand the incentives and behavior of both the firms that seek financial banking and the different suppliers of capital.

Profile of the Producing Firms

As in most economies, firms have dramatically different funding needs at different stages of their development. To provide an overview of the current status of the financing of Hong Kong firms, we first provide profiles of three types of target producers: start-up firms, mature larger firms, and finally subsidiaries of foreign multinationals. The differences between and similarities among these three groups provide illustrations of the flow of funds to current and prospective Hong Kong firms.

Typical Start-up Firms

Individuals looking to finance a start-up company in Hong Kong do not turn to the formal financial markets for backing.

The primary characterization of start-up firms is that they rely on family funds for financing. This is certainly not a feature that is unique to Hong Kong companies, it is true throughout much of Asia and indeed in the developed economies of North America and Europe. In Hong Kong, however, it is almost unheard of to find a company that did not begin with family money. Whether family financing is preferred as a means of ensuring control over the company, or whether there is little faith on the part of the entrepreneurs that they would receive financing, it is the case that members of the investment community rarely see applications from start-up firms.[5]

While it is true that most entrepreneurs start with family financing, it is also true that early on in the life of the firm there is a need for increased funds, typically to purchase equipment for expansion. If start-up firms do seek external finance, they usually approach banks and are extended trade credit. Such credit is short-term—90 days up to one year—and is secured by the receipts of the company, generally not collateralized by the firms physical assets and is often used to finance capital investment. Firms must roll over the loans as they come due to accommodate the longer term nature of the assets that have been purchased. In interviews with both customers and lender we found widespread acceptance of this use for trade credit, although both sets of participants recognized the advantages of intermediate-term debt especially for capital purchases. It is only after the company has exhibited success over a number of years that banks will consider giving firms project financing or longer term loans. In general, even the horizon of these loans is quite short, typically two to three years, although one occasionally sees a loan of five years. It is extremely rare to see loans of any greater length of maturity, and virtually all of them are related to commercial property development.

The implications of this short-term loan structure varies across activities. For a trading concern with cash flow from the outset of operations, rolling over this type of short-term note may be feasible, due to the incoming revenues, and beneficial, as the firm can vary its debt obligations on short notice. On the other hand, a start-up firm, in software development for example, trying to turn an idea into a new product line typically experiences a lack of revenues at the outset which essentially cuts off trade credit as a source of financing.

SOFTWARE COMPANIES

Software companies illustrate many of the challenges facing start-up, technology-related firms in Hong Kong. Of those interviewed, all were initially self-financed. None receive venture capital backing or were able to get extended bank loans. Firms have been able to grow, but internal flows of funds have been critical in providing expansion capital. The ITC did provide assistance for some, but the type of restrictions still limits the risk-taking entrepreneurs from expanding their businesses. When asked what recommendations they would like to see made, they expressed interest in ways to facilitate contacts between themselves and large firms requiring their services that could help establish partnerships to infuse the software companies with additional, needed funds.

The managing director of Company A recognizes the difficulty for smaller high-tech companies trying to raise capital; he noted that venture capital firms and banks would rather invest in real estate-related activities. He said that for his own company, he tried but could not get venture capital money; 'The VCs will tell you there is money, then you do the work but get nothing. One hundred percent of the high-tech start-ups can't get money from VCs.' Rather, the number one source of money is families, then personal money. (Company A is now 19 years old, employs 40 programmers and exports their software packages to Southeast Asia and Japan.)

The two top managers of Company B financed their financial engineering software company themselves in 1991. They were then selected to be in the ITC's incubation program. They discussed the two ways in which the government currently funds companies. First, there is seed capital from ITC. There are many requirements, and then the amount of money cannot exceed HK$1 million, which is not enough to finance a company. Second, there is the Applied R&D Fund. While there is no maximum on the amount of money, a company can apply only once. Fear of rejection keeps many from even trying to apply for the money. Also, the partners have to guarantee the loan; it is not a source of venture capital. They suggested modifying the loans to encourage firms to apply and then treat the funds as true venture capital investment.

Generally, successful software firms in Hong Kong begin their operations doing project work, just in order to have a flow of revenues from the outset of operations.

The difficulty in obtaining longer term financing is compounded for firms seeking to expand in China. Many manufacturing firms continue to expand their business in China,

They discussed their dream of becoming a listed company, but were extremely skeptical of their chances of listing on the Stock Exchange of Hong Kong (SEHK). Even listing on a Chinese exchange seemed more probable. In their opinion, the lack of a NASDAQ-type exchange and the high requirements of the SEHK mean that there is almost no way a small company can get capital. There is no mechanism in place in Hong Kong to allocate capital to risk ventures.

Many firms that do successfully start are restricted in their ability to grow due to capital constraints. For example, the general manager of Company C explained how their company, a software company designing software for architecture and engineering firms, tried to get venture capital backing for their expansion and failed. The venture capital firms claimed they were too risky. Banks also rejected them as they had no collateral to back the loans. They used personal finances to start the company seven years ago. Having failed to get venture capital or bank financing, they were fortunate to find a private investor who gave them some of the funds they needed to expand their services.

The president of Company D reiterated the fact that software firms have to rely on personal finances and software sales for financing. He also raised the point that one of the reasons firms like his do not seek or receive venture capital funding is that many managers are technology-oriented rather than business-oriented; they know all about the programming side of their company but not how to provide the financial statements required by the potential investors or banks. He said this, too, restricted some firms from seeking government funds. When asked whether taking the company public was a goal, he said no. He feared it would make the company too focused on short-term performance and that it would be run by analysts. He does need greater access to capital, but sees a 'synergy partner' as a superior outcome. The trick, he admitted, is finding such a partner.

and seek loans for the expansion. However, Hong Kong banks cannot rely on machines and property in China as collateral for loans and as a result will not extend loans for equipment destined for China without alternative, Hong Kong based collateral. Firms without such collateral again resort to higher interest rate trade credit to finance operations across the border.

This confluence of factors leads to a typical strategy of financing for smaller firms and new ventures. The path starts with a reliance on family finance, followed by extensive use

---

P-PLUS COMMUNICATIONS

P-Plus is a new company that just succeeded in receiving a license to be one of six suppliers of wireless communication services in Hong Kong. It brings together four partners, both as sources of capital and different types of expertise. The four partners provide half of the funding needed to develop the company; short-term trade credit provides the other half of the initial funding. Despite the reputation and resources of the partner companies and the successful bid for the license, it still will likely be one year before P-Plus will qualify for project financing. The venture will have sufficient financing, but only given the existing sources available from the current partners. There are three principal partners: Star Telecom is the largest shareholder and has considerable experience operating in the Hong Kong market; Telecom Finland is the partner that provides the specific technology to be applied in the company; Pacific Electronic Wire and Cable has both technology and regional market expertise. P-Plus exemplifies the use of global resources to strengthen a company's local position. In seeking partners, a good match of technology and local knowledge was very important, and the company hopes that this formula will help it succeed in expanding into neighboring markets.

---

of very short-term debt to raise money for expansions and capital expenditures. Occasionally firms will then qualify for project financing. Firms that attract the attention of institutional investors are those that have already established a degree of success, transferring a proven technology or differentiating existing products. An alternative source of capital, listing on a stock exchange such as the Hong Kong stock exchange (SEHK), is available only to well-established operations. Firms that list on the SEHK must have three years of consecutive profits above HK$20–30 million. Clearly, support from institutional investors and listing on stock exchange remain options well beyond the reach of most small firms as sources of capital in the initial stages of a company.

Typical Large Firm

Surprisingly, the financial structure of large companies is very similar to that of smaller, start-up firms. There is still a heavy reliance on internal financing or short-term bank loans. It is

GROUP SENSE

Group Sense, founded in 1988 as a software company, was started with personal and family funds. By reinvesting profits it was able to grow. In fact, for the first five years of its existence, Group Sense never relied on external financing. After two years, it expanded into product development and manufacturing. Now it licenses technology and produces a range of products sold in Hong Kong and much of Southeast Asia. Its products include digital Chinese–English dictionaries and electronic diaries. Group Sense moves quickly to take advantage of windows of opportunity; it tries to fill smaller niche markets before Japan or the United States expand into them. The company seeks local partners in overseas markets, not just as sources of capital, but as an important means of gaining outside expertise of the new markets. In 1993, it succeeded in going public with a market capitalization of HK$800 million. It saw increased recognition and an improved reputation as key benefits of listing on the Hong Kong stock exchange.

Group Sense does not invent the technologies it uses, but it does employ over 100 engineers to redevelop existing technology to adapt it to particular markets. It sees as its strength the ability to combine new technology with smaller regional markets' needs. The company believes Hong Kong is an idea location for its business as it is such a hub for technology vendors and buyers. Group Sense illustrates that small, self-financed companies that take advantage of local strengths and outside expertise can indeed succeed.

true that the larger, more established firms in Hong Kong have greater access to resources of the financial sector in Hong Kong, but even so, it is rare to find examples of longer term project financing and almost all firms cite internal funds as their primary source of expansion capital.

The goal for many of the larger firms is to be listed on the SEHK. Yet, significantly, many do not rely on it as an important source of new capital. They still rely to a great extent on internal financing. The single most important exception are infrastructure projects. The funds associated with the building of the new airport and the related infrastructure projects have lead to numerous partnerships with foreign investors and a significant amount of project finance extended by both local and foreign banks.

Of the large firms in Hong Kong, few are technology-related companies. There are some examples of success, such as

Group Sense (translators and electronic organizers, pagers, educational toys), Varitronix (liquid crystal displays), and VTech (electronics, computers, and telecommunications products). Technology companies, however, often face additional obstacles compared with other types of industries. First, they are often companies whose primary product is an idea or new way to do things. This can increase the difficulty in raising financial backing, particularly in a market that stresses the importance of tangible forms of wealth. Second, these firms often face global competition, right from the start. For example, firms in the software industry must compete with software providers in the United States and Europe as well as from emerging competitors such as Bangalore, India.

Multinational Corporations

The financial structure of multinational corporation (MNC) subsidiaries differs from that of their domestic Hong Kong counterparts. While MNC affiliates often make heavy use of internal funds from the parent company, they typically also have access to a greater range of instruments from financial institutions including long term loans and leasing arrangements. Often, they are customers of the same financial institution as the parent company and the good reputation, and often the assets, of the parent company provide backing for the loan to the affiliate giving them access to the same preferential interest rates. This is particularly true of Japanese MNCs, which deal predominantly with Japanese banks even in Hong Kong. This means that, unlike Hong Kong firms, both large and small, affiliates of foreign multinationals are not adversely affected by the relatively limited types of financing available in the local capital markets.

Profile of the Providers of Funds/ Sources of Capital

Banks

Banks remain the first contact most firms have with the financial sector, usually through the trade credit arrangements outlined above. Yet, manufacturing or manufacturing-related activities make up only a small fraction of banks' business. For domestic banks, the current portfolios and anticipated expansions remain heavily weighted towards the property and retail sectors. Most bankers could give only a single example of a high tech company they have financed, or a single example of non-property loan with a maturity of greater than two years, usually to a large, or listed, company.

Regulations restrict most foreign banks to operating only a single branch, ensuring that they do not operate large-scale retail businesses under their own name.[6] The activities of the foreign and domestic banks also differ on types of customers and preferred types of business. In general, foreign banks have as important customers affiliates of multinationals from their home country. The overseas offices or branches of the MNC vary greatly in their degree of activity and the amount of financial services they seek, but they can account for one-fourth to one-third of banks' business. Foreign banks are also involved in financing local property deals, but they play a smaller role in this regard than other domestic players. Their involvement with local companies varies. Their preferred customers are the large, established, listed companies. While they do consider smaller local Hong Kong companies, the chief concern is with information and the lack of disclosure of company information.

This concern is emphasized in particular by the Japanese banks. In their relationships with companies in Japan, they build on years of experience, inside information and personal contacts with senior managers of the firms. In Hong Kong they do not have such a network and proceed more cautiously. As a result of the perceived higher risk of lending to less well known companies, interest rates are often 1–2 percent higher than what a Japanese subsidiary would receive.

Banks, more than other financial institutions, face bigger impediments to doing business in China. Given the restrictions on banking in China, many banks use their Hong Kong branches to service clients in China. However, the issue of collateral remains. No-recourse loans are made, but at a higher cost. Branches in China are being set up, and are seen as the way in the future to serve clients based there. However, no one foresaw Hong Kong's role as a banking sector being eclipsed by China in the next 10 to 15 years.

As China is not yet seen as a viable area of growth for most banks, they see expanding business in Hong Kong as their top priority. Significantly, this translates, virtually without exception, into trying to expand their retail business. Mortgages are seen as particularly lucrative. As one investment banker noted, 'There is no "Chapter 11" (bankruptcy) mentality here. Defaults on loans, particularly mortgages are virtually zero.' The margins are also larger in retail banking, both on mortgages and credit cards than in corporate finance.

One commonly advanced explanation for the short-term nature of loans is the uncertainty surrounding the transfer of sovereignty in 1997. This has had some effect on term length and is reflected in interest rates charged on loans. However, a full explanation must go deeper than this. As most loans are of relatively short duration, it was not until 1994 or 1995 that the issue of loans that would mature post-June 30, 1997 had to be resolved. Some banks reacted by shortening the maturity to avoid the issue. But, loans that matured later in 1997 did get written: with a premium of 60–100 basis points. By the end of 1995, the premium had fallen somewhat, but it has remained at 30–40 basis points. Some bankers speculate that lending activity will not fully resume until 1998 or 1999, and at that time a surge in lending to fulfill pent up demand would be expected. One potential ramification of such a scenario is that the curtailing of lending could contribute to an economic slowdown in 1997–1998 that would then be blamed on China and the transition. Such a downturn would be due to a self-fulfilling prophecy rather than directly attributable to any action on the part of Beijing.

Another way in which uncertainty has translated into higher borrowing costs is the uncertainty regarding the stability of the Hong Kong dollar. Foreign banks are wary about being overexposed to the currency and so hedge against their holdings, up to 50 or 60 percent. This raises interest rates about 30 basis points.

It is surprising that there is a lack of three- to five-year loans to the extent that banks could be making money by investing in this area. However, given the low risks and high returns emphasis on retail banking, especially mortgages, banks are unlikely to be a source of capital for technology firms in the near future.

Venture Capital/Direct Investment

History of VC/DI in Hong Kong and China

Venture capital, or direct investment, firms blossomed in Hong Kong in the mid-1980s. This was a time of expansion for Hong Kong firms, particularly as manufacturers moved into the Pearl River Delta in China. It was also a time when institutional investors abroad became increasingly aware of the potential growth in the Southeast Asian region and the number of investors and investments grew rapidly. Growth rates peaked in the early 1990s and since then, activity in this area has grown more slowly as the Chinese economy has slowed, some investments have proven to be less lucrative than expected, and the competition for deals has increased. The Hong Kong Venture Capital Association started in late 1987 and had 16 members. Today it has over 55 full members and 32 associate members.

While there are now many companies that call themselves 'venture capital' firms, in fact very few companies perform true venture capital placement, i.e. provide equity capital to firms before the sale of their first product. One of the founding members of the Venture Capital Association of Hong Kong admitted 'I have not personally seen a young company where plant and equipment wasn't financed by 1 year loans.' Thus the 'venture capital' industry in Hong Kong would be more accurately labeled a 'mezzanine' capital industry, where investors provide funding for the expansion of existing companies. Companies seeking funding need to have a successful track record before outside investors will back them. As one investor put it, 'I doubt there are two guys in town who'd be willing to do seed capital. Everyone is in expansion capital, mezzanine financing.'

Interestingly, the sources of the investment funds have not changed dramatically as the industry has developed. As in the early years, the vast majority of the money in these funds comes from the United States, usually from institutions or pension funds. Significantly, without exception VC/DI firms report that very little Asian money is channeled through their investment funds. They speculate that Asian investors are either performing regional diversification, sending some fraction of their money to Europe and the United States, for example, or seeking investment opportunities through personal connections or other private sources.

By all accounts the flow of funds is continuing to increase. A decade ago there were few outside investors, competition was more limited and finding opportunities was not so difficult. A few cases of spectacular returns have raised interest in the area. By the early 1990s, more fund managers were located in Hong Kong, helping fund companies moving into China and also investing in property in China. This was the boom time for investors. Recently, firms have become more wary; there are more fund managers looking for opportunities so the competition is fiercer and they are more wary of accepting risky deals. As an American fund manager overseeing a China country fund said, 'the market in China suffers from saturation. No sooner is a market identified than it is flooded with new companies and people wishing to invest in them.'

Typical Venture Capital/Direct Investment Today

Today, the typical Hong Kong VC/DI firm is looking primarily at large investments with a substantial investment horizon. Possible investments are drawn from around the region, although they are most likely to be in China through a Hong Kong based firm. The past success of funds and the growing interest in the region by foreign institutional investors has increased the size of funds being managed out of Hong Kong. Whereas the average placement used to be US$1–3 million, it is now closer to $10 million, although placements of up to $20 million, or even $50 million are possible. With the new, larger size of assets under management, fund managers find smaller projects less desirable since the costs in terms of personnel and time for evaluating any given project is roughly constant. A number of fund managers mentioned that their own time commitment to set up an individual deal is the biggest constraint they face. Given the choice between one $5 million deal or five $1 million deals, the former represents a more cost-effective strategy. As a result, the typical project size has increased with the implication that many smaller start-ups may be going unfunded; potentially opening a niche for new investors. On the other hand, there is likely to be a warm reception for large projects, particularly those associated with infrastructure projects.

The horizon for the typical VC/DI fund varies, but today is generally in the range of five to seven years and can be as long as ten years, particularly when firms are looking at investments in China. Investment horizons have lengthened over time as investors have realized that to be successful they will need to take a longer view. Many funds have built in one or two years of leeway to make sure that they can successfully exit from all their investments. The longer horizons of the major players in the VC/DI community are a stark counterexample to the stereotype of Hong Kong businessmen as short-term investors.

VC/DI firms in Hong Kong consider a wide range of industries and countries for their activities but rarely invest in a Hong Kong company unless it is a partner in a joint venture in China. This is virtually the rule for manufacturing projects and means that most projects associated with Hong Kong firms are in the same industries for which Hong Kong was once famous, such as plastics, textiles, and light manufacturing in general. In many cases, the joint venture also includes another international partner.

There is at least one striking difference between investments in China and elsewhere in the region by most VC/DI firms. When they invest in China they take a majority stake, whereas when they invest elsewhere in Asia, they usually prefer a minority holding. Since the majority shareholder is usually the one that manages the company, this implicitly reflects the lack of confidence in the level of Chinese management. It also means that these same venture capital firms have gained experience in how to manage firms and to bring in relevant outside expertise. This particular activity is especially important for the successful financing of technology start-ups. Typical venture partners in the United States provide much more than just capital to the new firm. They also bring managerial and marketing expertise, contacts with suppliers and customers and a wide range of 'non-finance' activities. To the extent that this ability to bundle financial capital with management skills is especially important for technology firms, it must be part of the financing package for technology start-ups in Hong Kong.

While long-term projects are indeed considered by Hong Kong VC/DI firms, technology-related investments still receive relatively little attention. Of all the VC/DI firms, we found only one that had started (in the mid-1980s) with a strong focus on technology investments. Disappointing results and a low volume of potential investments over the intervening years have led the fund gradually to broaden its focus to include candidates in any field, not just high technology. At present there are no examples of venture funds operating in Hong Kong with a pure technology focus and most preclude technology-intensive investments altogether.

Of all the issues surrounding investments by Hong Kong VC/DI firms, none is rated more important than the development of a viable exit strategy from the investment. Every fund manager ranked exit strategy as a primary concern when considering a potential investment. With the preponderance of investments going to China and no immediate prospect of easy listing on existing Chinese stock exchanges, there are currently two basic exit strategies: listing on the SEHK and direct sale to a third party. By far the preferred exit strategy of VC/DI companies is to list, with the preferred exchange being the SEHK. In part this results from easier monitoring with the exchange nearby, but also because the SEHK is seen as the optimal market for stocks of Chinese companies. Of the 24 Chinese companies with permission to list abroad, 22 are in Hong Kong. Hong Kong investors are the most knowledgeable about these stocks and the market is the most liquid in Hong Kong.

While the listing on the SEHK is regarded as the preferred exit strategy, the characteristics of that exchange affect the types of companies and industries that are considered for investments in the first place. If they do not believe the company will be able to list, investors will not enter and the firm will lose an important source of capital. In the next section we discuss some of the advantages and drawbacks of the

SEHK to provide insight into possible solutions for the apparent shortage of investments in technology-related industries.

The Role of the Hong Kong Stock Exchange

The SEHK is now one of the top ten largest exchanges in the world.[7] It not only lists Hong Kong-based companies, it is also the exchange of choice for Chinese companies that gain permission to list abroad. Opened in 1986, it now has an average daily volume of 5,000 transactions representing HK$3.3 billion, with demand growing and the number of companies seeking to list increasing.[8] The companies listed are generally large—two thirds have HK$200 million or more in annual turnover. While much of the liquidity comes from the home market, 30 percent of its business comes from offshore investors.[9]

Listing is seen as by far the most attractive exit strategy for direct investment firms and is a goal for most start-up companies. The SEHK is viewed as prestigious and relatively stable and the exchange takes active steps to maintain this reputation. However, obstacles remain that hamper many start-up or technology firms from being able to use the exchange as a source of capital. Despite its obvious strengths, there exist several characterizations of the SEHK which may affect its performance and influence the types of stocks that seek to list. These include:

a) the relative absence of manufacturing and especially technology stocks;

b) the requirement of three consecutive years of profits;

c) the notion that most listed companies are still essentially family-controlled businesses;

d) the motivation for listing as a reputation enhancement or risk diversification instead of as a means of raising capital for future growth;

e) the reduced ability of the exchange to monitor the organization and assets of the firm after listing;

f) the area targeted for growth by the SEHK is broader regional coverage (China, for example) rather than broader sectoral coverage.

We emphasize that these items are as problematic in perception as they are in reality, as the beliefs of investors influence their actions.

In the course of studying the possibility of starting a NASDAQ-style exchange in Hong Kong, the Market Development Group of the SEHK counted all the high-technology companies currently listed. Even construing technology in very broad terms, they found only 15 such companies out of 542 listed and many of the 15 are actually manufacturing companies with a small technology component. With such a small base of existing companies, it is not surprising that technology start-ups do not consider listing on the SEHK as a part of their plans or that members of the investment community are reluctant to invest in technology-based firms in Hong Kong.[10] The depth of the expertise regarding technology companies in the Hong Kong investment community is relatively limited at present.

To provide assurance of the base quality of companies listed on the exchange, SEHK has instituted a number of requirements firms must meet before they can list. Firms must have been operating for at least three years, with a profit level of HK$20 million in the year prior to listing. They must also have a combined profit level of HK$30 million for the two years prior to that. Again, there are some exceptions, such as infrastructure investments (investments in the new airport and toll roads in China). While increasing the overall quality of firms on the exchange and increasing confidence of potential shareholders, these same requirements implicitly limit the range of companies that seek listings. The companies most likely to list are relatively mature with established product lines and stable earnings. Technology start-ups, especially software companies, are unlikely to meet these requirements early in their life cycle, precisely at the point when they need to raise capital for rapid growth.

There is a 'joke' in Hong Kong that there is only one truly public company on the SEHK—the Hongkong Shanghai Banking Corporation—with the rest remaining essentially family-owned businesses. Whether true in fact, or merely a common misperception among market participants, this characterization represents a potential problem for companies thinking of listing on the SEHK and is typical of the obstacles facing companies trying to raise capital. For many companies on the SEHK, it is indeed the case that even though they are listed, control remains firmly in the hands of the original family owners. Officials at the exchange recognize this problem (a requirement of listing is that at least 25 percent of the firm be offered), but privately concede that if they tried to raise that limit, most firms would forego listing. One investor described the problem as that of having to learn the characteristics of the family instead of the company.

Maintaining control is often described as very important for Hong Kong's family-owned businesses. Owner–managers may be willing to forego some growth and expansion if this means diluting their control of the company. The implications for potential investors are clear. Not only is there a question of how aggressively a company will try to grow, there is a broader question of whether the company is developing adequate internal resources to ensure future success. A disturbingly large number of owners could not describe their strategy for locating the next generation of managers.

In interviews with a small number of family owners of listed manufacturing and technology companies, we asked about the reasons for going public. Surprisingly, no one cited the need to raise capital for expansion or long-run growth as the primary motivation. While a couple of companies cited the need to bring in outsiders to monitor the second generation of family managers, many others discussed the reputational benefits and prestige of being a listed company. One founder indicated that his company did not have a plan for the use of the additional capital.

In looking for ways to expand, the SEHK is not considering increasing the range of companies listed; instead, it is looking for ways to increase its geographic scope. It believes its future lies in a greater regional focus, not in trying to bring in more technology-based companies. In this regard, they view as a major success the record of the 'H-shares'—Chinese joint stock companies that are selected by the Chinese Security Regulation Commission to be listed abroad. China features as important to many of its listed firms, but it is the Chinese companies themselves that hold the biggest promise. It is the growth of the H-shares, that the SEHK sees as one of its biggest achievements and looks to for continued growth. Almost all of the H-share companies, 22 out of 24, have chosen to list in Hong Kong. The focus by the exchange on expanding the number of Chinese companies, coupled with the impediments detailed above, make it unlikely that the SEHK can become a home for technology stocks in the near future.

All of the issues discussed above would be largely irrelevant if listing on the SEHK was thought to provide a 'good' return on VC/DI investments. However, the most common complaint about the SEHK heard in the business community in Hong Kong is the persistence of low Price–Earnings (P/E) ratios relative to comparable exchanges. The P/E ratio for the SEHK this year has been around 15.[11] The low P/E ratios in conjunction with the inherent disadvantages facing technology companies means that few such companies choose to list in Hong Kong.

Compounding the difficulties facing technology-based companies and would-be investors is an innate skepticism about stocks on the part of the average Hong Kong resident, who in general is not a shareholder. There exists a mentality that personal wealth should be accumulated in tangible forms and above all in property. As one institutional investor put it, 'When people [in Hong Kong] think of money, they do not think of securities, they think of property, property, property.' Another remarked that given a choice, the person on the street would always choose to buy a gold bar over a gold stock. In part, this disregard of the stock market as an investment vehicle is not surprising given the relative absence of domestic pension funds or other domestic institutional investors.[12] One fund manager advocated that for the stock exchange to really develop, there needed to be a larger presence of domestic institutional funds to invest. Currently the absence of domestic institutional investors limits the number of players in the market, hampers the development of more professionally based relationships between companies and investment firms rather than personal network connections, and is unlikely to change the bias of the average citizen against less tangible forms of wealth.

The suspicion of intangible forms of wealth also manifests itself in a general unwillingness to back a business founded on a concept or idea, the very basis of many technology firms.

Virtually every institutional investor interviewed was skeptical that a start-up firm in technology would receive much interest in Hong Kong. Part of this cynicism is driven by the lack of experience in dealing with such firms, however, almost every investor admitted that they never looked for such firms in Hong Kong.

There is a vicious circle in the case of investment and technology in Hong Kong. The recent history of firms in Hong Kong includes few examples of successful technology-based firms and numerous alternative profitable opportunities. The attributes of the SEHK make listing of technology stocks less likely. As a result, investors are unlikely to seek out technology start-ups for investment. Potential entrepreneurs in technology areas correctly estimate that the likelihood of raising capital in Hong Kong is low, and consider alternative locations or alternative opportunities. The result is a low density of both investors looking for technology firms and technology firms looking for investors. Each side correctly argues that they do not see the activity from the other. In the following section we discuss possible methods to break the circle.

Stimulating Investment in Technology in Hong Kong

This chapter has examined the existing structure of the capital market in Hong Kong, focusing on the provision of funds to Hong Kong industry. The conclusion of the study is that while there is plenty of capital available in Hong Kong in general, a surprisingly small fraction is directed towards local start-up firms, and in particular to local firms with a technology focus. The problem regarding investment and technology is relatively clear. While the financial sector in Hong Kong is large, active, and quite sophisticated, it is not supplying capital in sufficient quantities to technology start-ups to support a vibrant high-tech sector in Hong Kong. This gap is part of a vicious circle where the lack of investors and the lack of entrepreneurs feed on each other. The chapter identifies three main sources of the funding bottleneck. First, as documented elsewhere in this volume, historically there have been few entrepreneurs with a technology focus, although this is changing rapidly. Second, over the past decade, investors have had ample lucrative investment opportunities in other areas, most notably in local property markets and in the rapid expansion of Hong Kong manufacturing firms in the Pearl River Delta. Third, and arguably most important for the future of technology firms in Hong Kong, there are few viable exit strategies for potential investors to consider. This sections offers suggestions for both government and business to address these concerns.

At the top of most discussions of how to stimulate a technology-based sector in Hong Kong is the potential role for government action. Elsewhere in this volume, we discuss the issue of whether the government should be doing more to encourage the emergence of new technologies (such as science parks, funding for R&D, and the creation of other research facilities, among other efforts). Another proposal advocates that the government take a more active role in the financing of such projects. To the extent that there is a lack of adequate funding for start-up firms, one proposed solution is the formation of a venture-type fund by the government. Another possibility is that the government invest directly in particular projects, or put money in private sector investment funds with the stipulation that these funds invest a certain percentage in new or high-tech projects.

We do not think there is a need for the government to become directly involved in the financing activities of technology start-ups. As described above, Hong Kong has a sophisticated, dynamic financial sector with plenty of available capital. The issue is not the need to stimulate the flow of funds to Hong Kong, but rather directing them to the start-ups. Due to its long tradition of nonintervention on behalf of specific companies or industries, the Hong Kong government is not well-prepared to take on the role of lead investor in the emerging technology sector. In fact, companies and members of the financial community list the nonintervention of government as one of Hong Kong's greatest strengths.[13] While some firms express an interest in a general subsidy of industry, without exception both investors and corporate executives argued against a policy where the government would try to pick winners. Taxes are relatively low, and are cited as a reason for the success of the financial sector, so further tax breaks targeted at technology venture capital funds would most likely not boost investment. As for direct investment in technology firms by the government, this would require a level of expertise both about investing and about technology itself far beyond the current capabilities of the government.

Although the Hong Kong government is not well suited to the role of investor, either direct or indirect, it can play an important role in stimulating the flow of funds to the emerging technology sectors. Most importantly, the government can facilitate the exchange of information between investors and new technology companies through organizations such as the HKTDC. A case in point is the local Hong Kong software industry, described as 'one of the best kept secrets of Hong Kong' in the chapter on information technology in this volume (Chapter 11). Promotion of the software industry could include not only trade shows, or 'software fairs' to facilitate the interaction of software consumers and producers, but also companion events designed to introduce local software entrepreneurs to potential investors. The events would educate the investors about the potential of the companies and would inform the companies about the requirements of the investors.

Perhaps the most important obstacle to investments in high-technology companies from an investor perspective is the lack of a viable exit strategy. Existing exit strategies are limited to listing on the SEHK or sale to a larger company or foreign MNC. The former is infeasible for most companies due to the strict listing requirements, and the latter is available only to a limited number of firms in select industries. Possible solutions to the problem of exit strategies include the establishment of a Hong Kong or a regional version of a NASDAQ-type exchange, listing of Hong Kong companies on China's Shenzhen exchange, or relaxed requirements for listing on the SEHK.

However, difficulties exist with each of these potential solutions. Loosening the listing requirements for all firms on the SEHK might damage the good reputation of the exchange and the companies already listed there. A regional NASDAQ-type exchange or listing on the Shenzhen board moves the investment activity out of Hong Kong, while the establishment of a new, NASDAQ-style exchange in Hong Kong may be difficult in the short run given the relatively small number of technology firms at present.

Another, as yet unconsidered alternative is the creation of a new class of shares to be traded on the SEHK. These 'T-shares' would be designed to encourage the listing of technology-based companies on the existing exchange. The new type of shares would have more flexible listing requirements as in a 'small cap' exchange, including reduced restrictions on current profitability and lower initial capitalization. However, to encourage increased outside supervision and external expertise, these companies would be required to float a greater fraction of their equity. The separate designation as a 'T-share' would help insure the reputation of currently listed companies and the SEHK.

In addition, to prevent individual investors from exposure to excessively risky investments, trading could be limited to registered institutional investors. Individuals could gain access through new classes of financial instruments such as mutual funds. As trading volume and experience with this new class of shares grows, a separate, dedicated exchange might be established in due course.

The first, and most important, step to solving the exit strategy problem is increased communication between the major players. This might take the form of an *ad hoc* committee, including prominent officials of the SEHK, founders of large, successful technology companies (both listed and private), and most importantly representatives of the smaller start-ups, the very firms who crave the inflow of capital. There is no question that the resolution of these problems presents profitable opportunities for all parties.

While the current flow of funds to start-up companies, and technology companies in particular, is not adequate, future prospects are quite good if the issues identified in this report can be resolved. The sophistication of the Hong Kong capitals markets is substantial and local investors are eager to locate new investment opportunities. Complementing this financial savvy is a rapidly growing community of technology entrepreneurs. With progress in addressing these difficulties, Hong Kong has the potential to develop a thriving group of technology industries in the near future with ample opportunities for financial reward and growth.

Notes

1   Throughout this chapter we focus our attention on financing for technology-intensive firms.

2   It is not obvious that these high-return activities are also riskier.

3   What is striking, however, is that of the large property developing companies, all are Hong Kong companies with the exception of one Singaporean firm. One banking executive commented that if a foreign company started to make serious bids in this area, the Hong Kong property developers would close ranks and keep them out.

4   This question of why Hong Kong manufacturers have not 'moved up' is addressed in more detail in the other chapters of this volume.

5   The history of manufacturing in Hong Kong may play a role in the evolution of the financial structure of Hong Kong firms. Whether arriving from Shanghai in 1949, or more recently fleeing the Cultural Revolution, many of today's successful businessmen, or their fathers, started as entrepreneurs who fought to maintain direct personal control over their businesses and generally did not have access to the sophisticated financial community present in today's Hong Kong.

6   Foreign banks may still purchase a controlling interest in a domestic bank.

7   The Stock Exchange of Hong Kong ranks as the ninth largest in the world according to *Emerging Stock Markets Factbook*, International Finance Corporation, Wash., DC, 1996.

8   The Stock Exchange of Hong Kong, *Stock Exchange Fact Book 1995.*

9   It is not possible to determine whether or not this money is from overseas or local investors.

10 In fact, most fund managers expressed surprise that we were asking about high-technology companies in Hong Kong.

11 S. Webb, 'Heard in Asia,' *Asian Wall Street Journal,* November 26, 1996.

12 While stock ownership by individuals has a long history in the United States, the proliferation of mutual funds and private retirement vehicles in recent years has raised the awareness of stocks among the typical household.

13 There is considerable debate over whether or not the Hong Kong government is truly 'noninterventionist' (for example, in its land policy, housing policy). However, the perception that one industry or company will not be favored over another is viewed as a great asset for Hong Kong.

14   Manufacturing Capabilities: Hong Kong's New Engine of Growth?

Alice H. Amsden

Less than two decades ago, Hong Kong's economy was still driven by 'manufacturing'—conventionally defined (as in the US Government's 1987 *Standard Industrial Classification Manual*) to include 'establishments engaged in the mechanical or chemical transformation of materials or substances into new products.'[1] Over time, manufacturing in this narrowly defined form of production declined sharply in importance.[2] Instead, Hong Kong became an economy dominated by services. Value added per person (labor productivity) was higher in Hong Kong's service sector (trade, finance, transportation, and communication) than in its manufacturing sector as early as 1983 (see Figure 14.1).

Figure 14.1
Value Added Per Person Engaged in Major Economic Sectors,
1983 and 1993

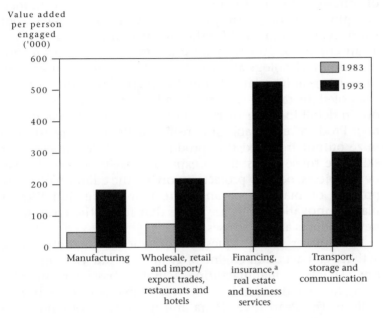

Note: a Percentages do not include the insurance sub-sector.

Source: Publications of the Hong Kong Census & Statistics
Department:
(1) Surveys of Industrial Production
(2) Surveys of Wholesale, Retail and Import/Export Trades,
     Restaurants and Hotels
(3) Surveys of Storage, Communications, Financing,
     Insurance and Business Services
(4) Surveys of Building, Construction and Real Estate
     Sectors
(5) Surveys of Transport and Related Services

The question is whether the accumulation of capabilities
(skills) related to manufacturing activity may be expected to
become Hong Kong's new 'engine of growth.' Manufacturing
activity is defined broadly here to include all the auxiliary
activities necessary for the support of production, ranging
from product design to distribution.[4] This is in recognition of

the fact that in practice, the dividing line between manufacturing and service activity has become blurred. 'Engine of growth' refers to a sector which is expanding faster than that of other sectors due to greater capital accumulation (human and physical) and possibly exports. Given Hong Kong's labor shortage, I presume that for the manufacturing sector to serve as an engine of growth it must accumulate skills or 'manufacturing/technological capabilities' (the terms are used here interchangeably) relatively rapidly. These capabilities include a set of skills related to three broad competencies, as spelled out in detail in Table 14.1: *production, investment, and innovation.* Production capabilities are the skills necessary to optimize output from existing production facilities. Investment skills are those necessary to expand capacity and undertake new projects, be they projects involving the addition of a new product or machine or an entire new production line or plant. Innovation skills are those that foster the creation of new products and processes.

The answer to the question of whether manufacturing activity can act as an engine of growth, in our view, depends on: (1) which manufacturing activities have remained in Hong Kong and which have been relocated elsewhere, principally to the Pearl River Delta and other parts of China; (2) whether the manufacturing capabilities sustaining Hong Kong-based manufacturing activities are world-class; and (3) the process by which such capabilities are being upgraded, if at all. I explore these questions below and hypothesize that the more the activities remaining in Hong Kong are of 'high value added' (the value of wages plus profits per worker); and the more Hong Kong-based activities 'benchmark' favorably with those in industrially advanced countries; and the more manufacturing capabilities are upgraded both incrementally and 'radically' (through the entry of new high-tech firms or the introduction of new technologies), the greater the likelihood that such activities will act as an engine of growth.

I examine these propositions for manufacturing with respect to a sample of companies in the electronics sector, which was selected because of its large share in the economy. In terms of the manufacturing sector it accounted in 1994 for approximately 15 percent of value added, 18 percent of gross output, 27 percent of exports, 10 percent of employment and 30 percent of foreign investment.[5] Its heterogeneity in terms of numerous market segments also contributed to the existence of a wide range of capabilities among firms. Using electronics I can therefore observe whether there has been a tendency over time for Hong Kong companies to move upscale or stay stationary with respect to their manufacturing capabilities. I also distinguish between the locational activities of locally owned and foreign firms, singling out Motorola as an example of a multinational with operations (I examine semiconductors and pagers) straddling the Pearl River Delta and Hong Kong. This chapter concludes with a discussion of what, if anything, the government can do to make Hong Kong's manufacturing capabilities into an engine of growth in a high-wage environment.

I am dubious that Hong Kong's manufacturing capabilities can (or necessarily should) act as a growth stimulant. Based on my observations, I would suggest that a major new element in Hong Kong's broadly defined manufacturing universe is likely to be enterprises from mainland China that come to Hong Kong to establish 'listening posts' for the purpose of upgrading their market information and technological capabilities. I would recommend that the government play an active role, comparable to that of the Singapore government's pursuit of multinational investment, in encouraging such Chinese firms to broaden the scope of the high-value-added activities they locate in Hong Kong. An influx of firms from China into Hong Kong is a mirror image of an outflow of firms from Hong Kong into China. The latter is discussed in the context of the electronics industry by Reif and Sodini (see Chapter 10), who also devote considerable attention to analyzing how Hong Kong's electronics sector can raise its capabilities and compete internationally in the future. I conclude by observing by contrast the advantages Chinese firms gain by locating in Hong Kong—advantages related to product development capabilities, administrative skills, distributional services, and so forth. With such investment, Hong Kong may be expected to benefit as well.

Table 14.1
Elements of Technological Capability

Production Capability[a]
- Production management—to oversee operation of established facilities
- Production engineering[b]—to provide information required to optimize operation of established facilities, including the following:
1. Raw material control: to sort and grade inputs, seek improved inputs;
2. Production scheduling: to coordinate production processes across products and facilities;
3. Quality control: to monitor conformance with product standards and to upgrade them;
4. Trouble-shooting to overcome problems encountered in course of operation;
5. Adaptations of processes and products: to respond to changing circumstances and increase productivity;
- Repair and maintenance of physical capital—according to regular schedule and when needed

Investment Capability
- Manpower training—to impart skills and abilities of all kinds
- Preinvestment feasibility studies—to identify possible projects and ascertain prospects for viability under alternative design concepts
- Project execution—to establish or expand facilities, including the following:
1. Project management: to organize and oversee activities involved in project execution;
2. Project engineering: to provide information needed to make technology operational in particular setting, including the following:
   a. Detailed studies: to make tentative choices among design alternatives;
   b. Basic engineering: to supply core technology in terms of process flows, material and energy balances, specifications of principal equipment, plant layout;
   c. Detailed engineering: to supply peripheral technology in terms of complete specifications for all physical capital, architectural and engineering plans, construction and equipment installation specifications
3. Procurement: to choose, coordinate, and supervise hardware suppliers and construction contractors
4. Embodiment in physical capital: to accomplish site preparation, construction, plant erection, manufacture of machinery and equipment
5. Start-up of operations: to attain predetermined norms

Innovation Capability
- Basic research—investigation to gain knowledge for its own sake
- Applied research—investigation to obtain knowledge with specific commercial implications
- Development—translation of technical and scientific knowledge into concrete new processes, products, and services through detail-oriented technical activities, including experimental testing

a   Activities listed refer to the operation of manufacturing plants, but similar activities pertain to the operation of other types of productive facilities as well.

b   This usage of the term departs from conventional usage in that the term
is used far more broadly to include all of the engineering activities related to the operation of existing facilities. In this usage, the term encompasses *product design* and *manufacturing engineering* as these terms are
generally used in reference to industrial production. See the entries
under these headings in the *McGraw–Hill Encyclopedia of Science and
Technology* (New York: McGraw–Hill Book Company, 1977).

Source: L. Westphal; L. Kim; and C. Dahlman, 'Reflections on the
Republic of Korea's Acquisition of Technological Capability,' in
International Technology Transfer: Concepts, Measures, and Comparisons,
N. Rosenberg and C. Frischtak (eds.), New York: Praeger, 1985.

Manufacturing Capabilities:
Mid-Technology

The performance of any manufacturing activity is based on
one or several technological capabilities, as defined above (see
Table 14.1). These capabilities are examined below in a sample of 32 Hong Kong electronics firms.[6] In this section I am
interested in merely describing the firms' capabilities by providing an indication of their depth and breadth. Later I summarize the distribution of the capabilities by geographic location—Hong Kong versus China.

The terms low-, medium-, or high-tech typically are applied
to a whole industry, and the electronics industry is usually
classified in the 'high-tech' category because of its high level
of manufacturing capabilities, measured as the share of R&D
expenditures in sales or value added per worker. Clearly, however, some segments of the electronics industry are not high-
tech; assembly operations tend to be low-tech and a subset of
other activities are what I would call 'mid-tech'. By 'mid-technology' I mean a set (or subset) of manufacturing activities
involving innovation capabilities that are not science-based,
and production and project execution skills that are dependent on more than mere raw labor power. Process and product changes in mid-tech industries are typically incremental
rather than radical. Technology, although expensive, is available from international suppliers and global demand is grow-

ing (in some cases, such as steel, simply because world population is growing). Major examples, in historical sequence, are electrical machinery, basic chemicals, automobiles, consumer electronics, and commodity semiconductors.[7]

Generally this sample suggests that electronics firms in Hong Kong are surviving at the middle or lower end of the capabilities spectrum and have not yet risen to the ranks of high-end producers. I argue later that both low-end and high-end manufacturing activities in electronics are likely to be located increasingly in China, while Hong Kong itself will remain a repository in exceptional companies for mid-tech skills.

Production Capabilities

The production activities which have tended to remain in Hong Kong embody a set of skills pertaining to (1) metalworking, in the case of machine building; and (2) process tending, in the case of chemical transformations, as exemplified by the following companies:

- ASM Assembly Automation Ltd. manufactures die bonders, wire bonders and trim/form systems. After relocating fabrication and assembly operations to China, it began to employ more skilled workers in Hong Kong than previously (total employment in 1996 was 800 in Hong Kong and 1,500 in China). Hong Kong workers tend to be relatively mature and experienced and ASM utilizes their skills to make machinery and tools.

- ALCO Holdings Ltd. , one of Hong Kong's biggest producers of radios, hi-fi boom boxes, and telephones, now employs 14,000 workers in China and 1,400 in Hong Kong. Its Hong Kong workforce manufactures tooling and molds for plastic injection (plastic injection molding itself is undertaken in China), whereas its China workforce performs relatively unskilled fabrication and assembly.

- The ACL Company, a spinoff from Motorola that produces substrates in Hong Kong with a workforce of 320 (it has no production in China), makes use of Hong Kong's highly skilled workforce to maintain strict quality control.

- Varitronix Ltd. produces liquid crystal displays in Hong Kong using a total workforce of 350 that is highly experienced in identifying and trouble-shooting process defects (in addition, Varitronix employs 500 people in the PRC and 350 in Malaysia).

Hong Kong's manufacturers of printed circuit boards (Elec & Eltek, Meadville, and Wong's) exhibit a similar division of labor, insofar as they tend to produce more complicated, multi-layer boards in Hong Kong and more simple boards in China owing to perceived differences in labor quality.

Some Hong Kong firms still maintain some production engineering functions in Hong Kong (such as materials control), but the stated intention is to move them to China as soon as skills permit, to locate them as close as possible to production. Therefore, as Chinese production managers gain experience, one would expect *production capabilities* related to managing labor-intensive or mass production operations to be cultivated more in China than in Hong Kong. The production capabilities that one would expect to improve in Hong Kong would be only those related to the employment of highly skilled labor. I infer this from the experience of those foreign firms operating throughout East Asia, including Hong Kong, which relatively quickly transferred management responsibility for production-related tasks to local partners, as such partners rapidly assimilated production capabilities.

Investment Capability (Project Execution)

'Flexibility'

Hong Kong's survival as a manufacturer after the loss of its low-wage advantage is commonly attributed to 'flexibility'. This term has acquired many meanings that range from flexibility in production (a shift from one to another model on the automobile assembly line, for example) to the emergence of new start-ups to replace bankrupted firms. My observations of Hong Kong's electronics sector, in keeping with those of Reif and Sodini in Chapter 10, suggest a meaning of 'flexibility' that relates to project execution: Hong Kong's dominant enterprises possess the ability to introduce new products and processes quickly owing to skills associated with machinery *prototyping* and simple *project engineering,* especially skills related to the redesign of products to suit modest changes in consumer tastes, an example being the 900 MHz cellular telephones supplied by VTech Holdings Ltd. under its own brand name. Firms in Hong Kong that do their own machinery design, tooling, and prototyping for their China production operations reduce costs by customizing the scale of their machinery—they can re-engineer the design and size of their production equipment to suit changing output characteristics and levels as dictated by demand conditions rather than by standard equipment specifications supplied by international machinery makers. A case in point is Johnson Electric, which designs key pieces of machinery in Hong Kong to use in China in order to produce its micromotors.

The skills inherent in tooling, prototyping, and product redesign are at the level of 'mid-technology' as defined earlier—they are not science-based but neither are they exclusively based on low-cost, unskilled labor. Hong Kong now excels at manufacturing activities that embody mid-technology skills, at least as exemplified by the electronics industry.

Source of Technology

Firms require technology to introduce a new product or expand production capacity. They can either make or buy such technology, but even if they buy it they must invest in their own capabilities (to varying degrees) to ensure that their technology works optimally. In this section I examine the technology sources of the Hong Kong electronics firms in the sample.

Joint Ventures, Strategic Alliances, and Overseas Acquisitions

Technology was typically acquired through a foreign partner in a joint venture or strategic alliance.[8] Aside from large multinational firms operating in Hong Kong's electronics sector (especially Motorola and at one time Philips), smaller foreign firms have also been prevalent. In 1993 the electronics and electrical products industries in Hong Kong accounted for 39.4 percent of the total stock of foreign investment in Hong Kong's manufacturing sector (the next most important manufacturing industry for foreign investment was textiles and clothing, but with only 9.6 percent of the total).[9] The following companies exhibited a typical pattern of technology acquisition through joint-venture investment.

- The ACL Company was restructured by American managers who formerly worked for Motorola (US). Currently ACL employs 80 people in the United States (located close to Motorola facilities) who are responsible for many of ACL's product designs.
- Albatronics, Inc. was founded by a Japanese engineer who became Sony's agent for distributing the CPUs (central processing units) for CD players in Hong Kong. The company has since diversified into other product lines but still employs Japanese engineers in Hong Kong (total employment in Hong Kong is 250 and in China is 3,000). Additionally, Albatronics acquires technology from Sony and other buyers, including Japan's NEC (Nippon Electronics Corporation).
- The Epson/Seiko Company, a wholly owned Japanese foreign investment, manufactures watch movements in Hong Kong using a highly mechanized production process designed in Japan (employment in Hong Kong is only 400, down from 1,000 in 1986). It also employs 12,000 workers in China using a labor-intensive process to produce printers for computers. The company uses Hong Kong as a regional headquarters to service operations in the PRC, as well as to make watch movements.
- Gold Peak Batteries, a division of Gold Peak Industries, has formed a joint venture with Toshiba for its 1.5 volt battery. Technology from the United States for other product lines is acquired through various strategic alliances and foreign licenses.

Hong Kong's overall reliance on foreign investment by comparison with other late-industrializing countries is indicated in Table 14.2. With the exception of the years 1986 through 1990, foreign inflows of direct (equity) capital was roughly 5.5 percent of gross fixed capital formation (GFCF) for all sectors, not just manufacturing. Assuming for all countries in Table 14.2 that the share of foreign investment in total GFCF is the same as the share in the manufacturing sector, the importance of foreign manufacturing investment in Hong Kong was high relative to that of some latecomers (Brazil, India, Indonesia, South Korea, and Taiwan) but low relative to that of others (especially Malaysia and Singapore).[10] Assuming Singapore is one of Hong Kong's major competitors for foreign investment—and that the lower the share of foreign investment in GFCF the greater the need for indigenous investments in new technology—then Hong Kong should be investing relatively more in its own technological capabilities than Singapore. In fact, it is not doing so.

Table 14.2
Foreign Direct Investment (FDI) Inflows as Share of Gross Fixed Capital Formation

	Annual Average (%)				
Country	1971–75	1976–80	1981–85	1986–90	1991–93
ARGENTINA	0.1	2.1	5	11.1	37.63
BRAZIL	4.2	3.9	4.3	1.7	1.47
CHILE	-7.3	4.2	6.7	20.6	8.53
CHINA	-	-	0.9	2.1	10.37
HONG KONG	5.9	4.2	6.9	12.9	5.70
INDIA	0.3	0.1	0.1	0.3	0.63
INDONESIA	4.6	2.4	0.9	2.1	4.50
KOREA	1.9	0.4	0.5	1.2	0.63
MALAYSIA	15.2	11.9	10.8	11.7	24.57
MEXICO	3.5	3.6	5.0	7.5	6.80
SINGAPORE	15.0	16.6	17.4	35.0	37.40
TAIWAN	1.4	1.2	1.5	3.7	2.60
THAILAND	3.0	1.5	3.0	6.5	4.70
TURKEY	-	-	0.8	2.1	3.17

Source: United Nations Council on Trade and Development, *World Investment Report,* New York, 1992 and 1995, as cited in A. Amsden and M. Mourshed, 'Scientific Publications and the Capabilities of Late Industrializers,' 1997. (See Note 18.)

NOTE: FDI Inflows comprise: equity capital, reinvested earnings, and intra-company loans.

Customers

A second source of technology for new investments, especially those involving new products, is *customers* from industrially advanced countries.

1. The designs and specifications of the ACL Company's substrates, for example, are determined by its customers, who pass on technical information to ACL. Motorola accounts for 40 percent of ACL's sales and its top six customers account for a total of 80 percent of sales. Such customer concentration allows for a relatively simple flow of new information.

2. Similarly, Albatronics relies on its Japanese buyers (especially Sony and NEC) for new information and product design suggestions.

3. The product designs for almost all of ALCO's consumer electronics come from information supplied by customers such as Aiwa of Japan.

4. The technology of Hong Kong's producers of printed circuit boards (PCBs) (Elec & Eltek, Meadville, and Wong's) is highly buyer-driven. Wong's, which recently expanded its production facilities in both Hong Kong and China, also exemplifies the sourcing of foreign technology for *process* expansions and not just product changes. The general manager of Wong's new production facility in Hong Kong is Japanese, formerly with Toshiba, with extensive experience in the world PCB business.

5. A typical buyer-driven electronics producer is Primatronix, which makes answering machines in China (2,000 employees), with a backup staff of 70 people in Hong Kong. Primatronix deviates from the standard path of technology acquisition only by having bought a US company in 1988 (Record-A-Call) with a lot of patents. (Another Hong Kong company, Gold Peak, also acquired a foreign firm with technological capabilities—and a familiar brand name, Clipsal.)

Innovation Capabilities: Absence of R&D

The three elements of an innovation capability are basic research, applied research, and development (see Table 14.1). Aggregate data on research and development (R&D) expenditures in Hong Kong are almost nonexistent, but a US National Science Foundation international study provides data for Hong Kong for one year only, 1989, on R&D expenditures as a percentage of gross domestic product (GDP). Hong Kong's percentage of 0.4 compares *un*favorably with that of Japan (2.9 percent), Singapore (0.9 percent), Korea (1.9 percent), and Taiwan (1.4 percent). It merely equals that of China (0.4 percent). Given a higher incidence of foreign investment in Singapore than Hong Kong (and even a higher incidence of foreign investment in China in 1991–93, as shown in Table 14.2), and assuming that Hong Kong's relative international ranking in R&D expenditure is similar for manufacturing only, then Hong Kong's seemingly negligible R&D activity does not inspire hope that manufacturing capabilities will become an engine of growth in the near future.

Based on my sample and additional evidence in Chapter 10, almost certainly no electronic firms in Hong Kong undertake basic research and probably few, if any, undertake even applied research, as these two terms are commonly understood in industrially advanced countries. Given the ambiguity of the meaning of 'development', the question is what type of activities under this rubric Hong Kong companies engage in, if any.

'Development'

The more firms carry out production under their own brand names (OBM, or original brand manufacture) and the less they produce on contract under other firms' brand names (OEM, or original equipment manufacture), the more they are likely to invest in their own technological capabilities. The two types of production tend to be mutually exclusive in the same narrowly defined industry; otherwise an OEM producer that badges its own products would be competing against its own customers. Some Hong Kong electronics companies, however, operate as an OEM producer in one market niche and an OBM producer in another niche.[11] The transition from OEM to OBM is difficult if there is a lack of skill in design and testing, and an absence of knowledge of international standards and marketing.

Two major original brand manufacturers in Hong Kong's consumer electronics industry—Team Concepts and VTech— both primarily produce educational toys. Team Concepts employs 2,000 workers in China and 250 in Hong Kong, of which 200 are engineers and 100 are design engineers. Team Concepts spends 5 percent of its sales revenues on 'R&D', by which it means product design engineering for electronic educational toys (whose designs change less rapidly than those of other toys). VTech, with 16,000 employees in China and 1,000 in Hong Kong, produces 60 percent of its output under its own brand names and spends 4 percent of its sales on 'R&D', which also involves simply product design engineering (although both companies also conduct 'R&D' overseas, as mentioned later). The two companies illustrate the strong connection between OBM and investment in in-house technological capabilities. They also suggest that in Hong Kong's consumer electronics sector R&D means development, and that development tends to involve product design (or redesign) engineering but not the invention of any basic new concepts.

Sources of technology for new product lines or process expansions, therefore, come from multiple sources: through foreign business contacts and investments in in-house capabilities. The latter, however, appear to be relatively small and almost nonexistent in the case of OEM suppliers. The competitive strategy even of OBM suppliers is deliberately not to undertake extensive research but instead, to follow industry leaders and to lag behind the world technological frontier by a few years. This is probably not so difficult in industries where technological change even at the world frontier is relatively slow. Companies such as Matsushita, with a similar strategy in industries with fast-changing technology such as consumer audio electronics, invest far more in R&D in order to stay even one or two years behind.

Latecomers to industrialization such as Taiwan, South Korea, Hong Kong, Singapore, and other fast-growing East Asian economies initially competed in world markets exclusively on the basis of costs, whether related to cheap labor or scale economies.[12] This contrasts with the economically advanced countries, which have typically competed internationally on the basis of novel, proprietary products and processes (ignoring raw materials).[13] In between these two extremes are mid-technology industries and related capabilities (defined earlier). I have explored the extent to which Hong Kong's business enterprises are shifting from competing almost exclusively on the basis of costs to competing increasingly on the basis of skills.

All in all, Hong Kong's electronics sector suggests that relatively little investment has been expended on developing more than the most basic technological skills. It is difficult, therefore, to see how manufacturing capabilities can serve as a dynamic engine of growth in the near future, particularly in the case of consumer electronics, where skills do not appear to have succeeded in energizing demand even in the recent past. Between 1990 and 1994, output of consumer electronics in Hong Kong fell sharply (see Table 14.3). Production of electrical machinery rose, but only with respect to machinery, equipment and apparatus, which may partially reflect the efforts of some firms to customize their own machinery for their Chinese plant expansions.

Instead, Hong Kong's electronics firms appear to continue to compete almost exclusively on the basis of costs; they survive by taking advantage of market opportunities after profit margins of world industry leaders have fallen, as noted in Chapter 10. Costs and capabilities do intersect, however, insofar as Hong Kong's competitiveness partially rests on 'flexibility,' and flexibility depends on project execution skills. Mostly, however, cost competitiveness has been achieved through locational decisions. It is to such decisions and their management that this study now turns.

Table 14.3
Electrical Machinery Production, 1990–1994

| | (volume indices: 1990=100) | | | | |
Year	1990	1991	1992	1993	1994
Electrical machinery, etc.	100	103	105	107	111
Consumer electronics	100	99	95	88	88
Mach, eqpt, and appar.	100	109	125	141	146
Total manufacturing	100	101	102	102	102

Source: Hong Kong Census and Statistics Department, *Hong Kong Monthly Digest of Statistics,* various issues.

Location of Manufacturing Activities: Hong Kong versus China

In this section I investigate why established firms (foreign and local) have retained certain manufacturing activities in Hong Kong. My analysis of locational choice is formulated in terms of cost, including sunk costs, which I take to reflect the dead weight of history. Relocating certain manufacturing activities to China, especially labor-intensive production to the Pearl River Delta, has helped Hong Kong firms remain cost-effective in world markets. Retaining certain activities in Hong Kong has also contributed to flexibility, which also reduces costs. A location in Hong Kong allows firms to benefit from: (a) skilled and experienced production workers (in machinery building and process control), which allows the production of new products to be quickly implemented; (b) excellent telecommunications, which allow flows of information to be managed efficiently between China, Hong Kong, and the rest of the world; (c) other top-notch physical infrastructure, including port facilities, which allow imports, exports, and re-exports to be quickly processed. In addition, government policies subsidize physical plant expansion in industrial estates that cater to mid-tech (and ideally high-tech) firms and that minimize transaction costs related to international trade, which is almost entirely free.

A rule of thumb among the electronics firms I investigated appears to be that every conceivable activity that can be relocated to China is a worthy target for relocation because differences in labor costs between Hong Kong and China are so sharp (estimated on the order of at least 10:1), not simply for production workers but also for managers and engineers.

China has eclipsed Hong Kong as an important venue for total manufacturing employment. Data from some of the electronic companies in this survey (as shown in Table 14.4) indicate that firms employ on average almost 13 times as many workers in China as in Hong Kong.

The type of employment that has tended to remain in Hong Kong over time, and the type that, in theory, may be expected to increase in the future, is analyzed according to the following categories: administration; development; high-end production; and distribution.

Table 14.4
Distribution of Employment Between Hong Kong and
China, 1996

(partial sample of electronics firms)

	Hong Kong	China
ACL	350	0
Albatronics	250	3000
ALCO	1400	14000
ASM	800	1500
Avantec	25	300
China Aerospace	50	15000
Elec and Eltek	670	2100
Epson	540	2000
Gold Peak	1300	10000
Johnson Electric	560	12530
Lafe	292	5000
Mabuchi Industry	400	30000
Meadville	700	1040
Primatronix	75	1500
QPL	800	0
Silcon Electrics	30	150
Team Concepts	250	2000
Valence Semiconductor	27	0
Varitronix	350	500
Vitelic (HK)	210	0
VTech	1000	16000
Wing Sang Bakelite	52	1000
Wong's Circuit	1130	610
Mean	460	5800

Source: Company data

Administration

Firms retain their administrative functions in Hong Kong
partly for historical reasons and partly for very rational economic reasons, assuming that administrative functions are
the brain of a company and that information is the brain's
sustenance. Given Hong Kong's economic openness, its fluency in the English language, and its excellent telecommunications, tourist and transportation infrastructure, Hong Kong
facilitates the rapid absorption of all types of global information, technical and commercial. Some companies report, for
example, that English speaking buyers/vendors prefer to con-

duct business in Hong Kong than in China. Facility in English is one of Hong Kong's key assets *vis à vis* China.

One firm, Company A, which makes consumer hair care electronics (such as curlers and hair dryers), car electronics, and kitchenware, exhibits the typical pattern of retaining a set of administrative activities in Hong Kong while transferring almost all other manufacturing activities to China. In 1996 the company employed 1,000 people in China and 52 people in Hong Kong (as noted in Table 14.4). Its Hong Kong workforce was engaged as follows:

5 engineers on 'R&D' who work with customer designs;

9 people in materials planning and control;

9 people in tooling;

8 people in three teams concerned with new projects for specific products;

2 people in marketing and sales;

4 people in accounting;

15 support staff.

Company A reports that its employees get training from exposure to other factories in Hong Kong, from the Hong Kong Productivity Council, and from internal learning. The company cooperates closely with Hong Kong Polytechnic University. Since 1992 it has brought in ten student interns. These students are industrial engineers or manufacturing process engineers who bring in know-how for the company's computer information systems. The salary of these students is shared 50:50 with Hong Kong Polytechnic University (under the 'Teacher Companies Scheme'). In this case, as in many others, the decision to locate in Hong Kong is enhanced by Hong Kong's expanding technical university system.

For Company B, Hong Kong serves as the site for its equipment to contact the rest of world (teleconferencing), and to control its China operations. Communications from China are considered to be difficult due to shortages of telecommunications links. The company spent a lot of money and effort to unite its Hong Kong and Shenzhen operations with fiber-optic lines installed by the Telecommunications Authority of China through Hongkong Telecom. Now Company B has six lines for data transmission and voice telephone (200 telephone system lines from China to headquarters). It also has video-conferencing from Hong Kong via satellite worldwide, and then onto customers. Video-conferencing is used to communicate orders from Europe to Shenzhen, which reduces production cycle time.

Development

'Development' in the context of the Hong Kong electronics industry (as noted in the previous section) tends to involve engineering activities related to product development. Value added per person tends to be relatively high given the engineering content of such activities and therefore 'development' is a prime candidate for expansion in Hong Kong's manufacturing sector of the future.

Nevertheless, given that much development activity in the electronics industry is customer-driven, product development is likely to occur close to where customers are located, and not necessarily at corporate headquarters. Co-development, in fact, appears to be an international trend.[14] It also appears to be a trend in leading Hong Kong electronics companies. They do a substantial amount of development work outside Hong Kong.

Sales of Company B's products by region are as follows: Hong Kong and China, 34 percent (there is no meaningful distinction between the two since production in China is distributed through Hong Kong due to Hong Kong's more reliable port facilities); other Asia, 13 percent; North America, 27 percent; and Europe, 26 percent. Given the importance of Company B's European and North American markets, in addition to its Asian market, 'R&D' (amounting to approximately 4 percent of total sales) was undertaken in Hong Kong as well as in Switzerland, Germany, and the United States. Moreover, R&D in Hong Kong is internationalized: about 10 to 15 long-term foreign engineers work in Hong Kong, including Chinese, Japanese, and Americans. The product development center in Germany is headed by a German engineer who first spent many years working for the company in Hong Kong (and who was responsible for many of its patents).

VTech, similarly, carries out product development not just in Hong Kong but also close to its customer bases in the United Kingdom and Canada.

Thus, the amount of development work that occurs in Hong Kong is likely to depend on: (a) the number of foreign firms that locate in Hong Kong to be close to their own customer base; and (b) the number of their customers that operate in the Pearl River Delta.

The extent of development activities that will be located in Hong Kong, then, depends critically on the customer base that emerges in Hong Kong and China. The expansion of high-value-added product development activity in Hong Kong depends critically on the extent to which Hong Kong's economy is integrated with that of China, and on the growth rate of China's economy, which creates customers for Hong Kong's manufacturing activities, such as development.

High-Skilled Production

The types of production activities that are retained in Hong Kong tend to be skilled, related to tooling and the prototyping of machinery (as in the case of Gold Peak, Johnson Electric, and VTech) or quality-driven process control [as in Varitronix, ACL, Tec Hill (customizing chips) and QPL (manufacturing casing and legs of chips].

The skill bias in Hong Kong-based production is evident from the example of Company C, the new production facility of which is being located in Hong Kong (at a government subsidized industrial site). Company C intends to produce more of its complicated, multi-layer printed circuit boards in Hong Kong, and generally its Hong Kong facility is designed to have higher productivity than its China (Huizhou) facility. Measuring productivity as square-foot panels per employee per week, virtually every function, from quality control to total employment, is expected to have higher productivity in Hong Kong than in China, a function of better training and tighter management control in Hong Kong. What is questionable is how long such an advantage will remain with Hong Kong as Chinese industry restructures and keeps investing in technological skills.[15]

Distribution

The strategy of most Hong Kong electronics companies—of quickly moving into a market niche that high-end producers begin to abandon (or neglect)—requires rapid response in terms of both production and distribution. Given Hong Kong's excellent port and air transportation facilities, it is not surprising that distribution activities usually are located in Hong Kong rather than in China.

As noted earlier, Company B distributes all of its China production through Hong Kong. Approximately 67 percent of its principal competitor's worldwide sales (equaling roughly one-fourth of total world sales) is run through Hong Kong. Epson/Seiko distributes 60 percent of its worldwide manufactures through Hong Kong. The competitive asset of both Tec Hil and QPL is fast distribution, and Hong Kong provides the marketing services both companies require.

Thus, the manufacturing activities that tend to be located in Hong Kong rather than in China are those that require the assets in which Hong Kong abounds: experienced managers, engineers, skilled machinists, and process control operators, as well as good distribution facilities. China, however, is likely to catch up quickly with Hong Kong in supplies of skilled production workers and even engineers (assuming current high levels of investment in restructuring continue). Moreover, given a global tendency towards co-development (buyer and seller jointly developing a product), the Hong Kong engineers' product development activities will increasingly depend on proximity to available customers, most likely operating out of China. The future of Hong Kong's locational advantage for high-value-added development, I would argue, will depend on how closely Hong Kong firms integrate with those on the Mainland.

Location and Ownership:
Motorola (China) Electronics Ltd.

The new entry of multinational firms seeking to take advantage of Hong Kong's locational assets is a conceivable source of dynamism in Hong Kong's future. If Motorola (China) Electronics Ltd. is any guide, however, multinational regional investment will be principally be in China, with questionable investments in Hong Kong, other than possibly skeletal administrative regional headquarters. Much depends on whether Hong Kong can provide *product development support services* that are cheaper/better than those provided by China. These services have been singled out because they are what Motorola (Hong Kong) [and Phillips Hong Kong/China] provides its semiconductor operations in China, and what Motorola (Singapore) provides its paging products operations in China. The support services provided by Singapore, however, are increasingly being transferred to China.[16]

Historically, Motorola's biggest business line in China has been pagers, and this line has developed from the manufacture of simple products, to the provision of technical support services, and finally to the establishment of China's own 'R&D' facility for the local market. Motorola in 1983 established a Singapore Design Center in order to be closer to its Asian customers. The Center's team of engineers and designers, who are dedicated to paging products, works with counterparts in the United States researching and developing new paging products for Asia and the rest of the world. The Motorola Confidant and Scriptor LX2 pagers are the result of the Singapore team's development efforts. After a decade, Motorola has begun to transfer this expertise to China with the establishment in 1994 of a China Design Center in Beijing. Equipped with the most advanced instruments from Motorola, the center has a mission gradually to develop expertise to support fully Motorola's China paging business, although currently the research work in Beijing is basically secondary, based on technology developed in the United States and Singapore. Most of the 20 to 35 employees of the China Design Center are Chinese technically oriented professionals with Masters or PhD degrees and some post-graduate work experience.

Semiconductor design tends to be more technically demanding than pager design, so the question is whether or not the design work now handled in Hong Kong for China's semiconductor production will be transferred to China. The most likely organization in China for such design work is the Motorola (China) Electronics Ltd.'s Semiconductor Products Sector (SPS), initially intended to provide customer service for semiconductor-, as well as computer-related products. SPS has established R&D liaisons with China's best universities and government laboratories.

The assessment by Western experts of China's high-tech capabilities in electronics varies, but influential champions exist:

> China may become a major competitor for the electronics industry's Japanese, European, and American powers that be. Last summer, Intel CEO Andy Grove told a group of FORTUNE editors that he thought his biggest competition in ten years would come from China. Asked recently if he stood by that forecast, Grove replied, yes—'but probably in eight years.' (Fortune)[17]

The point is that if Hong Kong wishes to act as a design development center for electronic products produced in China, it will face increasingly intense competition from Chinese design engineering centers and genuine R&D laboratories. The distribution of manufacturing activity between low-wage China and high-wage Hong Kong, therefore, may not take any simple labor-intensive versus skill-intensive dichotomous form. Quite possibly in the near future China will become the locus for low-tech production and high-tech research. Hong Kong's competitive advantage, therefore, will have to be sharpened in the domain of mid-technology activities and related skills.

The international benchmarking of such mid-tech capabilities is the subject of the following section.

Benchmarking Capabilities at the National and Firm Levels

International Comparisons

If Hong Kong's manufacturing sector is to act as an engine of growth, its manufacturing capabilities must be equal to or better than those of its international competitors. In this section I present a global comparison, assessing Hong Kong's technological strengths relative to those of other 'emerging economies,' including Argentina, Brazil, Chile, China, India, Indonesia, Korea, Malaysia, Mexico, Singapore, Taiwan, Thailand, and Turkey (in varying combinations, depending on data availability). 'Capabilities' here include three sets of skills related to production, project execution, and innovation. I compare indicators related to 'science and technology,' which probably most influences innovation. To proxy manufacturing capabilities as accurately as possible I use scientific publications in internationally respected, refereed journals (as compiled by the Institute for Scientific Information, Philadelphia, PA) and US patents.

Science and Technology Indicators

Scientific publications provide one surrogate to measure the scientific and technological capabilities of a country. In the case of the emerging economies, this surrogate also happens to correlate strongly with other indicators of scientific and technological skills.[18] Little published data on R&D for Hong Kong exists (except for the year 1989, which suggests Hong Kong's R&D expenditures are extremely low, as noted earlier). Such data for other emerging economies, however, suggest a fairly positive association with scientific publications. There is also a very high measured correlation (0.85), between growth in scientific publications and growth in US-registered patents. Scientific publications are also positively correlated (0.83) with scientists and engineers in R&D (per million population), as well as with gross fixed capital formation as a share of GDP. It is also worth noting a positive but small correlation between scientific publications and inward foreign direct investment as a share of gross fixed capital formation; foreign investment does not appear to be a strong complement of a country's own scientific publication capacity.

Bearing these correlations in mind, Table 14.5 looks at the average annual growth rate (starting in 1980) of scientific publications. Hong Kong's growth rate, of roughly 40 percent, is hardly trivial, but falls short of that of several competitors, including China and Taiwan (which started from a larger base) and Korea and Singapore (which started from a smaller base). In terms of the ratio of the growth rate of scientific publications to GDP growth, Hong Kong again falls behind that of China, Korea, Singapore, and Taiwan. The major subjects of the scientific publications also provide some suggestion of technological strengths and potential. In 1995, the most important subfields of Hong Kong's scientific publications tended to be engineering and electronics, biochemistry, and applied physics. These contrasted with the major subjects of China's publications, which were chemistry, materials science, and physics.[19] Although it is difficult to draw concrete inferences from these findings, one possible hypothesis is that Hong Kong's publications focus on relatively applied fields whereas those of China are in relatively theoretical ones. If this is correct, it suggests a compatible relationship between the two countries, with one specializing in 'development' and the other in more basic research.

Table 14.5
Growth Rates of GDP and Scientific Publications

	(Average annual growth rates, percentages)		
	(a) GDP 1980-93	(b) Science Pub. 1980-95	Ratio (b)/(a)
ARGENTINA	0.8	6.79	8.5
BRAZIL	2.1	14.07	6.6
CHILE	5.1	3.56	0.7
CHINA	9.6	90.01	9.4
HONG KONG	6.5	40.41	6.2
INDIA	5.2	0.62	0.12
INDONESIA	5.8	20.25	3.5
KOREA	9.1	280.98	30.8
MALAYSIA	6.2	11.08	1.8
MEXICO	1.6	11.30	7.1
SINGAPORE	6.9	82.85	12.0
TAIWAN	7.5	83.47	11.1
THAILAND	8.2	7.12	0.87
TURKEY	4.6	45.79	9.9

Sources: GDP figures: World Bank, *World Development Report*, Washington, DC, 1995.
Science publication figures: Adapted from SciSearch, Institute for Scientific Information, Phila., PA, as presented in Amsden and Mourshed (1997).

Turning to US-registered patents, it is worth noting that because patenting activity varies substantially by industry (and possibly firm), a country's patent record will be influenced by its industrial composition (and firm strategy). Bearing these limitations in mind, Table 14.6 presents data on patent growth. Hong Kong's patent growth rate is impressive, at 76 percent on average over the period 1980–95. By 1995 Hong Kong had many more US patents than China or Singapore. Still, Hong Kong's performance fell well below that of Korea and Taiwan in terms of both number and growth rate of patents.

My lukewarm assessment of Hong Kong's manufacturing capabilities, based on scientific publications and patents, and hence admittedly limited data, parallels that of the US National Science Foundation (NSF).[20] The NSF used five variables to construct a 'technological infrastructure' indicator: number of scientists in R&D; purchases of electronic data processing equipment; and data from a survey asking experts to rate a nation's capability to train citizens locally in academic science and engineering, its ability to make effective use of technical knowledge, and the linkages of its R&D to industry. Among eight Asian countries (Hong Kong, Singapore, South Korea, Taiwan, China, India, Indonesia, and Malaysia), Hong Kong ranked *lowest* (see Figure 14.2).

Figure 14.2
Comparison of Asian Technological Infrastructures

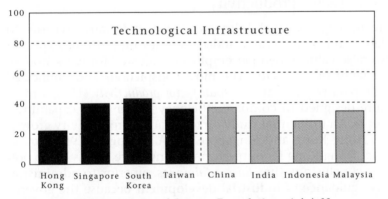

Source: United States National Science Foundation, *Asia's New High-Tech Competitors,* NSF 95-309, Washington, DC, 1995

Hong Kong's poor showing was due in part to the absence of data on the number of scientists and engineers in R&D, which understated its score. Yet Hong Kong's investments in R&D, as discussed earlier, appear to be minimal. It may also have been due to Hong Kong's traditional reliance on entrepreneurial expertise over formally conducted R&D. In addition, 'its comparatively small population may have played some part . . . since numbers of trained scientists and engineers and the size of the attendant R&D enterprise are compared with economies with much larger populations.'[21] Still, the NSF goes on to observe:

> Even though Singapore's population is smaller than Hong Kong's, Singapore's extensive national investments in information technology and its prominence in the region as a computer manufacturer more than compensated for any population bias. Singapore's technological infrastructure was rated nearly as high as South Korea's and better than Taiwan's.[22]

It is noteworthy that the NSF also ranked Singapore at the top in 'productive capacity,' which purports to measure the strength of a nation's current manufacturing infrastructure as a baseline for assessing its capacity for future growth in high-tech activities. For this indicator Hong Kong ranked below Singapore, South Korea, and Malaysia, although almost equal to Taiwan.

Total Factor Productivity

Technological capabilities are expected to raise returns to labor and capital (value added), so they may also be expected to raise value added per employee (adjusted for work hours), or labor productivity. The most conspicuous and publicized comparative data are for *total factor productivity* (TFP), a measure designed to compare efficiency rather than capabilities *per se*. An influential study on total factor productivity growth in Hong Kong and Singapore (by A. Young in 1994) found that Hong Kong far outperformed Singapore.[23] This led to policy conclusions that *laissez-faire* was superior to administrative guidance of industrial development because the government's economic role has been much smaller in Hong Kong than in Singapore. Nevertheless, when the same data set used to compare Hong Kong and Singapore is extended to include other countries, the results are counterintuitive (see Table 14.7). They thus call into question both the economic logic behind the TFP estimates and the accuracy of the statistics on which they are based. Countries with the highest measures of TFP, such as Pakistan and the Congo, are, in fact, among the worst international competitors, and exceptionally poor performers such as Uganda and Burma (Myanmar) outshine stellar economies such as Japan and Korea.

When a more simple measure of total factor productivity is used, namely value added (wages plus profits) per worker, the international comparison is less favorable to Hong Kong. As Table 14.8 indicates, when the prevailing US level of productivity is used as the standard, between 1973 and 1978 productivity in Hong's Kong's manufacturing sector and electronics sector specifically hardly rose. Moreover, Hong Kong's productivity rose much less than in South Korea or Singapore. Nevertheless, these data are not definitive either; large changes over short time periods may reflect exchange rate movements rather than underlying productivity trends.

Table 14.6
US-Registered Design and Utility Patents by Country of Origin

Country	1980	1985	1990	1995	% Change 1980–95	% Change 1980–85	% Change 1985–1990	% Change 1990–95
ARGENTINA	20	12	19	32	29%	-40%	58%	68%
BRAZIL	24	30	45	70	44%	25%	50%	56%
CHILE	5	2	2	7	63%	-60%	0%	250%
CHINA	1	1	48	63	1577%	0%	4700%	31%
HONG KONG	49	66	151	248	76%	35%	129%	64%
INDIA	4	11	23	38	116%	175%	109%	65%
INDONESIA	1	2	3	7	94%	100%	50%	133%
KOREA	9	50	290	1,240	421%	456%	480%	328%
MALAYSIA	1	3	6	8	111%	200%	100%	33%
MEXICO	43	35	34	45	4%	-19%	-3%	32%
SINGAPORE	3	10	16	61	192%	233%	60%	281%
TAIWAN	71	199	861	2,087	218%	180%	333%	142%
THAILAND	3	1	3	10	122%	-67%	200%	233%
TURKEY	1	1	3	2	56%	0%	200%	-33%
14 LI TOTAL*	235	423	1,504	3,918	165%	80%	256%	161%
Total Issued US Patents	66,297	77,361	99,452	114,870	20%	17%	29%	16%

Table 14.6 *continued*
US-Registered Design and Utility Patents by Country of Origin

Country	1980	1985	1990	1995	% Change 1980–95	% Change 1980–85	% Change 1985–1990	% Change 1990–95
FRANCE	2,150	2,516	3,093	3,010	12%	17%	23%	-3%
GERMANY	5,895	6,906	7,861	6,874	6%	17%	14%	-13%
JAPAN	7,401	13,351	20,743	22,871	49%	80%	55%	10%
USA	40,847	43,481	53,205	65,425	17%	6%	22%	23%
As Share of Total Issued US Patents:								
14 LI	0.35%	0.55%	1.51%	3.41%	1.02%	0.19%	0.97%	1.90%
FRANCE	3.24%	3.25%	3.11%	2.62%	-0.21%	0.00%	-0.14%	-0.49%
GERMANY	8.89%	8.93%	7.90%	5.98%	-0.97%	0.04%	-1.02%	-1.92%
JAPAN	11.16%	17.26%	20.86%	19.91%	2.92%	6.09%	3.60%	-0.95%
USA	61.61%	56.21%	53.50%	56.96%	-1.55%	-5.41%	-2.71%	3.46%

Source: CASSIS database, US Patent and Trademark Office, Washington, DC.
* LI = late-industrializing countries

Notes:

(1) Country of Origin is based on the residence of the first-named inventor.

(2) The 1980–95 percent change is an average of the three average percent changes for 1980–85, 1985–90, and 1990–95.

Table 14.7
Counter-Intuition: Annual Growth of 'Total Factor Productivity'(1970–1985)

1	Egypt	0.035	23	Guinea	0.014	45	Turkey	0.008
2	Pakistan	0.030	24	South Korea	0.014	46	Netherlands	0.008
3	Botswana	0.029	25	Iran	0.014	47	Ethiopia	0.007
4	Congo	0.028	26	Burma	0.014	48	Austria	0.007
5	Malta	0.026	27	Mauritius	0.013	49	Australia	0.007
6	Hong Kong	0.025	28	China	0.013	50	Spain	0.006
7	Syria	0.025	29	Denmark	0.013	51	Kenya	0.006
8	Zimbabwe	0.024	30	Israel	0.012	52	France	0.005
9	Gabon	0.024	31	Greece	0.012	53	Liberia	0.004
10	Tunisia	0.024	32	Japan	0.012	54	Paraguay	0.004
11	Cameroon	0.024	33	Luxembourg	0.012	55	Honduras	0.004
12	Lesotho	0.022	34	Yugoslavia	0.011	56	Portugal	0.004
13	Uganda	0.021	35	Tanzania	0.011	57	U.S.A.	0.004
14	Cyprus	0.021	36	Colombia	0.011	58	Belgium	0.004
15	Thailand	0.019	37	Sweden	0.010	59	Canada	0.003
16	Bangladesh	0.019	38	Malaysia	0.010	60	Algeria	0.003
17	Iceland	0.018	39	Malawi	0.010	61	CAR	0.002
18	Italy	0.018	40	Brazil	0.010	62	India	0.001
19	Norway	0.017	41	Panama	0.009	63	Singapore	0.001
20	Finland	0.015	42	U.K.	0.009	64	Sri Lanka	0.001
21	Taiwan	0.015	43	W. Germany	0.009	65	Fiji	0.001
22	Ecuador	0.014	44	Mali	0.008	66	Switzerland	0.000

Source: A. Young, 'Lessons from the East Asian NICs: A Contrarian View,' *European Economic Review*, 38 (1994).

Table 14.8
Ratio of East Asian to US Productivity, Selected Years
(Index of value per worker, US = 1.0)

	1973	1976	1982	1986
Hong Kong				
Manufacturing	0.22	0.22	0.27	0.26
Electronics	0.21	0.23	0.33	0.28
S. Korea				
Manufacturing	.29#	0.31	0.41	0.46
Electronics	0.27#	0.28	0.38	0.48
Singapore				
Manufacturing	.28#	0.34	0.44	0.55
Electronics	.31#	0.29	0.33	0.59

#=1970

Source: Adapted from D. Dollar and E. Wolff, *Competitiveness, Convergence, and International Specialization,* Cambridge, Mass.: MIT Press, 1993, #915, pp. 172–74.

Hong Kong's poor relative showing among its neighbors in technological and productive capacity is reflected in its relatively poor position in terms of wages for production workers in manufacturing. Table 14.9 presents comparative data on hourly compensation costs for manufacturing production workers for the period 1975–1990. At the beginning of the period Hong Kong tended to lead in wages. By the end of the period there was a convergence among Hong Kong, Singapore, South Korea, and Taiwan, but Hong Kong ranked at the lowest end of the spectrum. By contrast, other data indicate that Hong Kong's *per capita income growth* is keeping abreast with (or ahead of) these other countries' per capita incomes, possibly indicating a change towards more unequal income distribution in Hong Kong.

All in all, international comparisons of Hong Kong's manufacturing capabilities based on relatively up-to-date evidence lend some support to our more discursive findings on capabilities presented in the first part of this chapter. Namely, Hong Kong's capabilities are far from the top in Asia and are often wanting on their own terms. There is little to inspire hope that they will act as an engine of growth and propel manufacturing activity in the future unless they are substantially upgraded.

Table 14.9
Hourly Compensation Costs for Production Workers in Manufacturing: 1975–90

Region/Country	1975	1980	1984	1985	1986	1987	1988	1989	1990
Newly industrialized economies[1]									
Hong Kong	0.50	1.15	1.52	1.59	1.71	2.06	2.57	3.27	3.75
Singapore	0.76	1.51	1.58	1.73	1.88	2.09	2.40	2.70	3.20
South Korea	0.84	1.49	2.46	2.47	2.23	2.31	2.67	3.15	3.78
Taiwan	0.33	0.97	1.22	1.25	1.34	1.65	2.30	3.29	3.82
	0.40	1.00	1.42	1.50	1.73	2.26	2.82	3.53	3.95
China[2]	0.17	0.30	0.25	0.24	0.24	0.24	N/A	N/A	N/A
India	0.19	0.44	0.42	0.35	0.39	N/A	N/A	N/A	N/A

[1]Trade-weighted measure.
[2]China's data are for all employees.
N/A = not available

NOTES: Hourly compensation is defined as all payments made directly to the worker, before payroll deductions of any kind, and employer insurance expenditures. The compensation and other pay measures are computed in national currency units and are converted into US dollars at prevailing commercial market currency exchange rates which the US Bureau of Labor Statistics considers the appropriate measure for comparing levels of employer labor costs.

Sources: Data for all countries except China are from Bureau of Labor Statistics, 'International Comparisons of Hourly Compensation Costs for Production Workers in Manufacturing, 1975–90,' Report 817, Washington, DC, November 1991; data for China are published data from BLS, December 1990, as cited in US National Science Foundation, L. Rausch, *Asia's New High-Tech Competitors*, Washington, DC: US Government Printing Office.

Firm-Level Comparisons

This section benchmarks the mid-tech manufacturing activities of two sets of Hong Kong firms with their Japanese cohorts, one set (A) that manufactures a product we shall refer to as 'widgets' (the Hong Kong firm will be referred to as '1A' and the Japanese firm as '2A') and another set (B) that manufactures printed circuit boards (three Hong Kong companies and a Japanese firm 'B2').

Widgets

1A (the Hong Kong firm) and 2A (the Japanese firm) are both family-owned firms with some public equity ownership. Both companies have relocated their labor-intensive assembly operations in China. Both are considered to be well-managed enterprises by the business press. There are, however, two crucial differences between the two companies that impact on their technological capabilities: the proximity of their headquarters to their customer base and their size (2A is roughly three times larger than 1A). 2A's customer base is mainly in Japan, whereas 1A's is more global. 2A employs about three times as many people in China as 1A does. These two factors have been both cause and effect of *differences in the level of manufacturing capabilities*. My research suggests that 2A's skill level appears to be different in subtle ways from 1A's although both companies spend about the same percentage of sales on product development, and 1A outshines 2A in specific product lines. Moreover, the amount of development and R&D activity that 2A undertakes in Japan is proportionately greater than that which 1A undertakes in Hong Kong.

The issue of customer base has conditioned the *types* of products that each company produces. Given Japan's well-developed electronics sector, 2A specializes in components for video and audio equipment, among other products, whereas the Hong Kong firm, 1A, manufactures components for a more heterogenous customer and end-user base.[24] The demand for widget performance may be equally exacting in both product lines but 2A services customers whose products change relatively rapidly. Therefore, 2A's own product development must involve not simply incremental improvements to stable designs, but also a continuum of significantly new designs.

Variations in level of technological capability are suggested, not only by differences in product mix but also by differences in *patenting behavior*. A small sample of recent patents by each company indicates a relatively high level of design capability in *both* companies, and differences in the use of advanced electronics. Design capabilities reflect both education and training as well as the skills accumulated over the years of R&D in close conjunction with advanced manufacturing. Hong Kong's track record in these respects in companies and the universities needs to move along a trajectory that Japan, too, sought to pursue.

Given the need to work closely with customers (who are the real potential competitors of both 2A and 1A, should such customers decide to make their own widgets), the existence in Japan of a large and exceedingly demanding customer base has enabled 2A to keep the brains of its company entirely in Japan; almost all R&D and product development are done there. By contrast, 1A's product development is more globalized because its customer base is more geographically dispersed. Much of its engineering creativity is located in Western advanced industrial countries (some patents have come from foreign engineers working in overseas development centers).

As for differences in size, 2A's strategy is to mass-produce generic widgets and convince customers to accept standardization in the interests of lower costs. 1A's products, by contrast, are more customized. Therefore, the tooling and process equipment that both companies make for their assembly production are different. The Hong Kong firm, 1A, like other firms in its industry, buys its standard processing equipment and makes special feature assembly equipment that is very expensive to buy. The method it uses to make such machinery tends to require highly skilled machinists producing in small batches. By contrast, the Japanese firm, 2A, makes 70 percent of its machinery, including highly automated systems. Towards this end it established a separate company with high-precision tooling capabilities.

All in all, while 1A's technological capabilities should not in any way be disparaged, and are improved incrementally, they appear at the moment to differ from those of 2A along various dimensions (product mix, process development capabilities and R&D techniques). What is more, the activities that 2A retains in Japan appear to be more extensive than those that 1A retains in Hong Kong, although employment in both corporate headquarters is approximately equal.

Printed Circuit Boards (PCBs)

Differences in scale and proximity to discriminating customers also differentiate the activities of PCB manufacturers in Japan and Hong Kong.

Differences in scale are illustrated in Table 14.10.[25] A large Japanese PCB producer, '2B', had sales greater by a factor of 5.3 than '1B', a large Hong Kong producer. The demand potential for PCBs presented by the fast-growing Japanese economy led 2B as early as 1975 to make a risky investment in an expensive CAD system for design at a time when other competitors were designing boards by hand. Competitors also eventually introduced CAD, but 2B's standards had already been adopted by major customers. CAD enabled 2B not only to produce more accurate designs but also to design more quickly, in an industry where quick response is essential. Currently 2B conducts all of its R&D and almost all designing in Japan, through co-development with its electronic and automotive customers. Close interaction with customers and short lead times are 2B's strengths. Information about designs is transmitted to the Japanese company's other facilities in Singapore, Malaysia, Indonesia, and Belgium through fax.

In addition to being a leader in design, 2B has also created other aspects of PCB manufacture, which involves several different types of processes—machining, chemical transformation, printing, and so forth. At a time when other companies were making holes on boards by pressing, 2B introduced a novel drilling process. The company also innovated in its use of laser technology and electric beams. Innovativeness increased 2B's customer base which, in turn, allowed it to invest more in expensive equipment. In terms of process, scale enables the Japanese producer to use large automated production lines to achieve cost-competitiveness.

Table 14.10
World Sales of Printed Circuit Boards, 1995

Producers	Country	Sales (US$ Millions)
1. CMK	Japan	1120
2. Hitachi	"	520
3. Nippon Mektron	"	400
4. Ibiden	"	334
5. Mitsubishi Gas	"	na*
6. Photo circuits	USA	na
7. Hadco	"	na
8. Japan Circuits	Japan	na
9. Dae Duck Group	Korea	na
10. Compaq	Taiwan	226
11. Topan Printing	Japan	221
12. Elec & Eltek	Hong Kong	210
13. Daisho	Japan	190
14. Yamamoto	"	190
15. Nanya Plastics	Taiwan	180

Source: Elec & Eltek
*na=not available

1B, one of Hong Kong's largest PCB producers, and by all counts a well-managed company, differs from 2B in terms of design capability and automated production techniques. It does not compete directly against 2B, the Japanese producer, because it serves a different market niche, personal computers as opposed to more complex and demanding electronic products.

By way of conclusion of this section on benchmarking, our firm-level comparisons suggest one reason for the difficulties Hong Kong firms face in reaching the world technological frontier: an absence of end users in close proximity that create a big market and are technically challenging. Such a role, however, could conceivably be played by firms in China, including joint ventures, and it is to further integration between China and Hong Kong manufacturers that attention is now turned.

Hong Kong's New Engine:
Investments from China

My analysis thus far suggests that it is unlikely that an internal dynamic for growth will be created in the future by Hong Kong's manufacturing capabilities. If a dynamic is to emerge, it will have to emerge externally, most likely from a closer integration between manufacturing activities in China and Hong Kong.

Low wages in the Pearl River Delta have already been a source of energy, encouraging the 'Made By Hong Kong' rather than 'Made in Hong Kong' phenomenon. A low-wage advantage for Hong Kong firms in the Pearl River Delta, however, has a finite life span as wage rates there have already begun to rise sharply. Still, Hong Kong manufacturers, especially OEM firms, quite possibly can search out still lower-wage labor further afield, in inland China, Vietnam, and Myanmar, and continue to produce profitably despite higher transaction costs (witness the profitable activities of Korean OEM producers in Guatemala and the Dominican Republic). Such activity, however, may at best be expected to sustain Hong Kong's current manufacturing growth rate (which according to Table 14.3 has been stagnant), but not to create a new dynamic based on rising levels of skills.

There are, however, other benefits for Hong Kong's industries from closer ties with China. As pointed out in Chapter 10, China holds out an important source of demand for Hong Kong's goods. In what follows, however, I concentrate on the gains from an inflow of firms from China to Hong Kong.[26] Mainland firms appear to locate facilities in Hong Kong for the purpose of learning about technological and commercial developments worldwide. Hong Kong is the preferred venue because of all the competitive assets it possesses with respect to its cosmopolitan character, information technology, and transportation services. Such 'listening posts' may be expected to take different forms, from a sparse administrative headquarters to a design center undertaking R&D. *I would argue that one of the most important tasks the Hong Kong government can undertake to energize manufacturing activity is to recruit aggressively such Mainland firms (much as the Singapore government recruits global multinationals).* This should be done with a view towards encouraging them to extend the scope of their manufacturing activities in Hong Kong in the form of co-development projects with Hong Kong companies and universities.

Table 14.11
Overseas Investment in Hong Kong
Manufacturing Number, Cumulative Values, and
Employment in 1993 (Major Source Countries)

Country	Number of Investments	Investment (US$ Million)	Number of Employees
Japan	147	1,788	19,292
USA	89	1,474	18,499
China	37	565	6,099
Netherlands	12	213	9,319
UK	46	200	4,231
Switzerland	23	169	3,076
Singapore	20	79	2,567
Others	133	653	3,239
TOTAL	507	5,141	66,322

Source: Tables 1–6, Hong Kong Government Industry Department, *1994 Survey of Overseas Investment in Hong Kong's Manufacturing Industries.*

Notes:
Investment refers to total investment at original cost, which includes stock of fixed assets at original cost plus working capital. Exchange rate used US$1 = HK$7.8.

No official statistics are available on the amount of total PRC investment in Hong Kong, estimated at between US$20–25 billion at the end of 1994.

Table 14.11 presents data for 1993 on overseas investments in Hong Kong for the manufacturing sector only. If the data are correct, China was the third largest foreign investor in Hong Kong manufacturing, although well behind Japan and the United States. As footnoted in the table, unofficial data estimate that at the end of 1994, *total* investment from the PRC in Hong Kong in such sectors as real estate and other services was as much as US$20–25 billion. Manufacturing activity in Hong Kong by Mainland firms, therefore, may be just beginning.

Table 14.12 gives an indication of the manufacturing branches in which Chinese investment is located. Transport equipment is the most prominent, although what is classified as transport equipment probably spills over into other sectors such as electronics. A case in point is China Aerospace, a member of a Chinese conglomerate that manufactures satellites, cars, and trucks. China Aerospace's Hong Kong holdings include real estate, which supposedly has provided it with money to invest in production facilities in Shenzhen and to establish an R&D center in Hong Kong, which serves as a listening post, among other functions. The center employs roughly 40 engineers who design electronic parts. Despite legal restrictions on the inflow of personnel from China to Hong Kong, almost all these engineers are Mainlanders.

The level of China's technological capabilities by and large remains a black box, particularly with respect to the firm and industry. In China, as in Hong Kong, R&D laboratories and science and technology centers that are attached not to a firm but rather to a university or public entity (such as China's National Academy of Science) generally command professional respect. At the firm and industry level, however, there are not yet a large number of detailed studies to give a clear picture of technological skills. Conditions are in any event changing rapidly with respect to property rights, the regulatory regime, markets for intermediate inputs, firm structure, and the degree of competition.[27] All these changes are likely to have a major impact—mostly positive—on firms' investments in technological assets.

Table 14.12
Chinese Manufacturing Investment in Hong Kong by Industry
US$ Millions (%)

Industry	1991	1992	1993
Tobacco	N/A	N/A	N/A
Transport Equipment	270 (56)	355 (67)	373 (65.9)
Electronics	67 (14)	54 (10)	34 (6.1)
Textiles and Clothing	42 (9)	39 (7)	N/A
Metal Products	21 (4)	23 (4)	N/A
Electrical Products	12 (3)	14 (3)	17 (3.0)
Plastic Products	28 (6)	12 (2)	62 (11.1)
Chemical Products	10 (2)	10 (2)	39 (6.8)
Others	32 (6)	27 (5)	40 (7.1)
TOTAL	482	534	565

Source: See Table 14.11

Technological capabilities in China may be expected to vary substantially among industries and firms. The most accomplished sectors are likely to be those in the military-industrial complex, including nuclear power. As in Russia and India, these sectors appear to be quite advanced. In aerospace, for example, China has become an international satellite launcher. In petrochemicals and steel, selected enterprises have been undergoing extensive upgrading. Producer goods generally, therefore, may provide the nucleus for China's listening-post investments in Hong Kong as a way to source not just technology but also marketing expertise and financial resources.

Policies to Encourage High-Value-Added Manufacturing Activity

Given the endowments that make Hong Kong an attractive venue for creating a listening post, I would predict that the number of PRC firms establishing such a facility in Hong Kong will increase sharply after political unification in July 1997, assuming an inviting environment is created for this purpose. To maximize the high-value-added activity that Mainland firms locate in Hong Kong, I would recommend the adoption of the following generic types of government policy:

1. The government may wish to recruit PRC firms to Hong Kong, much as the Singapore government recruits multinational firms. The issue of *which* industry is probably less important than *the level of their manufacturing capabilities*. The government should try to recruit Chinese firms with high-caliber capabilities and skills whatever their industry (so long as it falls within a wide range of industries that are compatible with Hong Kong's own existing and projected capabilities).

2. A sound approach, in my view, would be to invite to Hong Kong those PRC enterprises that can be persuaded to undertake process/product development activities, R&D, and prototyping/tooling. The selection of firms to recruit should be decided in collaboration by government, business, and academia, and should reflect the needs and interests of business and academia for PRC partners. The benefits for Hong Kong in the form of greater manufacturing capabilities should be spelled out systematically in each case.

3. The system of incentives to attract developmental activities would need to be carefully formulated and implemented. Three potential minefields are: whether PRC firms would be allowed to bring their own engineers and skilled workers or would be induced or forced to hire Hong Kong engineers; whether PRC firms that establish only administrative head-quarters should be penalized if the effect for Hong Kong is merely to boost real estate prices; and how to impose finite limits on any form of subsidy.

4. Incentives to induce PRC firms to undertake co-develop-ment projects with Hong Kong firms or universities could include cheap finance and/or subsidized real estate prices in special 'enterprise zones.'

5. The finance for such incentives should also be considered; quite possibly such incentives could be financed from a small (1 percent) tax on goods being shipped from Hong Kong to the PRC. Such a tax might be acceptable to both sides if revenues were used to promote a science and technology infrastructure from which both Hong Kong and China could benefit.

6. Government policies to attract high-value-added activities to Hong Kong from China should be taken as a starting point for coordinating Hong Kong's science and technology policy with that of China.

A Summary of Findings and Recommendations for Manufacturing

The major findings, conclusions, and policy recommenda-tions of this chapter may be summarized as follows:

1. Based on a small sample of electronics firms, as well as aggregate data, I found that Hong Kong typically had culti-vated mid-technology manufacturing capabilities; high-tech-nology capabilities were not evident, and generally Hong Kong's 'technological infrastructure' was poorer than that of other East Asian late industrializers.

2. The source of new technology in the electronics sector sample tended to be foreign rather than indigenous. Firms

manufacturing under their own brand names (OBMs) tended to invest more in their own technological capabilities than original equipment manufacturers (OEMs), but the efforts even of OBMs (principally in the form of product redesign) were modest. R&D, as generally understood, is almost nonexistent in my sample of Hong Kong's electronics sector (the consumer electronics branch of which is sharply contracting in terms of output). Aggregate data suggest it is virtually absent in other sectors as well.

3. In all Hong Kong industry, modest investment in manufacturing capabilities was suggested by international benchmarking. Using internationally refereed scientific publications and patents as indicators, I found rapid growth in Hong Kong but not nearly as rapid as in Hong Kong's major East Asian competitors. Hong Kong placed at the bottom of a composite index on technological capabilities (and manufacturing wage rates) constructed by the American National Science Foundation as noted in (1) above.

4. The Hong Kong electronics firms in our sample continue to compete on the basis of cost, not skills. Costs and capabilities intersect insofar as 'flexibility' contributes to lower costs and arises as a consequence of project execution skills. Mostly, however, lower costs have been obtained by means of relocating labor-intensive production in China. Taking Motorola as a case study of multinational locational decisions, I found a strong preference for locating as many activities as possible in China rather than in Hong Kong, even high-value-added activities related to product development and R&D.

5. In our sample, the types of manufacturing activities that have remained in Hong Kong include administration and distribution (thanks to Hong Kong's excellent infrastructure services), prototyping and tooling (thanks to its experienced, skilled workforce), and product development (thanks to its engineering capabilities and university support services). But a comparison of Japanese and Hong Kong firms in two mid-technology industries—micromotors and printed circuit boards, suggests that somewhat less design work is done in Hong Kong than in Japan because of a smaller, less demanding, and less geographically proximate customer base, as well as a lower level of capabilities.

6. Given these trends the growth dynamic in Hong Kong's future manufacturing sector is unlikely to be internal, based on accumulated skills. It is likely to be external, partly as a result of foreign investment pouring into Hong Kong from China, which is now the third largest foreign investor in Hong Kong's manufacturing sector.

7. I would recommend that the government play an active role in attempting to induce more Chinese investment into Hong Kong in the form of high-value added manufacturing activities related to design and R&D. This would give a systematic focus to government efforts to upgrade the technological skill base of Hong Kong industry.

Author's Acknowledgements
I would like to thank Kheng Leong Cheah for excellent research assistance. I also benefited from help from Charles Sodini, Richard Lester, and especially Rafael Reif.

Notes

1 United States Executive Office of the President/Office of Management and Budget, *Standard Industrial Classification Manual,* Wash., DC, National Technical Information Service, 1987, p. 67. In turn, establishments are defined as 'an economic unit, generally at a single physical location, where business is conducted or where services or industrial operations are performed.' *(Standard Industrial Classification Manual,* p. 12.)

2 Within five years (1989–1993), the share of manufacturing in gross domestic product had fallen from 19.3 to 11.1 percent. Hong Kong Census and Statistics Department, *Estimates of Gross Domestic Product 1961 to 1994,* 1995.

3 It is tempting to make international comparisons of this statistic but difficult to do so accurately. Based on the early work of economists such as Simon Kuznets and Moses Abramovits, the conventional wisdom became that manufacturing had higher labor productivity than services. But accurate international comparisons depend on how the service sector is divided and especially on how variations in working hours across sectors are handled.

4 'Auxiliary' establishments are those 'primarily engaged in performing management or support services for other establishments of the same enterprise.' *(Standard Industrial Classification*

Manual, p. 13.) Examples of auxiliary establishments include central administrative offices, establishments primarily engaged in research, development, and testing for other establishments of the same enterprise, and warehouses and storage facilities primarily servicing other establishments of the same enterprise. The traditional classification of 'manufacturing' is blurred depending on the classification of auxiliary establishments. In theory, each auxiliary establishment should be classified according to its primary activity, which is.usually not manufacturing, but this is not always feasible, especially in the case of the small firms that are typical of Hong Kong's economy. In practice, therefore, there has tended to be a blurring of service-oriented and production-oriented activity at the level of the firm (enterprise), which is a summation of various establishments and my unit of analysis. The term manufacturing is used here in this broader sense.

5   For data on value added and gross output, see *Surveys of Industrial Production,* Hong Kong Census and Statistics Department; for data on exports, see *Hong Kong Trade Statistics,* Hong Kong Census and Statistics Department; for data on employment, see *Reports of Employment, Vacancies and Payroll Statistics,* Hong Kong Census and Statistics Department; and for data on foreign investment, see *1995 Survey of External Investment in Hong Kong's Manufacturing Industries,* Hong Kong Government Industry Department.

6   I do not pretend that this 'sample' is scientifically selected; the companies I examine were chosen merely for representativeness according to several criteria: their capabilities, size, ownership, and accessibility for study. Probably they include some of the most successful companies in the industry, although some unsuccessful cases (in terms of profitability and growth) were inadvertently uncovered. My aim initially was to study best-practice firms. If anything, therefore, my sample overstates the skill level of the average electronics enterprise. Note also that this sample overlaps with that of Reif and Sodini in Chapter 10.

7   T. Hikino and A. H. Amsden, 'Staying Behind, Stumbling Back, Sneaking Up, Soaring Ahead: Late Industrialization in Historical Perspective,' in *Convergence of Productivity: Cross-National Studies and Historical Evidence,* W. J. Baumol; R. R. Nelson; and E. N. Wolff (eds.), New York and Oxford: Oxford University Press, 1994, p. 291.

8   Historically, the formation of Hong Kong's electronics sector was a function of foreign investment. (M. Hobday, *Innovation in East Asia: The Challenge to Japan,* Aldershot, UK: Edward Elgar, 1995.)

9   Hong Kong Government Industry Department, *Survey of Overseas Investment in Hong Kong's Manufacturing Industries,* Hong Kong, 1994, p. 62.

10 The distribution of Hong Kong's foreign investments in manufacturing, by country, was as follows in 1993: in cumulative value (US$), Japan accounted for 35 percent and the United States accounted for 29 percent; in terms of number of investments, Japan accounted for 29 percent and the United States for 18 percent (Hong Kong Government Industry Department, Survey of Overseas Investment in Hong Kong's Manufacturing Industries, 1994, p. 61).

11 Out of 29 firms for which data were available, 21 had some OMB production, although the 21 included foreign firms.

12 Even cost-competitiveness based on low wages, however, depends on some sorts of skills, say, with respect to production engineering and quality control (see Table 14.1).

13 Hikino and Amsden, 'Staying Behind, Stumbling Back, Sneaking Up, Soaring Ahead.'

14 As noted in the general case by Flaherty, 'In globalizing companies headquarters managers no longer dictate product development and technology choice. Headquarters certainly is no longer the only place managers and technologists look for technologies and products; subsidiary professionals often lead technology development. . . . In companies like Ford, IBM, Ericsson, ABB and Procter & Gamble, product development is carried out jointly by experts who are located in different countries and draw on their individual experiences to create a better world product.' (M. T. Flaherty, *Global Operations Management,* New York: McGraw–Hill, 1996 p. 53.)

15 For data on China's heavy investments in restructuring existing enterprises, see A. H. Amsden, D. Liu, *et al.,* 'China's Macro Economy, Environment, and Alternative Transition Model,' *World Development,* 24, 2 (1996): 273–286.

16 W. Yao provides detailed information on the operations of Motorola (China) in 'Winning in High-Tech and Emerging Markets: How Motorola's Global Strategy Fits into China's Development Policy,' M.S., Urban Studies and Planning. Cambridge, Mass., Massachusetts Institute of Technology, 1996.

17 K. Schoenberger, 'Motorola Bets Big on China,' *Fortune* (May 27, 1996): 117.

18 For more details on the correlations between the growth in scientific publications and other science and technology indicators in emerging economies, including a list of coefficients, see A. Amsden and M. Mourshed, 'Scientific Publications and the

Capabilities of Late Industrializers,' MIT, 1997, 3-405, 77 Massachusetts Avenue, Cambridge, Mass., 02139.

19   These findings are taken from a more detailed analysis of the subjects of scientific publications of late industrializing countries, provided in Amsden and Mourshed, 'Scientific Publications and the Capabilities of Late Industrializers.'

20   United States National Science Foundation, L. M. Rausch, *Asia's New High-Tech Competitors,* Wash. DC: US Government Printing Office, 1995. Hobday also writes: 'Hong Kong lagged behind the other newly industrialized economies in technological capability.' (M. Hobday, *Innovation in East Asia: The Challenge to Japan,* p. 184.)

21   United States National Science Foundation, Rausch, *Asia's New High-Tech Competitors,* p. 32.

22   Ibid.

23   A. Young, 'Lessons From the East Asian NICs: A Contrarian View,' *European Economic Review,* 38 (1994).

24   The Hong Kong firm has begun to make significant inroads in 2A's home market with lower prices for comparable products.

25   Sales of American and Japanese PCB producers are not comparable because US demand tends to be for mounted PCBs, while Japanese demand tends to be for unmounted ones.

26   According to a *New York Times* article, 'With Beijing's rule arriving in Hong Kong next July, thousands of Chinese companies and entrepreneurs have flocked from China to stake their claim in this prosperous British-run enclave of capitalism.' [K. Chen, 'Chinese Firms Rush for Hong Kong Base Ahead of Takeover,' *New York Times,* December 22, 1966, pp. B1, B6.]

27   S. Gu, 'The Emergence of New Technology Enterprises in China: A Study of Endogenous Capability Building via Restructuring,' *Journal of Development Studies,* 32, 4 (April, 1996).

Index